Advance Praise for
The Risks of Simile in Renaissance Rhetoric

"*The Risks of Simile* is a landmark book of immense learning and profound originality. No treatise on rhetoric between the fifteenth and the nineteenth centuries, however obscure, has escaped the author's attention. The book is also solidly grounded in the rhetorical thought of Antiquity. By masterfully using a psychoanalytical framework, as well as a variety of twentieth-century methodologies, Shirley Sharon-Zisser demonstrates how aware Renaissance rhetoricians were of the links between sexuality and language. The book, which completely reshapes its own field of inquiry, will become and remain an indispensable scholarly tool for years to come."
Alexandre Leupin, Louisiana State University;
Author of Barbarolexis: Medieval Writing and Sexuality

"*The Risks of Simile in Renaissance Rhetoric* stands alone as a book that counters and remedies voguish but attentuated and often non-coherent work on sexuality and textuality in a presumed age of post-theory. Challenging both new historicists and formalists, Sharon-Zisser provides a rigorous and brilliant analysis of the connections between rhetoricity and eroticism in early modern rhetorical theory. I strongly recommend this important book to anyone working on the history of rhetoric, modern critical theory, feminism and gender studies, medieval and Renaissance poetics, and psychoanalysis. Sharon-Zisser's book is a vindication of theory's best achievements in modern intellectual work."
James J. Paxson, University of Florida;
Associate Editor of Exemplaria: A Journal of Theory in Medieval and Renaissance Studies

The Risks of Simile
in Renaissance Rhetoric

New Studies in Aesthetics

Robert Ginsberg
General Editor

Victor Yelverton Haines and Jo Ellen Jacobs
Associate Editors

Vol. 32

PETER LANG
New York • Washington, D.C./Baltimore • Boston • Bern
Frankfurt am Main • Berlin • Brussels • Vienna • Oxford

Shirley Sharon-Zisser

The Risks of Simile in Renaissance Rhetoric

PETER LANG
New York • Washington, D.C./Baltimore • Boston • Bern
Frankfurt am Main • Berlin • Brussels • Vienna • Oxford

Library of Congress Cataloging-in-Publication Data

Sharon-Zisser, Shirley.
The risks of simile in Renaissance rhetoric / Shirley Sharon-Zisser.
p. cm. — (New studies in aesthetics; vol. 32)
Includes bibliographical references and index.
1. Rhetoric, Renaissance. 2. Rhetoric and psychology.
3. Simile. I. Title. II. Series.
PN183. S53   808'.009'024—dc21   99-087806
ISBN 0-8204-4581-9
ISSN 0893-6005

Die Deutsche Bibliothek-CIP-Einheitsaufnahme

Sharon-Zisser, Shirley:
The risks of simile in renaissance rhetoric / Shirley Sharon-Zisser.
–New York; Washington, D.C./Baltimore; Boston; Bern;
Frankfurt am Main; Berlin; Brussels; Vienna; Oxford: Lang.
(New studies in aesthetics; Vol. 32)
ISBN 0-8204-4581-9

Cover art: Correggio, *Venus with Mercury & Cupid ('The School of Love')*
By Courtesy of the National Gallery, London.

The paper in this book meets the guidelines for permanence and durability
of the Committee on Production Guidelines for Book Longevity
of the Council of Library Resources.

© 2000 Peter Lang Publishing, Inc., New York

All rights reserved.
Reprint or reproduction, even partially, in all forms such as microfilm,
xerography, microfiche, microcard, and offset strictly prohibited.

Printed in the United States of America

Acknowledgments

This book could not have been completed and published without the help and support of many institutions and individuals. It is my utmost pleasure to acknowledge my debt to all those who have helped me fulfill the imperative for articulation.

Research for this book was supported by generous grants from the Cohen-Porter Fund for the Department of English at Tel Aviv University, the British Council, and the Fulbright Foundation. I am grateful to the staff of the British Library, the Bodleian Library at Oxford University, and the Kroch Rare Book Library at Cornell University, for facilitating this research and in may cases leading me to the obscure rare texts I had been searching for.

Some of the material in this book is reprinted by permission from articles listed below. Shirley Sharon-Zisser, "Wanting Word of Woman, Subversive Speech of Simile: Écriture féminine and the Erotics of Rhetoric," *Intertexts* 3:2 (1999), pp. 33–58. Copyright Texas Tech University Press. Shirley Sharon-Zisser, "From 'Guest' to Occupier? Unstable Hospitality and the Ahistoricity of Tropology in the Discourse of Rhetoric," *Philosophy and Rhetoric* 32:4 (1999); Copyright 1999 by The Pennsylvania State University Press. Reproduced by permission of the Pennsylvania State University Press. Shirley Sharon-Zisser, "'Illustrer nôtre langue maternelle': Illustrative Similes and Failed Phallic Economy in Early Modern Rhetoric," *Exemplaria: A Journal of Theory in Medieval and Renaissance Studies* 9:2 (1997), pp. 393–420. Pegasus Press, University of North Carolina, Asheville, NC 28804. "'Similes Hollow'd with Sighs: The Transferential Erotics of the Similaic Copula in Shakespeare's 'A Lover's Complaint,'" *Exemplaria: A Journal of Theory in Medieval and Renaissance Studies* 11:1 (1999), pp. 195–200. Pegasus Press, University of North Carolina, Asheville, NC 28804.

Correggio's *Mercury Instructing Cupid Before Venus* is reproduced on the cover of this book by courtesy of the National Gallery, London.

In the course of my work on this book, Evelyne Goldblatt and Marie Burgin extended technical and administrative assistance whenever it was necessary. The patience and expertise of Michal Semo and Meital Sharon of Tel Aviv University's Graphic Design Studio in the course of typesetting and preparing the book for press have been invaluable, as has the assistance of Jeffrey Galas at Lang's production department. Heartfelt thanks are due to Yael Ring for her help in meticulously proofreading drafts and in compiling the bibliography.

I have benefited immensely from the commentary and support of colleagues and friends. I wish to thank Gila Aloni, Terence Cave, Barbara Correll, Alexandre Leupin, Aim Luski, Jerome Mandel, James Paxson, Zephyra Porat, and Tzachi Zamir. They have all, in different ways, helped make this book better.

Hana Wirth-Nesher has long been an inspiration to me, as an intellectual and as a person. Her interest and encouragement helped launch this project. Her astute criticism sharpened and improved it immeasurably. Without Hana's sensitivity, her support, and her strength, the work presented in this book, and much else, would not have survived the hardships.

Stephen Whitworth's brilliant and groundbreaking work on the semiotics of the early modern pastoral has had a profound influence on my thinking about the psychic subtext of early modern theories of linguistic form, and resonates in many pages of this book. I am deeply grateful to Stephen for his scintillating brilliance, for his insistence on the aesthetic, for his uncompromising integrity and courage, for his encouragement and support, and for a challenging intellectual companionship which inspired, transformed thoughts and rhetoric, gave hope, and made it all possible, meaningful, and worthwhile.

Robert Ginsberg, the series editor, has made the publication of this book, in its present form, possible in significant ways. In him, I found the most supportive, most open-minded, most perceptive, and most demanding and exacting editor I could hope for. Whatever coherence and clarity this book manifests are to a considerable extent the result of his generous advice and superb editing, for which I shall remain eternally grateful.

Over many years, and in various locations, Eyal Zisser unfailingly created the spaces which functioned as the conditions of possibility for my work on this book. He has done so with understanding, devotion, patience, and generosity whose scope is most rare. This book owes much of its coming to be to Eyal's nobility of spirit, good humor, persistent optimism, and constant companionship.

My father, Moshe Sharon, first taught me the love of Renaissance music which may be heard in many of the following pages. My mother, Alisa Sharon, first taught me the love of/as language this book speaks, but did not live to see it through to publication.

I dedicate this book to her memory.

Ramat Hasharon, Israel, May 2000

TABLE OF CONTENTS

Introduction: The Erotics of Rhetoric in the Renaissance 1

Part One   The Archaic Substance of Speech 17
Chapter One: Renaissance Rhetoric and the Dialectics of the
Archaic Mother 19

Part Two   Fetishization/Colonization: The Brisuric
Binarism of Elocution 73
Chapter Two: Ornamentation: Figure, Fetishism, and Perversion 75
Chapter Three: Displacement as Detour: Tropology, the
Tropics, and the Troubadours 129

Part Three   Impaired Pair: Metaphoric Denial, Similaic Desire 165
Chapter Four: Master Trope/Trope of Mastery?: Metaphor,
Ontology, and Phallic Masculinity 167
Chapter Five: Transferential Approximations: Similes,
S(i)miles, Jouissance 213
Chapter Six: Simile and Maternality: From the Abject
to the Orgasmic 277

Works Cited 345

Index 369

Cicero in his book *de amicitia* these woords dooth expresse,
Saying nothing is more desirous then like is unto like
    — Ulpian Fulwell, *Like Will To Like* (1587)

It is not every day that you come upon something which
is constructed so as to give you the very image of your own
desire
    — Jacques Lacan, *Seminar II*

But when my glass shows me myself indeed…
Mine own self-love quite contrary I read
    — William Shakespeare, sonnet # 62

All I do is kiss you through the bars of a rhyme
    — The Dire Straits

INTRODUCTION:

The Erotics of Rhetoric in the Renaissance

Correggio's *Mercury Instructing Cupid Before Venus* (*The School of Love*) (1528) features three mythological figures. Apparently fascinated by such figures, Correggio made them the focus of five of his paintings. Three of these five paintings, *Ganymede, Jupiter and Io,* and *Leda* (1531–1532), depict seductive myths of abduction. These myths involve the abduction of objects of both sexes, Ganymede, Io, and Leda. The irresistible phenomenal beauty of these objects engenders in Zeus an attraction powerful enough to cross the boundaries between mortality and immortality, between the human and the divine. The sources for these myths of erotic abduction are the ancient texts of Apollodorus, Hesiod, Homer, and Ovid.

The ancient mythological texts do not provide a narrative parallel for the pictorial composition of *The School of Love*. No less erotic than Correggio's depictions of (bi)sexual abductions, *The School of Love* presents Cupid, Mercury, and Venus, her breasts supple and their nipples erect and suggesting sexual arousal, as minimally draped nude figures whose sensuality is accentuated by their dark and luscious backdrop. Correggio's three figures are eroticized because, like every "figure of love," they are expressly dynamized (Bataille, "The Solar Anus," *Visions of Excess*, p. 7). In this painting, not only Cupid has wings, and not only Mercury wears winged sandals. Venus too is unusually shown as having wings. Unlike the figure of Jupiter-turned-eagle in Correggio's three paintings of mythological abductions, the three sensuous figures in *The School of Love* do not exercise the erotic kineticism with which their wings potentially endows them to traverse the distance between the Olympian and the mundane. They do not use their wings to cross the ontological boundary separating the temporal and the eternal. Instead, their hands and arms, and the wings extending from those arms, are contiguous to one another and trace the shape of a heart. Correggio's Venus, Mercury, and Cupid form a self-contained, self-referential triangle in which they charge and recharge one another with libidinal energy.

The libidinal energy circulating in *The School of Love* is polymorphic and less than normative. The erotic links in Correggio's painting involve the heterosexuality binding Venus or Aphrodite to Mercury or Hermes. This binding is the mythological foundation for the non-phallic image of the androgyne, the Hermaphrodite. The erotic links in the painting include the homosexual pederasty binding Mercury and Cupid as older master and younger catamite. The remaining libidinal link in the painting is the incest binding Venus and her son Cupid. In Correggio's second mythological painting without classical narrative referent, *Venus and Cupid with a Satyr* (1528), the incestuous relation of Venus and Cupid is even more pronounced. In *Venus and Cupid*, Cupid and a naked Venus, her posture and expression bespeaking *jouissance*, are shown sleeping together, their hands touching.

Polymorphic erotic energy is not the only factor circulating in Correggio's erotic-mythological triangle. In this triangle, erotic energy is trascoded with rhetoricity. This transcoding is the effect of two of the painting's semiotic components: the placement of Cupid's shaft and bow, and the painting's title and sub-title. Cupid's love-arousing phallic shaft is a standard mythological image for erotic energy. This image appears in Correggio's *Venus and Cupid with a Satyr*. In *The School of Love*, Cupid's shaft is conspicuous by its absence. Instead of the missing shaft, Cupid holds another phallic instrument: a pencil or pen. An erotic instrument is replaced by an instrument of rhetoric.

Cupid's bow is analogous in function to the maternal as psychic point of origin and aim of the subject's desire (Lacan, *Seminar IV*, pp. 67–68). This bow, the literal point of origin for the erotic trajectories initiated by Cupid's shaft, is present in the painting, but in an unusual place. In *The School of Love*, his mother Venus unusually but appropriately holds Cupid's bow. The pen or pencil conflated with Cupid's shaft is not applied to Cupid's bow. The pen or pencil is applied to a sheet of paper transcoded with this bow. An instrument of love is replaced by an instrument of language.

The transcoding of love and language is reinforced by the painting's composition. In the painting, Mercury holds the sheet of paper transcoded with Cupid's bow. Mercury is transcoded with the simultaneously maternalized and eroticized figure of Venus, who holds the bow. The painting's composition suggests an affinity between the goddess of love and the god of eloquence.

The relation between the painting's title and sub-title suggests the same affinity. Since the painting's title is *The School of Love*, Cupid's inscriptions on the sheet of paper would appear to be amatory principles. The supposed source of these principles is the goddess of love Venus. The painting's sub-title, *Mercury Instructing Cupid Before Venus*, and the pictorial composition reflected by the sub-title, do not point to Venus as the source for Cupid's inscriptions. Cupid's teacher is not Venus but Mercury, whose domain is the precepts of eloquence, of rhetoric, not of love. Cupid is schooled in rhetoric as much, and at the same time, as he is schooled in eroticism.

What circulates in *The School of Love* is rhetoricity and erotic energy, and rhetoricity as a manifestation of erotic energy. In Correggio's painting, the principles of love and of eloquence, of the erotic and the rhetorical, are mapped onto one another. This mapping anticipates by centuries Jacques Lacan's fundamental psychoanalytical maxim according to which love is what "does not stop being written" (*Seminar XX*, p. 144).

The eroticism inscribed by Correggio's Cupid into the sheet held by Mercury is not exclusively the normative eroticism of matrimonial, reproduction-oriented heterosexuality. This norm gravitates to the phallus as "despotic signifier" (Hocquenghem, p. 95). It is dictated by the father function. Yet the father function is absent from Correggio's painting as from the myth of Cupid's birth.

The eroticism inscribed by Cupid into the sheet held by Mercury, the painting's pictorial composition suggests, is a hermaphroditic, bi-sexual, polymorphic eroticism beyond or before the phallus and the advent of the Name/No of the Father. What Cupid inscribes on the sheet held by Mercury is an archaic eroticism or desire. This desire is, in the words of Edmund Spenser, "Borne without Syre" ("Colin Clovts Come home againe," line 800). This de-sire "whose only name is the absence of the sign of the father" (Whitworth, "Far from Being," p. 171), is not definitively assignable to any gender. De-sire flows between the Hermetic and the Aphroditic, the masculine and the feminine. In *The School of Love*, de-sire flows between homosexuality, heterosexuality, incest, and pederasty suggested by the loving links between the limbs of Cupid, Mercury, and Venus who form the triangle of desire.

Correggio's pictorial conflation of the rhetorical and the erotic in its multiple forms is in no sense an anomaly in the culture of the European Renaissance. In this period, the art of rhetoric enjoyed a vogue manifest in an unprecedented outpouring of treatises theorizing the aesthetic categories of language (Rebhorn, pp. 1–2). Much of the literature published in this period, especially the poetry, whether pastoral or Petrarchan, thematizes forms of sexuality and desire and their affective consequences such as melancholy and despair. Frequently, early modern literary texts thematize sexuality and desire in relation to aesthetic categories. The conceptual and anagrammatical link between the rhetorical and the erotic suggested by Correggio's *The School of Love* is explicitly inscribed, for instance, in the title of a seventeenth-century English rhetorical treatise, Edward Phillips's *Mysteries of Love and Eloquence* (1658). The title page of this treatise, much like Correggio's painting, links images of the mythological figures of Cupid or Eros, god of love, and Mercury, god of eloquence and rhetoric, by means of the shape of a heart. In the same vein, Robert Greene's *Ciceronis Amor: Tullies Love* (1589), makes Cicero, the Roman rhetorician whose theorizations of aesthetic form reverberate in much early modern rhetorical theory, the paradigmatic lover at whom "young Gentlemen that aime at honour should levell the end of their affections" (title page).

The conflation of love and eloquence is inscribed in Renaissance treatises on grammar, where the Latin verb chosen almost invariably to exemplify the conjugation of verbs (the dynamic, and hence eroticized, category of syntax) is "to love," or its Latin equivalent *amare*. Love and eloquence are linked in treatises on rhetoric such as Abraham Fraunce's *The Arcadian Rhetorike* (1588), or Thomas Blount's *Academie of Eloquence* (1654), whose examples for aesthetic forms are consciously drawn from the amatory pastoral poetry of Edmund Spenser and Philip Sidney.

The authors of early modern amatory poetry reiterate the anagrammatic and conceptual links between the eroticism they thematize, and the aesthetic categories of grammar and rhetoric by means of which they thematize eroticism. In sonnet #11 of his *Ideas Mirrovr: Amovrs in Quatorzains* (1594), Michael Drayton speaks of language as a simultaneously rhetorical and erotic apparatus, an "Alphabet of love" (line 1). In this alphabet of love, "vowels" function as "Vows" (line 5), "liquids" as "liquid christall tears" (line 9), "dolefull Dyphtongs" as "dispaires" (line 11), and "accents" as "Redoubling sighs" (line 12). In John Dickenson's pastoral romance *Arisbas* (1594), the hero laments his separation from his beloved by means of a rhetoric not "limit[ed]…with distinct clauses" (p. 35). The amatory dejection of the female protagonist of William Shakespeare's "A Lover's Complaint" is characterized rhetorically, as marked by her shrieking "undistinguish'd woe" (line 20). In the second sonnet of the eighth decad of Henry Constable's *Diana* sequence of love sonnets (1594), the speaker implores his mistress to no longer "entertaine…[her] long disdaining" of his affections (line 3). He asks her to "Giue *Period* to [his] matter of complaining" (line 1, emphasis mine). Constable transcodes the psychological dynamic of the dissolution of erotic resistance with a punctuation mark. He anticipates by centuries Lacan's designation of "beneficent punctuation" as a means of gaining insight into the affective structures of the subject's unconscious (*Écrits*, p. 44). Most significantly for the conceptual context explored in this book, in Shakespeare's "A Lover's Complaint," the seductive gifts offered by the poem's male protagonist to his beloved, material manifestations of the intersubjective process contemporary psychoanalysis came to name "transference" (Lacan, *Seminar I*, pp. 108–112), are transcoded with an elocutionary category. They are described as *"similes...*Hollow'd with sighs" (lines 227–228, emphasis mine).

The incessant transcoding of the rhetorical and the affective in its erotic inflection is not peculiar to the amatory poetry and metalinguistic theory of the Renaissance. Contemporary psychoanalysts and philosophers too often speak of rhetorical categories in relation to erotic and sexual categories. Lacan theorizes desire as the "metonymy of our being" (*Seminar VII*, p. 321), and describes the basic intersubjective relation as resting upon the structure of the demand or question (*Seminar IV*, p. 182). According to Jacques Derrida, the affective relation of friendship has everything to do with apostrophe ("Politics of Friendship," p. 367). According to Georges Bataille, "the copula of terms" can be thought only in relation to "the copulation of bodies" ("The Solar Anus," *Visions of Excess*, p. 7). According to Michèle Montrelay, in the moment of orgasm, a woman is transported beyond the field of metaphor (pp. 80–81). In all these cases, contemporary theorists point to links between psycho-erotic categories and rhetorical-aesthetic categories.

The concern with the intersection between the rhetorical and the erotic shared by early modern writers and contemporary thinkers has two significant theoretical consequences. The first of these has to do with the pertinence of the study of early modern rhetoric to contemporary thinking of the psychic. The second has to do with the historical and conceptual relevance of contemporary philosophy and psychoanalysis to the study of early modern texts.

Psychoanalysis, especially Lacanian psychoanalysis, is a mode of thinking recognizing it has no medium but the subject's speech (*Écrits*, p. 40). It is a mode of thinking wherein speech is recognized as the joint where desire, the principle responsible for "the primary structuration of the human world," becomes manifest (*Seminar II*, pp. 224, 234).

Psychoanalysis is thus a mode of thinking to which theorizations of linguistic forms are most relevant. Lacan's famous claim, "the unconscious is structured like a language" (*Seminar III*, p.167), points to conceptualizations of structures of language as the function allowing psychoanalysis to map the operations of the psychic. For Lacan, psychic operations are primarily operations of desire, erotic operations. Lacan acknowledges "the ancient art of rhetoric" as the antecedent of psychoanalysis in the conceptualization of the categories in terms of which he theorizes these erotic operations (*Écrits*, p. 298).

Lacan is a psychoanalyst and philosopher, not an analyst of the rhetorical theory to which he acknowledges his intellectual debt. Yet this rhetorical theory, especially in the European Renaissance, when it reached its vogue, comprises detailed theorizations of many dozens of rhetorical categories. These rhetorical categories include metonymy, metaphor, apostrophe, and demand, associated with psychic structures by Lacan, Derrida and other contemporary thinkers. They include lesser-known categories such as anapodoton, homiologia, isocolon, syncrisis, and zeugma. Early modern rhetoricians do not always link those aesthetic categories with psycho-erotic structures as explicitly as do contemporary thinkers. However, the overall conceptual connection between the rhetorical and the erotic consciously insisted upon by early modern rhetoricians, poets, painters, and musicians encourages us to read early modern conceptualizations of rhetorical categories as implicit, symptomatic theorizations of links between linguistic and psycho-erotic structures.

The study of early modern rhetoric offers an invaluable resource to contemporary psychoanalysis and critical theory. The analysis of conceptualizations of numerous rhetorical forms in the texts of early modern thinkers who share the fundamental insight of contemporary thinkers concerning the co-imbrications of the linguistic and the psychic yields nuanced and detailed meditations on those co-imbrications. Contemporary theory, especially psychoanalytical theory, can build upon the results of such analysis for formulating more refined and precise insights into the domain of psychic structures.

The psychoanalysts Nicolas Abraham and Maria Torok are incorrect to point to psychoanalytical investigations of the linguistic structure of the psyche as "constitut[ing] new figures, absent from rhetorical treatises" (*The Shell and the Kernel*, p. 85). Feminist psychoanalysts Hélène Cixous, Luce Irigaray, and Catherine Clément are imprecise when they speak of theorizations of aesthetic forms in rhetorical treatises as univocal reflections of a male imaginary hostile to women. These feminist psychoanalysts make the destruction of theorizations of aesthetic forms in rhetorical treatises a task of feminist psychoanalysis. They believe such destruction would make it possible to access the archaic, maternal modes of signification purportedly repressed by the theorizations of aesthetic forms by male rhetoricians. Such destruction of the rhetorical tradition is impossible. Even were such destruction possible, it would result in the loss of aesthetic forms inscribed with femininity and non-phallic modes of desire (Sharon-Zisser, "Wanting Word of Woman"). Feminism and psychoanalysis cannot afford this loss.

The analysis of the theorizations of aesthetic forms in early modern rhetorical treatises can contribute to feminist psychoanalysis and psychoanalysis in general. The analysis of the inscription of multifarious forms of desire, pleasure, and other affects in early modern metalinguistic texts yields a detailed and nuanced grid for links contemporary thinkers seek to draw between structures of language and of subjectivity.

The second theoretical consequence of the shared concern with the intersection of the rhetorical and the erotic in early modern writing and contemporary thought has far-reaching implications for early modern studies. Critics such as Richard Halpern, Patricia Parker, or Wayne Rebhorn tend to read the metalinguistic theory of the Renaissance as a reflection of power relations, as an index to early modern ideologies of gender, race, or class. Richard Halpern describes "humanist style production" as "a mode of ideological control" (p. 38). According to Patricia Parker, it is not "necessary to read far in the handbooks of rhetoric or discussions of language in the English Renaissance...to perceive an intimate and ideologically motivated link between the need to control the movement of tropes and contemporary exigencies of social control" (*Literary Fat Ladies*, p. 98). In these handbooks, Parker argues, "definitions of figures, schemes, and tropes...frequently begin...to turn into illustrations of the social order the figure would rhetorically reflect" (ibid., p. 99). According to Wayne Rebhorn, Renaissance rhetoric is "deeply implicated in the social and political order that produces it" (p. 12).

These arguments claim to find their grounding in textual traces of the early modern past. However, their ultimate theoretical grounding, even when they disavow this, is in the contemporary critical fashion of new historicism. This fashion proclaims the purported difference of the past. New historicism, Stephen Greenblatt writes, is driven by "a search for textual otherness" ("Introduction," *New World Encounters*, p. xvii). In the words of Jonathan Goldberg, new historicism is "attentive to the alterity of the past" and committed to the delineation of "formidable differences even across relatively short historical periods [and of] disjunctions at any given moment from place to place" (pp. 18–20).

The new historicist insistence on disjunctions and differences guarantees blindness to continuities, including the continuity between early modern and contemporary thinkers where the lesions between love and language are concerned. Patricia Parker, one of the more subtle analysts of early modern rhetorical theory, rightly observes the preoccupation of early modern rhetoricians such as Thomas Wilson and Richard Sherry with the correlation of linguistic and inter-subjective joinings (*Shakespeare from the Margins*, p. 88). She avows a commitment to new historicist and cultural materialist methodologies (ibid., pp. 1–5, 10–11) wherein the impossibility of conceptual continuities between the early modern and the modern is a fundamental assumption. This assumption breeds repressive blindness. It leads Parker to elide the lesions between the erotic and the rhetorical fundamental to Lacanian psychoanalysis no less than to the early modern rhetoricians she cites. Such lesions, she states, "may seem to modern sensibilities completely unrelated" (ibid., p. 88).

This sample of repression suggests the new historicist critical fashion articulated by Greenblatt and Goldberg and relied on by Parker rests on a facile elision of the category of desire, especially in its inevitable interactions with the category of the aesthetic. The critical fashion of new historicism, and the arguments resting on this fashion recently articulated by scholars of early modern rhetoric, elide and repress, at their peril, the kind of reading early modern metalinguistic and poetic texts call for.

The articulations of early modern writers concerning conceptual links between rhetoric and eroticism do not invite us to read metalinguistic theories of the Renaissance as manifestations of contingent social, political, or ideological contexts. The incessant transcoding of the linguistic-rhetorical and the affective-erotic in the amatory poetry and the metalinguistic theory of the Renaissance invites us to read this theory as it has never before been read. The metalinguistic theory of the Renaissance insists on being read as a series of extended and complex meditations on the relations between linguistic and affective, especially erotic structures.

In avowing conceptual connections between the linguistic and the affective, between the rhetorical and the erotic, early modern metalinguistic and poetic texts do not, as new historicists would have it, stand out in their radical alterity and alien-ness to modern sensibilities. They do not speak from an irreducibly different past. In recurrently pointing to the connections between the erotic and the rhetorical, early modern literary and metalinguistic texts strikingly anticipate a fundamental concept of contemporary language-oriented psychoanalysis, manifest in the thinking of Jacques Lacan, Julia Kristeva, Michèle Montrelay, Luce Irigaray, Sarah Kofman, André Green, Nicolas Abraham, and Maria Torok. The idea of the co-imbrication of the rhetorical and the psychic is present in the post-structuralist philosophy of Jacques Derrida, Georges Bataille, Giles Deleuze, Jean-Joseph Goux, Jean-Luc Nancy, Emmanuel Levinas, Edmond Jabés, and Giorgio Agamben.

The work of contemporary theorists alert to the co-imbrications of the linguistic and the psychic Renaissance rhetoricians too insist on includes hermeneutic strategies. The hermeneutic strategies offered by contemporary thinkers sharing the fundamental insight of Renaissance rhetoricians concerning the links between love and language can be applied to the texts of those rhetoricians. This application is not anachronistic. It is recursive. Hermeneutic strategies offered by contemporary psychoanalysts and philosophers alert to the co-imbrications of love and language are most historically and conceptually appropriate to the analysis of early modern texts on the aesthetics of language. Given the early modern insistence on the co-imbrication of the rhetorical, the psychic, and the erotic, a philosophically-inflected psychoanalysis is a mode of reading early modern texts invite and insist on.

Language-oriented psychoanalysis and philosophy offer hermeneutic strategies for interpreting the links between rhetoric and Eros drawn by early modern thinkers. Unlike the historicist and materialist modes of reading all too often applied to early modern texts, the hermeneutics of contemporary thinkers such as Lacan, Goux, Derrida, and Agamben this study draws upon do not focus exclusively on the level of the signified, on what is consciously and explicitly avowed by the text's semantemes. Such hermeneutics ascribe greater significance to the sliding of the signifier, from text to archetypal or other intertext, from the structure of a given category to its isomorphs in other domains of discourse, from syllable to its phonic or etymological resonance in a different signifier, from letters to their anagrammatical inscription in another word. Such psychoanalytical and philosophical modes of reading do not, as does new historicism, seek the illusory factual stability of the anecdote as signified. They are true to Derrida's demonstrations of the constitutive instability of any signifier, any text. Demonstrations of the sliding of the signifier and the instability of the signified may be exemplified in Agamben's explorations of the affective and conceptual resonances of mythological archetypes in medieval semiotics, and in Goux's tracing of isomorphisms between economic, erotic, and psychic symbolic economies. They may be exemplified in Nicolas Abraham's and Maria Torok's uncovering of the psychic substance of the illness of Freud's Wolf-Man by following the phonic and etymological resonances of his words through many languages, in Sigmund Freud's analyses of parapraxes, in Ferdinand de Saussure's studies of anagrams. In all those cases, textual analysis does not remain trapped in the imaginary register of the signified, the register prone to misrecognition and alienation (Lacan, *Seminar III*, p. 146). Instead, the modern thinkers mentioned above focus on various dimensions of the signifier as symptoms, apparent on the text's surface or envelope, and follow those symptoms to their origin in the text's unconscious kernel. Such modes of interpretation require us to read not only with our conscious mind and with our eye to semantic significations. They require us to read with our unconscious and with our ear to the text's semiotic productivity, whether structural, phonic, etymological, grammatical, ungrammatical, anagrammatical, or intertextual.

The common fascination of early modern thinkers on language and contemporary psychoanalysts and philosophers with the co-imbrications of the linguistic and the affective encourages us to read early modern rhetorical and poetic texts by means of the aurally and semiotically inflected hermeneutic strategies offered by these psychoanalysts and philosophers. This commonality of early modern and modern concerns is not the only factor inviting us to read early modern texts in ways attentive to the semiotic and especially the acoustic as an opening up into the unconscious. Articulations of early modern writers too invite us to follow the seductions of the acoustic into the mainsprings of affect. The poetics of John Dickenson's pastoral romance *Arisbas*, Stephen Whitworth has brilliantly shown, are acoustic. These acoustic poetics invite a mode of reading attentive to the aural effects of sound and structure and to the readerly pleasures whose source contemporary psychoanalysis came to identify in the unconscious ("Far from Being"). Other examples abound. In George Chapman's *Ovid's Banquet of Sense* (1593), the most sensuous attribute of Ovid's beloved Corinna is her "sweet voice" (line 21). Ovid's "ardour" or passion is aroused primarily by the appeal of this "sweet voice" to his "ears" (line 18). In *The Arte of English Poesie* (1589), one of the most influential treatises on the aesthetics of rhetoric in the English Renaissance, George Puttenham speaks of poetic aurality as a sensuous experience. Poetic speech leads to the oral/aural satisfaction of the speaker, who autoerotically experiences it as "currant and slipper vpon the tongue" (p. 5), and as "pleasing" and "delicate to the eare" (p. 5). Poetic speech gives rise to the aural satisfactions of the addressees too. Those aural pleasures, those "impression[s] of the eare," Puttenham emphasizes, appeal to affect and determine "whither soeuer the heart...shal be most affectionatly bent and directed" (p. 5). In the dedication to Thomas Campion's *Observations in the Art of English Poesie* (1602), the "sweet[ness]" or sensuous, aural pleasure with which "numbers" (rhymes) "help...the eare" is described as making poetic speech "the chiefe beginner, and maintayner of eloquence" (unpaginated). Samuel Daniel's *Defence of Ryme* (1603) was published in response to Campion's pamphlet and engages in a polemic with Campion's invective against rhyme. Yet Daniel too speaks of the sensuous aural pleasure of "delighting the eare" as enabling poetic verse to "stir...the heart" (p. 10).

The declarations of the centrality and affective significance of aural aesthetics on the part of early modern poets and theorists of language demand a particular critical engagement from the readers of early modern poetic and meta-poetic texts. The consistent exploitation on the part of early modern English writers of the semiotic productivity enabled by the non-standardized spelling and pronunciation of the time demands a special type of critical engagement too. Like the critical engagement contemporary psychoanalysis insists on, the critical engagement demanded by early modern texts requires us to read with more than our rational, conscious minds. Early modern texts encourage us not to rest content with the deceptively determinate, semantic meaning of the signified. The critical engagement early modern texts call for requires us to follow the aurally and structurally effected productivity of the constitutively unstable signifier through its slidings and slippages from the text's envelope to the text's unconscious kernel. These slidings and slippages extend beyond the rational and conscious to the pleasures and other affects of the unconscious.

Listening for the unconscious of early modern texts requires a letting go of the obsessional insistence on the extrinsic new historicists phobically seek to enforce. Listening for the unconscious requires us to recognize the in-verse of the deceptively secure extrinsic as the source of veracity or truth (Lacan, *Seminar XVII*, p. 61). Veracity is in verse, in language (ibid., p. 71). But it is in aspects of language we have been trained to ignore as not sufficiently, securely objective, in details we have been taught to disregard as trifles.

Freud was not the first to discern the importance of such trifling details of the in-verse. In *The Arte of English Poesie*, Puttenham speaks of the importance of the hermeneutic of the anagram, the "breed[ing]" of "one word out of another" (p. 82). This hermeneutic, Puttenham says, involves attending to "trifles" of language (ibid., p. 84). Paying attention to the trifles of language, Puttenham recognizes, leads to the apprehension of "gratefull newes" (ibid., p. 82), to insight. This hermeneutic is psychically beneficial and transformative, leading to "solaces and recreations of mans wit" (ibid., p. 85). The psychically transformative insight and solace effected by the listening to trifles is accompanied by "pleasure" too (ibid., p. 82). This is pleasure of the type Puttenham recognizes as being of the order of the "primitiue" (ibid), of the archaic psychic site psychoanalysis would identify as the unconscious.

Listening to trifles, Puttenham knew, yields pleasure, solace, and insight for the subject, yet runs the risk of arousing the defensive anger of those given to the cathexis of the seemingly definite and objective, always a symptom of the repression of desire and the unconscious. Puttenham responds to those "reprehendours" of the trifling, those given to the cathexis of the definite, those who care "for nothing but matters of pollicie, & discourses of estate," and esteem "nothing that sauereth not of Theologie" (ibid., p. 84), the early modern equivalents of the new historicists of today. The refusal of the imperative to listen to trifles, he implies, comes from "suppress[ion]," a psychic function he identifies, centuries before Freud, as the function of the "seuere censor" (ibid., p. 85). Trifles, Puttenham adds, are worthy of "the most serious studies of man" (ibid). Inherent in trifles is what is "profoundest" (ibid) in human existence.

For Puttenham, the "profoundest" and "most serious" aspects of existence have everything to do with "pleasure" and with the "primitiue" or archaic (ibid., p. 82). Psychoanalysis would identify those aspects of existence achieving the primary structuration of the human world as desire and the unconscious (Lacan, *Seminar II*, p. 224). Those "profoundest" aspects of existence are not subject to limiting appeals to history. They are, Puttenham says, "come from many former siecles vnto our times" (p. 95).

The "profoundest" matters of desire and the unconscious remain constant across the "siecles." They are "vncontrolled...by any Pope or Patriarch" (ibid), by any agent of the Name/No of the Father. These matters may, Puttenham suggests, be discerned through attending to "trifles": anagrams, phonic resonances, linguistic and metrical forms. All of these seeming "trifles" are structures. They are thus unaffected by the vicissitudes of temporality. Puttenham devotes his treatise to meditations about these fundamental "trifles." He invites us too to respond to the seductions of the seemingly trifling. Puttenham asks us to not capitulate to censorship of the play of the forms of language, not to focus on the extrinsic and seemingly objective. He invites us to replace the "suppression" involved in the cathexis of the definite with a response to the seductions of the structures constituting the unconscious.

This book responds to Puttenham's imperative to listen to and for desire and to give up the search for a reassuring but small sense of groundedness such as new historicists seek when interrogating early modern texts for "matters of pollicie, & discourses of estate." It responds to Puttenham's call to attend to the in-verse and the seemingly trifling. In line with psychoanalysis, this book identifies the attention to trifles Puttenham recommends as a means of listening for the unconscious.

This book brings a critical engagement conceptually co-extensive with early modern texts and with contemporary theory, especially psychoanalytical theory, to bear on early modern treatises on the aesthetics of rhetoric. The book's focus is one aesthetic category among the many dozens theorized in such treatises, simile. This category is nevertheless granted a special status within early modern rhetorical treatises. In those treatises, simile, and the category of figure in terms of which simile is usually classified, are major sites of the inscription of the unconscious. Although subordinated to the most privileged aesthetic form in Renaissance treatises on rhetoric, metaphor, simile is the sole object of a rhetorical sub-genre invented in sixteenth-century Europe, the compendium of similes. Simile is a rhetorical category most often remarked upon in early modern amatory literature, especially in relation to excessive forms of eroticism beyond the phallic norm of matrimonial heterosexuality. Despite this crucial and paradoxical conceptual status of simile in early modern language theory, this aesthetic category has never before been the subject of serious scrutiny in studies of rhetoric and of the Renaissance. Simile has never before been a subject of philosophical and psychoanalytical inquiry at all.

Attending to the many ways in which aesthetic categories of linguistic form in early modern rhetorical treatises are interwoven with those of desire, sexuality, and other forms of subjectivity, and to the pressure this entanglement has on the deployment of the similaic as a register of desire and sexuality in literary texts, this book raises the following questions: what are the psycho-conceptual stakes of the simultaneous devaluation of and fascination with simile in early modern rhetoric? Why was this aesthetic category, whose systematic debasement still resonates in contemporary theory, simultaneously theorized in early modern rhetoric as perilous feminine excess and made the exclusive focus of a new rhetorical sub-genre? Why do Shakespeare, Spenser, Lanyer, Donne, and other early modern writers so often articulate meta-rhetorical reflections on simile when they thematize polymorphic forms of desire or intense eroticism?

In this book, I analyze theorizations of simile in early modern rhetoric in reference to early modern conceptualizations of several interrelated categories: the primal substance of semiosis, and the aesthetic categories of figure, trope, and metaphor. Each of these categories in relation to which simile is conceptualized in early modern language theory is the subject of a separate chapter. Each of these categories is shown to be theorized in terms of a different psycho-conceptual dynamic:

the primal substance of semiosis is shown to be aligned with femininity in its archaic maternal deployment;

"figure" is shown to be theorized in terms of seduction, fetishism, and perversion;

"trope," erroneously conflated with "figure" in contemporary theory, is shown to be theorized in terms of the phallic drive to colonization and possession;

"metaphor" is shown to be theorized in terms of de-subjectifying phallic desire and the fallacious insistence on Being and self-identity.

Of these categories, the primal substance of semiosis, figure, and simile are aligned with femininity and the unconscious, with manifestations of the archaic within the symbolic. Trope and metaphor are aligned with the symbolic in its repressive, prohibitive deployment. They are aligned with the psychic function of the phallus as bar rather than nurturing omphalos, with what seeks to bar the unconscious. Theorizations of trope and metaphor inevitably deconstruct in a way bespeaking the yearning for the archaic, for a primordial, unconscious eroticism underlying the humanist effort to construct a hyper-rational theory of signification.

My analysis of early modern theorizations of simile as an articulation of the archaic and omphalic within the symbolic in the last two chapters of this book is enabled by the analysis of categories related to simile in the first four chapters. My mode of argumentation proceeds by means of accretion, aiming at a constellation of concepts which clarify the omphalic aesthetics of simile. Proceeding by accretion, I demonstrate the inextricable intertwining of the simultaneous devaluation of and obsession with simile in early modern metalinguistic texts with a pervasive anxiety of female sexuality in its maternal deployment. My final chapter shows how, given the function of the maternal as the psychic grid for all objects of desire, simile is theorized in early modern rhetoric in relation to multiple forms of sexuality. These forms include matrimonial heterosexuality and forms beyond the phallic norm inscribed into the privileged categories of metaphor and trope: adultery, male and female homosexuality, and incest. Most significantly, as my penultimate chapter demonstrates, simile is conceptualized in early modern language theory at once in relation to multiple and excessive forms of sexuality, and as the linguistic substrate of a particular, non-phallic, omphalic, and non-ontological structure of desire and eroticism cutting across sexualities. This mode of desire, the most authentic articulation of the archaic within the symbolic, involves an embracing of intersubjective separation, transference, and approximation as necessary conditions for a constitutively fragmentary *jouissance*.

Part One
The Archaic Substance of Speech

CHAPTER ONE

Renaissance Rhetoric and the Dialectics of the Archaic Mother

> It is by embracing the mother-tongue, the blessed moment wherein the mother becomes words, that language first deploys itself.
> —Claude Louis-Combet, *Le don de langue*

Early modern treatises on the aesthetics of rhetoric often symptomatically describe the primal substance of semiosis as perilous and far from neutral. Richard Sherry's *Treatise of the Figures of Grammer and Rhetorike* ends in such a symptomatic moment. At the end of his treatise, Sherry refers to a "dissolute" semiosis "wau[ing] hyther & tyther, as it were without synewes and iointes, stading [sic] surely in no point" (fol. lxi).

Sherry theorizes the "dissolute" substance he describes in terms of liquidity. This substance, he says, "waueuth [waveth] hyther & tyther." Since liquidity has been ubiquitously associated with the feminine (Irigaray, *Marine Lover*, p. 32; Bachelard, pp. 20, 171), Sherry's transcoding of dissolute semiosis with the aquatic weights this type of semiosis toward femininity.

Other metalinguistic texts of the Renaissance offer similar conceptualizations of the substance of semiosis. Like Sherry's *Treatise of the Figures of Grammer and Rhetorike* (fol. ii), Henry Peacham's *Garden of Eloquence* of 1577 (sig. A3) speaks of the "great…floud of Eloquence." In *The Foundacion of Rhetorike* (1563), Richard Rainolde refers to the substance of semiosis as "flowing" (fol. ii). In *The Mysterie of Rhetorique Unvail'd* (1657), John Smith describes the substance with which his treatise is concerned as "streams" (unpaginated). In *De Arte Poetica* (ca. 1517), Marco

Girolamo Vida speaks of the "prolixity" of the substance of language (p. 87). In *Vocal Organ* (1665), Owen Price theorizes the classical languages as the "Fountains" of English, and the letters "m, n, r, and l" as "liquids" (unpaginated). In Erasmus's *De Copia*, the "speech of man" is imagined as a "river [of] thoughts and words pouring out in rich abundance" (p. 295). In all these cases, the substance of semiosis is liquefied and hence feminized. In Peter Erondell's *The French Garden* (1605), the feminization of the substance of semiosis is explicit. Erondell refers to this substance as "*Lingua Mulierum*" (woman-tongue) (unpaginated).

The semiotic substance Sherry speaks of is maritime and aquatic: it "waueth." Vida too speaks of the "prolix" substance of semiosis in terms of the maritime image of a "flowing wave" (*mobilis unda*). The imagining of semiotic substance as maritime activates one of the "most constant" archetypes of the maternal (Bachelard, p. 156), symptomatically registered in the phonic resonances between *mer* (sea) and *mère* (mother) in French. This archetype of the maritime as maternal conceptually links the waters of the ocean with the "milk" of the primal, archetypal Great Mother, the source of all life (ibid., p. 170).

The substance of semiosis Sherry describes as maritime is "dissolute," undivided. Centuries later, Freud was to describe a conceptually similar substance. In *Civilization and Its Discontents*, Freud theorizes an affective substance of "indissoluble connection" and "limitless extension" (pp. 2–4). Like Sherry, Freud speaks of this substance in terms of a feminizing aquatic image. He calls it "oceanic" (ibid., p. 1). The feminizing aquatic image in terms of which Freud theorizes the dissolute substance of oceanic affect is maritime and hence maternalizing. Like Freud's category of the boundless oceanic feeling, Sherry's category of dissolute semiosis taps into the archetype of maternal origin as boundless infinity.

The idea of the boundlessness of origin has a long history. In Greek mythology and its Babylonian and Egyptian sources, life is said to have been created out of "primeval...boundless waters" (Kirk and Raven, p. 12), conceptually coeval with Freud's limitless "oceanic." In Anaximander's early philosophical conceptualization of origin, the "cause of coming-to-be" is described as infinite (ibid., p. 107). In Greek mythology, and in early Greek philosophy, the embodiment of this boundless origin is Okeanos, "the source of all waters" and "origin of all things" (ibid., p. 11).

Although as origin, Okeanos is conceptually maternal, Plato, citing Homer, makes Okeanos a male "begetter of gods" (*Theaetetus*, 152e). In Renaissance representations Okeanos is at once archaic, conceptually maternal, and female. In the beginning of *The Shepheard's Complaint*, John

Dickenson speaks of "aged," archaic "Oceanos" as "she," and foregrounds her maternal function of nurturing the earth "with her morning tears" (p. 5). Sherry's invocation of the maritime to speak of a substance of signification harkens to ancient mythological inscriptions of origin as ocean. These inscriptions are informed by the archetype of the primal Great Mother. This archetype resonates in Dickenson's *Shepheard's Complaint* and other Renaissance texts.

The maternality ascribed to the substance of semiosis by Sherry and other early modern thinkers on rhetorical aesthetics is primal and archaic in individual yet archetypal terms. This is underscored in early modern formulations more explicit than Sherry's about the maternality of the substance of semiosis. The title of Richard Rainolde's treatise, *The Foundacion of Rhetorike*, references rhetoric's foundation or substance of origin. Rainolde describes this substance of origin as "flow[ing]" (unpagninated), liquid, and hence conceptually feminine. The rhetorician's task, Pierre de Courcelles writes in La Rhétorique (1540), is to enrich *"nôtre langue maternelle"* (our maternal language) (unpaginated). Referring to the primal substance of language as "maternal," de Courcelles, like Sherry, invokes the archetype of origin: the Great Mother and her oceanic inscriptions. In addition, de Courcelles invokes the manifestation of this archetype in the early stages of life: the signification heard by the subject-to-be in the earliest interactions with his/her mother or maternal surrogate.

In his *Syncrisis* (1677), the grammarian Elisha Coles too invokes the archetype of the archaic mother, and the concrete, individual manifestations of this archetype in early linguistic interactions between mother and child. Emphasizing the conceptual link between the substance of signification and a primal, archaic maternality, Coles describes the grammarian's task as rendering "familiar" a "Mother-Tongue" as "Ancient as Nature itself" (sigs. A1–A2). In the early modern aesthetic metalanguages of Coles and de Courcelles, as in the contemporary theorization of Claude Louis-Combet, the substance of signification is imagined as the "maternal language," traceable to the origin where "the mother is made words" (*Le don de langue*, p. 33).

The substance of semiosis described by Sherry is maternalized for another reason: its conceptualization as "sta[n]ding surely in no point" because it lacks stabilizing form. Similar conceptualizations of an amorphic substance of semiosis appear in other early modern metalinguistic treatises. In *De Copia*, Erasmus repudiates a substance of semiosis lacking "discrimination" and imaged as a "meaningless," formless "heap" (p. 295). John Smith describes the semiotic substance clarified by the figure of "hirmos" as a "confused heap of matter" (sig. A3). These conceptualizations of a semiotic substance without form are underlain by a "maternal semantic archaeology" whose source is in Aristotle. In this semantic archaeology, "(maternal) matter is the changing...receptacle that possesses no determination or consistency" in and of itself (Goux, *Symbolic Economies*, p. 5).

The associations drawn in early modern thinking on language between the primal substance of affect and signification, between the aquatic and maritime, and between the amorphic, the material, and the maternal, are made even more explicit by Sherry's near contemporary, the poet John Dickenson. In his pastoral romance *Arisbas*, of 1594, Dickenson speaks of the substance of semiosis as an "infinite...engulf[ing]...Ocean" of "copious matter" (p. 31). Just as in Sherry's rhetorical text, in which the substance of semiosis is imagined as limitless because lacking "sinewes" or discrete components, and "iointes" or links among them, in Dickenson's romance the substance of aesthetic signification is imagined as boundless, "infinite" (ibid.). Later in the same text, Dickenson speaks of this infinite substance of semiosis as amorphic and "not limit[ed]...with distinct clauses" (ibid., p. 35). Dickenson speaks of this boundless substance, which he explicitly associates with an "Ocean," as "exceed[ing]" and potentially "engulf[ing]" the subject. Dickenson describes the oceanic substance of language and affect as something in which the subject may be "Drowned" (ibid., p. 34). He anticipates by several centuries Freud's characterization of the "oceanic" as an affective state in which "the boundary line" separating self from other, and self from world "becomes uncertain" (*Civilization and Its Discontents*, p. 3).

Like Sherry, Dickenson speaks of the primal substance of semiosis as amorphic. This substance, he writes, "admit[s] no methode" (*Arisbas*, p. 34), no conceptually paternal pattern (Goux, *Symbolic Economies*, p. 222). Instead, Dickenson describes the primal substance of semiosis as conceptually maternal "matter" (*Arisbas*, p. 31). Similar descriptions of this substance appear in Thomas Wilson's *Arte of Rhetorique* (1560) (p. 49), and in Richard Rainolde's *Foundacion of Rhetorike* (fol. ii).

These descriptions of the substance of language as "matter" tap into the conceptual link forged in Aristotelian and post-Aristotelian philosophy between the material and the maternal, between matter and *mater* (Goux, *Symbolic Economies*, p. 228). In Sherry's *Treatise of Schemes and Tropes* (1550), "matter" is explicitly described as the "receptacle of all formes" (unpaginated), and in Smith's *Mysterie of Rhetorique Unvail'd*, the "substance" of semiosis is identified as "matter" and contrasted with "form" or "inward principle" (unpaginated). In the two cases, the Aristotelian distinction between "matter" as female and "form" as the "male" she "desires" (Goux, *Symbolic Economies*, p. 232) is even more clearly at work. In the tradition of thought looking back to Aristotelian philosophy within which Dickenson and the Renaissance rhetoricians write, matter is conceptualized as the archaic "All-Mother," the "source of things in the sense of being their underlie" (Irigaray, *Speculum*, p. 179).

The maternalization of the substance of signification in Dickenson's text is underscored by its characterization as "copious," in terms of the rhetorical category of *copia*. The category of *copia* carries associations with "abundance, fertility, and fruitfulness...crystallized in the image of the cornucopia" (Cave, "Copia and Cornucopia," p. 59). Dickenson invokes these associations when speaking of the "copious matter" of language as "plentie" (*Arisbas*, p. 31). Rhetoricians of Dickenson's time too speak of the substance of language in terms of fertility. Thomas Wilson describes this substance as "plentiful matter" (*Arte of Rhetorique*, p. 49). Richard Rainolde speaks of the substance of language as characterized by "aboundaunce and plentuousness" (fol. ii). John Smith theorizes this substance as a "fruitful field" (unpaginated).

In all these cases, thinkers on language of Dickenson's time link the substance of language with the fertility inscribed in the rhetorical category of *copia* (Parker, *Literary Fat Ladies*, p. 15). Dickenson's image of "copious matter" conceptually aligns the substance of aesthetic signification with the fertility of the female body. This association overdetermines the maternalization of the substance of signification established by means of its conceptual links with the material, the liquid, the maritime, and the amorphic, in Dickenson's romance and in the rhetorical texts of Sherry, Peacham, Rainolde, Smith, and Erasmus.

The theorizations of the primal substance of aesthetic signification as maternal in the texts of early modern rhetoricians, grammarians, and poets has intriguing affinities with theorizations of primal language by feminist psychoanalysts such as Hélène Cixous and Julia Kristeva (Sharon-Zisser, "Wanting Word of Woman"). In Bernard Lamy's *Art of Speaking* (1676), the "material" and hence conceptually maternal "Body" of semiosis is identified with "sound" (pp. 181–182), with the orality at the focus of the drives oriented toward the maternal body in the primal, oral stage of the psyche. Centuries later, Cixous postulates an archaic "Voice" of "first, nameless love" (*Newly Born Woman*, p. 93). She locates this "Voice" at "a time before the law" (ibid.). She identifies this time as the time of "the relationship to the 'mother'" who is "always...repairing and feeding, resisting separation" (ibid.).

Cixous's archaic "Voice" is distinctly maternalized. This "Voice" is described as "milk that could go on forever" (*Newly Born Woman*, p. 93), in terms of a "material imagination" for which "any blissful drink is maternal milk" (Bachelard, p. 158).

Cixous's notion of primal maternal Voice is akin to Kristeva's concept of the archaic register of the "semiotic": the "vocal and kinetic rhythm[s]...oriented and structured around the mother's body" before "the establishment of the sign" (*Kristeva Reader*, pp. 94–95).

Cixous and Kristeva idealize the archaic maternal substance of semiosis. The idealization of the archaic substance of language imagined as maternal makes its recovery, assumed to be possible, imperative. Cixous calls for a retrieval of a "voice mixed with milk," and identified with "the lost mother" (p. 93). This retrieval, she insists, must be effected through the destroying "explosion" of the "masculine...economy" of signification (*Newly Born Woman*, p. 93). Cixous identifies "rhetoric" as part of this masculine economy (ibid.). For her, the "masculine" language of rhetoric is the "locus of repression" of archaic maternal Voice ("Laugh of the Medusa," pp. 245, 249).

For Kristeva, the archaic substance of signification is the incantatory register of the "semiotic." This register mediates the relation of the subject-to-be to the mother's body. The register opposed to the semiotic is the "symbolic." For Kristeva, the symbolic is the register of codified metalanguages, including, implicitly, the metalanguage of rhetoric. Kristeva identifies the symbolic as a "phallic" register. According to Kristeva, the register of the symbolic supplants and seeks to "censor" the maternal semiotic register. The advent of the phallic register of the symbolic marks the scission of the subject from the maternal body as "receptacle and guarantor of demands" (*Kristeva Reader*, pp. 101–102, 113).

Less militantly than Cixous but no less nostalgically, Kristeva applauds instances where codified language breaks down, allowing the maternalized semiotic to irrupt. She identifies such instances in poetic language. Instances of poetic language, and conceptually akin instances in pictorial art, are, for Kristeva, samples of "aesthetic practice[s]" whose effect is to "shatter" the "phallic" register of the symbolic "seal[ing] off...and...censur[ing]" the "archaic basis" of semiosis, a basis she identifies with the *jouissance* in/of the primal maternal body (*Desire in Language*, pp. 241–243, 269).

Cixous and Kristeva celebrate and advocate the practice of a form of aesthetic semiosis they portray as archaic and maternal. They portray this form of signification as archaic and maternal more explicitly but no less profoundly than Renaissance thinkers on language such as Sherry, Peacham, Dickenson, Smith, Rainolde, Price, Coles, and de Courcelles.

The attitude of these and other male Renaissance thinkers on language to the archaic substance of signification is complex and dialectical. This attitude to the origins of signification as inseparable from the origins of infants inadvertently and uneasily echoes in the theories of feminist psychoanalysts. The attitude of Renaissance rhetoricians to the primal substance of semiosis is at the same time undeniably different from the attitude of feminist psychoanalysts to this substance.

Sherry, for instance, places a negative value-judgment on the infinite, dissolute, oceanic, conceptually maternal, and archaic substance of semiosis. He labels this substance "fawtye" (faulty), and associates it with the inverse of the affect of being "sure" (*Grammer and Rhetorike*, fol. lxi). Dickenson articulates the dangers posed by the "Ocean" of primal semiosis he transcodes with the "plenty" and fecundity of the maternal body. He speaks of this substance as "ouerwhelm[ing]" the subject (*Arisbas*, p. 31). Erasmus too is wary of the maternality he ascribes to the substance of semiosis. In the same passage wherein he describes the liquidity, "abundance," and amorphousness of this substance, Erasmus describes engagement with it as an enterprise of "considerable risk" (p. 295).

In those formulations, Dickenson, Erasmus, and Sherry represent the archaic maternality they attribute to the primal substance of signification as threatening and entailing risk. They point to this substance as a cause for anxiety. They imply the use of this substance should be avoided. The practitioner of rhetoric, Sherry cautions, should not "come...nie unto it" (*Grammer and Rhetorike*, fol. lxi).

Another symptomatic indication of the anxiety generated by the association of the primal substance of signification with an archaic maternality preceding all separations and scissions occurs at the end of Thomas Wilson's *Arte of Rhetorique*. "I fear none," Wilson claims in the closing sentence of his rhetorical treatise, "because I stand upon a safe ground" (p. 244). Wilson ends his treatise with a disavowal of anxiety. Because disavowal is an implicit recognition of what is denied (Evans, p. 44), Wilson's disavowal indexes his relation to the substance of semiosis he had theorized throughout the preceding text as anything but "safe." The substance of semiosis itself induces the disavowed "fear."

Wilson's statement of disavowal indexes an anxiety as intense as its totalizing denial. This statement of disavowal points to the source of the rhetorician's anxiety. Indirectly linking the preceding exposition of the precepts of rhetoric with a *terra firma* or "safe ground," Wilson's statement points to the substance of semiosis to which he had applied these precepts as neither safe nor firm. The substance Wilson imagines is something in relation to which "ground" seems a "safe" place of refuge. Like the pre-verbalized affective-semiotic substance with no "distinct clauses" in Dickenson's *Arisbas*, the substance Wilson anxiously imagines at the end of his treatise is one in which the subject might be "Drowned" (Dickenson, *Arisbas*, p. 34). In Wilson's *Arte of Rhetorique*, as in the texts of Dickenson, Sherry, Peacham, Smith, and Erasmus, the primal substance of semiosis is related to an engulfing liquidity conceptually coeval with the psychic state Freud would label "oceanic."

In Wilson's *Arte of Rhetorique*, as in Sherry's *Treatise of the Figures of Grammer and Rhetorike*, where dissolute oceanic liquidity is associated with a state of not being "sure," the liquidity attributed to the primal substance of semiosis is indexed as a major cause for the rhetorician's anxiety. The phobic articulations of early modern thinkers on language concerning the liquidity of what constitutes signs verify one of Lacan's insights. "All use of language," Lacan was to write centuries later of the same anxiety, "incurs fright." What is most "frightening" about language, Lacan adds, is the "prolixity" of its substance (*Seminar III*, p. 227).

Dickenson's conceptualization of the primal substance of semiosis indicates the reasons for the anxiety of the oceanic liquidity attributed to this substance in his text, just as in the phobic formulations of Erasmus, Wilson, and Sherry. Such a substance, Dickenson suggests, "ouerhelme[s]," "engulf[s]," and potentially "Drown[s]" the subject. Such a dissolute substance, he further suggests, potentially drowns the "distinct clauses" of language (*Arisbas*, pp. 31, 35). Erasmus too identifies the lack of a differentiating "discrimination" in the oceanic substance of primal semiosis as the source of the "risk" this substance entails (*De Copia*, p. 295). Sherry similarly expresses unease over the absence of "perfecte...woordes" from the primal, dissolute substance of signification. For Sherry, the codified system of language consists of particular sounds "coprehend[ing]" (*sic*) particular "thyng[s]" or ideas (*Grammer and Rhetorike*, fol. lxi). The dissolute substance of language, Sherry implies, threateningly lacks distinct and self-contained units. In the texts of Dickenson, Wilson, Erasmus, and Sherry, the primal, oceanic substance of semiosis is imagined as posing a threat of inundation. Such inundation, these early modern thinkers on language fear, would dissolve differentiating limits. These limits, the transcoding of chaotic language and emotional chaos in Dickenson's romance and in Wilson's rhetorical treatise suggest, are limits defining and differentiating subjects as much as words.

In thinking of codified language as system of particular and distinct elements, Dickenson, Wilson, Erasmus, and Sherry anticipate Saussure's theorization of language as a medium "in which there are only differences" (p. 129). In thinking of subjects as defined by differentiating limits, Dickenson and Wilson anticipate Lacan's theorization of subjectivity as separation, as a "discontinuity in the real" (*Écrits*, p. 299). In anxiously theorizing a dissolute substance of signification, the early modern thinking of rhetoric anticipates fundamental concepts of contemporary linguistic and psychoanalytical theory.

This anticipation notwithstanding, the attitude of early modern thinkers to a substance of origin lacking discontinuities and separating limits seems to be different from the attitude of contemporary thinkers to such a substance, whether of language or of affect. For Lacan, an undifferentiated substance of origin is unimaginable. Kristeva does imagine an archaic psychic substance of non-differentiation. Although even biologically speaking, the embryo is separated from the mother's body by the placenta, Kristeva theorizes an archaic psychic substance of "fusion with the mother" (*Kristeva Reader*, p. 101). The oral manifestation of this fusional substance is the pre-linguistic register of the "semiotic," an unpredictable register lacking the differentiating scissions of the symbolic. Kristeva's attitude toward the fusional psychic substance registered in the semiotic is extremely positive. She speaks of it as a substance of "maternal *jouissance*" (*Desire in Language*, p. 242). For Dickenson, Wilson, Erasmus, and Sherry, the primal substance lacking limits, discriminations, and distinctions appears to be unequivocally inducive of an anxiety of inundation. These early modern thinkers appear to conceive of this primal substance without limits as, in Dickenson's terms, an "auncient Chaos, wherin [sic] all things (if things) were confounded" (*Arisbas*, p. 33), a chaos in which the particularity of "things" is frighteningly lost.

The anxiety of the substance of origin expressed in early modern texts has more to it than the threat of the loss of differentiating boundaries constituting subjects and signs. This anxiety proceeds from the imagining of this substance as "limitless," like Freud's category of the oceanic (*Civilization and Its Discontents*, p. 1). Limitless in itself, the substance of origin imagined by early modern thinkers is inducive of anxiety because, like Freud's oceanic, it "threatens to obliterate" other, discrete substances (ibid.). Another source of the anxiety expressed by Renaissance thinkers in relation to the liquid substance of semiotic origin is the imagined maternality of this liquidity. Given the imagined maternality of the primal substance of semiosis, the anxiety of this substance articulated by Dickenson, Sherry, Wilson, and Erasmus is a manifestation of the fear of the archetypal Terrible Mother.

In the primal stages of life, the mother is "world and self in one" for the subject-to-be (Neumann, *Fear of the Feminine*, p. 231). While the child develops toward individuation, the identification between mother and child becomes progressively less total. During stages of individuation, the mother becomes associated with the archetype of the Terrible Mother because the engulfing nurturing she provides "hinders the development" of the child toward subjectivity as separation (ibid., p. 239).

The fear of an archetypal, archaic maternality thwarting the development toward distinctness is, Neumann argues, "concentrated in fear of the female body" (ibid., p. 259). The maternal body, Kristeva too argues, becomes a locus of aversion and repugnance, a not-I "disturb[ing] identity," from which the subject must differentiate (*Powers of Horror*, p. 4). In Kristeva's terms, the potentially engulfing maternal body is "abject" (ibid., p. 8). For Kristeva, the abject is the maternal body in each subject's history, and the archetypal "archaic Mother goddess" from which the subject must separate (ibid., p. 100) by way of relating to her as horrifying and repulsive (ibid., p. 54).

Kristeva describes the maternal body in its abject inflection as a site of fear and of repulsion (ibid., p. 38). The fear she identifies in relation to the archaic maternal body is the fear of the loss of differentiating boundaries incurred by the "fusional...archaic dyad" of mother and embryo (ibid.).

This fear of inundation appears to univocally underlie the phobic expressions made by Dickenson, Wilson, Sherry, and Erasmus regarding a primal substance of signification imagined in oceanic terms. Yet the fear Kristeva identifies in relation to the maternal body is, dialectically, the fear of the loss of imaginary fusion with the archaic mother with the advent of subjectivity as separation (ibid., p. 41). Several separations from the archaic mother mark the course of the subject's early psychic life. The embryo is separated from the mother's body by the placenta, and biologically separates from the placenta at birth, a process described by Freud as the "model" for any subsequent anxiety (*Symptoms, Inhibitions, and Anxiety*, p. 63). The fall from the placental is followed by physical separation from the mother in the early stages of life, when the infant is totally dependent on her for nourishment and the removal of outside dangers (ibid., p. 66). Kristeva discusses this type of separation as causing fear (*Powers of Horror*, p. 40). Most traumatic and anxiety-inducing is the psychic separation from the archaic relation to the mother with the advent of subjectivity (ibid., p. 46).

The anxiety expressed by early modern thinkers in relation to the primal substance of signification they transcode with the primal maternal body is not categorical or unequivocal but dialectical. According to Claude Conté, anxiety in general has a dialectical structure (pp. 17, 22). The anxiety related to the maternal body is an anxiety of the loss of the separateness constituting subjectivity. This is an anxiety of the subject's being inundated and obliterated by a dissolving substance threatening the subject from the outside. Because this dissolving substance is threatening to the subject, it is imagined as repulsive and abject. The anxiety related to the maternal body with which Renaissance thinkers transcode the primal substance of semiosis is simultaneously an anxiety of the loss of the fusional substance imagined to precede the separateness subtending subjectivity. For Renaissance thinkers on language, this loss is irremediable. Unlike Cixous and Kristeva, they do not regard archaic fusion with the mother as even momentarily recuperable.

The anxiety of losing the primal unity with the archaic mother is closely linked with the mouth, the organ by means of which the infant holds on to the mother's breast and incorporates the physical nurturing she provides. The mouth is the organ by means of which the mother provides the aural satisfactions attendant upon her production of the "rhythmic and intonational...vocal modulations" of the pre-linguistic register of the "semiotic" (*Kristeva Reader*, p. 96), the "mother-tongue" (Jacobus, p. 160). The anxiety of losing primal fusion is a predominantly oral anxiety, focussed on the "oral object...that sets up archaic relationships between the human being and...its mother" (Kristeva, *Powers of Horror*, pp. 75–76).

The phobic articulations of early modern theorists of language in relation to the primal substance of semiosis are symptoms of this anxiety of losing the primal oral object and, simultaneously, of the anxiety of being engulfed by this object. Kristeva describes "any verbalizing activity, whether or not it names a phobic object related to orality," as an attempt to psychically "confront" the phobic oral object. For Kristeva, any verbalizing activity involves an attempt to undo the anxiety of loss induced by the oral object. The essence of this attempt to undo anxiety is the substitution of words for the lost mother's breast, the major corporeal site of imagined archaic fusion with her (*Powers of Horror*, p. 41).

Lacan too theorizes language as a symbolic substitute for the primal oral object, the mother's breast (*Seminar IV*, p. 175). For Lacan as for Kristeva, the systems of signification constituting the register of the symbolic, including the codes of logic, grammar, and rhetoric, are symptoms of the anxiety related to the loss of the primal oral object. According to Lacan and Kristeva, these codes are generated in an attempt to allay the anxiety related to the loss of the primal oral object. The codes of language, including rhetoric, are substituted for "the good maternal object that is wanting," for "maternal care," for "the good breast" (Kristeva, *Powers of Horror*, p. 45).

Lacan and Kristeva theorize linguistic codes as counter-phobic operations. In light of these theorizations, the systems of rhetorical aesthetics constructed by Erasmus, Sherry, Wilson, Peacham, Smith, Coles, and the other Renaissance rhetoricians I discuss in this book are attempts to compensate for the loss of an archaic oral object. These attempts to compensate proceed by theorizing forms of rhetorical aesthetics as objects to be placed in the mouths of subjects who have lost their primal oral, maternal object. Kristeva calls the process of placing words in empty mouths "introjection" (*Powers of Horror*, p. 41). Nicolas Abraham and Maria Torok do the same (*The Shell and the Kernel*, p. 128).

The idea of language as substitute oral object is not an invention of the psychoanalysts of this century. In *The English Parnassus* (1657), Joshua Poole explicitly transcodes "poesie," the object of his aesthetic reflection, with the primal oral object, the "first milk" (unpaginated). In the dedication to his treatise, Poole fantasizes about "babes" who "lugge" this lactic-linguistic substance from "nipples." He proceeds to describe these nipples as "coral." This description phonically links these nipples with the *chora*, the primordial substance Plato speaks of in the *Timaeus* as "nourishing and maternal" (*Kristeva Reader*, p. 94), and, inseparably, with the oral.

The postulation of Renaissance rhetoric as an oral substitute for the lost satisfactions afforded by the primal oral object is suggested by the close engagement of Renaissance rhetoricians with the literary genre of pastoral. Pastoral's psychological object of representation is the "eternal polymorphism" of the "archaic libido" characterizing the primal, oral stage of psychic development (Lacan, *Seminar VII*, p. 92). Pastoral texts thematize the polymorphic libido in its relation to the "erogenous zones," orifices, or "mouths at the body's surface," where "Eros...find[s] his source" (ibid., p. 93). Stephen Whitworth has appropriately termed this genre past-oral. This genre enjoyed a vogue in the English Renaissance, whose psychological and rhetorical complexities Whitworth has begun to unfold in a series of dazzling readings.

The pastorals of the English Renaissance include well-known texts such as Sidney's *Arcadia*, Spenser's *Shepheardes Calender*, and Shakespeare's similaically entitled *As You Like It*. Lesser-known pastoral texts of the English Renaissance are Shakespeare's unjustly neglected "Lover's Complaint," Angel Day's *Shepheards Holidaie* (1587), Richard Barnfield's *The Affectionate Shepheard* (1594), Michael Drayton's *Shepheard's Garland* (1593), William Smith's *Chloris: The Complaint of the Passionate Despis'd Shepheard* (1596), and John Dickenson's undated *Shepheard's Complaint*. Other English Renaissance pastorals include works stylistically and conceptually allied with John Lyly's *Euphues: The Anatomy of Wit* (1587). Among these are Thomas Lodge's *Rosalynd: Euphues' Golden Legacy, found after his death in his cell at Silexedra* (1592), John Dickenson's *Arisbas: Euphues Amidst his Slumbers* (1594), and Robert Greene's *Menaphon: Camilla's Alarum to Slumbering Euphues in his Melancholie Cell in Silexedra* (1589).

Like all pastorals, the Euphuistic pastorals of Dickenson, Greene, and Lodge are related to the oral conceptually and psychologically, in their representation of a polymorphic sexuality characterizing the primal, oral phase of the libido. Euphuistic pastorals are linked with the oral stylistically too. Their style, influenced by John Lyly's *Euphues*, is euphonic, "made and measured by the ear" (Child Griffin, p. 80). Euphuistic style privileges and foregrounds the acoustic effects of assonance, alliteration, symmetry, and formal balance. In *Orpharion* (1599), Robert Greene defines Euphuism as a style involving the "musicall concorde of...sweet moodes graced with...harmonious discords" (title page). According to Greene, the desired effect of Euphuistic style is to "sound...pleasure...to the eare" (ibid.). Greene describes Euphuism as a style in which the orality of poetic voice aims not at the communication of ideas but at the aural pleasure of an other. "The voyce is made the eare for to reioce: / And your eare giueth pleasure to my voice," the speaker of the first sonnet in Henry Constable's *Diana* sequence (1594) says to his beloved, in a poetic formulation of the Euphuistic aesthetics of oral/aural joy-giving linguistic joining (lines 12–14).

In Euphuistic, past-oral aesthetics, "the ear of the Other," to use Derrida's term, functions as an erogenous zone with the same "invaginated folds and...involuted orificiality" of the mouth (Derrida, *The Ear of the Other*, p. 36). In Euphuistic aesthetics, the ear accepts poetic voice as a pleasure-giving stand-in, bearing the signature of the maternal" (ibid., p. 21), for a lost primal oral object. The "ear of the Other," Derrida remarks, is "an orifice for the mother-tongue" (ibid., pp. 21, 35).

The concern with euphony, with the aural pleasures afforded by the orality of voice underlying the aesthetics of the Euphuistic writers of pastoral was not foreign to the rhetoricians who were their contemporaries.

The list of figures of speech in Sherry's *Treatise of Schemes and Tropes* includes "tasis" or "extensio." Sherry theorizes tasis in terms of a pleasure-giving orality as "a turning of voyce in pleasaunte pronounciation," or "a swete and pleasaunte modulacion or tunablenes of wordes" (*Schemes and Tropes*, unpaginated). Sherry's theorization of tasis is similar to Puttenham's definition of "musicall speech" as "tunable...melodious," and "delicate to the eare" (p. 5). Sherry's sensitivity to the acoustics of speech, and his desire to make rhetoric a medium of pleasure-giving orality, are apparent in the first sentence of the dedication of the *Treatise of Schemes and Tropes*. In this opening sentence, Sherry declares his worry of his treatise's appearing "straunge unto our Englyshe *eares*" (unpaginated, emphasis mine).

Other Renaissance rhetoricians express the view of rhetoric as pleasure-giving orality. In the dedicatory epistle to *The Garden of Eloquence*, Peacham describes the function of his treatise as providing "delight [to] the eares...as running poyntes in Musick" (sig. A3). In the dedicatory epistle to *The Academie of Eloquence* (1654), Thomas Blount describes eloquence as "mak[ing] use of...voice...to enchant the Eares, with the cadence of periods, and the harmony of Accents" (unpaginated). Marco Girolamo Vida celebrates the abilities of the rhetorician to send an "impulse of delight" into the "ears" of his listeners, thereby causing them a "boundless pleasure" (p. 87). Puttenham devotes five chapters of *The Arte of English Poesie* (1589) to "auricular" figures, described as "pleasant and agreable to the eare" (p. 234). In all these cases, Renaissance rhetoricians offer their theorizations of linguistic forms as oral objects whose insertion into the aural orifice affords pleasure.

These theorizations of aesthetic forms conceptually resonate with the Euphuistic aesthetics informing a strain of Renaissance pastorals thematizing the archaic, as do all instances of the pastoral genre (Lacan, *Seminar VII*, p. 89). This conceptual resonance between Renaissance theorizations of aesthetic forms in terms of a pleasure-giving orality and the thematic and psychological concerns of Renaissance past-orality inflects the oral/aural pleasure of which the rhetoricians speak as an attempted re-creation of an archaic bliss whose focus is the maternal body. Puttenham's theorization of auricular figures paronomastically suggests this. The purpose of auricular figures, Puttenham states, is to provide the "eare" with "a certain *recreation*" (p. 236, emphasis mine).

The notion of language as an oral object attempting to substitute for archaic contact with the mother is not the only point of connection and overlap between Renaissance rhetoric and Renaissance pastoral.

Renaissance rhetoricians often cite passages from pastoral texts to elucidate aesthetic forms. Abraham Fraunce makes Spenser's *Shepheardes Calender* the source of examples in his treatises on logic and rhetoric. In the *Treatise of Schemes and Tropes*, Sherry cites "Bucolicall" poetry "where y herd men do speke of nete and shepe" (unpaginated). In the *Treatise of the Figures of Grammer and Rhetorike*, Sherry cites "the peace worlde in the fourth Egloge of Virgill" as an example of "chronographia" (fol. xlvil). Peacham exemplifies metalepsis by means of Virgil's use of "eares of Corn [to] signify...haruesters" in his *Eclogues* (*Garden of Eloquence*, unpaginated). In Marco Girolamo Vida's *De Arte Poetica*, Virgil, primarily in his capacity as a writer of pastoral who "exalted above the heavens the hallowed rites of the countryside," is invoked as the "father" of rhetoric (p. 123). In Thomas Blount's *Academie of Eloquence*, figures are said to be "exemplifi'd out of" a contemporary pastoral, Sidney's *Arcadia* (unpaginated), cited as the "fountain" of the examples in the epistle to the reader in John Smith's *Mysterie of Rhetorique Unvail'd* (unpaginated) too. In such cases, the rhetorical treatise grants resonance to the text of pastoral. It becomes a substitute in the second power for the lost archaic state. The rhetoric book functions as a textual substitute for the gratifications of primal orality, and disseminates a thematization of this past-orality.

Some Renaissance theorists of language create an even stronger link between rhetoric and pastoral. In addition to using passages from pastoral texts to exemplify their metalanguage, they transcode their metalanguage with pastoral. The title of Peacham's treatise, *The Garden of Eloquence*, collapses the metalinguistic concept of "eloquence" with the image of the "garden," an image whose biblical inflection carries associations of primal, pre-lapsarian, past-oral bliss. The titles of Peter Erondell's *The French Garden* and John Bodenham's compendium of similes, *Belvedere or the Garden of the Muses* (1600), similarly pastoralize language by transcoding it with the image of the garden. Henry Vaughan's entitling his treatise on rhetoric, published in 1600, *The Golden Grove*, conflates the domains of language and of a pastoral grove. The imaging of this "grove" as "golden" further inflects Vaughan's idea of rhetoric toward pastorality. This image taps into the topos of pastoral a golden age. Peacham and Bodenham were not the first to collapse rhetoric with the image of the garden as a blissful, pleasure-giving pastoral site in the titles of their meta-linguistic treatises. One of their French predecessors, Antoine Vérard, entitled his treatise on rhetoric, published in 1501, *Le Jardin de Plaisance* (the garden of pleasure).

In the sub-title of Peacham's treatise and in Bodenham's epistle to the reader, the forms of rhetoric are collapsed with "flowers," components of the pastoral world traditionally linked with desire and "amorous emotions" (Bataille, "The Language of Flowers," *Visions of Excess*, p. 11). The same collapsing of rhetorical forms into flowers occurs in the subtitle of Antoine Vérard's *Jardin de Plaisance: Fleur de Rhétorique* (flower of rhetoric) and in Girolamo Mascher's eponymous *Il Fiore Della Retorica* (1560). The "excellent flowres" to be found in the "Muses Garden," Bodenham tells the reader in his dedicatory epistle, are "most learned, graue, and wittie sentences" (unpaginated). In Vida's *De Arte Poetica*, the forms of rhetoric are imaged as "a thick shower of blossoms" *(florum)* (86). A similar mapping of rhetoric onto pastoral in terms of images of gardens and flowers occurs in *The Treatise of Schemes and Tropes*. In Sherry's dedicatory epistle, the experience of learning rhetoric is compared to the experience of going "into a goodlye garden garnyshed wyth dyuers kindes of herbes and flowers" (unpaginated). In the commendation for publication of John Smith's *The Mysterie of Rhetorique Unvail'd*, the author is applauded for having made a "collection of so many choice Flowers of Rhetorique" (unpaginated). The epistle to the reader of this rhetorical treatise refers to the treatise as "a pleasant garden, bedecked with flowers" (unpaginated). In all these cases, the elocutionary is mapped onto the fl-oral and situated in the conceptual and psychic field of past-oral.

The mapping of the elocutionary onto the floral found in early modern treatises on rhetoric has medieval precursors. A prominent medieval rhetorician, Alberic of Montecassino, entitles his metalinguistic treatise *Flores Rhetorici* (rhetorical flowers). In the *Ars Versificatoria* of Matthew of Vendôme, another prominent rhetorician of the European Middle Ages, the space of "the form of words" is imaged as the space of "Flora, the portress of spring, [who] adorned...the earth with a many-colored mantle of flowers" (p. 61). Matthew of Vendôme describes this space of aesthetic forms qua flowers as a space of "dedicated desire[s]," of amorous passions thematized in pastoral texts from as early on as Longus' *Daphnis and Chloe* and the Biblical Song of Songs. Even more intriguingly, Matthew of Vendôme images the space of rhetoric qua pastoral in terms of the most primal, archaic forms of amorous passions, those connected with "the beginnings of birth," and with "delicate infancy" (p. 61). Overdetermining the psychic orality accruing to rhetorical forms by virtue of their encoding into flowers situated in the space of pastoral, Matthew of Vendôme describes the primal libidinal affects he transcodes with these forms as "striv[ing] to indulge in half-formed laughter" (p. 61), in an oral expression of nascent archaic *jouissance*.

Matthew of Vendôme's early modern successors foreground the psychic orality involved in rhetorical/past-oral pleasure. Erondell speaks of the oral inflection of "pronounciation" as the "gate through the which" one "enter[s]" the meta-linguistic field of his treatise as pastoral garden. Sherry speaks of this entry as an experience not of intellectual enlightenment but of "corporall...pleasure" (*Schemes and Tropes*, unpaginated). Like the most primal, corp-oral *jouissance*, the pleasure Sherry speaks of is predicated on the corporeal, on the material, and on the conceptually maternal.

Other Renaissance rhetoricians habitually speak of the pleasures offered by the "flowers" of rhetoric primarily not as orally-expressed but as orally-experienced by an organ "circumscrib[ing] an internal space," a cavity within which pleasure resonates (Montrelay, p. 88). Predicated on a distinct structuring of a surface of pleasure rather than on the anatomical specificity of an organ, oral pleasures include "tastes, sounds, perfumes" sensed by the ear, the nose, and the mouth (ibid.).

In view of the multifarious sensuousness of orality, we should not be surprised by the ease with which Renaissance rhetoricians move among the olfactory, the aural, and the gustatory when collapsing rhetoric into pastoral and describing the delights offered by rhetorical forms as flowers. Vida, for instance, speaks of the "blossoms" he transcodes with the forms of rhetoric as affording sensuous "pleasures...fit for the gods" (p. 86). These sensuous pleasures are multiple, and they are all psychically oral. Vida collapses his rhetorical forms qua flowers into the "liquid essence" extracted from them, the orally-consumed "liquor of ambrosia" (*ambrosiae liquor*) (ibid.). He implicitly references the "divine voluptuousness" (*divina voluptas*) these forms qua flowers offer as a gustatory voluptuousness. For Vida, the voluptuous "pleasures" afforded by the ambrosia he transcodes with rhetorical forms are olfactory too. This ambrosia, he says, yields "sweet fragrance" (ibid.). At the same time, Vida describes this fragrance as orally-emitted "breath" whose effects are aural (ibid.). In Vida's text, gustatory delights shade into olfactory, and potentially into aural delights.

The sliding of olfactory into aural pleasure suggested in Vida's text is actualized in the text of his contemporary Francis Bacon. In his essay *On Gardens*, Bacon speaks of the olfactory "delights" of flowers (p. 73). He describes the fragrance of flowers as "Sweete...in the Aire" (ibid.). Like Vida, Bacon describes floral fragrance as an orally-emitted "Breath," whose effects are aural. Bacon explicitly mentions the aural pleasures afforded by the breath he transcodes with floral fragrance. He speaks of this breath as a "Warbling of Musick" (ibid.). In George Chapman's "Ovid's Banquet of Sense" too, aural and olfactory pleasures shade into one another. In this poem, Ovid is described as lured by the "sweetness of voice" of his beloved Corinna (Argument) to draw physically nearer to her and sensually experience "Her odours" (p. 25). These "odours" are "odour'd" with the maiden's "breast" (ibid.). They are "odour'd" with her aurally effective "breath" too (ibid.). In Chapman's poem, as in the texts of Bacon and Vida, the sensuous pleasures of "perfumes and sounds" (p. 27) shade into one another phonically and conceptually.

Centuries after Chapman, Bacon, and Vida, Michèle Montrelay was to speak of olfactory pleasures as structurally and psychically related to aural pleasures. For Montrelay, olfactory pleasures are circumscribed by an organ whose "surface dynamizes vibrations and breaths, transforming them into sonorities resonating in an interior space," and "functioning as a prototype of all musical instruments" (p. 88). The above examples from Vida, Bacon, and Chapman show how Montrelay's idea of the pleasures of odors and sonorities as conceptually related to one another through the category of orally-emitted breath was not foreign to Renaissance thinkers. The idea of olfactory and aural pleasures as structurally and psychically oral too is not altogether an invention of contemporary psychoanalysis. This idea is implicit in early modern theorizations of orally-emitted and aurally-received rhetorical forms as flowers offering olfactory pleasures. The phonic and conceptual link emphasized in Renaissance treatises on rhetoric between the fl-oral and the past-oral inflects these pleasures as related to the archaic, to the most primal psychic state Freud was to theorize as oral.

The conceptual relation between the elocutionary qua floral and archaic *jouissance* is foregrounded in John Bodenham's *Belvedere*. Bodenham associates the rhetorical "flowers" collected in his treatise with a "happinesse" consisting of their "affoord[ing]" every conceivable "delight or pleasure" (sig. A4). For Bodenham, this "happinesse" is primal and archaic. This is suggested by Bodenham's description of the rhetorical qua pastoral space of his treatise as the space "where these flowres [of rhetoric] had their first springing" (sig. A4). Bodenham speaks of his text as an object made of the most archaic substance of semiosis. He then offers the text as having the power to "heale":

> If thy conscience be wounded, here are a store of hearbs to heale it: If thy doubts be fearfull, here are flowres of comfort. Are thy hopes frustrated? here's immediate helpes for them. In briefe, what infirmitie canst thou haue, but here it may be cured? (sig. A4)

Bodenham offers his rhetorical object as able to cure fears, frustrations, and pains of loss. His characterization of this object as archaic inflects these fears, frustrations, and pains as incurred by the scissions attendant upon the emergence from the imagined archaic fusion of mother and subject-to-be. This is an emergence into subjectivity as separation, and into the frustration-inducing prohibitions imposed on subjectivity, into the "state of Not...the state of emergency in life" (Lacan, *Seminar VII*, p. 46). The power of the rhetorical object to allay the frustration and fear attendant upon the loss of imagined archaic fusion, Bodenham suggests, accounts for its ability to "afoord" pleasure.

In Bodenham's treatise as in all cases rhetoric is pastoralized, forms of language, collapsed into their "first spring[s]" (unpaginated), are "substituted for maternal care" such as is expected by the subject-to-be in its earliest phase of development (Kristeva, *Powers of Horror*, p. 45). In this primal phase, the mother is expected to cure any infirmity, assuage every anxiety, meet every need, and preclude every possible privation or lack of a real object (Lacan, *Seminar IV*, p. 66). The mother's fulfillment of these expectations leads to the translation of the satisfaction of particular real needs into the generalized, symbolic structure of the satisfaction of the demand for love, which is then internalized. For Lacan, the symbolic satisfaction of the demand for love is coeval with the allaying of frustrations Vida too speaks of (*Seminar IV*, pp. 180–182). For Lacan and for Kristeva, such symbolic satisfaction is offered by language. In Bodenham's text, language, by virtue of which, Kristeva would argue, "the speaking being" is "a separate being who utters only by separating" (Kristeva, *Powers of Horror*, p. 46), is paradoxically adduced as tempering or assuaging the infirmities and pains attendant upon separation. This ability to allay symbolic frustration accounts for Bodenham's theorization of language as offering glimpses of imagined fusional *jouissance* in/of the archaic maternal body. Much like Kristeva, Renaissance rhetoricians and their medieval precursors imagine this *jouissance* as preceding the scissions, privations, and frustrations involved in the emergence of subjectivity.

The adducing of rhetoric as a past-oral object able to offer glimpses of archaic *jouissance* noticeable in Bodenham's *Belvedere* is most marked in the texts of Abraham Fraunce, a humanist whose accomplishments include a translation, published in 1591, of Tasso's pastoral *Amyntas*. Fraunce claims he "reformed" the title of this text. He re-named the text *The Countesse of Pembrokes Yuychurch*. This re-forming aligned Fraunce's translation with an already famous English pastoral dedicated to the same woman, Sidney's *The Countess of Pembroke's Arcadia*. The name of

Arcadia, the mythical locale of pastoral, resonates in the title of Fraunce's contribution to early modern aesthetic theory, *The Arcadian Rhetorike*. Fraunce's designation of his handbook of rhetoric renders the linguistic forms the handbook comprises fragments of the archaic pleasures of which Arcadia is the mythical site.

Fraunce's conception of the forms of the symbolic register as signs potentially substituting for, if not proffering, archaic, Arcadian pleasures is suggested in his two works dedicated to logic, a discipline supposedly subtending the symbolic register in its repressive deployment. In 1588, Fraunce published a treatise on logic whose title, *The Lawiers Logike*, emphasizes the conceptual connection of the discipline of logic with the repressive dimension of the symbolic: logos (word), and law. Contemporary thinkers such as Kristeva and Cixous view the law and logos subtending the symbolic register in its repressive deployment as barring the archaic *jouissance* whose re-presentation, re-presentification is the goal of pastoral literature. For Fraunce, pastoral and the law and logic of the symbolic were inseparable. In *The Lawiers Logike*, examples are furnished from pastoral texts: Virgil's *Eclogues* and Spenser's *Shepheardes Calender*. The "disiunctive syllogisme" (p. 112) is exemplified by means of a citation and translation of Virgil's second eclogue, recounting the story of the shepherd Corydon who "lou'd hartily faire lad Alexis, / His maisters dearling, but saw no matter of hoping" (ibid., p. 121). The "thinge caused" (ibid., p. 29) is exemplified by means of Piers's description of "the effects of loue" in Spenser's pastoral (ibid.).

For Fraunce, pastoral is more than a source of examples for logical precepts. The persona of the lawyer is, for Fraunce, interchangeable with the persona of the shepherd. The earlier version of *The Lawier's Logike*, apparently never published, and available only in handwritten form, was entitled by Fraunce *The Sheapheardes Logike*. This treatise on logic avowedly follows the fine logocentric taxonomies of the Ramist theory of argumentation. Yet Ramist logocentricity is deconstructed already in the dedication to Fraunce's treatise. In the dedication, Fraunce describes the substance of logic in terms of the same aquatic image used by Sherry, Peacham, and Erasmus to describe the primal substance of semiosis. Fraunce describes the substance of logic as a liquidity, feminized as "shee," whose "streames do flow" everywhere, dissolving the boundaries between "Kings aboade" and the "feyld" where shepherds "keepe...theyr sheepe" (p. 2). The substance of logic, Fraunce implies, is, like the substance of rhetoric as imagined by Sherry, Peacham, Erasmus, and Dickenson, a substance of primal, oceanic liquidity. Within this liquidity, the logocentric hierarchies of the symbolic in its repressive deployment, the hierarchies differentiating "Kings" as purveyors of the Law of the Father from "simple countrey m[e]n" (ibid.), are not recognized. For Fraunce, all subjects, "law-yers" by virtue of their constitutive partaking of the laws of the symbolic, at the same time carry within themselves residues of the archaic substance of semiosis, of logic and of rhetoric. All subjects are incarnations of the type of fictional character predominant in the genre of pastoral thematizing the archaic: "shepheards" (ibid.).

The perennial presence of the shepherd within the king and lawyer, of the archaic within the symbolic, has a significant psycho-rhetorical consequence. Because of the presence of the archaic within the symbolic, every utterance made in the symbolic, every deployment of rhetoric and logic, accesses the most primal psychic substance. Every utterance of rhetoric or logic potentially activates the primal past-oral *jouissance* in/of the maternal body with which the primal psychic substance is transcoded. Every deployment of rhetoric is an injunction to re-experience the most archaic joy, the oral joy of the subject-to-be whose mouth connects it with the physical and psychic nurturing provided by the mother's breast. The belief in the possibility of every deployment of rhetoric to re-presence archaic pleasures informs Fraunce's dedication of his translations of the pastoral tales of Amyntas and Corydon to the Countess of Pembroke. In this dedication, Fraunce enjoins the readers of his deployment of rhetoric as pastoral to pleasure, and pleasure alone:

> If anie begin to reade, when hee beginneth to take no delight, let him leaue off, and go no further. If he folowe on in reading without pleasure, let him...reprehend himselfe, who could continue in reading, without anie pleasure taking. (unpaginated)

The adducing of rhetoric as a conduit to archaic, past-oral delights and pleasures in the texts of Fraunce and other Renaissance rhetoricians causes rhetoric to fall prey to the dialectics of the oral object. The oral object circumscribes an interior space psycho-conceptually coeval with the horrifying "inside of the maternal body" (Kristeva, *Powers of Horror*, p. 54). This space is, in Kristeva's terms, abject.

In Vida's *De Arte Rhetorica*, the imagining of rhetoric as pleasure-giving oral object, as the "anti-phonal song" of the Muses (p. 91), underscores its inflection by a "surface of pleasure" functioning as a psycho-structurally oral "musical instrument" (Montrelay, p. 88). A psycho-structurally oral surface of pleasure similarly inflects the olfactory experience of "fragrance" (Vida, p. 86), and the gustatory experience of the "liquid essence" or "liquor" with which Vida transcodes the aesthetic forms of rhetoric (ibid.).

The experience of the liquor of ambrosia with which Vida transcodes rhetoric is literally and structurally oral. This experience involves the oral consumption of the "liquid essence" (ibid.) nourishing the gods. When Bodenham offers the "flowres" transcoded with the forms of rhetoric as potential herbal "cure[s]" for any "frustration" incurred by the loss of the archaic maternal body as source of complete satisfaction, he too conflates them with orally-consumed herbal potions. In the texts of Vida and Bodenham, rhetoric is adduced as a "counterphobic object" placed in the subject's mouth in the place of the maternal breast and the nurturing substance emanating from the breast (Kristeva, *Powers of Horror*, p. 41). In those texts, and more implicitly in all rhetorical theory, this theory, as substitute oral object, is transcoded with a digestible substance. This transcoding of rhetoric with a digestible substance renders rhetoric "liable to defile," abject (ibid., p. 75).

Digestible substances such as beverages, potions, or food are oral objects of satisfaction whose loss induces anxiety. They are material substances entering the body from the outside, and transformed by the bodily fluids released in digestion. Their residue is eliminated from the body as excrement. Drink, food, and medicine are substances crossing the body's boundaries. They are substances connected with the body's anal and oral orifices, and with bodily waste. In Kristeva's terms, these substances are abject (*Powers of Horror*, p. 75).

The abject nature of rhetoric as oral object worried Renaissance rhetoricians, especially with respect to the oral part of rhetoric, pronunciation, one of the two parts of delivery, which together with gesture, constitutes the fifth and last part of rhetoric in the classical division. The "fear" Thomas Wilson disavows and thus confirms at the end of *The Arte of Rhetorique* has to do with an anxiety of defilement as much as of inundation. Both anxieties stem from the imaginary conceptualization of the primal substance of semiosis as the archaic maternal body from which the subject-to-be is not distinct. The archaic maternal body is imagined in Wilson's rhetorical treatise in terms of the oceanic. The threat posed to the distinctness and individuality of the subject by the archaic maternal body gives rise to the fear of inundation by this body. This fear of inundation is what is indexed by Wilson's anxious search for "a safe ground" (p. 244).

The search for separateness from the archaic maternal body is manifest in the conceptualization of the maternal body as abject. The imaginary captation of the maternal body as abject generates the drive to define this body as the not-I from which the subject separates (Kristeva, *Powers of*

Horror, p. 2). The imaginary captation of the archaic maternal body transcoded by Renaissance rhetoricians with the primal substance of semiosis as abject comes to the fore in Wilson's theorization of pronunciation. This theorization immediately precedes Wilson's imaginary captation of the primal substance of semiosis as oceanic and inundating. Like Wilson's conceptualization of the primal substance of semiosis, his theorization of pronunciation has an anxiety of non-individuation at its psychic root.

All faults in pronunciation are, technically and anatomically, oral faults, involving the orifice of the mouth. Wilson's list of "faults" in pronunciation, however, includes cases in which faults of the oral orifice are inflected by other orifices, in their function not as surfaces of pleasure but as grotesque sites of excretion of abject substances of bodily waste. In one such instance, Wilson requires the orators' noses to be "without blowing" (p. 243), and denounces speakers who "blow...at their nostrils" (ibid., p. 242). In another, anally-inflected instance, he speaks disparagingly of "one Theophrastus Tausricus...said to declaim arsy-versy" (ibid., p. 243).

The excretion of an abject substance interferes with pronunciation, with the use of the oral orifice for the articulation of rhetoric as an oral object substituted for the primal object, the mother's breast. In a certain condition, this interference becomes most troubling for Wilson. Wilson is most troubled by the idea of an excretion interfering with pronunciation when this excretion is neither nasal, nor anal, but oral, involving the mouth. Wilson's catalogue of faults in pronunciation includes being "hoarse," "rattl[ing]," "cackl[ing]," or "chop[ping]" one's words. These are faults caused by a malfunction of the vocal cords partly constituting the oral cavity. In Wilson's words, these mispronunciations are caused by a "default of the windpipe" (*Arte of Rhetorique*, p. 242). Two of the faults mentioned by Wilson whose source is the oral cavity, "spit[ting]" and "cough[ing]" (ibid.), do not derive from a malfunction of the vocal cords within this cavity. They derive from the throat's being simultaneously involved in an act of elimination of phelgm, one of the abject "flows from within" conceptually related to the horrifying contents of the primal maternal body (Kristeva, *Powers of Horror*, p. 53).

In two other instances, the images of a person speaking "as though he had plums in his mouth," and "as though a good ale crumb stuck fast" (*Arte of Rhetorique*, p. 242), the oral cavity engaged in speech is imagined as involved in ingestion rather than excretion. An activity taking place on the confines between body and world, ingestion is by definition grotesque (Bakhtin, p. 317).

The ingestion of food or drink is an act involving "a partial rupture of physical equilibrium" (Bataille, "The Use Value of D. A. F. Sade," *Visions of Excess*, p. 95). Ingestion is all the more embroiled in the grotesque and abject when the simultaneous involvement of the oral cavity performing it in speech compromises the ability of the oral cavity to appropriate food and drink. In Wilson's images of a person who speaks with "plums in his mouth," or with "a good ale-crumb stuck fast" in his throat, food and drink are in the process of being digested. Because in these cases the mouth is simultaneously involved in speech, the digested substances evoked are on the verge of being transformed from substances of appropriation whose abjectness is hidden within the body to substances of excretion whose abjectness is overt.

In Wilson's two images of speaking with a full mouth, the oral cavity involved in introjection, in the emission of speech qua oral object substituting for the lost archaic mother, is simultaneously involved in the potential emission of abject substances. One of these substances is the saliva produced in the oral cavity. Saliva is produced in the oral cavity as a primal substance of semiosis, a store of "milk" ever supplied by the archaic "mother of eternities" so as to enable the tongue to "deplete" this store by way of introjection (Louis-Combet, *Le don de langue*, p. 13). At the same time, saliva is produced in the oral cavity as a digestive liquid, one of the abject flows from within involved in oral consumption.

Wilson's two images of introjection simultaneous with ingestion come disturbingly close to the possibility of the simultaneous emission of words and of semi-digested food and drink from the oral cavity. In those two images, a manifestation of rhetoric as a substitute for the archaic maternal body as cause of longing is on the verge of conflation with a sign of the archaic maternal body as an abject cause of aversion and repulsion. An anxiety of simultaneous ingestion and emission of an abject liquid substance surfaces shortly before the end of Wilson's rhetorical treatise. The surfacing of this anxiety gives an additional inflection to the anxiety Wilson expresses by disavowal at the end of the treatise, the anxiety of the archaic maternal body in the imagined form of the inundating oceanic, inscribed by inversion in Wilson's closing image of the "safe ground." The surfacing of the anxiety of vomiting while speaking shortly before this closing image inflects the anxiety this image indexes as an anxiety of the abject inscribed as potential in the images conflating rhetorical delivery and ingestion.

Wilson's anxiety of the oral cavity as a site of material traces of the archaic maternal body as blissful yet abject is intense. Commensurately with this intense anxiety related to the oral cavity, the defenses Wilson generates in abreaction to this anxiety are focussed on components of the oral cavity. The orator's teeth, Wilson instructs, should be "without grinning"; his lips should "not [be] laid out" (*Arte of Rhetorique*, p. 243). In Wilson's treatise, as in Owen Price's *The Vocal Organ*, a treatise geared toward the production of the "Harmony of the voice" through the manipulation of the "Lips, Teeth, Tongue, Palate, [and] Throat" (unpaginated), and elsewhere in the tradition of rhetoric, decorous delivery requires strict oral regulation.

At its extreme, such regulation would give rise to an aesthetics of silent incorporation. In such an aesthetics, the substance of speech would be physically buried within the mouth. Such an aesthetics of extreme oral regulation would involve physical incorporation and psychic incorporation as theorized by Abraham and Torok in *The Shell and the Kernel* (pp. 114–117) and *The Wolf-Man's Magic Word* (pp. 80–81). In Abraham and Torok's theorization, incorporation involves a burial within the psyche. In the case of an aesthetics of extreme oral regulation, what would be buried within the psyche is the imaginary transcoding of the substance of semiosis with the archaic maternal body. The phenomenal manifestation of this psychic burial, of the anxiety-driven aesthetics of extreme oral regulation, would be "the magisterial look of the face with a closed mouth, as beautiful as a safe" (Bataille, "Mouth," *Visions of Excess*, p. 60).

The physical incorporation of the substance of semiosis transcoded with the archaic maternal body would prevent the conflation of this imagined substance with orally-related abject body fluids. Orally-related abject bodily fluids are unconsciously regarded in early modern metalinguistic theory as imaginary traces of the threat of inundation, of the loss of individuation, signified by the archaic maternal body transcoded with the primal substance of semiosis. The anxiety induced by the archaic mother qua primal substance of semiosis leads to the postulation of an aesthetics of extreme physical incorporation of orally-related abject bodily fluids as an attempt to allay this anxiety.

The ultimate result of an aesthetics of extreme physical incorporation would be silence, the annihilation of rhetoric. The ultimate result of the conceptually related aesthetics of psychical incorporation would be perilous too, yet has its allure. Since psychic incorporation involves a "regress[ion] to [an] archaic level of magical satisfaction" (Abraham and Torok, *The Shell and the Kernel*, p. 117), a psychic incorporation of the primal substance of semiosis transcoded with the archaic mother would offer an imaginary, hallucinated rehearsal of what is imagined to be the most archaic and absolute fulfillment: the fulfillment of psychic fusion with the primal mother before the advent of subjectivity. The psychic incorporation of the archaic mother qua primal substance of semiosis would simultaneously provide a relief from the anxiety of the archaic mother, and the hallucinatory fulfillment of the nostalgic desire for primal fusion with her.

Subjectivity is predicated upon separation. The "forward-striving nature" of subjectivity "demands separation from the [archaic] mother" (Jung, *Aspects of the Masculine*, p. 17), and dictates a "[t]hirst…for introjection" as a means for psychic "growth" (Abraham and Torok, *The Shell and the Kernel*, pp. 113, 115). Incorporation becomes an inverted, "disguised" statement of the "desire to introject" (ibid., p. 115). Like any instance of incorporation, the fantasy of gaining complete control over the primal substance of semiosis qua archaic mother implied by Wilson's meticulous instructions for the manipulation of the oral cavity indexes "introjection" as "its nostalgic vocation" (ibid., p. 129).

The aesthetics of physical incorporation implied by Wilson as a means of allaying the anxiety induced by the archaic mother qua primal substance of semiosis demands the enclosure within the oral cavity of the vocal incarnation of this substance, voice. The sealing of the lips would provide such enclosure of the voice. Wilson, gesturing toward the fantasy of vocal incorporation, insists on lips not being "too laid out" (*Arte of Rhetorique*, p. 243). Yet since voice is a psycho-corporeal category born "in the epiphany of the visceral" (Louis-Combet, *Le don de langue,* p. 45), its incorporation intensifies and exacerbates the drive to "ceaselessly force open" the lips potentially sealing the oral cavity (ibid., p. 21).

The intensity of the vocal drive indexing a desire to introject is betrayed in Wilson's fixation on a particular component of the oral cavity toward whose closure his fantasy of the incorporation of voice gestures: teeth. The last set of faults in pronunciation mentioned by Wilson consists almost entirely of dental images:

> Some sets forth their lips two inches beyond their teeth…Some shows all their teeth. Some speak in their teeth altogether. (*Arte of Rhetorique*, p. 243)

Teeth have a psycho-conceptual significance. "Teething marks the first great transition" in psychic development (Abraham and Torok, *The Shell and the Kernel*, pp. 123–124). This transition marks the emergence from the oral stage in which the infant's incorporation of the mother's breast provides total and instantaneous satisfaction into the stage of greater individuation in which the infant can process nutritive substitutes for breast-fed milk (ibid.). Because they mark a crucial psychic stage, teeth "lend themselves" to the representation of the psychic passage from incorporation toward introjection (ibid.).

Although incorporation provides instantaneous satisfaction, it is a dangerous mechanism since it inhibits the introjection of desires, the mark of psychic growth and a condition for joy. Incorporation blocks joy. The affective correlative of incorporation is melancholy (Abraham and Torok, *The Shell and the Kernel*, pp. 126–127). Melancholy is an affective state whose corporeal marks include the absence of non-verbal oral expressions of *jouissance* in which teeth play a crucial part: smiles. The anagrammatic and conceptual links of smiles with the aesthetic category of simile did not, as I show in my penultimate chapter, escape Renaissance rhetoricians and poets.

In Wilson's rhetorical text, the drive toward the incorporation of voice as incarnation of the primal substance of semiosis transcoded with the archaic maternal body and phobically imagined as inundating and abject gives rise to an overt banning of smiles. The orator's teeth, Wilson instructs, should be "without grinning" (p. 243).

Yet the very invocation of the dental in this attempted foreclosure of joy-enabling introjection is more than a disguised expression of a nostalgia for introjection. Wilson's invocation of the dental is a trace of an already operative introjection. This invocation is a record of the failure of the fantasy of allaying the anxieties of inundation and abjection generated by the transcoding of the primal substance of semiosis with the archaic maternal body by means of deploying an aesthetics demanding the physical and psychic incorporation of this substance.

The placement of Wilson's invocation of the dental in the context of an insistence on incorporation indexes the desire to introject paradoxically involved in this insistence. Wilson's invocation of the dental in the context of his aesthetics of incorporation occurs in the theorization of an aspect of rhetoric entitled "delivery." The name of the rhetorical category in whose context Wilson demands the regulation of smiles underscores its embroilment in a psychic process of deliverance from a troubling affective state. At its deepest roots, the troubling affective state is subtended by the process of obstetrical delivery, the scission from the placenta already separating the infant from the maternal body. Even the fantasies of the incorporation of the archaic maternal body informing Wilson's theorization of delivery are undergirded by a desire for the delivery and deliverance from the perils of non-individuation imagined to be posed by archaic maternality.

The surfacing of the desire to introject even within the attempted deployment of an aesthetics of incorporation is not incidental. For most of Wilson's rhetorical treatise, what predominates is not the incorporation of the imagined primal substance of semiosis but its introjection, its processing by means of language. For most of his treatise, Wilson, like the other Renaissance rhetoricians examined in this book, uses introjection, not incorporation, in an attempt to allay the anxieties of inundation and abjection accruing to the primal substance of semiosis qua archaic maternality. Like all "reconstruction[s] of languages" as systems of signification, the aesthetics of rhetoric in the Renaissance betrays symptoms of an anxiety whose root is the archaic, engulfing maternal body necessarily imagined as abject by a subjectivity constitutively dependent on separation from it (see Kristeva, *Powers of Horror*, p. 45).

Separation and differentiation, the "basic acts" of the establishment of subjectivity as individuation (Neumann, *Origins and History of Consciousness*, p. 121), are the most prominent formal features of early modern texts on the aesthetics of rhetoric. Rhetorical treatises are elaborate taxonomies proceeding by a meticulous breaking down of the substance of semiosis into discrete forms. Many Renaissance texts on rhetoric look back to the traditional, Ciceronian division of rhetoric into five parts: invention, disposition, elocution, memory, and delivery. Each of these parts is broken down into further components.

Invention is broken down to a list of potential topics of argumentation. In Ralph Lever's *The Art of Reason, rightly termed, Witcraft* (1573), the topics mentioned are judicially-inflected, and include "Substance, Quantity, Quality, Respecte, Doing, Suffering, Where, When, Placing, [and] Having" (p. 8). In Wilson's rhetorical treatise, the topic of the judicial "Circumstances" of an action which features in Lever's text as the "When [and] Where" is broken down into seven components:

1. Who did the deed
2. What was done
3. Where it was done
4. What help had he to it
5. Wherefore he did it
6. How he did it
7. At what time he did it. (*Arte of Rhetorique*, p. 60)

Disposition is traditionally broken down into six parts: exordium, narration, partition, confirmation, refutation, and conclusion. Foregrounding the impulse toward separation driving this taxonomy, Wilson divides the Ciceronian category of partition into "proposition" and a double reiteration of the principle of separation: the "division or several parting of things" (*Arte of Rhetorique*, p. 50).

In most cases, elocution, the part of rhetoric with which I am concerned in this book, is broken down into the categories of "figure" and "trope," each of which is broken down into yet more discrete forms of style. Theorizations of memory include listings of a variety of mnemonic techniques. Delivery is divided into pronunciation and gesture, and the theorization of each of these parts involves listings of sanctioned and prohibited instances.

The drive toward meticulous differentiation marks those Renaissance rhetorics deviating from the traditional Ciceronian taxonomy. Ramist rhetorics such as Fraunce's *Arcadian Rhetorike* dispense with invention, disposition, and memory, limiting themselves to elocution and pronunciation. Yet Ramist rhetorics too are dedicated to meticulous differentiations. Fraunce speaks of elocution, the category with which his treatise is most concerned, as having "2 parts, Congruitie and Brauetie." The second of these two categories, Fraunce continues, "consisteth in Tropes…and in Figures." Each of these two elocutionary categories includes particular linguistic forms, some of which are divisible into separate "kindes." Metonymies, for example, are broken down by Fraunce into metonymies "of the cause," "of the thing caused," "of the subject," and "of the adjunct" (*Arcadian Rhetorike*, unpaginated). In *The Mysterie of Rhetorique Unvail'd*, John Smith provides an even more refined taxonomy of the aesthetic form of metonymy. Smith's taxonomy includes metonymies "of the Efficient," "of the Matter," "of the Instrument," "of things going together," "of the end," and "of the form" (unpaginated). Smith's treatise includes a detailed breakdown of the aesthetic form of synecdoche into "*synecdoche Speciei, Synecdoche Partis, Synecdoche Generis, Synecdoche Totius,* [and] *Synecdoche Numeris*" (unpaginated).

Unlike Ramist rhetorics focussing on elocution but treating memory and delivery, figurist treatises such as Sherry's *Treatise of Schemes and Tropes*, Puttenham's *Arte of English Poesie*, and Peacham's *Garden of Eloquence* deal with elocution alone. These figurist treatises consist entirely of an attempt to provide a "diuision of figures" (Puttenham, p. 132) or to "thorowelye" furnish the readers with "definicions" of linguistic forms enabling them to "kno[w] of eueri one the name & propertye" (Sherry,

Schemes and Tropes, unpaginated).

Manuals purporting to teach rhetoric by example rather than definition such as Angel Day's *English Secretoire* (1586) and Joshua Poole's *Practical Rhetorick* (1663) are no less committed to differentiation. Such manuals consist of a quoted text, and of a hyper-text in the margin of the quoted text. The function of the hyper-text is to point out instances of discrete rhetorical forms in the quoted text. The hyper-text carves up the substance of the quoted text into distinct units.

These examples suggest Renaissance rhetoricians of all schools are involved in an attempt to carve up the primal substance of semiosis qua archaic maternality by means of the introjection of this substance, its linguistic re-formulation as a system of distinct categories. The purpose of the rhetorical treatise, John Smith declares on the title page of *The Mysterie of Rhetorique Unvail'd*, is to help the reader "discern" the "tropes and figures" from one another, to tell them "apart." Students of rhetoric, Joshua Poole writes in the epistle to the reader in his *Practical Rhetorick*, should "be taught to *distinguish* [in] their Writing"; they should learn "Notes of *distinction* of all sorts" that "run thorough [sic] almost all the Figures of Rhetorick" (unpaginated, emphases mine).

In Renaissance texts on the aesthetics of rhetoric, distinction and differentiation are the name of the game. The substance subjected to differentiation is imagined as maternal. This substance is imaged as "plentiful matter" (Wilson, *Arte of Rhetorique*, p. 49), and as the "Plenty of Words and Matter" (Poole, *Practical Rhetorike*, unpaginated). In such instances, the primal substance of semiosis is transcoded with the fertile maternal body. In Renaissance rhetoric books, the maternal fertility transcoded with the primal substance of semiosis functions as a psychic category rather than as the cultural category Parker imagines it to be (*Literary Fat Ladies*, pp. 114–118).

The Renaissance rhetoricians' reproduction of the primal substance of semiosis they imagine in terms of the archaic maternal body as a system of differences fits Saussure's definition of language as "purely differential" (p. 120). This reproduction of the primal substance of semiosis as a system of differences is motivated by an attempt to allay an anxiety of inundation consequent upon the imagining of this substance as oceanic. This reproduction fits Kristeva's theorization of all linguistic systems as "counter-phobic" operations (*Powers of Horror*, p. 41).

These continuities between early modern and contemporary linguistic theory notwithstanding, there are differences between early modern and modern thinkers on language. Saussure regards language "as a form and not a substance" (p. 122). Lacan never imagines any substance preceding the advent of the symbolic. Unlike Saussure and Lacan, and like Cixous, Kristeva, and Louis-Combet, Renaissance rhetoricians do theorize their systems of differential linguistic aesthetics in reference to an imagined substance of semiosis transcoded with archaic maternality.

In Renaissance rhetoric, the introjection of the primal substance of semiosis qua archaic maternality resulting in the differentiation of this substance is conceived of as a victory over the threats of non-differentiation imagined as posed by this substance. This non-differentiated substance is imagined as posing a threat of amorphousness. Amorphousness is conceptually maternal (Goux, *Symbolic Economies*, p. 222). The amorphousness attributed by Renaissance rhetoricians to the primal substance of semiosis generates anxieties of maternality similar to those generated by the imagining of this substance as non-differentiated, conceptually connected with the state of fusion with the archaic mother imagined to precede the advent of language. Amorphousness generates a different anxiety too: the anxiety of the amorphic matter's unpredictable congealing into an infinity of possible forms.

Because the primal substance of semiosis is imagined by early modern thinkers on language as amorphic and thus malleable into an infinity of forms, this substance is conceptually protean. The amorphic primal substance of semiosis imagined by Renaissance rhetoricians has affinities with Proteus, the "ever-changing god of the sea" (Jung and Kerényi, p. 49). The mythological association of Proteus with the maritime, one of the archetypal inscriptions of the primal Great Mother, links him with the archaic.

Proteus is associated with the archaic for other reasons too. He is linked with the archaic by virtue of his name, whose meaning is "the first being" (ibid.). He is linked with the archaic because, like Oceanos, he is mythologically associated with "timeless birth" (ibid.). The mytheme of Proteus involves transcodings between the archaic and the oceanic, two categories inscribed by Renaissance rhetoricians into the primal substance of semiosis.

The mytheme of Proteus too becomes inscribed into the primal substance of semiosis Renaissance rhetoricians seek to control by introjection as differentiation. Appropriately, one of the products of Renaissance rhetoricians is a metalinguistic tract published by Thomas Willis in 1655, whose title, *Proteus Vinctus* (Proteus vanquished), rather phobically protests its victory over the protean primal substance of signification.

The differentiations characterizing early modern theorizations of rhetoric are, as all "thresholds and limits" in theorizations of language, symptoms of what Michel Foucault diagnoses as "profound logophobia" ("The Discourse on Language," p. 229). Yet in Renaissance rhetoric, the phobia of the "ponderous, awesome materiality" of the substance of semiosis has to do not with a general fear of political "domination" by social forces with which Foucault associates language (ibid., p. 216). Nor does the phobia of the materiality of the substance of signification noticeable in Renaissance rhetorical theory have to do exclusively with the fear of female sexuality uncurbed by patriarchal law diagnosed by Parker within this theory (*Literary Fat Ladies*, pp. 113–118). The theorizations of the substance of semiosis in Renaissance rhetorics inflect the anxiety roused by this substance and setting in motion the mechanisms of partition characterizing those rhetorics as more primal and psychically fundamental than the ideologically and historically informed analyses of Foucault and Parker allow for. What underlies the elaborate mechanisms of partition featuring in early modern texts on the aesthetics of rhetoric is an anxiety of the archaic maternal body imagined as a boundless substance of origin. The archaic maternality Renaissance rhetoricians inscribe into the primal substance of semiosis induces anxiety because although it initially provides "utter contentment" and "absence of suffering" (Neumann, *Origins and History of Consciousness*, p. 33), it eventually poses a threat to the subjectivity whose necessary condition of emergence is separation (ibid., p. 45) and "disentangle[ment]" from it (ibid., p. 109).

In separating the primal substance of semiosis they imagine into discrete aesthetic categories through introjection, Renaissance rhetoricians perform a ritual of scission from what they unconsciously imagine as a semiotic incarnation of the primal Great Mother. In performing this ritual, Renaissance rhetoricians assert themselves as distinct subjects. They do so at the moment they rearticulate a catalogue of distinct linguistic forms proffering a reassuring grid of control over the anxiety-inducing primal substance of signification qua archaic maternality.

The separations and partitions structuring Renaissance rhetoric are supposed to function as instruments of controlling archaic maternality through differentiation. These separations and partitions are symptoms of the operation of Renaissance rhetoric as part of the register whose deployments, whether repressive or pleasurable, are designed "to divide up, distribute, or reattribute everything that counts as *jouissance*," the register of the symbolic (Lacan, *Seminar XX*, p. 3). In its repressive deployment, the symbolic register is especially committed to censoring manifestations of the most archaic *jouissance*, the *jouissance* associated with the primal maternal body transcoded, in Renaissance rhetoric, with the primal substance of semiosis.

The differentiating partitionings manifest in early modern treatises on the aesthetics of rhetoric are conceptual operations constitutive of any manifestation of the symbolic. Yet Renaissance rhetoricians' introjection of the primal substance of semiosis involves more than the rearticulation of this substance as a list of differentiated aesthetic forms. Renaissance rhetoricians systematize those aesthetic forms, and place them in relation to one another. According to Sherry, rhetorical theorization involves the "placyng and setting" of aesthetic forms "in order" (*Grammer and Rhetorike*, fol. ii). Fraunce conceptualizes the category of "Trope" as including "single words," in contradistinction to "Figure" as involving words "coopled and conioyned" (*Arcadian Rhetorike*, unpaginated). Thomas Hobbes, drawing upon Aristotle, theorizes "Similitude" in relation to metaphor (p. 111), as does John Smith in *The Mysterie of Rhetorique Unvail'd* (p. 3).

The existence of divisions and subdivisions of aesthetic categories makes the definition of a given aesthetic category depend on its positioning, as, for example, one of Puttenham's "auricular" figures, or as one of Sherry's "schemes," within the conceptual structure of the rhetorical treatise as a whole. The theorization of aesthetic forms in relation to one another makes Renaissance rhetoric books into more than catalogues based on the paratactic, list-like form of organization suggested in the title of Thomas Farnaby's *Index Rhetoricvs* (1625). The theorization of aesthetic forms in relation to one another makes Renaissance rhetoric books into systematized codes. The status of Renaissance rhetorics as systematized codes is implied in titles such as Dudley Fenner's *The Artes of Logike and Rhetorike* (1588), and Lamy's *Art of Speaking*. This status of systematicity is explicitly recognized in the title of a slightly later treatise, John Stirling's *System of Rhetoric* (1733).

Because Renaissance rhetorics are systematized theorizations of aesthetic forms in their difference from one another, and in their position within the conceptual structure of language at large, Renaissance rhetorics are manifestations of what Lacan defines as the symbolic register, the register of "organized structure" (*Seminar III*, p. 9). In this register, "every element" is defined in its relation to others (ibid., p. 34).

The symbolic is a register of differentiation. In its repressive function, the symbolic is the register of regulation, including regulation by prohibitions. The prohibitions of the symbolic include stylistic prohibitions of "vices" such as barbarism and solecism. Psycho-structurally, prohibitions are part of the Father function, the "Name of the Father" (*le nom du père*). The symbolic in its repressive deployment is a register subtended by the father's limit-imposing interdictions (*le "non" du père*) (Lacan, *Écrits*, p. 67).

The theorization of rhetoric in the Renaissance involves a conceptual transition from preoccupation with the primal substance of semiosis to the articulation of systems of linguistic differences. This conceptual transition seems to index a psychic transition from an anxious preoccupation with the primordial mother to an assumption of the law of the symbolic Father, whose function is the introduction of an order subtended by prohibition (Lacan, *Seminar III*, p. 320).

Renaissance rhetoricians provide a mythic articulation of this psychic transition from the chaos of the archaic maternal body to the regulated domain of the Law of the Father. This mythic articulation is the often-told story, traceable to Cicero's *De oratore*, of the birth of rhetoric, in which the rhetorician leads humanity from a pre-civilized state of nature to the reassuring structures of civilization. The political and ideological stakes of this myth have been thoroughly explored by Eric Cheyfitz in the *Poetics of Imperialism*, by Stephen Greenblatt in *Learning to Curse*, and in Wayne Rebhorn's *Emperor of Men's Minds* (pp. 23–79).

However, the implications of this myth of origin extend beyond the political and ideological into the psychological. Psychoanalytically speaking, the myth of the birth of rhetoric is a myth of transition from the archaic into the symbolic in its repressive deployment as the domain of the Father. In Wilson's version of this myth, the rhetorician who rescues humanity from an archaic existence in which "all was against order" and lacked structure is described as a better substitute for the lapsed "first father" (*Arte of Rhetorique*, p. 41). In *The Garden of Eloquence*, Peacham refers to this mythical rhetorician as "the emperor of men's minds" (unpaginated), the embodiment of paternity as law.

The identification of the mythical rhetorician as a Father who rescues humanity from a chaotic state transcodable with archaic maternality and institutes it in the domain of paternal law, and the identification of rhetoric as an instance of the symbolic in its repressive deployment as the register of the Law of the Father, do not necessarily, as Kristeva implies, make all of the aesthetic forms comprised in rhetoric "phallic function[s]" alienated from the "maternal enclosure" of the lost primal substance of semiosis (*Kristeva Reader*, pp. 101–102). The status of rhetoric as an instance of the symbolic does not necessarily, as Cixous believes, thoroughly implicate rhetoric in the repression of primal, boundless maternal "Voice" (*Newly*

Born Woman, p. 93). The inclusion of rhetoric in the symbolic does not, as Cixous implies, define rhetoric as consisting only of forms from which the feminine, and in particular the maternal, "have been driven away...violently" ("Laugh of the Medusa," p. 245).

Renaissance rhetoric is more than a manifestation of the symbolic in its repressive deployment. What makes it so is the dialectical attitude of Renaissance rhetoricians to the substance they attempt to systematize. Renaissance rhetoricians simultaneously imagine the primal substance of semiosis as a site bespeaking the threat of inundation and as a site of lost pleasure nostalgically longed for. This dialectical attitude of Renaissance rhetoricians to the primal substance of semiosis qua archaic maternality is manifest in the imaginary dimension of Renaissance rhetoric.

The system of rhetoric as an instance of the register of the symbolic, of the signifier, is generated by means of the introjection of the imagined primal substance of semiosis. However, the imagining of the primal substance of semiosis as the archaic maternal body, and the description of each one of the categories into which this substance is divided in the process of its introjection, are procedures occurring in the register of the imaginary. This is the register of "relations of understanding" (Lacan, *Seminar III*, p. 9), of "meaning," of the "signified" (ibid., pp. 53–54).

In the following chapters of this book, I demonstrate how the introjection of the imagined primal substance of semiosis underlying the system of rhetoric is carried out by means of an unstable crossing of vocabularies relating to different fields of meaning. Jean-Joseph Goux in *Symbolic Economies: After Marx and Freud* convincingly maps the model for this crossing of vocabularies. The domains of meaning involved in the production of Renaissance rhetoric as a symbolic economy are mainly erotic and amatory. Gendered, gynecological, sexological, economic, religious, and political domains of meaning are, albeit to a lesser degree, involved in the production of Renaissance rhetoric as a symbolic economy too.

What makes possible the semiotically-productive crossing of domains of meaning whose result is the system of early modern rhetoric is a structural feature of these domains. The domains of meaning involved in the production of early modern rhetoric through an imaginary contamination of and exchange with one another are undergirded by the same symbolic structure. They all involve attributions of value whose significance derives from the postulation of one of their component signifiers as a "master signifier" (Lacan, *Seminar XVII*, p. 20), an idealized measure, or, in Goux's terms, a "general equivalent."

Goux describes the genesis of the general equivalent as involving an act of *"excommunication"* of the form elected for general equivalency from the symbolic set of which it is a member. The "sovereign element, as universal equivalent," Goux explains, "itself has no equivalent; it is *out of the ordinary*, placed for this reason outside the community that it governs. It is cut out, subtracted, withdrawn. It legislates *as an exception*" (*Symbolic Economies*, p. 31). The general equivalents analyzed by Goux include the father in the field of subjects, the phallus in the field of objects of drive, gold in the field of products, and language in the field of signs (*Symbolic Economies*, p. 13, emphases Goux's).

Goux's analysis of symbolic economies does not include the domain of rhetoric. However, Goux's theorization is crucial to the understanding of early modern rhetoric as a would-be symbolic system. Goux's theorization of symbolic economies makes it possible to discern the general equivalent of early modern rhetoric. The general equivalent in the field of elocutionary forms is metaphor (see Chapter Four below). Renaissance rhetoricians seek to postulate rhetoric as a symbolic economy gravitating to the general equivalent of metaphor. This would-be symbolic economy of rhetoric consists of a system of signifiers, including the aesthetic forms of elocution such as synecdoche, apostrophe, asyndeton, simile, or aposiopesis. All aesthetic forms gravitate to the form elevated to the rank of master signifier or general equivalent, metaphor. The determination of the meaning of the signifiers included in the symbolic economy of rhetoric, a determination enabling the production of metaphor as a general equivalent in relation to which all other elocutionary forms take their value, is an imaginary procedure, involving the interpermeation of various fields of signification. What this interpermeation of fields of signification is designed to yield is a symbolic economy of elocution.

Symbolic economies, and the logic of general equivalence structuring them, are deployments of the symbolic in its repressive deployment as a register subtended by the Name of the Father. They thereby have a phallic, "masculine profile" (Goux, *Symbolic Economies*, pp. 5–6). The symbolic economy of Renaissance rhetoric too is a would-be phallic system driven by an impetus for "the break with…bad matter, source of all evil" (Goux, "The Phallus," p. 52). In Renaissance rhetoric, the "bad matter" whose exclusion is sought is the primal substance of semiosis qua archaic maternality.

The exposure of Renaissance rhetoric as a would-be phallic symbolic economy throws unexpected light on traditional conceptualizations of the relationship between rhetoric and philosophy, from Plato's *Gorgias* onwards. In the philosophical tradition documented by Jacqueline Lichtenstein in *The Eloquence of Color* (pp. 1–90), rhetoric is feminized. The gender-informed conceptualizations of the relation of rhetoric to philosophy have always overlooked the complex gendering of rhetoric itself. The domain of rhetoric is disparagingly theorized by philosophers in the Platonic tradition as feminine with respect to the rational and conceptually phallic master discourse of philosophy. Yet in the Renaissance rhetoric itself is theorized as a would-be phallic symbolic economy, in which feminized signifiers such as the categories of figure and simile are subordinated to would-be phallicized categories such as master trope or metaphor.

Although produced as a would-be phallic symbolic economy, Renaissance rhetoric fails as a system gravitating to a phallic general equivalent. This failure is indexed in the imaginary dimension of Renaissance rhetoric: in the significations, produced by an unstable crossing of a variety of semantic fields, attributed to the signifiers, the aesthetic forms of elocution constituting the symbolic economy of elocution. For example, the attempt to produce the category of trope as phallic through the introduction into rhetoric of vocabularies of heroism and colonization is belied by the inevitable deconstruction of these discourses, their haunting by specters of de-phallicizing decolonizations (see Chapter Three below).

Another example of the deconstruction of the attempt to produce Renaissance rhetoric as a symbolic economy has to do with the category of metaphor. I show in the fourth chapter of this book how the attempt to crown metaphor as the general equivalent of elocution by associating it with the general equivalents of phallus and gold runs into difficulties. Debased binaries of these general equivalents, displaced person rather than hero, borrower rather than possessor of gold, irrupt into the discourse on metaphor, undermining its status as master signifier. The debased binaries of displaced person and borrower deconstruct the phallic general equivalent of metaphor. They undermine the imaginary construction of metaphor as a marker of ontological plenitude. In Lacanian terms, these debased binaries castrate the category of metaphor.

Because Renaissance rhetoric is subtended by a phallic drive to erect a symbolic economy, this castration of the would-be phallic categories of trope and metaphor cannot be the paternal castration theorized by Freud in relation to the Oedipal stage. The castration undergone by the category of metaphor is a castration for which paternal castration "is a substitute": maternal castration, defined as the frightening possibility of being "totally devoured by the [archaic] mother" (Lacan, *Seminar IV*, p. 367), the trace of the archetypal Great Mother.

The archetypal Great Mother is terrifying because of the danger she poses to individuation. Renaissance rhetoricians transcode the archetype of the Great Mother with the primal substance of semiosis. Yet the archetype of the Great Mother inscribed into the primal substance of semiosis remains in excess of the attempts of Renaissance rhetoricians to fully control this substance. The archetype of the terrible Great Mother returns to castrate the forms to which Renaissance rhetoricians attribute phallic power.

The castrative return of the Terrible Mother is manifest in the theorization of several forms in Renaissance treatises on rhetoric. In the third and fourth chapters of this book, I identify trope and metaphor as the aesthetic categories occupying the phallic position of master signifiers in the symbolic economy of Renaissance rhetoric. In these chapters, I show how the phallic categories of trope and metaphor are de-phallicized and castrated in the imaginary register of Renaissance rhetoric, where archaic maternality resisting the drive toward individuation continues to be inscribed and to inscribe its power.

The archaic mother's feared power to punitively de-erect whoever dares separate from her is registered in the theorization of other forms in terms of the incurring of lack in all registers. Peacham theorizes tapinosis as occurring when a "hygh" topic, associated with the "maiestie" of the monarch form, the political general equivalent isomorphic with the phallus, is "brought downe and muche defaced" (*Garden of Eloquence*, unpaginated), or, as Sherry puts it, has its "dygnitye…diminished" (*Schemes and Tropes*, unpaginated). In Sherry's *Treatise of the Figures of Grammer and Rhetorike*, "diminution" is theorized more generally, as the loss of value of "any thyng that is excellent" (fol. xxxvii), anything occupying the supreme symbolic position of a phallic general equivalent. In Puttenham's treatise too, tapinosis is related to symbolic castration. The "impairing" diminution tapinosis involves, Puttenham writes, is of "dignitie" or "maiestie." This diminution is a loss of stature in the symbolic system of political power (p. 316). Puttenham theorizes tapinosis in terms of the loss of "viguor" or sexual prowess too (ibid.). For Puttenham, tapinosis is implicated in sexual im-pairing, castrated in the Freudian sense. In Lacanian terms, wherein the inscription of lack in the register of the real is privation, not castration (*Seminar IV*, p. 269), the loss of vigour Puttenham associates with tapinosis is a mark of a real privation of sexual potency.

Traces of the archaic mother as a force resisting and punishing drives to individuation are writ large in the representation of the figure of anapodoton. Peacham theorizes anapodoton as "an Oration wanting one member" (sig. F2). Stephen Whitworth has shown how Peacham's theorization of anapodoton relates it to castration ("Far from Being," p. 165). The "want" or lack inscribed in the figure of anapodoton is symbolic or structural, embodied by a syntactical lacuna. This lack is imaginary, involved in the significance of a situation of "want" or frustration. Anapodoton is related to real privation, to castration in the literal sense too. In Renaissance English, the term "member," used to describe what anapodoton "want[s]" or lacks denotes not only a "short sentence or clause" but "a mans priuy member" (Florio, p. 307).

Another rhetorical form Renaissance rhetoricians link with symbolic castration, imaginary frustration, and real privation is apocope, theorized by Sherry as a "cuttynge awaye" of part of a word (*Schemes and Tropes*, unpaginated). Sherry's theorization of apocope is echoed verbatim by John Smith (unpaginated). Aposiopesis is another rhetorical form related to lack and castration. Aposiopesis is theorized in Renaissance rhetoric as a "break[ing] off" of speech (Peacham, *Garden of Eloquence*, sig. N2), or as the "cut[ting] off" of speech (Lamy, p. 229). In *Practical Rhetorick*, Poole exemplifies aposiopesis by the phrases "Love made Jove _____ but we must speak nothing rashly of the gods" (p. 23), or " So blind is Self-love; that _____ but shame forbids me to utter it" (ibid., p. 53). The typographical mark furnished by Poole in his examples of aposiopesis is a horizontal line of the length of several characters. This typographical mark marks an absence or lack on the text's structural, symbolic level. Poole's typographical mark is a horizontalization of the erect "I," the typographical mark of the phallus (Lacan, *Écrits*, p. 287). This typographical mark graphically signifies de-erection, frustrating lack on the imaginary level. Sherry theorizes aposiopesis as occurring when "any thing lacketh to the perfectness of speache" (*Grammer and Rhetorike*, fol. xvi). Because this theorization of aposiopesis foregrounds a "lack" on the symbolic level of the structures of "speech" and the loss of stature within a hierarchical system, it is conceptually linked with symbolic castration. Symbolic castration involved in the diminution of stature in a hierarchical system similarly informs Farnaby's reference to aposiopesis as a "relinquishing" of "sense" whose result is "imperfection" (p. 25).

Early modern theorizations of aposiopesis are conceptually linked with literal castration or real privation by virtue of the affects associated with this aesthetic form. The major affect in relation to which Peacham theorizes the form into which he inscribes manifestations of lack on all registers is "feare" (*Garden of Eloquence*, sig. N2). Fear is the affect Freudian psychoanalysis would come to associate with literal castration (Laplanche and Pontalis, pp. 57–59). Peacham specifies the fear he associates with aposiopesis as usually "feare of shame" (ibid., sig. O4). Freud too would relate the two affects of fear and shame. In *Symptoms, Inhibitions, and Anxiety*, Freud speaks of fear as a cause of inhibition (p. 4), a psychic function whose manifestation is shame. For Freud, fears leading to inhibition are fears related to the sexual function (ibid.). The co-presence of the affects of fear and shame in Peacham's theorization of aposiopesis and in Freud's theorization of inhibition suggests an unconscious sexual inflection to the "break[ing] off" Peacham relates to aposiopesis.

The affects of fear and shame Freudian psychoanalysis would associate with the anxiety of literal castration remain connected with aposiopesis in Puttenham's theorization of this form. The syntactic lacuna involved in aposiopesis occurs, Puttenham observes, when we are "ashamed" or inhibited and "afraid" or anxious (p. 139). Bernard Lamy too theorizes aposiopesis as a figure involving a syntactic "cutting off" of speech, a structural lack indexing symbolic castration. Lamy theorizes this structural lack in relation to a situation involving the fear accruing to the idea of literal castration. Aposiopesis is "used most commonly," Lamy says, upon the occasion of a "threat" (p. 229). All those instances of early modern theorizations of apocope and aposiopesis in relation to manifestations of lack in all registers and to the affects related to literal castration are traces of the terrifying, castrating aspect of the archaic maternality inscribed into the primal substance of semiosis. These unsettling traces, indicative of the depth of the rhetoricians' fear of archaic maternality, are present even within the symbolic economy endeavoring to regiment and regulate this maternality.

Archaic maternality, terrifying because of the danger it poses to individuation and thus imagined as horrifying and abject, is inscribed in the imaginary register of Renaissance rhetoric in direct images of the abject insides of the maternal body, and in indirect marks of lack and castration. In the final chapter of this book, I show how images of maternal abjection feature prominently in the imaginary dimension of theorization of simile, wherein a gynecological field of signification is crossed with the rhetorical field. Simile is imagined in early modern rhetoric as a maternal body "contract[ing]" to produce metaphor as a phallic issue (for instance, Hobbes, p. 110). Simile's association with rhetorical length or "dilation" (for instance, Hobbes, p. 110; Smith, p. 211) similarly brings an obstetrical semantic field into play. In another instance, occurring in a treatise devoted solely to simile, Robert Cawdray's *Treasvrie or Storehovse of Similies* (1600), this aesthetic form is described in terms of an abject maternality. Cawdray theorizes simile as allied with "women in trauaile...in child-birth," with "bloud" and "milke," the two most distinctively maternal abject bodily fluids, and with "the secrets and bowels of nature" (sig. A2), the archetypal embodiment of "the horrors of maternal bowels" (Kristeva, *Powers of Horror*, p. 53).

In another case, the abject interior of the female womb is referenced in the name of a vice of speech, in which "the preposition is...put unto...the verbe," and proper grammatical order is reversed: "hysterologia," the speech of the womb (Sherry, *Grammer and Rhetorike*, fol. xviii). According to Parker, the early modern theorization of syntactic reversal in relation to the womb has to do with early modern cultural anxieties of a reversal in the patriarchal hierarchy (*Literary Fat Ladies*, p. 68). The early modern theorization of hysterologia has to do with early modern conceptualizations of hysteria, or, as Shakespeare's King Lear refers to it, "*Hysterica Passio*" (Act 2, scene 4, line 45). This "hysterical affect" (Jorden, p. 9), or as it is called in the title of Edward Jorden's treatise on the subject, the "suffocation of the Mother," is conceptualized in early modern England as a condition of anatomical reversal. Shakespeare's Lear refers to hysteria as a "climbing sorrow," wherein the "mother" or womb "swells up toward [the] heart" (Act 2, scene 4, lines 54–55). The anatomical reversal characterizing hysteria in early modern texts is isomorphic with the grammatical reversal structuring the rhetorical form of hysterologia. Hysterologia in its early modern theorization is allied with hysteria etymologically, phonically, structurally, and conceptually.

According to Jorden, the symptoms of hysteria or the "rising of the Mother" (p. 6), include "suffocation in the throate" (p. 2), leading to the vocal disturbances. These vocal disturbances include "frenzies, convulsions...laughing, singing, weeping, crying, &c" (ibid.), vocal expressions exceeding the rules of proper speech. Centuries later, Freud too would describe vocal expressions exceeding rules of speech as symptoms of hysteria (*Studies in Hysteria*, p. 25). In hysteria, Freud says, the subject "loses her command of grammar and syntax" (ibid.). In early modern and in modern theorizations of hysteria, this condition is associated with articulations in which grammatical rules of ordering are relinquished. Hysterologia in its early modern theorizations is an instance of such relinquishing of grammar. Hysterologia is one of the symptoms of hysteria in its early modern and modern theorizations. Hysterologia is a linguistic trace of an illness early modern physicians such as Jorden associate with the womb, with the abject insides of the maternal body.

Another factor relating hysterologia to the abject dimension of the maternal body thought to be involved in the condition of hysteria is the reference to it as "prepostera" (Sherry, *Schemes and Tropes,* unpaginated), or the "preposterous" (Smith, sig. A4). These references inflect hysterologia as a disturbance. Jorden's early modern theorization of hysteria speaks of its symptoms in their entirety a disturbance of order. These symptoms, he says, "can hardly be comprehended within any method or boundes" (p. 2). Centuries later, Kristeva would describe disturbance as an attribute of the abject. According to Kristeva, the abject "disturbs identity, system, order" (*Powers of Horror*, pp. 2–4). Because hysterologia in early modern rhetoric is defined as a "preposterous" disturbance, it is structurally and conceptually related to maternal abjection in its early modern and modern theorizations.

The early modern vocabularies of rhetoric and of hysteria intersect in the theorization of other rhetorical forms. One of the symptoms of hysteria mentioned by Jorden is "syncope." When this symptom occurs, "the pulse is scarcely or not at all perceyued, the breath of respiration being gone" (Jorden, p. 9). "Syncope" is the name of a rhetorical figure too. In rhetorical syncope, a syllable is removed "from the myddeste of the worde" (Sherry, *Schemes and Tropes*, unpaginated), or, in Smith's terms, "taken away" from a word (p. 171). In the texts of Sherry and Smith, syncope as an aesthetic form is structurally coeval with the hysterical symptom described by Jorden. In early modern rhetoric, syncope as figure is related to syncope as symptom in the imaginary and symbolic registers. The figure of syncope is gynecologized and hystericized, inscribed with traces of the abject maternal body.

Abject maternality is inscribed into the last part of rhetoric in its traditional division, "delivery," a term in which aesthetic and obstetric semantic fields cross. In this case, as in the case of syncope, rhetorical vocabulary crosses with a medical vocabulary related to the abject aspect of the maternal body. The imaginary embroilment of rhetorical and obstetrical delivery is underscored in Lamy's *Art of Speaking*, where voice is described as produced by obstetrically-inflected operations of the lungs: "dilation," in which the lungs "draw...in the Air," and "contraction," in which the lungs "expel" air (p. 180). The obstetrical term "contraction" itself is the Latinate name of a rhetorical figure in which "two vowels or syllables" are made into one, for which the Greek term is "synaeresis" (for instance, Smith, sig. A). In this case too, an aesthetic vocabulary crosses with medical vocabulary on the abject aspects of maternality.

The above examples begin to reveal the maternal as in no way excluded from the symbolic economy of Renaissance rhetoric. Renaissance rhetoricians transcode the primal substance of semiosis with the maternal as real origin. Terrified by the engulfing and castrating aspects of maternal origin, they seek to control and regiment the substance they transcode with this origin. Yet the maternal Renaissance rhetoricians seek to control keeps returning in the imaginary dimension of Renaissance rhetorical theory. The archetype of the Terrible Mother returns in early modern rhetoric as the abject and horrifying dimension of the meaning of the rhetorical categories of simile, hysterologia, syncope, dilation, contraction, and delivery. This archetype returns in the castrative dimension of the imaginary signification of the aesthetic categories of trope, metaphor, tapinosis, apocope, anapodoton, and aposiopesis. The return of archaic maternality imagined as real within a symbolic system seeking to repress it grants (pre)-historical resonance to Lacan's characterization of the archaic mother as structurally positioned "at the limit between the symbolic and the real" (*Seminar IV*, p. 82). In Renaissance rhetoric, this limit is the imaginary traces of archaic maternality in the theorizations of aesthetic forms related to abjection or to the threat of castration.

Imaginary traces of archaic maternality index the constitutive failure of Renaissance rhetoricians to achieve total control over and separation from the substance of origin they imagine and fear. Another reason why traces of archaic maternality appear in the symbolic economy of Renaissance rhetoric is the ultimate recoil of Renaissance rhetoricians from such total separation and control. The attitude of Renaissance rhetoricians to the archaic maternality they transcode with the primal substance of semiosis is, as are all attitudes to archaic maternality, dialectical. Inscriptions of the archaic mother exceed the imaginary captation of maternality as an inundating, devouring force resisting and punishing separation from it.

In the symbolic register, archaic maternality is inscribed differently. The archaic mother is the locus of the "primal relation" of satisfaction (Lacan, *Seminar IV*, p. 223), and provides the structural, symbolic substrate for all future love objects. The primal maternal object is irretrievably lost in the series of scissions through which subjectivity comes to be. Its imprint remains in the psyche. All love objects which "succeed" the lost primal maternal object can only be imagined or experienced in relation to this imprint or structural trace. Structurally speaking, all objects are the lost maternal object "found again" (Lacan, *Seminar IV*, p. 83; *Seminar VII*, p. 58).

Archaic maternality postulates and structures the field involving "the union of two individuals, wherein they overreach themselves, and for a more or less fragile and transitory moment...find themselves parts of [a] unity" re-enacting primal fusion imagined to have been and to have been lost (Lacan, *Seminar IV*, p. 85). This field of momentary joinings of constitutively separate subjects (Lacan, *Seminar I*, p. 108) "achieves the primitive structuration of the human world" (Lacan, *Seminar II*, p. 222). This field of joining is the field of the erotic, of desire, "desire as unconscious" (ibid.). Desire or Eros "bind[s]" separate "subjects together" (Lacan, *Seminar I*, p. 108). The Eros or desire binding separate subjects in the perpetual hope of momentary glimpses of imagined archaic non-differentiation from the archaic mother does not manifest itself in sexual copulations. Desire "becomes manifest at the joint of speech" (Lacan, *Seminar II*, p. 234), in language.

The correlation between erotic and linguistic, rhetorical joining did not escape Renaissance rhetoricians. Their recognition of language as the field of the erotic, where the satisfactions of past-orality are "revive[d]" but "revived verbally" (Lacan, *Seminar I*, p. 171) is manifest in the importance they grant to oral/aural pleasures. Another manifestation of the early modern recognition of the correlation of love and language is the special attachment of many Renaissance rhetoricians to the poetics of pastoral. Renaissance rhetoricians' recognition of rhetoric as the field of the erotic, as distinct from the sexual, wherein archaic bliss may be momentarily re-created, is manifest above all in their theorizations of aesthetic forms.

The aesthetic forms of rhetoric in their entirety, Richard Sherry writes, consist of words "alone," and "words iogned together" (*Figures of Grammer and Rhetorike*, fol. xxvii). Peacham too speaks of the field of elocution as consisting of meaning units "eyther coupled or uncoupled" (*Garden of Eloquence*, unpaginated). Similarly, Fraunce speaks of aesthetic forms as including meaning-units "coopled and conioyned" (*Arcadian Rhetorike*, unpaginated). Puttenham describes a particular form of elocutionary joining, "syneciosis," as the "Crosse-couple," who takes "two words," and "tieth them as it were in a paire of couples, and so make them agree like good fellowes" (p. 172). In these statements, Sherry, Peacham, Fraunce, and Puttenham implicitly transcode rhetorical with inter-personal couplings.

What is the nature of the inter-personal couplings Renaissance rhetoricians transcode with linguistic joinings? What is the conceptual relation between the rhetorical couplings Sherry, Fraunce, Peacham, Puttenham, and other early modern rhetoricians speak of, and sexual, bodily copulations? Does Puttenham's theorization of syneciosis inflect the "good fellowes" referenced in it primarily as bodies? Do early modern rhetoricians conceive of rhetorical couplings as analogues, reflections, or isomorphs of bodily copulations?

The answer to this last question may sometimes appear affirmative. Peacham calls the meaning-units of language joined in rhetorical couplings *"membri"* (*Garden of Eloquence*, unpaginated), a term used to signify the male organs of sexual copulation. When theorizing the category of elocutionary joining of which Puttenham's syneciosis is a particular case, Sherry and Peacham use the term for sexual intercourse, *"copulatio,"* (Sherry, *Grammer and Rhetorike*, fol. xxx; Peacham, *Garden of Eloquence*, sig. S2). The term used by Sherry, Peacham, Smith, and other Renaissance thinkers on language to name the grammatical part performing linguistic joinings and creating rhetorical/erotic "couples" is the "copula" or "copulative." In John Florio's *New World of Words*, this term is lexically indexed as "a copulation" (p. 317). In all these cases, rhetorical couplings appear to be theorized as linguistic analogues of bodily contact of sexual members, of sexual intercourse.

Yet the joinings of words of which Sherry, Fraunce, Peacham, Puttenham, and Smith speak are more than analogues of inter-personal couplings. These joinings of words are manifestations of rhetoric itself as a medium of inter-personal couplings. In Renaissance rhetoric, as in Lacanian psychoanalysis, the domain of rhetoric is inflected as constitutively erotic. Rhetorical copulas are, by virtue of their partaking of the domain of rhetoric, and by virtue of their structural function of linking and separating, constitutively erotic, regardless of their imaginary and symbolic links with organs of sexual copulation. The rhetorical couplings Renaissance rhetoricians speak of are erotic couplings independently of being analogues of sexual couplings.

Rhetorical couplings are at least doubly erotic. They are erotic in the imaginary sense because they are part of the domain of rhetoric transcoded with eroticism by Renaissance rhetoricians. They are erotic in the structural, symbolic sense, because their function is to keep separate as much as to connect. Rhetorical qua erotic couplings connect and separate constitutively separate meaning-units of language isomorphic with constitutively separate subjects. In Renaissance rhetorical theory, meaning-units isomorphic with subjects, but not the category of the subject itself, are eroticized along with all components of rhetoric. Subjects may pair with one another in an erotic pact which has the potential to approximate, and momentarily, verbally, fragmentarily re-create archaic *jouissance*. Because in early modern rhetorical theory, the category of components of rhetoric is more eroticized than the category of the subject, inter-subjective couplings are less intensely eroticized than the rhetorical couplings transcoded with them. In the conceptual terms set up in early modern rhetoric, sexual couplings, dependent on the contingencies of time and space, are even less eroticized. Sexual couplings mirror the structure of the pairing of separates subtending intersubjectivity and language, but unlike rhetorical couplings, they are not in and of themselves erotic.

In its implicit theorization of the interrelations between linguistic, intersubjective, and sexual couplings, early modern rhetorical theory again anticipates Lacanian psychoanalysis. For Lacan, the erogenous zones of the body, the "cuts expressed in the anatomical mark of a margin or border the lips...the rim of the anus, the tip of the penis, the vagina, the slit formed by the eyelids...the...aperture of the ear" (Lacan, *Écrits*, pp. 314–315), reflect the structure of subjectivity as a "cut" or separation (ibid., p. 299), and the differential structure of language. Language, not the body, Lacan reiterates in *Seminar XX* (for instance, p. 146) is the medium of love and the point of emergence of desire. In the early modern rhetorical treatises of Peacham, Sherry, Puttenham, Fraunce, and Smith, as in Lacanian psychoanalysis, rhetoric is the primary medium of intersubjective erotic coupling. Sexual, corporeal coupling is a possible but not necessary reflection of rhetorical qua erotic coupling.

If Eros is what binds yet tears asunder (Montrelay, p. 90), the most intensely eroticized components of Renaissance rhetoric are rhetorical copulas binding meaning-units yet keeping them distinct. Rhetorical copulas function and are theorized as elocutionary erogenous zones. Among rhetorical copulas, the apostrophaic copula "O," and the related "wanting" part of anapodoton inviting the reader to "provide that missing part as the mark of [his/her] own desire" (Whitworth, "Far from Being," p. 165), most markedly function as elocutionary erogenous zones.

The conventional sound of apostrophe, the copula by means of which it links the speaking subject with the object toward which the subject "flye[s] out" (Peacham, *Garden of Eloquence*, unpaginated) in approximating passion is the typographical cut "O." The "O" is the marker of loss, of the "absence" of the object to which Peacham and Sherry define it as possibly addressed. However, the apostrophaic "O" is not a mark of melancholy occasioned by absence and separation. The apostrophaic "O" is the mark of the introjection of separation and absence into the conditions of coupling. The sound of O, as Joel Fineman has put it, is associated with "a mark of the real, the object...that occasions desire in the first place" ("The Sound of 'O' in *Othello*," p. 44). Addressed to an object qua cause of desire in what Peacham describes as "a sodein remouing, from the thirde person, to the seconde" (*Garden of Eloquence*, unpaginated), the apostrophaic copula acquires the psychic force Lacan too attributes to the use of the second person pronoun: the force of effecting a "soul murder" (*Seminar III*, p. 305).

Originating in the lack, in the "wanting" Shakespeare speaks of in sonnet #87 as the "cause" of the "fair gift" of a desiring other structuring subjectivity as desire, apostrophe passionately, desperately, cruelly addresses itself to the "wanting" of the other it hails and exacerbates. The apostrophaic copula has the "cut" of subjectivity as discontinuity and hence desire, the cut which it painfully and lovingly expands in its hailing of the "you," as its cause and its address. The apostrophaic copula rhetorically enacts the cruelty of an Eros incorporating the death drive "as a force...aimed at whatever opposes its expansion" (Green, *Tragic Effect*, p. 14).

The cruel intersubjective kinesis of the apostrophaic copula enables apostrophe to function as, in Derrida's terms, "a desire, a request, and a promise, one could even say a prayer" regarding an absent other. This intersubjective kinesis inscribed into the apostrophaic copula enables it to function as an "appeal" to the other which makes a "sign toward the future" (Derrida, "Politics of Friendship," p. 367). The apostrophaic copula is a memory toward the future, a proleptic "remembraunce," in Peacham's terms, transcending static, melancholic lack.

The apostrophaic copula is conceptually coeval with what Heidegger describes as the threshold qua pain. Pain in Heidegger's theorization is structurally co-extensive with Eros in Montrelay's theorization. Pain for Heidegger is what "tears asunder [and] separates." Pain is the "joining agent," the affective copula effecting an "intimacy" which can only be less than a "fusion." The intimacy Heidegger speaks of is an "intimacy of striving," of subjects' continually "overreaching" themselves (*Poetry, Language, Thought*, pp. 50–54, 202–204), and performing what Lacan defines as the basis of the erotic relation (*Seminar IV*, p. 85).

The apostrophaic copula is a mediator of an intersubjective erotic coupling, an oscular scission in separating boundaries through which coupling erotic content is diffused. In Heidegger's terms, the apostrophaic copula is a rift of wrenching, separating pain functioning as a "threshold" (*Poetry, Language, Thought*, p. 204) through which the intersubjective amatory exchange or transference between two subjects yearning toward one another and hence pairing with one another takes place. The apostrophaic copula structures apostrophe as a figure of erotic transference. Puttenham speaks of it as an "exchaunge" that "breedeth" a "certaine recreation to the hearers minds" (p. 199), strikingly anticipating the Lacanian notion of transference, the structure subtending Eros, as a linguistic exchange "which changes the nature of the two beings present" (*Seminar I*, pp. 112, 109).

The erotization of apsotrophaic and other copulas in Renaissance texts on the aesthetics of language conceptually and anagrammatically postulates rhetoric as the field of the erotic. In this field, the archaic mother is inscribed not only in traces of the abject, and in troubling marks of inundation, devouring, and castration. In the field of the rhetorical as the erotic, the archaic mother is inscribed as the structuring and dynamizing principle of object relations, the primordial cause of all desire enabling the love objects qua substitutes for it to be addressed. In the metalinguistic theory of the Renaissance, rhetoric, the domain of the copula, is postulated as the field of the erotic. In this field of rhetoric qua eroticism, desire is played out as the part of the demand addressed to the other which remains in excess of any satisfaction in the contingent domain of sexual copulations (*Écrits*, p. 263).

The erotization of rhetoric is manifest, most significantly so, in forms gynecologized or inscribed with castration. Simile, the form most closely associated with female genitality, is inscribed with a structure of non-phallic, non-possessive, open-ended desire, a desire recognizing and embracing approximation (see Chapter Five below).

Syncope, the form whose name is the name of a hysterical symptom, is theorized as a castrative "cut[ting] away." Syncope is theorized as the removal of a "letter or syllable...from the midst of a word" (Smith, p. 171; Farnaby, p. 38), as the creation of a gap, of an empty interval. In Lacan's terms, such an empty interval is the only space in which desire can deploy itself (*Écrits*, p. 263).

Aesthetic forms theorized in relation to literal castration include apocope, aposiopesis, and anapodoton. Apocope is theorized as occurring "when the last syllable of a word is cut off or taken away" (Smith, p. 171). Aposiopesis is theorized as the abrupt suspension of speech (for instance, Lamy, p. 229). Anapodoton is theorized as occurring when an oration's most crucial member is missing (Peacham, *Garden of Eloquence*, unpaginated). All three of these figures are theorized as postulating a lack, an empty space. This lack indexes a painful deficiency, whether of real privation, imaginary frustration, or symbolic castration. An instance of symbolic and structural rather than literal castration, the lack theorized as involved in the figures of apocope, aposiopesis, and anapodoton functions as does castration, according to Lacan. The lack involved in these figures functions an invitation to "reach...[*jouissance*] on the inverted ladder of desire" (Lacan, *Écrits* , p. 324), as an opening up of a space of wanting, the only true space of eroticism.

The postulation of rhetoric as the space of the erotic as a wanting, as what is hollowed out within the demand to the object substituted for the (m)Other as cause of desire is anagrammatically and symptomatically registered in the theorization of the form of "erotema," whose name phonically resonates with the name of eroticism, of desire. This aesthetic form is conceptualized by Peacham as "demaunding...something stronglye" (*Garden of Eloquence*, sig. L4). Erotema is glossed by Puttenham as "the Questioner or inquisitive" (p. 176). The theorizations of erotically-resonant erotema in terms of demand in the rhetorical texts of Peacham and Puttenham anticipate another insight of Lacanian psychoanalysis. These theorizations underscore the links Lacan would point out between the psychic function of the demand, the syntactic function of the question, and the psychic category of eroticism or desire. Peacham's and Puttenham's theorizations of erotema bring together the categories of demand and question, and the category of eroticism resonating in the name of this rhetorical form. Lacan would elaborate on the connections between these categories, suggested by Renaissance rhetoricians centuries before. He would underscore the implication of demand, a structure addressed to a particular love object (*Seminar XX*, p. 126), in the question posed by the lack of Being instituted by the primal scission from the (m)Other qua cause of desire.

Renaissance rhetoricians attempt to offer a response to the erotematic demand for an impossible One-ness, an impossible plenitude of Being, in the aesthetic form of asyndeton. Asyndeton is theorized as a "fygure which keepe[s] the partes of...speech together, without helpe of anye coniunctions" (Peacham, sig. I3; Sherry, *Figures of Grammer and Rhetorike*, fol. xxxi). This figure is "without a copulative" (Smith, *Mysterie of Rhetorique*, unpaginated). The copula, the rhetorical component safeguarding separation, is declared superfluous to it. Asyndeton has the structure of a psychic state in which the boundaries separating subjects are all but obliterated. In *Civilization and Its Discontents*, Freud would theorize such a psychic state. This state occurs, he would say, at the height of the condition of being in love (p. 3). At this point of maximal libidinal intensity, subject and love object experience an affective state in which they imagine themselves to be on the verge of oceanic merger (ibid.).

The imagined approximation to oceanic merger, which Freud would theorize in relation to the psychic structure coeval with the structure of asyndeton as theorized in the Renaissance, had been indicated by Sherry. Sherry nominates the form of asyndeton, which "lacketh coniuccions," "dissolutio" (*Schemes and Tropes,* unpaginated). "Dissolution" is the term Sherry uses in the later *Treatise of the Figures of Grammer and Rhetorike* to conceptualize the primal, oceanic substance of language (fol. lxi). In Sherry's thinking, the aesthetic category of asyndeton is aligned with the primal oceanic substance of semiosis.

Although asyndeton lacks the "conjunctions copulative" doubly eroticizing rhetorical forms, asyndeton too is, as Sherry and Peacham put it, composed of "partes." Even the structure of asyndeton participates in the pairings and partings constituting the erotic in rhetorical and intersubjective terms. Puttenham's slip from referring to asyndeton as "loose language" (p. 145) to referring to it as "lose language" (p. 146) is thus symptomatic. Puttenham's slip indexes even the loose(ning) of linguistic boundaries between words and isomorphic boundaries between subjects as taking place within the field of intersubjectivity and language to which imagined archaic One-ness, a condition whose experiencing would require one to "lose language," has been irretrievably lost. Puttenham's slip from "loose language" to "lose language" when speaking of asyndeton involves the loss of an "o." Theorizations of apostrophe predicated on the "o" as copula or elocutionary erogenous zone inflect "o" as a typographical mark of lack. "O" is the phonemic trace of orgasmic joy and of pain. Puttenham's slip from "loose language" to "lose language" when speaking of asyndeton parapractically postulates the "o" lost in its course as subtending and hence intensely eroticizing the form of asyndeton.

This intense erotization of asyndeton in Renaissance rhetoric relates it to the aesthetic form whose name is the name of orgasmic pleasure, "climax," which for Lacanian psychoanalysis is a psychic, not a biological category. The structure of rhetorical climax as theorized in the Renaissance is a gradational structure of "reduplication by…degrees" (Fraunce, *Arcadian Rhetorike,* unpaginated). This structure of gradation coincides with the "mounting of pleasure and its apogee in the moment of orgasm" (Montrelay, pp. 79–80). At this moment, the subject, "far from being reduced to the pleasure of an organ," is momentarily "transported," within "the field of the signifier," to "the archaic situation of which [the] maternal is the sole organizer" (ibid.). Gradationally-reached orgasm functions as an experience of momentary, sublime transcendence within language. Orgasm offers a fleeting grasp, from within the condition of language, subjectivity, and hence separation, of a "fragment of *jouissance*" (ibid., p. 39), of archaic past-oral bliss. The structure of orgasm as psychic transcendence within the field of the signifier as theorized by Montrelay is already implicit in Peacham's theorization of elocutionary climax as "incrementum, when by degrees we ascend to the top of some thing, or rather aboue the toppe" (*Garden of Eloquence*, sig. D3). Rhetoric, Peacham suggests long before Montrelay, is the point wherein language reaches its point of "maximum incandescence," which for Montrelay would be the point of the orgasmic pleasure of a woman, experienced "within the field of the signifier" (p. 79). Rhetoric, Peacham suggests long before Lacan, is the site where one finds a "ladder," deployed from the point of lack and symbolic castration, through which one may reach *jouissance* (*Écrits*, p. 324).

Archaic maternality remains inscribed in Renaissance rhetorics in a dialectical fashion, as an object of longing fundamentally structuring all longing or desire, and as an object of aversion and anxiety. Archaic maternality as cause of desire is inscribed in Renaissance rhetorics as the structuring principle of the erotic as an empty field hollowed out within the demand by the satisfaction of need. This structuring principle appears in the theorization of the rhetorical form of "demaund" itself, a question lacking a response, as erotically resonant "erotema." The principle of lack and hence desire appears in theorizations of aesthetic forms predicated upon missing such as syncope, apocope, aposiopesis, and anapodoton. Renaissance rhetoricians' theorization of the copula as the agent of cutting and linking isomorphic with Eros eroticizes copula-mediated forms such as simile, apostrophe, metaphor, and epizeuxis. The aesthetic forms of asyndeton and climax are theorized in Renaissance rhetoric as structures isomorphic with the psychic structures of love at its most intense and of orgasmic joy, as identified by psychoanalysis.

I show in the following chapters how the dialectical relation to archaic maternality as object of the most intense desire and anxiety structures and informs the theorizations of the major aesthetic categories of figure, trope, metaphor, and simile. Theorizations of these aesthetic categories in Renaissance rhetoric are in various ways parts of the attempt to introject the primal substance of language transcoded with archaic maternality so as to rearticulate this primal substance as a symbolic economy of "rhetoric" whose components gravitate to a phallic general equivalent. In all cases examined in this book, these attempts to repress and control archaic maternality inevitably deconstruct, indexing archaic maternality as the object-cause of all desire too. The attempts of Renaissance rhetoricians to repress archaic maternality flow into what Wilson, tellingly re-telling one of the discipline's founding myths, the story of Demosthenes' oral castration, his "not being able to pronounce the first letter of that art which he professed," calls "'letolic'" (*Arte of Rhetorique*, p. 242).

The ostensibly nonsensical term "'letolic'" is semiotically productive. This term exploits the phonic and semiotic connections between "letter" or signifier and "let" as a marker of possibility. Shakespeare frequently plays upon these connections. Joel Fineman has demonstrated in an exemplary analysis of Shakespeare's *Rape of Lucrece* how in this poem, "let" and "letter" are a fundamental "Shakespearean constellation" used to explore the interconnections among temporality as the domain of desire, subjectivity, and language ("Shakespeare's Will: The Temporality of Rape"). In Shakespeare's famous "Let me not to the marriage of true minds / Admit impediments" (sonnet #116, lines 1–2), or "Let me confess that we two must be twain" (sonnet #36, line 1), or "Let the bird of loudest lay" ("The Phoenix and Turtle," line 1), Shakespeare's poetics suggestively postulate the field of rhetorical signification, of let-ters, as the field of let-ting, of temporal potentiality wherein desire as an expression of eternal prolepticism can play itself out.

The term "'letolic'" in Wilson's rhetorical treatise harkens back to phonic and semiotic connections more archaic than those between "let" and "letter" made possible by the English language. In the language of Demosthenes Wilson seeks to emulate, the signifier "'letolic'" phonically resonates with *lethos*, a light summer dress. Eugenie Lemoine-Luccioni shows in *La robe* how in psychoanalytical terms, all vestments function as a substitute placenta, a prosthetic replacement for the primal envelopment afforded by the archaic mother. In psychoanalytical terms, all love objects too are substitutes for the archaic mother as primal object-cause of desire. The *lethos* resonating in Wilson's "'letolic'" is analogous in function to the subject's objects of desire, substitutes for the primal maternal object. Since this primal object is incestuous, it must undergo a forgetting, a psychic function whose archaic Greek signifier, *lethe*, resonates with "'letolic'" too.

Wilson's "'letolic'" evokes the historical archaic of ancient Greece. "'Letolic'" invokes the archaic as a psychic category, the category of the object cause of desire expressible only in and as rhetoric. This signifier postulates a productive semiotic field. The signifier's first syllable, "let," is the first syllable of "letters," the most basic constitutive units of rhetoric. The syllable "let" phonically invokes the primal la(c)tic liquid of the archaic mother transcoded with the substance of letters and all other components of language. In the Greek language in which Wilson invokes the signifier "'letolic,'" its first syllable is phonically associated with sartorial substitutes, *lethoi*, for the archaic mother. In Greek, the first syllable of "'letolic'" resonates with *lethe*, forgetting, the psychic function to which the primal incestuous maternal object must be subjected.

The second syllable in Wilson's "'letolic'" is "o," a gap and a marker of joy. This signifier, I have argued above, typographically, phomenically, and structurally indexes the space of desire. The last syllable in "'letolic,'" "lic," is the archaic, Old English origin of "like," the name of an erotic affect, and, significantly for the conceptual context explored in this book, of the common copula of simile. The syllable "lic" phonically invokes the constitutively erotic function of "li(n)king" as well.

Centuries before Lacan, Wilson's seemingly nonsensical "'letolic'" links the categories of desire, lack, temporality, language, alphabetical letters and communicational letters, and the archaic, categories linked in more detailed fashion in Lacanian psychoanalysis. To the links made in psychoanalysis, Wilson's signifier adds the category of the similaic, which language-oriented psychoanalysis has never addressed, but which, I suggest, should be seminal to such psychoanalysis.

Wilson's "'letolic'" indexes a dimension of Renaissance linguistic theory never explored before. This signifier inflects early modern linguistic theory as more than a phallic symbolic economy committed to censoring and repressing the archaic. "'Letolic'" inflects this theory as a domain of rhetoric qua eroticism, where let-ters are deployed across the gap structuring desire to create links of libidinal lik-ings, links momentarily, fragmentarily performing, re-creating the archaic. I show in the following chapters how this field of "'letolic'" in which the forgotten archaic mother is inscribed not as a threat but as a source of joy, is one of infinite possibilities of pleasure. In the field of "'letolic," where pleasure is recognized as an effect of language, everything to do with "lic(k)ing," and/as "li(n)king," affective and erotic, can be "let," allowed to happen — or not.

Part Two
Fetishization/Colonization:
The Brisuric Binarism of Elocution

For all of the seductive allure of origin as ocean, the oceanic threatens to engulf the One of subjectivity as separation in uncontrollable and unpredictable diffusion. In the oceanic condition of infinite identity, boundaries keeping signifiers separate would be unpredictably dissolved. Renaissance treatises on the aesthetics of rhetoric are caught up in a constitutively ambivalent and dialectical relation to the limitless extension of the oceanic as origin, to the primal substance of semiosis transcoded with the archaic maternal body. Renaissance rhetoricians struggle to abject the primal substance of semiosis and re-produce language as a hyper-rational medium of expression for a phallocratic symbolic economy. Yet they repeatedly find themselves irresistibly drawn to the affective, irrational, erotic dimension of semiosis as archaic femininity. The treatises of Renaissance rhetoricians become a locus for the negotiation of a conflict between the rational, egoic drive toward schizmatization, separation, taxonomization, economization, systematization, legislation, symbolization, and between the pre-rational drive toward feminine origin, toward infinite identity. In Renaissance rhetoric, the dialectical relation of attraction and repulsion, desire and anxiety toward the archaic, maternal femininity transcoded with the primal substance of semiosis is manifest in an inaugural scission. This scission is the grand taxonomizing gesture of partitioning elocution into the categories of "figure" and "trope." These categories are polarized yet dialectically interrelated. Figure is associated with the veil hiding and circumscribing the hollow at the center of subjectivity which is the cause of desire. Trope is associated with a phallic disavowal of this hollow.

Chapter Two

Ornamentation:
Figure, Fetishism, and Perversion

The aesthetic category of "figure" retains the conceptual association of the substance of semiosis with the material, the maternal, the feminine. In the theorization of this category, however, femininity is deployed differently, perversely. Figure is imagined as what Bataille would call a supreme, "exemplary" object of desire: a seductive female body (*Accursed Share*, vol. 2, p. 137), made even more seductive by its visually apprehended veils. This seductive female body is imagined as the inverted, specular image of oceanic femininity threatening to engulf and dissolve the One of subjectivity as separation in uncontrollable and unpredictable diffusion. The female body associated with the aesthetic category of figure is imagined as a One, singular female body repeatedly penetrated, violated by the many. This body is imagined as perversely offering itself as an instrument for the *jouissance* of others, and as generating in others a perversion which takes the form of a desire to subserve it by fetishistically adulating its visually scintillating beauty.

The Latinate signifier "figure" and its Greek correlate "scheme" have the "form" or "shape" of an object as one of their denotations. Another denotation of the Latinate "figure," especially in its verb rather than noun form, is "to make apparent" or "show." In classical Greek, *schema* means appearance. Yet *schema* in ancient Greek is not simply appearance as an object's phenomenal facade. In Plato's *Republic* (365c), *schema* is "a 'seeming' masking the reality," a veil. *Schema* in classical Greek denotes a particular kind of veil for the body: a woman's outfit. For instance, in Euripides' *Bacchae*, *schema* denotes the women's clothes Pentheus is to wear so as to be able to watch the frenzied Maenads (line 832).

The signifiers "figure" and "scheme" denote two dialectically interrelated aspects of female phenomenality: the contours of an object, and the veils, especially the sartorial veils, by means of which this object is made visible to the world. Early modern theorizations of the aesthetic category of figure bring into play the two denotations of the signifier "figure." These theorizations invoke the "figure" of the female body as an object with a particular, traceable form in the register of the real as "speaking body" (Lacan, *Seminar XX*, p. 131). In these theorizations, the body transcoded with the aesthetic category of figure is imagined as offering itself "to the temptation of a possessor" (Bataille, *Accursed Share*, vol. 2, p. 139).

The sense of figure as body is related in Renaissance rhetoric to the visually apprehended fetishes by means of which a female body is "figured" or represented to the world, by means of which this body functions as a "surface of figuration" (Lemoine-Luccioni, p. 24).

Early modern theorizations of the aesthetic category of figure amplify the dialectical interrelation between the two aspects of phenomenality inscribed into the signifier "figure." In early modern theorizations, the category of figure is aligned with a fetishized female body functioning as subject and object of desire qua perversion.

In most cases, the fetishizing veils, not the flesh beneath them, predominate in early modern theorizations of the aesthetic category of figure. In most of these theorizations, the fantasy of figure as a seductive female body is powerful and close to a scenario of incest involving the body of the archaic mother who is "the primal seductress" (Kofman, *Don Juan*, p. 119), and the cause of all desire. This scenario of maternal incest informing early modern theorizations of figure is a scenario whose name cannot be sung, cannot be explicitly named in the domain contrasted yet dialectically interrelated with the domain of shadow as unconscious.

Yet, among the rhetoricians of the English Renaissance, a few did articulate the conceptual links between the aesthetic category of figure and maternal incest. Boldest among them was a theoretician and lover of language as a space of "corporall...pleasure," for whom figure was explicitly linked with archaic, past-oral, incestuous delight. Richard Sherry's *Treatise of Schemes and Tropes* of 1550, the earliest figurist rhetoric to be published in the English language, offers a theorization of the first aesthetic category mentioned in its title which would remain idiosyncratic in the history of English rhetoric.

Sherry was an esteemed philologist and translator of the classical languages (Sharon-Zisser, "Richard Sherry"). Echoing Quintilian's theorization of figures as the "gestures [*gestus*] of language" in the *Institutio oratoria* (bk. 9, ch. 1, sec. 13), Sherry describes "scheme," the Greek equivalent of the Latinate term "figure," as a "Greeke word" signifying "properlye the gesture dauncers use to make, when they have won the best game" (unpaginated). He conceptually links the category of figure with three concepts allied with an archaic, past-oral domain: (1) the gestural and corporeal, (2) the choreographic, and (3) the ludic.

The conflation of figure with gesture Sherry adopts from Quintilian aligns it with a corporeality, with a conceptually maternal materiality. The maternality accruing to the concept of gesture is intensified by its phonic proximity to gestation, child-bearing. "Gesture" resonates with an erotic femininity too. The signifier "gesture" is phonically close to the Latin *gestio*, a term denoting erotic frenzy and thought to derive from an archaic signifier referencing the sexual heat of female animals. Sherry's restatement in English of Quintilian's conflation of figure and gesture endows the term with connotations at once maternal and sexually feminine.

This restatement phonically associates figure with "jest," with a jocular playfulness granting access to the primal pleasures of the unconscious (Freud, *Jokes*, pp. 225–238). These unconscious pleasures are beyond the super-egoic inhibitions imposed by the conscious mind, the psychic locus of the Name/No of the Father. Freud describes the unconscious as the "ancient dwelling place" of pleasure (*Jokes*, p. 227). When Sherry theorizes figure in terms of gesture, he phonically associates this aesthetic category with jest, with the ludic which involves the opening up to the unconscious as site of pleasurable celebration. The phonic association of figure with ludic jest is confirmed by Sherry's explicit positioning of figure within the domain of "game," of the ludic. This is a domain exceeding the "'ordinary' life" (Huizinga, p. 13) subject to the prohibitive, super-egoic strictures of the symbolic in its repressive function. In Freud's yet more radical terms, the ludic is a domain situated even beyond the pleasure principle exceeding the super-ego, a domain "more elementary, more instinctual than the pleasure principle it overrides" (*Pleasure Principle*, p. 25).

For Sherry, figure is associated with more than the ludic as an archaic domain beyond the pleasure principle. Sherry associates figure with what is celebrated within the ludic. In Greek antiquity, to which Sherry's theorization of figure alludes, the most marked celebratory rites were the inebriate, ecstatic, frenzied celebrations of the cult of Dionysus. Dionysus is the "god of intoxicated delight" (Otto, p. 65). The Theban King Pentheus, who embodies the Law of the Father in Euripides' *Bacchae*, refers to

Dionysus as the "god who frees his worshippers from every law" (line 652). In the wildness of Dionysian celebration, all "laws and institutions" were "mocked" (ibid., p. 92). Sherry's theorization of the aesthetic category of figure in terms of archaic celebration and play associates this category with a Dionysian liberation from sobriety and rationality in a ritual enactment of "ecstasy and…enraptured love" (Otto, p. 49).

Sherry's alignment of figure with Dionysian celebration has a non-phallic inflection. Dionysus is an androgynous, non-phallic god, whom Euripides describes as characterized by a "feminine beauty" (Otto, p 143). The rituals of Dionysus involved frenzy, the suspension of rationality and logos. Jacques Derrida (*Dissemination*, pp. 80–84) and Jean-Joseph Goux (*Symbolic Economies*, pp. 44–45), show how the category of logos transcodes with the privileged yet repressive categories of Father and phallus. The suspension of logos in Dionysian rituals implicitly involves the suspension of the phallic function. The phallic function in its repressive inflection bars primal psychic forms, conceptually aligned with the archaic mother. The consequence of the suspension of the phallic function as repression would be the irruption of these archaic psychic forms. The association of the Dionysian with an archaic maternality exceeding the phallic function as repression is confirmed by the characterization of the madness involved in Dionysian rituals as inspired by "the madness inherent in the womb of the mother" (Otto, p. 143). Sherry's alignment of the aesthetic category of figure with the Dionysian links figure with psychic categories exceeding the phallus qua repressive function.

Sherry's theorization of figure aligns it with the Dionysian for another reason. Figure in Sherry's theorization is aligned with the Dionysian because this theorization involves the explicit association of figure with "daunce." This association has philological grounds. In Greek, *schemata* are dance-steps. In the *Laws*, Plato uses the signifier "*schema*" to refer to the dance composed by the Muses (669d). The signifier *schema* is used in the sense of dance-step in Herodotus' *Histories* (vol. 6, sec. 129), in Euripides's *Cyclops* (line 221), and in Aristophanes' *Peace* (line 323) and *Wasps* (line 1485).

The category of dance with which the rhetorical category of figure is philologically associated is a marked characteristic of Dionysian myths and rites. Dionysus is said to have danced already in the womb of his mother, Semele (Otto, p. 144), who was herself, during her pregnancy, "seized by an irrepressible desire to dance" (ibid., p. 96). The frenzied and intoxicating god Dionysus is said to have inspired in his female worshippers a "maddening desire to dance" (ibid., p. 81). The chorus in

Sophocles' *Antigone* refers to Dionysus as the god for whom the stars "delight / To dance," and as the god who causes the "nymph-train" to "rejoice" in his dance (lines 1126–1128). The chorus in Euripides' *Bacchae* describes Dionysus as setting the feet of women dancing (line 151) and as causing those women to "dance, delirious, possessed" (line 154). Sherry's theorization of scheme in terms of "daunce" conceptually aligns this aesthetic category with the Dionysian.

Elsewhere in Greek classical literature at the backdrop of Sherry's theorization of scheme, this signifier denotes the ecstatic, delirious dance characterizing Dionysian celebrations. In Aristophanes' *Wasps*, Philocleon speaks of a form of "dance" (*schema*) his interlocutor, Xanthian, proceeds to call "madness" (*manias*) (line 1485). A similar moment wherein scheme qua dance is thematized as frenzied possession occurs in Aristophanes' *Peace*, when Trygaeus characterizes the "dancing" (*schema*) of the chorus as a force "possessing" it and threatening to "wreck" decorum (line 323). This alignment of dance with delirium is confirmed by the chorus's description of dancing-qua-scheme as a force making the legs of its members involuntarily "bound with delight" (*hedonus*) (line 325). In Xenophon's *Symposium*, a dialogue thematizing a drinking banquet whose patron is Dionysus, Socrates speaks of choreographic gestures (*schemation*) danced by "young people" and "depicting the Graces...and Nymphs" as elements which might "greatly enhance" the banquet (sec. 7, line 5). In all those cases, the signifier "scheme" is used to thematize a form of choreography Dionysian insofar as it is manic, expressive of a celebratory intoxication beyond the control of the conscious, rational mind, the psychic domain where the Name/No of the Father, and the phallus as forbidding master signifier, reign supreme.

Dionysus, the god to whose myths the ancient thematizations of scheme as dance allude, is associated with psychic and sexual forms in excess of the phallus as a repressive function. The choreographic rituals associated with Dionysus, Jung and Kerényi argue, are a "reflection" of the god's "hermaphroditic nature" (p. 68), his polymorphic, non-phallic sexuality with which the category of figure or scheme thus becomes conceptually allied.

The category of the choreographic, in terms of which Sherry theorizes figure, has "polysexual signatures" (Derrida "Choreographies," *Ear of the Other*, pp. 183–184). These polysexual signatures are, Derrida argues, "beyond homosexuality and heterosexuality" (ibid.), and thereby beyond the rule of the phallus insisting on and enforcing the polarization of these two modalities of desire.

The primal, polymorphic, non-phallic signatures of the choreographic are inscribed in its etymological and historical proximity to the chorus as an archaic mythic/theatrical group of dancers (*schemation*) and singers in religious ceremonies and dramatic performances. The function of the chorus combines non-individuated plurality which is conceptually feminine (Irigaray, *This Sex*, p. 30) with the conceptually maternal orality of verse and song, and with the gestures of dance. The choreographic has a phonic, etymological, and conceptual proximity to the choric. Like the choreographic, the choric is associated with the Dionysian.

The association of the choric and the choreographic with the Dionysian implicit in Sherry's theorization of figure is made explicit in Marco Girolamo Vida's *De Arte Poetica* (*ca.* 1517). In his early modern treatise on the aesthetics of rhetoric, Vida points to the "summit of the lofty [Aonian] mountain" where the Muses can be seen "dancing choruses" (*Plaudentes celsae choreas*), as the rhetorician's "goal" (p. 121). In the Ciceronian version of this journey, the orator's destination is the *polis*, the place of civilization, of the Law and Name of the Father. In Vida's version of the archetypal journey of the orator, his destination is not the *polis* but the archaic, literally and conceptually feminine domain of the Muses.

The Muses who populate the domain of rhetoric in Vida's treatise are mythical-aesthetic embodiments of ardor and arousal. The plurality of the Muses is indicative of the multiplicity of the sensuous pleasures afforded by the arts they represent (see Nancy, *The Muses*, pp. 1–17). The ardor, arousal, and sensuousness conceptually characterizing the Muses characterize Dionysian rituals too. In Vida's narrative of the orator's journey to the domain of rhetoric, the Muses are involved in choric song and choreography, characteristic of Dionysian rituals.

The domain of the Muses conflated by Vida with the domain of rhetoric is Dionysian for mythological reasons too. More than one myth "tells of the persecution Dionysus underwent...either as a handsome boy or as a delicate, half-womanly stripling resembling Adonis or Attis...through having seduced...women into madness" (Kerényi, *Gods of the Greeks*, p. 262). According to several ancient traditions, the domain of the Muses was the refuge of the persecuted Dionysus (Otto, p. 144). In these mythological traditions, Dionysus, a persecuted, conceptually castrated, non-phallic god, is absorbed into the choric/choreographic-schematic and the orgiastic rituals of women (ibid., p. 60). Vida's conflation of the domain of rhetoric with the domain of the Muses strengthens the Dionysian inflection of rhetoricity.

The domain of rhetoric in Vida's narrative is Dionysian because of the mythological associations of its geographic locale, a mountain, too. In Euripides' *Bacchae*, the locale where love-maddened women ecstatically perform their "holy dance" is a mountain. The choreographic-schematic rituals of Dionysus are performed on Mount Cithaeron, beyond the bounds of the *polis* of Thebes (line 89). For Vida, the domain of rhetoric in its entirety is the domain not of law, of the *polis*, of logos, and of the phallus in its repressive function, but the mountain of Dionysian ritual beyond the *polis*.

The mountain Vida transcodes with rhetoric is the domain of the orgiastic and polymorphic, of the choric, and of the choreographic. In classical Greek, the domain of the choreographic is literally the domain of *schemation*, dance steps, whose name is identical with the name of the aesthetic category of scheme mentioned in the title of Sherry's *Treatise of Schemes and Tropes*. The aesthetic category of scheme or figure, whose importance for Sherry is indicated by his mentioning it first in his title and theorizing it first in the body of his treatise, carries associations of the choreographic, orgiastic category of the Dionysian.

In psycho-conceptual terms, the Dionysian is a category beyond the phallus as a repressive function; it is conceptually linked with the archaic mother. The Dionysian inflection of Sherry's theorization of scheme or figure maternalizes this category.

The aesthetic category of figure in the Dionysian, choric, and choreographic inflection Sherry gives it is connected with the maternal in another, tragic way. The Dionysian is invoked several times in Sophocles' *Antigone*. The function of the Dionysian in this tragedy in its entirety, Lacan says, has everything to do with the positioning of Antigone "at the limit where her life is already lost" (*Seminar VII*, pp. 280–282). The passage in the play invoking the conceptual complex linking the Dionysian with the choric and choreographic around which Sherry's theorization of figure revolves occurs at the threshold of the play's revelation of Antigone's having pushed the collusion of desire and the death drive to its limit. At this point, the desire of the mother in its tragic dimension of the possible annihilation of limits, diagnosed by Lacan as "the founding desire of the whole structure" of the play (ibid., p. 283), is revealed as "the origin of everything" (ibid., pp. 282–283). The Dionysian as choreographic has etymological and mythic links with the choric as site of a healing and celebratory maternality and of the breaching of limits subtended by the desire of the archaic mother qua death-drive.

The Dionysian as the choreographic and the choric has several conceptual links with the maternal. The Dionysian is connected with the maternal because like the maternal, it is structurally aligned with a primal and plural orality. The mytheme of Dionysus is strongly maternalized because it involves the sheltering of the castrated Dionysus by the Muses. The Sophoclean moment of the Dionysian is linked with the maternal because at this moment, maternal desire is pushed to the limit of the death drive.

The choric and choreographic marking Dionysian rites are etymologically and conceptually linked with the chora as the archaic, maternal substance of the universe, the substance imagined as preceding differentiation. The Dionysian world, Otto emphasizes, is "above all a world of women" (p. 142). This world has "motherliness in its primal form" and is at the same time "genuinely erotic" (ibid.). Sherry's theorization of figure in terms of the Dionysian and the choreographic brings this category into conceptual proximity with the archaic maternality he, like many of his peers, transcodes with the primal substance of semiosis. In the case of the theorization of figure, the alluring and seductive, even if dark and tragic, aspect of the archaic mother predominates over her abject and horrifying aspect.

An esteemed philologist and translator of ancient Greek, Sherry constructed a theorization of figure bringing into play its interrelated phonic, etymological, and mythical associations with the archaic, non-phallic, conceptually feminine categories of the Dionysian, the choric, the chora, and the choreographic. The phonic connection between the choreographic-as-schematic and the chora implicit in Sherry's theorization of figure foregrounds the archaic dimension of the choreographic. The choreographic is the register of the most primal traces of human movement. Dance is the first-born of the arts (Sibony, *Le corps et sa danse*, pp. 147–148). The choreographic consists of "the primal human material" (ibid., p. 148). Choreography is the site where one can observe the conceptual connection "between *mater* and material in its coming to be" (ibid., p. 148).

The constitutively archaic category of the choreographic consists of "gestures," elements in terms of which Sherry theorizes the aesthetic category of figure. Bodily movements are necessarily "repetitions of archaic gestures" (Sibony, *Le corps et sa dance*, p. 152), inhabited by and charged with desire for "contact with the Other" (ibid., p. 97–98). Gestures are thereby inscriptions of "the erotic act" (ibid., p. 152). Sherry's theorization of figure or scheme in terms of the choreographic, a term which in classical Greek semantically overlaps with the schematic, grants it an erotic charge.

Sherry's theorization of figure also aligns this aesthetic category with the Dionysian. The eroticism inscribed into the category of figure becomes linked with archaic, non-phallic, orgiastic, polymorphic forms of eroticism such as those celebrated in Dionysian choreographic rituals to which Sherry's theorization alludes.

In the world of Greek antiquity which Sherry's theorization of figure invokes, dances were part of the rituals involved in the mysteries of Dionysus and of the rituals of the Eleusinian mysteries, described in early Byzantine sources as an "imitation of Dionysian happenings" (Jung and Kerényi, p. 159). The Eleusinian mysteries center upon another simultaneously menacing and alluring manifestation of primal, polymorphic eroticism: the mother-daughter incest implicit in the myth of Demeter and Persephone. The similarities in the ritual expressions of the Dionysian and Eleusinian mysteries are undergirded by the mythological links between the two mysteries. In Euripides' *Bacchae*, the seer Tiresias points to Demeter as goddess of food and Dionysus as god of the "clear juice of the grape," the complement of food, as the two "supreme" powers "in human affairs" (lines 73–80). In addition to being Demeter's functional and mythological complement, Dionysus may be her son or grandson. An Orphic hymn describes Zeus as having begat Dionysus by Demeter or by Persephone (Kerényi, *Gods of the Greeks*, p. 25). Orphic hymn #44 describes the honors accorded to Dionysus' mother in the festival of Dionysus as owed by her to Persephone (Otto, p. 71). Dionysus is endogamously linked with Demeter and with Persephone as either a brother or a son.

The mythic links between Dionysus and Persephone are stronger than the links between Dionysus and Demeter, close to the point of total identification. Like Persephone, Dionysus is "a sacrificial victim and one who is doomed," (Jung and Kerényi, p. 139). In terms of his structural function in myth, Dionysus is Persephone's "counterpart" (ibid.), her narratological twin or double. In an Orphic hymn, the boundaries between Persephone and Dionysus are obfuscated even more. Dionysus is said to have resided with Persephone for two years in her underworld home (Otto, p. 79), a domain beyond the daylight of consciousness, beyond the law and the Name of the Father. In the domain of underworld, the distinctions separating Dionysus and Persephone in the mythological accounts, distinctions between the categories of mother and son, sister and brother, self and double, become blurred.

The rituals of the Eleusinian mysteries of Demeter and Persephone with whom Dionysus is so closely allied were, no less than the Dionysian rituals, emphatically choreographic. Because in classical Greek, the signifier *schema* denotes dance steps, the choreographic rites of Dionysus and Eleusis are semiotically schematic. Eleusinian rituals involved a torchlight procession and dance of the initiates along the "Sacred Road" leading to Eleusis (Kerényi, Eleusis, pp. 9–10). The rites reached an apex in a dance performed round the "Well of the Beautiful Dances" in Eleusis (ibid., pp. 70–71). Demeter was believed to have descended from this well into the unconscious depths of the underworld, depths to which Dionysus too was thought to have journeyed (Otto, p. 79). Because Demeter was believed to have descended from this well to retrieve her daughter, this well was known as *"eleusis,"* the "place of happy arrival" (Kerényi, Eleusis, p. 13).

Demeter's Well of the Beautiful Dances is a site linked through mythology with the underworld as a "place of happy arrival," (ibid., p. 23). This site of happiness is not subject to the interdictions of the Father. Instead, this site is "the realm of the blessed" (Kerényi, Eleusis, p. 23), and can be the locus of an incestuous passion between mother and daughter.

The Well of the Beautiful dances is an aquatic site. Because of the archetypal resonances of water, the well is linked with a feminizing liquidity. The feminization of Demeter's well is underscored by the well's location near the maternal element of the sea, in the Bay of Eleusis. According to Euripides, at this maternalized site of the well, the goddesses of the sea, the Nereids, who according to an Orphic hymn were the first to reveal the mysteries, joined in the dancing (ibid., p. 25). The category of the Eleusinian resonating in Sherry's theorization of figure links and subsumes the categories of the aquatic qua maternal, the choreographic, and the archaic scenario of mother-daughter incest. Figure in Sherry's theorization is maternalized and inscribed with what Derrida describes as the polysexual signatures of the choreographic.

Sherry's theorization of figure in terms of the archaic manifestations of the ludic, the Dionysian, and the choreographic, associates it with one of the most primal myths of the maternal, the category he transcodes with the primal substance of semiosis. The maternal, as inscribed in the myth of Dionysus and the related yet more transgressive myth of Demeter and Persephone, is incestuous and homoerotic. The maternal in the inflection inscribed into Sherry's theorization of figure is not abject, engulfing, and devouring like the maternality he inscribes into the primal substance of semiosis. In its Dionysian and Eleusinian inflection, the maternal is a manifestation of a pre-phallic, om-phalic sexuality linking mother and daughter in a umbilical bond. One of the sites of the choreographic "dancing out" of this umbilical bond is named the omphalos (ibid., p. 80).

The omphalic or umbilical is at the heart of the Eleusinian mysteries implicitly invoked in Sherry's theorization of figure, mythically and topologically. The mysterious event at the heart of the mysteries, the "primal Eleusinian theme," is the birth of the Primordial Maiden, the goddess Aphrodite Anadyomene, from the maternal element of the sea (Jung and Kerényi, p. 146). Anadyomene, who is the "closest to the origins" of all the goddesses of the ancient Greeks (ibid., p. 103), was thought to rise from the sea on a mussel-shell which functioned as an omphalos or umbilicus connecting her to the sea erotically and maternally (ibid., p 103). Rising from the maternalized waves to which she remained sensuously connected, the beautiful Anadyomene, literally "she who rises from the sea," was believed to appear naked before the initiates in Eleusis (ibid., p. 151).

Sherry's theorization of scheme alludes to the appearance of this goddess. This is confirmed by the structural proximity of her mythic birth from the sea to the mythic epiphany of Dionysus, whose cult is invoked in Sherry's theorization of figure, from the same watery element (Otto, pp. 63–64). The most forceful confirmation of the conceptual connection between the mytheme of Anadyomene rising from the waves and the aesthetic category of figure appears in an ancient text by Sopastros. Sospartos' account of the birth of Anadyomene involves the climactic moment when "a figure — *schema ti* — rose above the ground" (quoted by Kerényi, *Eleusis*, p. 95).

"*Schema*" is a signifier for an elocutionary category and for an ecstatic choreography. In Sherry's *Treatise of Schemes and Tropes*, the elocutionary and the choreographic significations of "scheme" are lexically and conceptually allied. In Sospartos' text, the signifier "*schema*" is collapsed with the action of rising above a surface. In Eleusis, the surface above which Anadyomene rises is the surface of the sea or of its shore. Sospartos' text describes the action of rising above the surface of the sea which, in Greek, is the name Anadyomene. In this text, the name of Anadyomene and the mytheme of her birth from the sea are collapsed with the signifier for ecstatic choreography such as was involved in the celebrations of this birth. For Sherry, who was aware of the choreographic resonance of the signifier "scheme," this signifier was primarily the name of an elocutionary category. The elocutionary category to which the signifier "scheme" refers becomes charged with the mythic resonances inscribed into it in Sospartos' text and other ancient texts describing the mysteries of Eleusis and their choreographic rituals.

The apogee of these mysteries, the Primordial Maiden Anadyomene, is a "beauty omnipotent" (Otto, p. 161), the essence of the object of desire (Bataille, *The Accursed Share*, vol. 2, p. 145). This Primordial Maiden, invoked in one of the most famous manifestations of the pictorial art of the Renaissance, Botticelli's *The Birth of Venus* (Otto, p. 103), is at once child-like, virginal, and "hetaera-like" (ibid., p. 150). She is reported to have once been represented to the initiates by the beautiful courtesan Phryne (ibid., p. 151). Anadyomene, whose naked body rising from the sea is at the heart of the Eleusinian mysteries, has a courtesan dimension. By virtue of this dimension, choreographic gestures of seduction are included among her attributes. Such choreographic gestures "make the body into an appeal" (Sibony, *Le corps et sa danse*, p. 64), and "announce there will be a sexual act" (ibid., p. 154).

Choreographic gestures (in classical Greek, "*schemata*") are included in the ritual movements of the women initiates dancing near the sea from which Anadyomene rises. Such gestures are attributed to Anadyomene too because her rising is a birth. Birth is a "mixture of bodies (mother-child)...followed by a separation followed by other mixtures and improbable separations" (ibid., p. 73). The only appropriate mode of celebrating birth, as Sibony argues (ibid.) and as the choreographic rites of Eleusis well demonstrate, is dance. Those choreographic rites index the vision of birth "as a source from which life, growth, and replenishment spring in inexhaustible plenty" (Jung and Kerényi, p. 146). The birth of the naked, sensuous Anadyomene from the waves is "the essence of dance: the dancing femininity giving body to its birth" (Sibony, *Le corps et sa danse*, p. 73) and dancing its *jouissance* (ibid., p. 16). The primal, archetypal magnitude of the birth at the heart of the Eleusinian mysteries invoked by Sherry's theorization of figure intensifies the choreographic import of this theorization.

The psychic core of Sherry's theorization of figure is the exemplary feminine beauty constituting the essence of the object of desire (Bataille, *The Accursed Share*, vol. 2, p. 145). The incarnation of this feminine beauty inscribed into Sherry's theorization of figure, Anadyomene, dances its *jouissance* on the primal maternal substance of the waves from which she emerges.

Yet the archaic, choreographic, omphalic, incestuous femininity of Anadyomene is not easily confronted. The primal mother-daughter eroticism such as Anadyomene's image invokes cannot be "faced directly" (Kofman, *Enigma of Woman*, p. 20). Confrontation with this image is an act of considerable psychic risk: an encounter with origin as femininity and maternal incest founding the "enigma of woman" (ibid., p. 83). This enigma, Sarah Kofman comments, has to do with "the desire for and the fear of incestuous relations" with "a forbidden Mother" (ibid.).

Not for nothing was this femininity placed at the heart of the Eleusinian mysteries, to be revealed only to the initiates. The primordial, unconscious desires Anadyomene embodies are desires barred from the domain of the conscious and rational, of the phallus and the Name in their repressive inflection. These desires threaten the paternal prohibition of incest subtending the repressive aspect of the symbolic domain. The Eleusinian maiden is referred-to only negatively, as an "unutterable something" (Jung and Kerényi, p. 147). Euripides refers to her as "the maiden not to be named" (quoted by Jung and Kerényi, p. 147). In Thelpusa, another site where her mysteries were celebrated, she was "not to be named at all before the uninitiate" (ibid., p. 47) . In the ritual choreographic procession leading to Eleusis, "the head of the initiate was wrapped in darkness just as in antiquity brides and those vowed to the Underworld [the domain of the unconscious] were veiled" (ibid., p. 139). Even within Eleusis, Anadyomene, the choreographic incarnation of *jouissance* omphalically emerging from this maternalized yet eroticized substance of the sea remained largely unnamed, shrouded in silence and darkness, hidden behind veils. She was masked, like Dionysus with whom she shared the mythic birth from maternal waves and the embodiment of a non-phallic, orgiastic sexuality not easily confronted from within the domain of the phallus as repression (ibid., pp. 86–91).

The ancients realized the non-phallic Dionysus in his polymorphic orgies embodies a sexuality too frightening yet too alluring to be confronted head on, and so hid his image behind a mask. In Euripides' *Bacchae*, Dionysus refers to his "mortal shape" as androgynous. This shape, he says, involves "long flowing hair and a youthful, almost feminine beauty." This beauty, Dionysus adds, "[v]eils [his] godhead" (lines 1–5), the psychic essence of the polymorphic sexuality such corporeality incarnates.

The ancients realized Anadyomene omphalically connected to the sea was the incarnation of an even more forbidden sexuality involving mother and daughter. This form of sexuality has the essence of the most seductive femininity. It involves maternal incest and a female homoerotic bond on which the prohibition of the Father, who is totally excluded from this bond, is even stronger than the prohibition on incest veiling this form of sexuality (Wittig, p. 28). In their prudence, the ancients "interpose[d] the veil" (Lemoine-Luccioni, p. 76) between themselves and the myth of maternal incest, even in the choreographic, and hence, in terms of classical Greek, schematic, celebrations of mother-daughter incest in Eleusis.

The veils the ancients interposed between themselves and the myth of archaic incest were sartorial and linguistic. Hymns sang of the prohibition on the initiates' revealing anything of what they had seen, felt, or heard. Such hymns "guard[ed] the unspeakable by speaking it" (Agamben, *Language and Death*, p. 13). They served as a veil for the unspeakable. At the same time, the language of the ancient Greeks recognized what Lacan would articulate centuries later: the veil itself is a substitute for the incestuous object choreographically/schematically celebrated in Eleusis. The name they gave to the veil, the sartorial outfit covering and on occasion camouflaging an object's naked flesh, was *schema* (Euripides, *Bacchae*, line 832).

The philosophy of subjectivity and of aesthetics has always retained the veil enshrouding the subject's primordial bisexuality incarnated in the androgynous image of Dionysus, and the subject's primordial incestuous yearning "for an Other [the maternal Other] who will never assure [this yearning]" (Delrieu, p. 130). The veil performs a psychically necessary function. The veil enshrouds a primal androgyny, incarnated in the image of Dionysus, and even more so a scenario of omphalic incest with the maternal Other, embodied in the image of Anadyomene. Because of its psychic necessity, the veil has become "one of the most fundamental images of the human relation to the world" (Lacan, *Seminar IV*, p. 155). The veil is necessary to the subject (ibid., p. 157) because it facilitates the subject's relation to a primordial (bi)-sexuality wherein even male beauty, as incarnated in the androgynous image of Dionysus, is feminine. The veil facilitates the subject's incestuous relation to the primordial maternal Other for which all other objects are substitutes by keeping the primordial (m)Other "at a distance" (Derrida, *Spurs*, pp. 47–59). Promising the presence of the primordial (m)Other beyond it (Lacan, *Seminar IV*, p. 156), the veil makes possible for the subject to inscribe upon it an imaginary captation of the (m)Other projectable onto objects of desire (ibid., p. 157). The veil institutes and subtends intersubjective erotic relations within the symbolic (ibid.). It becomes the symbolic, structural "support of love" (ibid., p. 156) and of desire for other objects. Desire would be impossible should the veil "be suspended, or even fall a bit differently" (Derrida, *Spurs*, p. 59) to reveal the "truth," or rather, as Derrida puts it, "the untruth of truth" (ibid., pp. 51, 55) of the primordial feminine object beyond it.

In the Dionysian cults, the feminine "untruth of truth" never to be revealed behind the veil was the androgynous Dionysus. In Eleusis, the place devoted to the celebration of the rebirth of Dionysus' female double Persephone, the essence of feminine truth never to be revealed was the Primordial Maiden, the naked goddess Anadyomene. The ancients spoke of another naked goddess, to be discovered in "unveiling" but "never completely unveiled": *Aletheia*, truth (Kofman, *Enigma of Woman*, p. 95; Detienne, pp. 52–69, 107–37). For the ancients, truth was the truth of origin, the truth of the primordial, incestuous, maternal object of desire. This truth of the primal maternal object is the psychic spring of Renaissance rhetoric. Renaissance rhetoric, or, to use Wilson's more semiotically and psychologically accurate term, "letolic," shrouds this truth of origin by means of the linguistic veils or *lethoi* of rhetorical forms. In Renaissance rhetoric, veils or *lethoi* function as psychically legitimate substitutes for the primal maternal object of incestuous desire, incarnated in the image of Anadyomene. Those veils conceal the primal object of incest yet obliquely point to it as the mainspring of all eroticism.

The classical Greek informing the aesthetic theorizations of Wilson, Sherry, and other Renaissance rhetoricians had yet another name for *lethoi* or sartorial veils concealing the real of the primal incestuous object. Those veils were called "*schemata*." In Euripides' *Bacchae*, *schema* is used in the sense of an outfit by means of which Pentheus veils or disguises his sex so as to observe the dancing Maenads (line 832). In Plato's *Republic*, *schema* is used to denote the "seeming" masking the "reality" (365c). In ancient Greek, the sartorial veil whose psychic function is to mask the primal incestuous object is named by means of the same signifier Renaissance rhetoricians like Sherry used to name one of the elocutionary veils performing this same psychic function. In the ancient text of Sospartos, the signifier "*schema*" is used to refer to the primal incestuous object, Anadyomene. Inscribed into the Greek signifier for the aesthetic category of figure is the dialectic between a primal incestuous object (*schema*) involved in the seductive choreographic gestures (*schemation*) of rising from the waves, and the sartorial veils (*schemata*) shrouding this object. This dialectic of the veil resonates within the aesthetic category of scheme or figure more forcefully than in other aesthetic categories performing the psychic function of veiling the primal incestuous object.

Tantalizingly pointing to the naked body of truth and/as the (m)Other who cannot and must not be seen, the veil sets in motion a seduction from a distance. This seduction promises but never fully delivers an unveiling of the body of the "invisible (m)Other" (Sibony, *Le corps et sa danse*, p. 58). This is a seduction of the type involved in the sensual dance of Salomé (ibid.), and any sensuous dance in which unveiling opens onto the joy of the flesh (ibid., p. 16). The same type of seduction in unveiling is suggested in the theorization of scheme as "daunce" by Richard Sherry, a Renaissance rhetorician for whom rhetoric was a domain of "corporall...pleasure," and, as indicated by his recognition of the relation between rhetoric and "dreames" at the end of his treatise, of erotic wish-fulfillment.

Sherry was not the only Renaissance rhetorician to allude to the androgynous image of Dionysus and the omphalic image of Anadyomene at the heart of Eleusinian mysteries, images which must remain veiled if desire is to deploy itself. In the beginning of his *Arte of English Poesie*, published three decades after Sherry's first treatise, George Puttenham re-articulates the Ciceronian myth of the primordial orator-as-civilizer with significant differences. The art whose invention Puttenham describes is called not rhetoric but "poesie." The term "poesie" references a literary domain. Puttenham's use of this term to name the domain of rhetoric suggests his sense of rhetoric as the domain of the aesthetic. This sense of rhetoric is quite different from the idea of rhetoric as the conceptually masculine and phallic domain of the political, suggested, for example, in Peacham's reference to the primordial orator as "the emperor of men's minds" (*Garden of Eloquence*, unpaginated). Unlike Peacham and Wilson, and unlike Cicero who is the source for the myths of the invention of rhetoric they retell, Puttenham speaks not of one but of several inventors. All of the inventors of rhetoric Puttenham mentions are poets of archaic Greece: Amphion, Orpheus, Linus, Museus, and Hesiod (p. 4). For Puttenham, rhetoric is the product of a multiple origin. The multiple has been associated with the feminine at least since the Pythagorean table of opposites cited in Aristotle's *Metaphysics* (986a). Puttenham's invocation of a multiple origin for rhetoric intensifies the feminization of this domain.

Renaissance rhetoricians often regarded ancient Greece as a conceptually phallic domain of politics and warfare. In his *Arte of Rhetorique*, Wilson invokes the political orator Demosthenes (p. 242). Rainolde alludes to a military hero, Alexander the Great, at the outset of his treatise (sig. A2). Puttenham relates to ancient Greece differently. For Puttenham, ancient Greece is the domain of Orphic hymns singing the polymorphic myths of Demeter, Persephone, and Dionysus, of the mystery cults, including those of the Pythagoreans, who made use of these myths, of Hesiodic mythologies, and of poetry in general. Puttenham harkens to ancient Greece as seductive origin of the aesthetics of language, as does Sherry in his theorization of figure. Ancient Greece as place of origin is for Puttenham the domain of the many rather than of the conceptually phallic "one" (Irigaray, *This Sex*, p. 26), the sole "father" of the art of rhetoric postulated by Wilson (*Arte of Rhetorique*, p. 41).

Puttenham's inventors of the art of language are more than inhabitants of the archaic as the domain of the multiple and polymorphic rather than the singular and phallic, of poetry and/as affect rather than of political oratory. Puttenham describes the inventors of rhetoric as "the first Priests and ministers of the holy mysteries" (p. 4). These priests are the hierophants of Eleusis, the singing priests whose connection with orality is underscored by their being descendants of Eumolpos, "he who sings beautifully" (Kerényi, *Eleusis*, p. 23). These priests conducted the choreographic rites to which Sherry's theorization of scheme alludes. The title of these priests, "hierophants" ("*heiro*" holy + "*phainai*" appear) indicates they were believed to reveal "the ineffable, holy thing," the omphalic image of the naked goddess who rises from the maternal waves yet can never be completely shown (Kerényi, *Eleusis* pp. 90–92). Given Puttenham's articulation of the conceptual connection between the art of language in its entirety and the Eleusinian mysteries, we should not be surprised by his being, as Peacham and Sherry were before him, a "figurist," a rhetorician who theorizes only about the third part of classical rhetoric, elocution. Sherry, the first of the English figurists, betrays an intense cathexis of the Eleusinian mysteries in his theorization of the aesthetic category of scheme in terms multiply resonating with these mysteries and then foregrounding this category at the expense of its phallic binary, trope (Sharon-Zisser, "Richard Sherry"). Puttenham may have had an even stronger cathexis of the Eleusinian mysteries. He alludes to these mysteries in his account of the origins of rhetoric. He is also the only rhetorician of the English Renaissance who does away with the phallic category of trope and refers to all forms of elocution as "figures," the Latinate version of "scheme," the signifier used to refer to the appearance of the goddess at Eleusis.

Two other rhetoricians of the English Renaissance allude to the conceptual connection between elocution, the aesthetic category of figure, the mysteries of Dionysus, and the Eleusinian mysteries of mother-daughter incest which the Greek name of this category echoes. One of these rhetoricians was John Smith, a seventeenth-century figurist, who chose to entitle his treatise *The Mysterie of Rhetorique Unvail'd* (1657). Another was his contemporary Edward Phillips, who entitled his treatise *The Mysteries of Love and Eloquence* (1658). In entitling their rhetorical treatises "mysteries," Smith and Phillips stress the conceptual link between rhetoric and the two interrelated ancient mysteries to which Sherry's theorization of figure alludes. These include the mysteries of Dionysus, at whose center is an image of an androgynous god. The joy and ecstasy choreographically, or, in terms of classical Greek, schematically, expressed in relation to this god is a fleshly veil, in classical Greek, *schema*, for the bisexuality he incarnates. The ancient mysteries resonating in the titles of the rhetorical treatises of Smith and Phillips include the mysteries of Eleusis, at whose core is the veiled omphalic image of Anadyomene rising from the waves, revealingly named by Sospartos "*schema*." The ancient mysteries resonating in the titles of the rhetorical treatises of Smith and Phillips are most strongly related to the rhetorical category of scheme or figure Sherry had already theorized in terms of those mysteries.

The titles of the rhetorical treatises of Smith and Phillips unmistakably make the conceptual, anagrammatical, and phonic connections between the rhetorical and the erotic characterizing early modern theorizations of language. The title of Phillips's treatise syntactically conjoins "love" and "eloquence," eroticism and rhetoricity. Phillips's title relates love and eloquence to "mysteries" such as those of Eleusis and Dionysus informing Sherry's earlier theorization of the rhetorical category of figure.

Sherry's theorization of figure is informed by mysteries of polymorphic eroticism beyond the phallus, and thereby conceptually om-phalic, feminine. These are myths of a loving bond between mother and daughter and of the mythically related frenzied attraction to an androgynous god. The title of Phillips's treatise alludes to these myths. This is suggested by the visual images accompanying Phillips's title. The frontispiece to Phillips's treatise includes three images. The top and bottom images feature a Renaissance courtier in a token posture of obsequious genuflection underscoring his conceptual castration with respect to his empowered and phallicized female object of desire. The central image of the frontispiece, the image bespeaking its title graphically and orthographically, does not postulate the domain of love as the domain of male castration complemented by female phallicization, the hallmarks of Petrarchan poetics.

The central image of Phillips's frontispiece postulates the domain of love as the domain of castration writ large, of the total absence of the phallus in its repressive function. At the center of this image is a heart bearing the inscription of the treatise's title with a significant difference in spelling. The word "mysteries," bespeaking the conceptual connection the treatise implicitly draws between eloquence as the domain of love and the omphalic myths of Dionysus and Eleusis, is spelt "misteries." The signifier "misteries" postulates the domain of love and/as eloquence not as the domain of the totalizing phallic master, a function Renaissance rhetoricians associate with the category of metaphor. This signifier postulates the domain of love and/as eloquence as the domain of the master's female and feminine counterpart, the mistress, in her amatory-erotic function.

Phillips's feminization of the domain of eloquence as the domain of love is underscored by the pictorial representations of the two mythological-allegorical figures standing for the functions named by the title and holding the heart at the center of the frontispiece: Cupid, god of love, and Mercury, god of eloquence. Both these figures are male, yet in Phillips's frontispiece, neither is phallically masculine. Cupid's arrows are sheathed in a pack barely visible behind his back. Mercury's phallic symbol, the caduceus, is not foregrounded, as it is, for instance, in Guillaume du Vair's *Traitté de l'Eloquence Françoise* (1621), where it is described as a conceptually phallic instrument of mastery through which Mercury "commands the powers of heaven, earth, and hell" (p. 395). In the frontispiece of Phillips's treatise, Mercury's phallic caduceus, like Cupid's phallic shaft, is partially hidden from view behind his back. Phillips's Mercury is clearly feminized. His body is thoroughly veiled by a long dress whose upper folds trace breast-like curves, corporeal traces of the primal body-part-object of the (m)Other.

The feminization of Cupid and Mercury in the frontispiece of Phillips's *Mysteries of Love and Eloquence* inflects the domain of eloquence as the domain of a particular kind of love. The love transcoded with eloquence in the frontispiece of Phillips's treatise is a non-phallic love not seeking mastery. This love gives itself up to mysteries such as those of Dionysus and Eleusis, recognized in the frontispiece as feminized, omphalic misteries.

The feminized allegory of Mercury on the frontispiece of Phillips's treatise inflects the domain of eloquence, Mercury's domain, as a domain where, as in this allegory, a veil traces yet conceals the archaic, incestuous maternal object. I have shown above how in Sherry's *Treatise of Schemes and Tropes*, the primal incestuous object is transcoded with the aesthetic category of scheme or figure. In the visual allegory of Mercury on Phillips's frontispiece, the visual trace of the archaic object, the object at the core of the Eleusinian mysteries to which the title of Phillips's treatise alludes, is the breast. In the frontispiece, the veil concealing the breast-object is a dress, a sartorial veil. Later in this chapter, I show how Renaissance rhetoricians, Sherry among them, transcode sartorial veils with the category of figure. The feminized allegory of Mercury on the frontispiece of Phillips's treatise evokes the primal incestuous object of the Eleusinian mysteries

94   *Fetishization/Colonization: The Brisuric Binarism of Elocution*

and the sartorial veil concealing it. In Renaissance rhetoric, the primal incestuous object and its veil are both associated with the category of scheme or figure. The allegory of Mercury inflects the domain of eloquence to which the title of Phillips's treatise alludes as, conceptually speaking, primarily the domain of figure, the domain of the aesthetic category closest to origin.

For Phillips, the title and frontispiece of his treatise suggest, more than for Wilson, eloquence was the domain of "letolic." Phillips's "letolic" is the domain where the incestuous maternal object thematized in the mysteries of Eleusis to which his title and the breasted Mercury of his frontispiece allude must undergo a conscious forgetting, a relegation to Let-he. In this domain, the incestuous maternal object may be granted a let-ting to be expressed in substitute symbolic forms of object love, of libidinal li(c)k-ing. In the domain of "letolic" postulated by Phillips's title and frontispiece, such substitutional objects, like the dress of the maternalized Mercury of the frontispiece, function as sartorial veils for the primal incestuous object. In the language of ancient Greece, to which Phillips's title and frontispiece allude, signifiers for sartorial veils included *let-hoi* and *schemata*. The first of these signifiers resonates in Wilson's "letolic," a term postulating rhetoric as the domain of erotic possibility. The second is the name of an elocutionary category Sherry associates with the Eleusinian mysteries.

The semiotic proximity between ancient Greek terms for veils, sartorial substitutes for the primal object, and early modern signifiers for rhetorical qua erotic categories has two conceptual consequences. First of these is an intensification of the inflection of rhetorical categories theorized in early modern treatises as linguistic analogues, analogues consisting of let-ters, formalized means of signification within the symbolic, for sartorial veils substituting for the primal oral object logically, not temporally preceding the symbolic. The second consequence of the proximity between archaic signifiers for sartorial objects and early modern signifiers for rhetorical qua erotic categories is an intensification of the psychic function of early modern rhetorical categories as veils tracing yet concealing the oral object for which they substitute. Of the two ancient Greek terms for sartorial objects resonating within early modern rhetorical categories, one (*lethoi*) resonates within a term ("letolic") referencing the domain of rhetoric in its entirety, and one (*schema*) resonates within a term (scheme) referencing a discrete elocutionary category within this rhetorical domain. This discrete elocutionary category, scheme or figure, is the most intensely related to the veiled mysteries of origin to which the title of Phillips's rhetorical treatise alludes.

The title of John Smith's treatise on the aesthetics of rhetoric, *The Mysterie of Rhetoric Unvail'd*, similarly bespeaks a conceptual, anagrammatical, and phonic connection between the el-ocutionary and the El-eusinian. This title alludes to ancient mysteries and to their unveiling, indexing Smith's desire to confront and access the primal bisexuality and incestuous desire the veils involved in those mysteries enshroud. Openly voicing a bisexuality and a desire for the maternal incest shrouded "behind the last veil" (Lemoine-Luccioni, p. 76) may have been too risky an enterprise for a Renaissance rhetorician, even one whose predecessors included Sherry and Puttenham, who had voiced their fascination with the Eleusinian and Dionysian mysteries. Despite the title of Smith's treatise, its Dionysian and omphalic dimension remains veiled.

The "mysteries" to which he refers, Smith avows in the epistle to the reader, are those of the Scriptures, in which "many…things [are] folded up," veiled (unpaginated). Although Smith does supply scriptural, alongside English and Latin vernacular, examples for the figures and tropes he conceptualizes, his avowal, as is frequently the case, is a disavowal. Even technically speaking, Smith's treatise is not concerned with an exegetical "unvailing" of the "mysteries" of the Scriptures. Smith's treatise is concerned with the "mysteries" of the archaic "Greek tongue" in which the aesthetic properties of the forms of elocution are "folded," "masked," or veiled to those "altogether unacquainted" with this tongue (unpaginated).

Similarly to Vida, who imagines himself as the leader of a procession toward a choreographic, polymorphic, Dionysian orgy, similarly to Puttenham, who makes the primal orator not the first civilizer but one of the hierophants of Eleusis who revealed the mysteries of homoerotic, maternal incest, Smith posits himself as one who mediates, through the theorization of the categories of rhetoric, a primal (bi)-sexuality situated beyond the phallus and within cavernous, conceptually maternal "folds" such as those of Mount Cithaeron which Dionysus invokes in *The Bacchae* as the place of the dancing Bacchants (line 62) and which is revealed only to the "initiates" (line 479).

Smith was an aesthetician of the Baroque. Leibniz, a major philosopher of the Baroque, was much concerned with "folds," with the infinite unfurling of curvilinear surfaces (Deleuze, *The Fold*, pp. 3–15). Like his contemporary, Leibniz, Smith was fascinated by folds, curvilinear surfaces made cavernous and conceptually maternal. Smith casts himself as an officiant of Dionysian "mysteries" ecstatically, choreographically unfurling within the "folds" of Mount Cithaeron. These folds to which Smith's epistle alludes exceed and shatter the straight walls of the palace/*polis* where Dionysus is imprisoned (Euripides, *Bacchae*, line 605). These folds are physically and conceptually isomorphic with the "long curls / Cascading most seductively over [Dionysus'] cheek" (ibid., lines 457–458). Smith's invocation and conflation of the categories of the archaic, the mystery, and the veil, allude to the cult of Dionysus and to the structurally, mythically, and conceptually related cult of Eleusis. Invoking the Eleusinian, Smith postulates himself as a hierophant of elocution, who purports to make an image of omphalic, homoerotic, maternal incest appear from behind the "abstruse" veils of the archaic Greek names of rhetorical forms.

Although Smith makes omphalic figures and phallic tropes the object of his inquiries into the "mysteries" of rhetoric, he describes the most ineffable, "abstruse" rhetorical objects as "neither Tropes nor Figures." For Smith, the most ineffable mysteries to be revealed in the study of rhetoric are mysteries whose meaning would be "incident to the unvailing divers of the Figures" (unpaginated). For Smith, ineffable mysteries are to be revealed through the "unvailing" of the aesthetic category of figure. Figure is the category Sherry, and more implicitly, Puttenham, had already associated with the omphalic, incestuous "scheme" of Anadyomene rising from the waves, the scheme at the veiled core of the Eleusinian mysteries. Figure is the elocutionary category Sherry, Phillips, and, as I will show below, other Renaissance rhetoricians transcode with the sartorial and psychic category of the veil. The mysteries to be revealed in the study of rhetoric, Smith implies, are the mysteries of Eleusis inscribed into the category of figure, transcoded with the two crucial components of the mysteries: the primal object and the veils tracing yet concealing this object. The mysteries of the primal object and its veil inscribed into the category of figure are, Smith implies, to be revealed through the analysis, of the kind we moderns would call psychoanalysis, of this category, which psychically functions as a veil.

Other Renaissance rhetoricians were not as bold as Sherry, Puttenham, Phillips, and Smith in articulating the conceptual links between the aesthetic category of figure, primal, Dionysian bisexuality, and the symbolic (m)Other, the object cause of all desire, as incarnated in the Eleusinian image, or, in Sospartos' terms, scheme, of Anadyomene rising from the waves. In theorizations of figure by other Renaissance rhetoricians, the archaic (m)Other as object cause of desire is inscribed only on veils. Those veils heraldize the presence of the archaic (m)Other beyond them, yet keep it safely enshrouded, offering themselves as substitutes. Instead of alluding to the archaic (m)Other, many early modern theorizations of figure recreate her reassuring envelopments in veils functioning as "reconstituted placenta" (Lemoine-Luccioni, p. 73). As "fascinating objects" on which "erotic life" focuses, the veils featuring in Renaissance theorizations of figure are, in Lacanian terms, of the order of the fetish (*Seminar IV*, p. 160).

The creation of veils as recreations of the "lost envelope" of the (m)Other is most evident in Renaissance theorizations of figure or scheme in terms of literal veils of the body, clothes, one of whose names in classical Greek is *schemata*. Echoing Quintilian's inaugural conceptualization of figures as "habits" (*habitus*) of thought analogous to "habits" of "bodies" (*corporibus*) (bk. 9, sec. 1, line 4), Erasmus writes in *De Copia*: "[s]tyle is to thought as clothes are to the body," able to "dis-figure" or to "enhance" (p. 306), and thus, implicitly, to "figure." Similarly, Mark Beumley conceptualizes figures as the "vestments" (*vestitus*) and "habits"(*habitus*) of the body (*corporis*) in his *Rhetoricae* (1598) (unpaginated). John Smith speaks of figures by means of the sartorial category of "apparel" (p. 4). Quintilian, Erasmus, Smith, and Farnaby, who refers to figures as *"habitus"* (20), theorize figure in terms of an enveloping surface. This surface is not the body. The surface early modern rhetoricians associate with figure envelops the body. This enveloping surface is the *habitus* of the body. The term *"habitus"* denotes "habit" as dress and is etymologically proximate to *habito* (dwelling). The theorizations of the category of figure in terms of "habit" conceptually link this aesthetic category with material encasements — clothes and houses — in which bodies are phenomenally contained.

These encasements, the habits and habitats of the body with which Quintilian and Erasmus associate figure, possess a phenomenality which is exterior, apprehended by the eye as scopic "surface of pleasure," not by the aural/oral orifices circumscribing an "internal space" (Montrelay, pp. 87–88). Because the habits and habitats of the body to which Quintilian and Erasmus allude in their theorizations of figure are scopically-apprehended envelopes, they function as repetitions of the primal specular image. This is the image generated by the reassuring yet intermittent and fragile maternal gaze enveloping the constitutive lack or hollow of the nascent subject (Lemoine-Luccioni, pp. 82–85, 90). Because the habits and habitats in terms of which Quintilian and Erasmus theorize figure are repetitions of the primal maternal gaze, they have two distinct yet related psychic functions. They are spherical envelopes, recreations of the lost placenta. And they are reconstitutions of the umbilicus (ibid., p. 81), of the omphalos structuring the image of archaic incest, which resonates in Sherry's formative theorization of the aesthetic category of figure in the English language.

Elsewhere in his inaugural theorization of figure, Sherry gestures toward the maternal incest resonating in the even more archaic origins of this aesthetic category in rhetoric's mythological pre-history. Figures, Quintilian writes, "spare modesty the embarassment of too naked an exposition" of "offensive" facts such as incest (bk. 9, sec. 2, lines 70–85). The sartorial veils in terms of which Quintilian theorizes figure, he implies here, are a recreated placenta omphalically and reassuringly enveloping the subject. They are veils protecting the subject from confrontation with omphalic incest and thus with a *"jouissance* menacing because it portends the annihilation of the desiring subject" (Delrieu, p. 147). Like all manifestations of the interdiction against incest, Quintilian's reference to figures as sartorial guarantors of "modesty" serve to "veil the nature of [incest as] desirable" (ibid., p. 146).

The "taboo of language's nudity" Roland Barthes identifies in Quintilian's theorization of figure ("The Old Rhetoric," p. 85) is a manifestation of the incest taboo. The "naked" body referenced in Quintilian's theorization of figure is the naked body of the subject who reinvents sartorial veils as substitutes for the lost placenta because she has been "disengaged" from it (Lemoine-Luccioni, p. 37). This naked body is also the naked body involved in a scenario of incest, like the scenario of Anadyomene haunting Sherry's theorization of figure.

Quintilian's theorization of figure as what veils/envelops nudity qua the absence of the placental and what veils/conceals nudity in incest is echoed in Joachimus Camerarius's *Elementa Rhetoricae* (1540), where figures are described as *"habitus"* (habits) rescuing the oration from the state of being *"a nuda"* (nude) (p. 154). Quintilian's theorization is also echoed in Bartolomeo Cavalcanti's *La Retorica* (1559), where figures are represented as means of transmuting *"le cose nude"* (nude things) into *"le cose belle"* (beautiful things) (p. 249). Puttenham too taps into the conceptual link between figure and the veil of nudity and incest when he describes "Poesie" as unable to tolerate the state of "any lymme" being "left naked and bare and not clad in his kindly clothes," just as "Madames of honour" would never do without "habillements or at leastwise such other apparell as custome and ciuilitie haue ordained to couer their naked bodies" (p. 114).

Yet for Puttenham there is more to figures qua clothes than the compensatory enveloping of bodies and the concealment, or as he puts it, "disguising," of the desirability of maternal incest. The "Madames of honour" of whom he speaks in his theorization of figure, would, he writes, "be halfe ashamed or greatly out of countenaunce to be seen" in clothes whose only function is to serve as a "couer" or veil for nakedness, literal or symbolic (the veiling of the desirability of maternal incest). Instead, he continues, such women "thinke themselues more amiable in euery mans eye, when they be in their richest attire, suppose of silkes or tyssewes & costly embroderies, then when they go in cloth or in any other plaine and simple apparell" (p. 114). For Puttenham, the function of "figures or figuratiue speaches" is conceptually isomorphic not with the veiling of literal or symbolic nudity of which Quintilian, Erasmus, Camerarius, and Cavalcanti speak. For Puttenham, the function of figures is isomorphic with the function of clothes which veil and make women "more amiable in euery man's eye," arousing of amorous passions, seductive. The function of figures for Puttenham is to seduce, to *"allure* as well the mynde as the eare or the hearers" (p. 114, my emphasis). What subtends and enables the sartorial and rhetorical seduction in terms of which Puttenham theorizes the aesthetic category of figure is a system of signification conceptually associated with the feminine. Centuries before Barthes's *Fashion System*, Puttenham spoke of this system of signification as "fashion" (p. 114).

Puttenham's near-contemporary Phillip Stubbes has recourse to the same conceptual links between the categories of fashion, femininity, and seduction in the *Anatomie of Abuses* (1584). In this moralistic treatise, Stubbes complains about "[n]ew fashions" appearing "euery day" (p. 76), which include "sumptuous apparel" of "silke or veluet" (p. 74) such as Puttenham was to speak of, which are used by women to procure the sexual interest of men (p. 88).

New historicists and cultural materialist critics of the past two decades have been wont to read early modern references to fashion such as Puttenham's and Stubbes's as instances of the construction and promotion of a self through cultural discourses Stephen Greenblatt has influentially termed "self-fashioning." Applying Greenblatt's influential idea of "self-fashioning" to the domain of fashion, Anne Hollander traces the "ineluctable movement of fashion" in Renaissance England to the "presumption" of courtiers in the post-feudal and increasingly mobile society of the Renaissance to fashion their selves through clothes as members of the higher classes. Such courtiers, Hollander states, used fashion in socially-motivated attempt "to imitate something better...more beautiful and shining, which [they] could not actually aspire to be" (p. 362). For Hollander as for Frank Whigham, fashion in the Renaissance was one among a repertoire of instruments, including manners and eloquence, deployed in the process of the "ostentatious practice of symbolic behavior taken to typify aristocratic being" (Whigham, p. 33).

While critics such as Hollander and Whigham may be right in pointing out the social and cultural function of fashion in the early modern period, they ignore the more fundamental psychic function of fashion. The psychoanalyst Daniel Sibony diagnoses fashionable clothes as "objects of the transmission" of the "subtle and indefinite substance called the feminine" (*Le corps et sa danse*, p. 292). Women's psychic investment in fashionable clothes, Sibony says, is an attempt to appropriate this quintessential substance of femininity (ibid., p. 300) so as to become what he calls "the Other-woman" (*Autre-femme*): a "feminine figure of the Other supposed to have confiscated all the attributes of the feminine" (*Le féminin et la seduction*, p. 5).

What is at stake in Puttenham's theorization of figure as sumptuary "fashion," is not, or at least not only, a feminine version of "Renaissance self-fashioning," the construction of identity through social, in this case, sumptuary, codes such as new historicists have been wont to speak of. Instead, what is at stake in the transcoding of the aesthetic category of figure and women's fashion in early modern treatises on rhetoric including Puttenham's *Arte of English Poesie* (p. 114), Peacham's *Garden of Eloquence* (unpaginated), Fraunce's *Arcadian Rhetorike*, (sig. B9), and Sherry's *Treatise of Schemes and Tropes* (unpaginated), is a psychic function. This psychic function involves women's use of fashionable clothes to access a quintessential femininity which renders them desirable, capable of seducing men (Sibony, *Le corps et sa danse*, p. 305), or in Puttenham's terms, "amiable in euery man's eye" (p. 114). Manifestations of the use of clothes as transporters of the seductive aspects of femininity, such as the manifestations of which Puttenham and Stubbes speak, are necessarily historical. But because the use of clothes as transporters of the seductive aspects of femininity is a psychic function, this function itself, the function subtending theorizations of figure from Quintilian onwards, is not historicizable.

Sarah Kofman speaks of women's need to "veil themselves" as corresponding to "a certain fetishism" (*Enigma of Woman*, p. 49). The sartorial veils, the fetishes of fashion with which Puttenham, and more implicitly Peacham, Fraunce, and Sherry transcode the aesthetic category of figure are objects of the transmission of the feminine "giving birth to the feminine" within a woman (Sibony, *Le corps et sa danse*, p. 300). These veils qua fetishes are omphalic objects connecting a woman with the

Other-woman, with the "primal, matricial mother" (ibid., p. 301). The fashionable feminine clothes Renaissance rhetoricians transcode with the category of figure make possible a re-enactment within the symbolic of the omphalic and homoerotic scenario of maternal incest. The fashionable feminine clothes with which Renaissance rhetoricians transcode the category of figure are means of accessing the scenario of maternal incest at the most archaic root of this aesthetic category, beyond even its polymorphic and orgiastic Dionysian veils. This Eleusinian scenario conceptually saturates the aesthetic category of figure in its early modern theorizations, on all levels.

Puttenham speaks of the fashionable feminine clothes he transcodes with the aesthetic category of figure as enabling women to become "amiable in euery man's eye" (p. 114). Sibony speaks of such clothes in conceptually isomorphic terms, as fetishes whose function is to establish a transferential relation with the Other-woman, the primordial feminine, and through this relation, to give birth to seductive, desirable femininity (*Le corps et sa danse*, p. 299). In his theorization of figure, Puttenham refers to the dialectic between nudity and its sartorial veils. This dialectic informs the theorizations of figure by Quintilian, Camerarius, and Cavalcanti too. In the context of the conceptualization of the fashionable feminine clothes Puttenham and other Renaissance rhetoricians transcode with the category of figure as enabling a woman to give birth to a desirable woman within herself the category of figure takes on another resonance, the resonance of seduction.

Connections such as rhetoricians draw between figures and garments, Barthes remarks, "make speech desirable" ("The Old Rhetoric," p. 85). More accurately put, such connections introduce into meta-language a particular, sartorial and scopic, dynamic of desire in which women make use of the fetishes of fashion to seduce. Within this dynamic, "the use of clothes" grants to female nudity the "allure of a thing, of a seizable object" (Bataille, *The Accursed Share*, vol. 2, p. 140). Because the garments Puttenham associates with figures are means of rendering a woman "amiable" or seductive, these garments are more than enveloping substitutes for a lost placenta. They are participants in a dialectic of seduction, "speaking where the body does not" (Lemoine-Luccioni, p. 31) in an "invocation" for an amorous "unveiling" (ibid., p. 28), for their own "spoli[ing]" by desire (Barthes, *Lover's Discourse*, p. 127). This seductive "dialectic of the garment" Barthes too identifies in the rhetorical category of figure ("The Old Rhetoric," p. 85) by virtue of its etymology ("*schema* means costume, *figura* appearance" [ibid., p. 85]) arouses desire "by hiding its object" (ibid.).

The dialectic of the garment underscores the seductive function of clothes of which Sarah Kofman speaks (*Don Juan*, p. 90). In this dialectic, parts of the female body are erogenized by their concealment behind veils such as the "silkes or tyssewes" Puttenham refers to (p. 114). Other parts of the female body become even more erogenized and seductive. These are the body parts exposed in the sartorial "intermittences," where "the garment gapes" (Barthes, *Pleasure of the Text*, pp. 9–10). These intermittences or "apertures" of the garment, Lemoine-Luccioni explains, "make sexual play possible" (p. 65). Puttenham's theorization of the aesthetic category of figure in terms of a sartorial seduction of men by women implicates this aesthetic category in a dialectic of the garment structured by the "staging of an appearance-as-disappearance" (Barthes, *Pleasure of the Text*, p. 10). The dialectic of the garment inscribed into Puttenham's theorization of figure involves the veiling of the "naked body" of a "Madam" with sartorial "couers" (p. 114). The intermittences and concealments of those sartorial "couers" work toward enticing men whose "eye" they solicit (ibid.) to what Eugenie Lemoine-Luccioni calls "the erotic game of undressing, of amorous denudation" (p. 69).

Using fashionable garments as means of making themselves "amiable in euery man's eye," the "Madames" Puttenham inscribes into his theorization of figure, like the prostitutes discussed by Bataille, who use "sumptuary expenditures" to "make them[selves] more desirable" (*The Accursed Share*, vol. 2, p. 142), postulate a particular structure of desire. Their self-fetishization through fashion, obtained through the appropriation of the Other-woman qua quintessence of femininity, is not solipsistic and narcissistic. Nor is their self-fetishization phantasmatic, structured by an imaginary captation of another object by the women as subjects. The self-fetishization of the "Madames" Puttenham inscribes into the category of figure does not stop short at obtaining quintessential femininity. The self-fetishization of Puttenham's "Madames" harnesses quintessential femininity to obtaining the objective of being "amiable in euery man's eye" (p. 114). The goal of this self-fetishization is the *jouissance* of the men at whom it is directed rather than of the women who perform it. The sartorial fetishism of the "Madames" Puttenham inscribes into the aesthetic category of figure is structured by a desire which does not question and unequivocally seeks the *jouissance* of an other. In Lacanian terms, this desire has the form of perversion (*Écrits*, p.320).

Women fetishists, Lacan says, make themselves "instruments of the other's *jouissance*" by more than "fancy dress" (*Écrits*, pp. 320, 322). Nor is fashionable dress the only fetish by means of which a woman gives birth to her seductive femininity. Other objects are enlisted for creating a veil which might visually proclaim the woman as an object of *jouissance*, denying the symbolic castration, the lack constituting her as subject (Lemoine-Luccioni, p. 117). In his theorization of figure, Puttenham speaks of other fetishes making women "amiable in euery men's eye": the "costly embroderies" on their garments, made by the "embroderer" with "stone and perle" (pp. 114–115). Puttenham transcodes the name of these fetishes with the aesthetic category of figure in its entirety. The entire section of his treatise devoted to the figures of elocution is entitled: "Of Ornament Poeticall."

Ornament is the concept used most frequently and consistently to theorize the category of figure in Renaissance rhetoric. Peacham mentions ornament as one of the attributes of figure in *The Garden of Eloquence* (1597) (unpaginated). In a treatise published in 1570, John Sturmius distinguishes tropes from "ornaments and beautifications of sentences" (p. 38), conflating these "ornaments and beautifications" with the binary opposite of tropes, figures. Richard Rainolde's *Foundacion of Rhetorike* (1563) mentions figures as the means whereby the "matter" of oration, the maternalized primal substance of semiosis, is "beutified and adorned" (unpaginated). Mark Beumley's *Rhetoricae* aligns figure with *"ornatum corporis"* (the ornamentation of the body) (unpaginated), a formulation repeated in John Smith's *Mysterie of Rhetorique Unvail'd* (p. 4). Obadiah Walker's *Instructions Concerning the Art of Oratory* (1659) lists "ornaments" as one of the synonyms of "figures" (p. 51). Bartolomeo Cavalcanti mentions figures as a means of *"adornare I suoi concetti"* (adorning one's conceits) in his *La retorica* of 1559 (p. 298). The anonymous *Rhetoricae Synopsis* of 1693 refers to figures as a means of making style *"ornatus"* (ornate) (p. 61). Dominico Decolonia's *De Arte Rhetorica*, published already into the eighteenth century, in 1705, represents figures as *"schema...ornamentum quoddam orationis"* (schemes ornamenting the oration) p. (17).

Like the "habits" of "fashion" Renaissance rhetoricians use to conceptualize figure, ornament is a feminized category. The category of ornament is marked by an association with the feminine which "goes back to the rhetorical manuals of classical antiquity" (Schor, p. 19). Since antiquity, ornament has been identified with feminine taste (Gombrich, p. 116; Brody, pp. 197–202). The feminization of ornament is inscribed by negation into Plato's metaphysics of austerity which privileges the insipid and unornamented and seeks to confine ornamentation to the constrained space of the pharmacy. The pharmacy is a feminine space, taking its name from Pharmacia, a nymph who is "the quintessence of femininity," and who is associated with acts of self-adornment whose mastering is imagined as involved in one's "becom[ing] a woman" (Lichtenstein, p. 42). This metaphysics of austerity is still at work in Nietzsche's aesthetics, where "self-adornment" is said to "pertain...to the eternal womanly" (quoted by Derrida, *Spurs*, p. 66). Ornamentation too, then, is a woman's means of accessing archaic, seductive femininity and giving birth to the feminine within herself in order to serve as an instrument for the *jouissance* of others.

Nietzsche's rearticulation of the conceptual connection between the ornamental and the feminine has to do with the seductive dimension of femininity (Derrida, *Spurs*, p. 67; Lichtenstein, p. 53). Ornament, as Derrida puts it in his study of this aesthetic category, has to do with what "seduces by attraction" (*The Truth in Painting*, p. 64). Ornament "dazzles...and tempts the mind to submit without proper reflection" (Gombrich, p. 17). If ornament is connected with the feminine, as philosophers of the aesthetic from Plato through Nietzsche to Gombrich have insisted, then it is connected with a femininity of a particular type: the femininity of the temptress or seductress. This is an archaic, archetypal femininity, a femininity which lures to transgress stabilizing law and "turns around Woman as the 'primary' form of the Other" (Sibony, *Le féminin et la séduction*, pp. 80, 88).

The seduction inscribed into the aesthetic category of figure via its ubiquitous association with ornament has to do with an "unconscious umbilicus" (ibid., p. 61). The mussel shell connecting the Primordial Maiden Anadyomene, the apogee of female desirability inscribed into Sherry's theorization of figure, to the maternal waves from which she emerges, is a phenomenal analogue for the psychic structure of the unconscious umbilicus of seduction. The unconscious umbilicus of seduction inscribed into the category of figure connects seducer and seduced, who become indistinguishable one from the other (ibid., p. 9) to the archaic femininity of the (symbolic) mother as primal seductress (ibid., pp. 56–57). This archaic femininity is "the carrier of life and of *jouissance*" (Sibony, *Le corps et sa danse*, p. 209). Within seduction as "a performance that two people put on together" (Forrester, p. 161), the seducer and the seduced bring into play and rebirth this archaic femininity. Because the aesthetic category of figure in its early modern theorizations is aligned with seduction via its ubiquitous association with ornament, figure is conceptually charged with archaic femininity accessed through seduction as unconscious umbilicus.

The association, so frequent in Renaissance treatises on rhetorical aesthetics, of rhetorical ornament with seduction, in particular with a seductress, is an ancient one. In his *De planctu naturae* (*The Complaint of Nature*), the twelfth-century rhetorician and theologian Alain de Lille links rhetorical ornaments with the figure of the archetypal seductress Venus and theorizes them as "inflaming passion" (*flammarent ardoribus*) (Migne, p. 439). In Tacitus' first-century *Dialogue on Orators*, a style loaded with linguistic ornaments Renaissance rhetoricians tend to associate with figures is imaged as glittering with "gaudy and meretricious attire" (p. 26). Such a style, Tacitus continues, is appropriate for speeches "sung or danced" (ibid.). Tacitus associates style loaded with figures with ornamented attire and with the eroticized feminine order of the choric and choreographic. In *Le corps et sa danse*, Daniel Sibony locates this order beyond the seduction principle. Invoking the order of the choreographic, Tacitus suggests a conceptual connection between stylistic ornament, which Renaissance rhetoricians associate with figure, ornamented attire, and the choric and choreographic beyond of the seduction principle.

In the mythic/ritualistic dimension of the ancient world, this choreographic beyond of the seduction principle to which Tacitus' theorization of ornamental speech as meretricious attire alludes was the domain of the love-maddened women dancing in erotic frenzy in the inebriate rituals of Dionysus. In the ancient world, this eroticized feminine beyond of the seduction principle was the domain of Anadyomene, the apogee of feminine beauty and desirability, rising from the waves before the initiates dancing on the shore of Eleusis.

The femininity of the women situated in the mythic/ritualistic beyond of the seduction principle in the ancient world was highly eroticized. The women maddened by Dionysus are, as this god puts it in Euripides' *Bacchae*, "sent raving from their homes" (line 43), leaving behind "[t]heir spinning and their weaving" (ibid., line 108). These women are driven to "run away from domestic life" and rush in erotic frenzy to the "choral dances" Dionysus inspires (Otto, pp. 134, 179). Structurally speaking, the women involved in Dionysian rituals move toward what Irigaray argues is the polar opposite of domestic and domesticated femininity of the virgin and mother: the femininity of the courtesan, the hetaera (*This Sex*, p. 186).

The Eleusinian Anadyomene is "more hetaera-like than virginal," and is said to have been once impersonated by a beautiful courtesan (Jung and Kerényi, p. 150). In the mundane world of ancient Rome in the context of which Tacitus produced his dialogue on oratory, the "meretricious attire" he associates with elocutionary ornament characterized the prostitute. In ancient Rome, courtesans wore outfits of "many-colored cloth, ornamented with bouquets" (De Beauvoir, p. 83). Tacitus' theorization of ornamented style alludes to prostitutes of his time and to the hetaera-like female participants in the choric and choreographic rites of Dionysus and of Eleusis.

In the writing of Dionysius of Halicarnassus, a Greek rhetorician who lived in Rome during the reign of Augustus, the association of ornamented style with the image of the woman who is lured and allures others from the domain of the Father is even more explicit. Identifying this style with a "harlot" who is "bent on destroying" the "estate" of the "lawful wife" of the patriarchal household, Dionysius describes this style as having sprung up "from some Asiatic death hole" (sec. 1, line 415). Like Cicero, to whose theorization of ornamented style Tacitus alludes in his dialogue (p. 25), Dionysius associates ornamental style with the "Asian," as opposed to the plain or "Attic." Jacqueline Lichtenstein (pp. 105–107) and Jane Sutton (pp.101–103) have shown Dionysius' theorization of the category of ornate style to associate this category with the seduction embodied by the image of the meretriciously attired prostitute of the ancient world.

The earliest institutional prostitutes of ancient Greece, whom Solon brought to brothels, or *dicterions*, located near the temple of Venus at Athens, were "Asiatic slaves" (De Beauvoir, p. 83). The prototype of the prostitute of the ancient world, whose image informs the theorization of ornamented style in the classical treatises of Cicero, Tacitus, and Dionysius of Hallicarnassus, is more than a threat to the patriarchal household. She is a trespasser of national boundaries, a foreigner or barbarian, who embodies the presence within Greek patriarchy of "other social forms and values, sometimes matrilinear and matrifocal" (Nye, p. 48).

The Asian prostitute of the ancient world with whom classical rhetoricians conceptually link the ornamental style their Renaissance heirs associate with the aesthetic category of figure embodies a threat to the Name of the Father writ large. This is a threat to the patriarchal household and to the entire edifice of the *polis* of which the patriarchal household is a constituent and a miniature reflection. Associated through its inaugural conceptualizations with an Asian prostitute, a barbarian, and a whore, the aesthetic category of figure in Renaissance rhetoric comes to signify the possible destabilization of the boundaries differentiating and demarcating the *polis* from its environs. This destabilization of boundaries on the level of culture and national identity is isomorphic with, and an externalized reflection of, a much more menacing destabilization on the psychic level beyond the vicissitudes of history. This destabilization would involve the psychic boundaries and bars functioning as super-egoic inscriptions of the Name of the Father. The consequence of such destabilization would be an admission into the conscious of structures of the unconscious, linguistic structures bespeaking a primordial, polymorphic eroticism. Resistant, the conscious mind would seek to bar the structures of the unconscious. The resistance of the conscious would manifest itself as anxiety of the inscriptions of the unconscious, or of aggression towards these inscriptions.

Mythological conceptualizations of the structures of the unconscious include the feminine homoerotic and incestuous myths and rites of Eleusis, and the orgiastic myths and rites of Dionysus. Dionysian rites center on a non-phallic, mad and maddening god, divorced and divorcing from rational sobriety. Dionysus is said to have been driven mad by Hera after his discovery of the vine (Apollodorus, bk. 3, sec. 5, line 2). He is said to have maddened the women of Argus (ibid., bk. 1, sec. 9, line 12), the pirates who took him captive but felt compelled to jump into the sea (ibid., bk. 3, sec. 5, line 3), and Lycourgous, who was driven to kill his own son (ibid., bk. 3, sec. 5, line 1). The psycho-sexual allure of the unconscious structures Dionysus embodies is intense to the point of it driving women to physically and psychically transgress the Law of the Father, "to desert their houses and abandon themselves to Bacchic frenzy on Mount Cithaeron" (ibid., bk. 3, sec.5, line 2).

The category of the Asian is historically aligned with the Dionysian thematization of structures of the unconscious through the historically and culturally specific image of the Asiatic prostitute of the ancient world. The category of the Asian is aligned with the Dionysian mythically and conceptually too. In Euripides' *Bacchae*, Asia is repeatedly mentioned as the place of origin of Dionysus and of his ecstatic, choreographic cult (lines 17–20, 57, 64, 457, 465). In the context of the Dionysian, however, Asia ceases to be a merely geographic category. In the mythological context, Asia is a psychic and conceptual category. In *The Bacchae*, the forces of the unconscious, of the polymorphic eroticism Dionysus incarnates, are of such magnitude they cause the walls of the palace of Pentheus, King of the *polis* of Thebes, to crumble. The magnitude of the forces of the unconscious embodied by Dionysus causes the women of Thebes, who respond to them, to psychically shatter the boundaries structuring their patriarchal homes. At the moment Dionysus, incarnating the structures of the unconscious, emerges from these crumbled walls, spatial analogues of the bars blocking the admission of the unconscious into the conscious, he addresses the women of Thebes who respond to the beckoning of the unconscious he embodies as "[w]omen of Asia" (line 604).

The category of "Asia" is more than the historical and geographical place of origin of the meretriciously ornamented courtesans with whom the ancient orators associate rhetorical ornament, the aesthetic function their Renaissance heirs associate with the elocutionary category of figure. Asia is more than the place of origin of Dionysus and of the Dionysian cult. *The Bacchae* thematizes the Dionysian as a psychic state of an erotic frenzy. In this play, the state of erotic frenzy drives women to abandon the patriarchal home and shatter the psychic boundaries structuring this home, so as to choreographically celebrate and seduce an androgynous object of desire. In *The Bacchae*, the "Asian" is the name of the psychic state of Dionysian erotic frenzy. "Asian" as the name of a psychic state wherein unconscious structures destabilize the strictures of the Name of the Father renders "Thebes," the signifier of the geographic and historical identity of the women involved in Dionysian rites, irrelevant, erasable. At the moment of their erotic frenzy, those women are addressed not as Thebans but as "women of Asia."

The category of Asia is aligned with the mytheme of Dionysus historically, mythically, and conceptually. Classical rhetoricians such as Tacitus, Cicero, and Dionysius of Halicarnassus theorize rhetorical ornament in terms of this image. In doing so, these rhetoricians point to the category of rhetorical ornament as one of the linguistic structures of the unconscious thematized in the mytheme of Dionysus. In Renaissance rhetoric, ornament is theorized as a conceptual substrate of the category of figure. The ancient transcoding of rhetorical ornament with the Dionysian as a psychic category involving a seductiveness born of an attraction so powerful it drives women to psychically and spatially transgress the domain of the Father so as to access an archaic eroticism beyond it reverberates in Renaissance theorizations of figure.

Symptoms of the reverberation of ornament as a psychic category indexing a primordial eroticism abound in Renaissance rhetoric. Sir Philip Sidney speaks of rhetorical ornament in his *Apology for Poesy* (1581) as manifesting a "courtesan-like painted affectation" (p. 246). In William Webbe's *Discourse of English Poetrie* (1586), rhetorical ornament is theorized in a way bespeaking an anxiety of the Dionysian. Rhetorical ornaments, writes Webbe, "must not be adventurous, neither must they be used everywhere and thrust into every place" (sig. I8). Webbe theorizes linguistic ornament in reference to a body in motion, a body "ad-venturous" because it ventures beyond spatial boundaries phenomenally manifesting psychic bars. The body imagined in Webbe's theorization of linguistic ornament "thrust[s]" itself beyond these bars and boundaries and may reach "everywhere." The body with which Webbe transcodes rhetorical ornamentation is incapable of stopping. Centuries before Webbe, the Bible had represented the kinetic body he invokes in his theorization of rhetorical ornament in sexual terms. In the Bible, the transgressively seductive woman with whom classical and early modern rhetoricians transcoded rhetorical ornament is the prostitute, whose "feet never stay at home," who "lurks" at "every corner," who is "now in the street, now in the squares" (Proverbs 7: 11–12).

More than the biblical image of the prostitute reverberates in Webbe's conceptualization of the rhetorical category of ornament. In Euripides' *Bacchae*, a pagan intertext resonating in Webbe's early modern rhetorical text, as in the Bible, the female body in motion is identified as the body of the prostitutes who "go creeping off / This way and to lonely places and give themselves / To lecherous men" (lines 223–225). In *The Bacchae*, prostitutes as female bodies in motion are transcoded with their mythic prototypes. These are the "Maenad priestesses" (ibid., line 225) who "have left their homes" (ibid., line 217), the domain of the *polis* and the law, to dance in erotic frenzy on "the wooded mountain-slopes," the pastoral space exceeding the *polis*, in honor of Dionysus (ibid., line 220). Centuries after Webbe, Bataille would characterize the body in ceaseless motion, the body "rapidly [passing] from one place to another," the body whose manifestations include the prostitute and the Maenad, as the incarnation of eroticism qua kinesis ("The Solar Anus," *Visions of Excess*, p. 7).

Webbe's theorization of rhetorical ornament conflates a form of language with a form of female motion charged with sexual attraction and a will to attract so powerful it is capable of engendering a shattering of psychic and physical confines upholding the Law of the Father. This conflation brings together the two functions Freud would point out as generating inhibiting interdictions because of their constitutive predisposition, as concepts, to "assume...the significance of copulation": writing and walking. "As soon as writing...assumes the significance of copulation, or as soon as walking becomes a symbolic substitute for treading upon the body of mother earth," Freud observes, "both writing and walking are stopped because they represent the performance of a forbidden sexual act" (*Inhibitions, Symptoms, and Anxiety*, p. 240). The seduced and seductive female body in erotic motion incarnates a Dionysian frenzy indexing primordial, unconscious eroticism. The possibility of admitting this primordial eroticism into the domain of the conscious generates anxiety born of resistance to the unconscious. This anxiety generates inhibition. The same psychic dynamic structures Webbe's theorization of rhetorical ornament as a seduced and seductive female body in erotic motion. In Webbe's theorization, the anxiety of primordial, unconscious eroticism as kinesis or ad-venturous motion transcoded with the category of linguistic ornament is indexed in a twice-repeated barring of the excessive use of ornament. Excessive ornament, Webbe repeats, betraying the association of ornament with unsettling erotic kinesis, and the anxiety this association generates on the level of the Name/No of the Father, of the repressive law the rhetorician purports to lay down, "must not" be allowed.

In Obadiah Walker's *Instructions Concerning the Art of Oratory* we find a similar attempt to inhibit the feminine seductiveness inscribed into the aesthetic category of rhetorical ornament. In this treatise, "ornaments," which Walker uses in apposition to "figures," implying the synonymity of the two categories, are theorized as means of "setting out the matter…speciously" (p. 51). Walker theorizes linguistic ornaments as doing something to the "matter" of semiosis his peers transcode with a female body: "setting [it] out," placing it as an object on display in a space which is "out" there, exterior to the home, the domain of the Name/No of the Father. The result of the display of figure as ornamented female body outside the domain of the Father is its becoming "specious," a term denoting aesthetic pleasure and etymologically pointing to the source of this pleasure in the *specere* or look. Figure in Walker's theorization seems to be an object of what Laura Mulvey has termed "scopophilia," a form of (male) pleasure predicated upon the reduction of the female body to an object the male's gaze fixes, controls, and possesses (pp. 21–22). In Walker's theorization, the female body with which figure is transcoded seems to be subject to a procedure described by Peter Brooks in a different context. This body seems to be placed as eroticized spectacle in a "field of vision" in which "looking is essentially an erotic activity associated with male sexuality and the object of vision…an exhibited female" (Brooks, pp. 100–101). In Walker's theorization, the category of figure is transcoded with a fleshly "matter" "set out" on seductive display on the "out"-side of the home. In early modern Europe, this out-side of the home would have been the space of the prostitute (Parker, *Literary Fat Ladies*, pp.104–110; Wills, p. 214). In Walker's theorization, the female body transcoded with figure is implicitly related to the gaze. The gaze, as Mulvey theorizes it in relation to female bodies, and as Foucault theorizes it in more general terms (*Discipline and Punish*, pp. 195–228), is predicated upon an attempt to control. In the light of the theorization of the gaze by Mulvey and by Foucault, Walker's theorization of figure seems to be informed by a will to control the meretriciously ornamented female body with which the category of figure is transcoded.

Foucault's notion of the panoptic gaze is in contradiction with Lacan's theorization of the gaze as the object always eluding the subject looking at it and eluded by what it looks at (*Seminar XI*, p. 103). Critics like Mulvey and Brooks, who transport the Foucauldian notion of the panopticon into psychoanalytic criticism, conflate the panopticon with the desiring gaze, thereby producing a mis-theorized concept of the gaze of the male subject of desire as an instrument of control (Copjec, pp. 34–37). For Lacan, the subject of the gaze "is not...of the reflexive consciousness, but...of desire" (*Seminar XI*, p. 89). The gaze to which Walker's "instruction" subjects figure as ornamented female body is not what controls or even reflects its object. This gaze is what refracts the object given only in its perpetual slipping away. The phrase "setting out the matter...speciously" does not and cannot stably signify the scopophilic, panoptical control of the ornamented body of a soliciting female. Walker's phrase slips into an inverted, perverted signification in which the "matter" of the female body is not transitively "set out" on display by a mechanism seeking to control it, but intransitively "set[s] out" on a transit of its own. For Lacan, what "set[s] out," what is in a transit wherein it "slips, passes...from stage to stage, and is always in some degree eluded" by what looks at it and it looks at, is the "gaze" as object (*Seminar XI*, pp. 73, 103). When the subject in love solicits a look, Lacan writes, "what is profoundly unsatisfying and always missing is that — you never look at me from the place from which I see you" (ibid., p. 103). In Lacan's terms, the female body inscribed into Walker's theorization of figure is not an object of a controlling gaze but a gaze qua object, "the object-cause of the subject of desire in the field of vision" (Copjec, p. 35).

Walker's theorization of figure as "setting out the matter more speciously" does not mark the circumscription of an eroticized, implicitly prostituted female object of desire by masculinist, panoptical mechanisms of control. Walker's theorization of figure marks the seductive female body's constitutive excess and elusion of such mechanisms. The eroticized female body is inscribed in this theorization as what would not be controlled by means of the possessive, scopophilic look of the male. The female body inscribed into Walker's theorization of figure is very different from the female body in another early modern text, the body of the mistress in

Donne's Elegy 19. In this elegy, the male speaker runs "through the titillating commands that would disrobe [the desired female body] to a position of global and gynecological specularity" (Correll, "Symbolic Economies," p. 495). In Walker's theorization, the seductive female body transcoded with figure is a body soliciting the look through its meretricious appearance and at the same time necessarily eluding the impossible demand for fusion with it subtending this look (Lacan, *Seminar XI*, p.103).

Etymologically and conceptually, the female body soliciting visual-erotic attention is what se-duces, leads aside (Baudrillard, *Seduction*, p. 22; Forrester, p. 80). Like the ancient rhetoricians, and like Webbe, Walker transcodes the aesthetic category of figure with an ornamented female body soliciting visual-erotic attention on the literal and symbolic outside of the space of the Father. Those classical and early modern rhetoricians align this aesthetic category of figure with the psychic category of seduction as a leading aside. Since seduction is "a performance two people put on together" (Forrester, p. 161), the leading aside inscribed into the category of figure in its early modern theorizations involves the seductive female and those she seduces.

The leading aside of seducer and seduced structuring seduction involves a disturbance of the Law. The law of seduction, Sarah Kofman observes, is to abolish law and disturb the Name of the Father (*Don Juan*, pp. 96, 118). According to Baudrillard, seduction is a "principle of uncertainty" (*Seduction*, p. 12) disturbing and challenging the Law (ibid., pp. 16, 24), and "impl[ying] a reversible, indeterminate order" (p. 22). Seduction leads seducer and seduced away from the locus of the Law, of the "matrimonial," into an "enchanted sphere" (Baudrillard, *Ecstasy of Communication*, p. 61). This enchanted sphere beyond the Name of the Father seduction opens up is the unconscious as state of "primal phantasy" (Baudrillard, *Seduction*, pp. 55–56). For Webbe and Walker, the aesthetic category of ornament is aligned with the psychic operation of seduction. The seduction inscribed into the theorizations of figure by Webbe and Walker involves a breaking beyond the interdictions of the Law of the Father enabling access to the primordial femininity of the unconscious.

Regardless of the sex of those involved in it, seduction involves access to the primordial femininity of the unconscious. Seduction as a psychic category is constitutively "of the order of the feminine" (Baudrillard, *Seduction*, p. 7). The association of the category of figure with femininity as seduction is overdetermined by its frequent representation, in Renaissance rhetoric, as a deviation. In Richard Sherry's *Treatise of Schemes and Tropes*, schemes or figures are defined as a way of speech which is not "after the common usage" (unpaginated). In Peacham's *Garden of Eloquence*, figure is theorized as a deviation from "the common manner and custom" of words (unpaginated). In Fraunce's *Arcadian Rhetorike* (1588) figure is theorized as a departure from the "usual and simple" mode of speech (sig. B9). The early modern theorizations of figure as deviation are structurally coextensive with the idea of seduction as a leading away. These theorizations underscore the implication of the category of figure in a psychic dynamic of seduction.

"Common," "ordinary," "usual," the terms in opposition to which figure is defined in Renaissance rhetoric, signify the epistemological order of a "custom" or code which is ubiquitous and known. They signify what is canny and familiar and thus etymologically and conceptually akin to the familial, the locus of the Name of the Father. In the theorizations of Sherry, Peacham, and Fraunce, figure is associated with a departure from the familiar/familial domain and a movement toward an alluring "Dimension" known, in the words of John Smith, only as "sweet and pleasant" (p. 6). In all these cases, figure is allied with a trajectory of deviation, of a leading away from the familiar/familial. Structurally and etymologically, this trajectory is the trajectory of seduction as what "deviates, turns...away from the path" or the place marked by the Law (Baudrillard, *Ecstasy of Communication*, p. 71).

Fraunce theorizes figure as a deviation from the "simple" in addition to the "usual." This theorization adds an aesthetic and geometrical inflection to the epistemological and legal deviation inscribed into the category of figure. The geometrical category of the "simple" involves the most basic geometrical figure, the straight line, and the simplest object, the level surface. Aesthetic simplicity involves the austere and non-ornate Cicero had termed "Attic" and opposed to the "Asian" as an aesthetic category conceptually aligned with the Dionysian, with the ecstatic shattering of paternal Law. In Dudley Fenner's theorization of figure, the conceptual association of this category with the deviation from geometric and aesthetic simplicity is accentuated by its description as a deviation from the "plain" (unpaginated). The term "plain" derives from the Latin *planus*, a signifier denoting a level surface, the most uncomplicated three-dimensional object. The theorization of figure as what is not "plain" aligns it with shapes and objects whose geometry is complicated by the folding of the "simple" straight line or level "plane" into conceptually maternal folds or caverns. Because it is theorized in terms of a deviation from simple geometrical forms, figure is aligned with an aesthetics of ornamentation which became predominant in the Renaissance (Fumerton), especially in the late

Renaissance or Baroque. Baroque aesthetics privileges complicating "curvilinear" folds over the "plain tangent" (Deleuze, *The Fold*, pp. 12–14). This aesthetics shows the fold to be always potential in the straight line (ibid.).

The intricate, cavernous objects resulting from the complicated foldings of planar surfaces are often ornaments, another category of objects frequently associated with the aesthetic category of figure in Renaissance rhetoric. Like the garments with which figure is frequently associated, ornaments are objects enabling a woman to access the primordial femininity of Anadyomene, to give birth to primordial, unconscious femininity within herself, and to seduce others with this femininity. At the same time, in the psychic function of fetishes or veils, the ornaments so often associated with the aesthetic category of figure guarantee a distance from archaic, incestuous, omphalic femininity whose intensity might be too anxiety-inducing, too threatening to subjectivity as part of the symbolic, for it to be confronted head-on.

Seduction does not depend only on the ornament which early modern rhetoricians such as Webbe, Walker, Fraunce, Peacham, Sturmius, Smith, Cavalcanti, Beumly, and Puttenham associate with the aesthetic category of figure. Nor does seduction depend only on the "sumptuary expenditure" to which seductresses resort so as to make themselves "more desirable" (Bataille, *Accursed Share*, vol. 2, p. 142), on the clothes Erasmus, Smith, Farnaby, Peacham, Fenner, Sherry, Camerarius, and Cavalcanti associate with figure, harkening back to Quintilian's formative sartorialization of this aesthetic form. Seduction "dwells in and on appearance" (Baudrillard, *Ecstasy of Communication*, p. 85), and is an "enchanted simulation" (Baudrillard, *Seduction*, p. 61). Because seduction involves all aspects of appearance, it necessitates the deployment of an entire array of artifacts: clothes, ornaments, and cosmetics. The artifacts enabling a woman to access and express a primordial femininity and to make the female body seductive, the "focal point...of luxury and lust," include "sparkling finery...jewels," and "make-up" (Bataille, *Accursed Share*, vol. 2, p. 141). Make-up is a form of ersatz at work in yet another conceptual category used to theorize the aesthetic category of figure in early modern rhetoric: color.

The association between rhetoric, especially the rhetorical category of figure, and color, is ancient. This association is as ancient as the associations between figure, clothing, and ornamentation. Quintilian had described "artificial dyes" and "false hues" as rendering a style "effeminate" (bk. 8, sec. 3, line 7). Tacitus' *Dialogue on Orators* speaks of "poetic coloring" as what creates an "attractive surface" for language and elicits "pleasure" (pp. 20–21), as a form of oratorial seduction. In the twelfth century, Alain de Lille spoke of rhetorical ornament as the "meretricious [*vulgaritatem*] dye of desire" (Migne, p. 475). In "The Dye of Desire," Andrew Cowell has shown how in other medieval texts rhetorical "color" is associated with carnal lust. In Tacitus' dialogue and in the medieval texts associating rhetorical dye with sexual attraction, rhetorical color, which Renaissance rhetoricians would align with the aesthetic category of figure, is theorized as what allures, as what awakens desire with a promise of pleasure, as what seduces.

In the early modern aesthetic theory of painting, too, color is theorized as what promises "a satiation of desire, or, in other words, pleasure" (Marin, p. 5). In early modern aesthetic theory of painting, color is theorized as what proffers "a pleasure exceed[ing] the sphere of discursiveness" (Lichtenstein, p. 210), the sphere of logos, of the Law of the Father, the sphere gravitating to the phallus as general equivalent. The effects of color as described in the early modern theory of painting are commensurate with a suspension of the Law of the Father and thereby with symbolic castration. The "beauty of coloris is Medusa's" (Lichtenstein, p. 195), the bleeding Gorgon head described in Greek mythology as stupefying its viewer and aligned in Freudian theory with literal castration. Any aesthetic theorizing about the "stupefying" effects of "color" in painting, Louis Marin says, "must deal...with the workings of Medusa" (pp. 108–109). Theorizing rhetorical figures by means of the category of color aligns them with the symbolically castrative effects of a medium the theory of visual aesthetics constructs as "indecent...illicit," and "[f]eminine" (Lichtenstein, p. 195).

Tapping into the ancient tradition aligning color, seduction, and an unconscious eroticism beyond the phallus in its repressive function, Puttenham's *Arte of English Poesie* links figuration with the seductive artifice of ornament and of face-painting. Puttenham refers to all poetic ornaments as the "colours in our arte of Poesie" (p. 115), associating them with a notion of seduction inscribed into the category of figure since its most ancient theorizations (Barthes, "The Old Rhetoric," p. 85). Puttenham describes figures as "rich Orient colours" (p. 115), aligning them with the Asian as the psychic and geographical site of meretricious seduction, of the Dionysian. Puttenham proceeds to describe the ornaments qua colors of rhetoric in terms of a class of colors used to increase a woman's seductiveness qua femininity, face-color or make-up:

> If the…colours in our arte of Poesie…be not well-tempered, or not well-layd, or be used in excesse, or ever so little disordered or misplaced, they not onely give it no maner of grace at all, but do disfigure the stuffe and spill the whole workmanship, taking away all bewtie and good liking from it, no lesse then the crimson tainte, which should be laid upon a Ladies lips, or right in the center of her cheekes, should by some ouersight or mishap applied to her forehead or chin, [when] it would make…but a very ridiculous beauty. (p. 115)

Theorizing rhetorical figures (or, better, "dis-figures") in reference to face-painting which makes "Ladies" look "ridiculous," Puttenham seems to allude to early modern attitudes to cosmetics as an art characteristically feminine (Whigham, p. 166; Lichtenstein, p. 42) yet "spurious, marginal and illegitimate" (Dolan, p. 231). In early modern moralistic tracts, cosmetic coloring, in relation to which Puttenham theorizes the aesthetic category of figure, is linked with disparaged female attempts to increase the seductiveness of the body. For instance, in King James's *Basilicon Doron*, "fairding" and the "painted preened fashion" are described as "baites to filthie lechery" practiced by "vnchaste women" (p. 175). King James condemns the use of face-painting along with "long haire or nailes" which he describes as "excrements of nature" (ibid., p. 177). A woman's self-ornamentation through color is moralistically disparaged as an attempt to defy death and corporeal decomposition. In the *Anatomie of Abuses*, Philip Stubbes censures "Colored Faces, abhord of God" (p. 64), and condemns women who "colour their faces" (ibid., p. 64) as "more than whorish" (ibid., p. 65), and as "presumptuous[ly]" attempting to "adulterate the Lord's workmanship" (ibid., p. 64).

Puttenham's attitude toward the feminine face-painting with which he associates the category of figure is far from being phobically moralistic and condemning as the attitudes of Stubbes and King James. Unlike them, Puttenham objects not to the act of face-painting itself but to cases in which "by some ouersight or mishap" it is "misplaced" and thus fails to fulfill its role of creating "bewtie" as artifice and appearance and eliciting "good liking" or desire.

Puttenham's invocation of "liking" as a signifier of desire in the context of his theorization of figure has significant repercussions for the theorization of simile in his treatise and elsewhere in Renaissance rhetoric. Puttenham uses the verb "liking," whose root is identical with the root of the similaic copula "like," to theorize the effect of feminine seduction in relation to the category of figure in terms of which simile is usually classified. For Puttenham, face-painting is a practice which can either elicit or fail to elicit constitutively similaic "good liking" or desire. Women's "crimson tainte" is what calls attention to bodily "places" (lips, cheeks, and nipples, which Elizabethan women colored so as to increase their erotogenicity) and erogenizes them with a promise of pleasure which can produce in the bodies of their beholders a physical tint signaling sexual attraction.

The property of artificial "taintes" applied to erogenous and erogenized zones of the female body to produce the physical tint of desire in the bodies of others, to tempt others, underlies the condemnation of such taint by moralists like Stubbes and King James as "tainting" the bestower and receiver of this tint with guilt or sin. Andrew Cowell has shown how in medieval literature and rhetoric at the cultural backdrop of Puttenham's text, "taint" had the multiple meanings of artificial color, sin, and physical tint produced in the body by amorous passion. In Italian, a language of much influence on the English Renaissance, the word *"tentura"* deriving from the same Latinate root as the Old French *"teindre"* to which Cowell refers, is phonically close to *"tentatione,"* temptation (Florio, pp. 556–557). The "crimson tainte" or erogenizing dye Puttenham refers to can, if "placed" strategically, evoke sexual attraction which physically dyes the body with a promise of orgasmic "dying." The "crimson tainte" of women Puttenham associates with the category of figure can tempt and ti(n)tillate, can arouse or fail to arouse desire and its physical correlates. Because it can make desire "appear and disappear," the "crimson tainte" of women, like the clothes and ornaments with which figure is associated in Puttenham's treatise and other early modern texts on rhetoric, is of the order of seduction (Baudrillard, *Ecstasy of Communication*, p. 67).

Accessories, including "eyeshadow, rouge, [and] jewelry" of the type early modern rhetoricians associate with the aesthetic category of figure, are means of making the female body into an "artifact that is the object of desire" (Baudrillard, *Political Economy of the Sign*, p. 94). The category of figure in Renaissance rhetoric is transcoded with various accessorial veils of the female body functioning as objects of the transmission of the feminine: habits, ornaments, and colors. All of these serve the purpose of what the early modern rhetorician John Sturmius calls "beautification" (p. 38): the purpose of creating a sensuous surface of a beauty which would elicit desire, of seducing. As Lacan puts it with regard to habits, these objects are best characterized as a *"pro-ménade,"* as what "promises a Maenad" as an incarnation of archaic feminine *jouissance*, provided these objects be dispensed with, taken off (*Seminar XX*, p. 12). Associated with such promenades which veil the female body yet seduce by eliciting an imaginary captation of a wished-for beyond, the category of figure, as theorized in Renaissance rhetoric, is also of the order of the fetish (Lacan, *Seminar IV*, p. 157).

The fetish is a philosophical category whose etymology (from the Latin root *factitius*) and conceptual history straddle dying (Spanish *afeitar*), fabrication (including of fabrics and the dyed clothes fabricated from them), and the facticity of fabricated objects, including ornaments (Spanish *afeite*) (Baudrillard, *Political Economy of the Sign*, p. 91). All these etymological and conceptual resonances of the category of the fetish are at work in theorizations of the rhetorical category of figure in Renaissance rhetoric.

The fetish is a "fascinating object, inscribed on the veil, around which erotic life revolves" (Lacan, *Seminar IV*, p. 160). The diverse veils with which figure is associated in early modern rhetoric: clothes, ornaments, and colors, are associated with a dimension of erotic life which is constitutively feminine insofar as it is implicated in seduction as an opening up into the primordial femininity of the unconscious. Like the fetishes analyzed by Emily Apter in a different cultural context, the fetishes involved in early modern theorizations of figure are points of signification where the categories of the fetish and of the feminine "dovetail, collide, and mutually refract" (p. 65). The femininity with which the fetishes transcoded with figure are associated is unconscious, Dionysian, implicated in deviance from the space of the Father. This femininity has to do with sex related not to procreation and the perpetuation of the Name of the Father but to recreation and play, to the space of the ludic Sherry locates at the archaic origins of the category of scheme. In *Dialogues on Eloquence* (1679), a later Renaissance rhetorician, François Fenelon, defines the ludic space of figural ornament as "effeminate" (p. 116) and as "frivolous" (ibid., pp. 114–115).

The frivolous is what is "hollow" (Derrida, *Archaeology of the Frivolous*, pp. 119, 125). It is what constitutively cannot be connected with the fulfillment of any "purpose" (ibid., p. 118). Lacan too speaks of a category manifesting itself in a structural hollow. The hollow Lacan speaks of is the hollow opened up within the demand by the satisfaction of need. Lacan identifies this hollow as desire (*Écrits*, p. 263). Derrida too talks of the hollow he associates with the frivolous as being of the order of Eros, of desire (*Archaeology of the Frivolous*, p. 130). For Derrida, the frivolous, with which Fenelon associates the category of figure, is of the order of a "desire...without any object or of a floating desire" (ibid.), which becomes the affirmation of the "need to desire" (ibid., p. 134), of the essence of the erotic.

The frivolous space of a seductive femininity whose desire is not focussed on any particular object but floats, attracting all possible objects, is the space of the temptress. The temptress incarnates a deployment of femininity conceptually aligned with figure in its theorization as a Dionisian Maenad, an incarnation of the Primordial Maiden of Eleusis. The category of the temptress or seductress is related to the aesthetic category of figure in another way too. The seductress uses the fetishistic veils with which figure is transcoded in its early modern theorizations (sumptuous attire, cosmetic dying, and ornament) so as to "turn herself into pure appearance, an artificial construct with which to trap the desires of others" (Baudrillard, *Seduction*, p. 86).

In early modern culture, the seductress using the fetishistic veils of sumptuous attire, cosmetic dying, and ornament, so as to elicit attraction was often described as the prostitute. King James writes of female bodies "artificiallie trimmed & decked" as analogous to the body of "a Courtizane" (pp. 171–173). Phillip Stubbes speaks of face-painting as a trademark of the "strumpet" (p. 65), and he denounces "ornament" as indelibly linked with "whoredom" (p. 88). Given the explicit association, in early modern culture, of the classes of fetishes with which the rhetorical category of figure is transcoded and prostitution, we should not be surprised to find this transcoding announced in an anonymous seventeenth-century text entitled *The Whores Rhetorick* (1683), an English adaptation of Ferrante Pallavicino's *La Retorica delle Putane* (1642).

This text, offered by an author who identifies himself only as "Philo-Puttanes" (p. 16), "to the most famous University of London Courtesans" (p. 11), is a manual of instruction in linguistic and other forms of seduction. The manual, however, is "vague and general" in terms of "descriptions of foreplay" or of positions for intercourse (Thompson, p. 37). In the eighteenth century, the conceptual nexus between rhetorical figuration and prostitution surfaces in an anonymous French text by a similar name, *La Rhétorique des Putains*. This handbook for courtesans offers them a catalogue of positions for sexual intercourse, this time described precisely and elaborately.

Despite the vagueness in sexual detail, the anonymous author of *The Whores Rhetorike* is explicit with regard to the function of his text. This function, he tells his interpellated addressees, is to help "the Female Orator...make the best of...substantial Flesh and Blood" (p. 125). She must, he instructs, have recourse to "solid kisses, and sensible Touch," and, should these fail to sufficiently excite her lover, she "must not be unprovided of lascivious Pictures, obscene Images and Representations to raise her...lover's joys" (p. 125). This instruction of the courtesan as rhetorician demonstrates the psychic structure underlying and enabling the overdetermined association of figure with seductive fetishes, with the effect of seduction as a leading away, and with the ludic and ex-static space which seduction opens up. This psychic structure involves a woman's placing herself in a situation in which "her body and desires are no longer her own" (Baudrillard, *Seduction*, p. 86) but the instruments for the "joy" of an unspecified, ever potential "lover." Lacan was to describe just such an intersubjective situation in which a subject makes herself into an instrument for the *jouissance* of an other, in which a subject assumes the position of the object-instrument of the will-to-enjoy. Lacan defines this structure of intersubjectivity as perversion (*Écrits*, p. 320).

Perversion involves a scenario wherein a female body covered with fetishistic veils connecting it with archaic femininity at the same time they cover yet accentuate its individual seductiveness offers itself as an instrument of the other's *jouissance*. This scenario is implicit in the interplay between two senses of and investments in the term "figure" (and its Greek equivalent, "scheme"): figure as the fetishizing veils of the female body, and figure as the tangible shape of the body.

In the *Treatise of Schemes and Tropes,* Sherry describes schemes as "the fourme...of any thynge" (unpaginated), a formulation Peacham reiterates in *The Garden of Eloquence* (unpaginated). Similarly, Dudley Fenner refers to figure as the "frame of speech" in *The Artes of Logike and Rhetorike* (1588) (unpaginated), and Hobbes describes this aesthetic category as the "fine shape or form of speech" in *The Art of Rhetoric* (1681) (p. 138). In all these cases, figure is theorized in reference to the contours of a material, and hence conceptually feminized, object. Figure becomes transcoded with the conceptually feminine, if not female flesh veiled by the fetishes of clothes, ornaments, and colors psychically linking it with the femininity of origin and enabling it to seduce by promising a glimpse of this femininity.

In Sherry's *Treatise of Schemes and Tropes*, Peacham's *Garden of Eloquence*, Fenner's *Artes of Logike and Rhetorike,* Fraunce's *Arcadian Rhetorike*, and Smith's *Mysterie of Rhetorike Unvail'd*, the sense of figure as feminine body and figure as the fetishistic veils by means of which this body becomes seductive coexist in one and the same theorization. These theorizations of figure seem to play out the entire trajectory of male heterosexual desire such as is inscribed in the progressive divestment of the woman in Donne's "Elegy 19: To His Mistress Going to Bed." In those theorizations of figure, as in Donne's elegy, the desire of the woman seems to be inscribed as perversion, as a means for the "joyes" (line 35) of a male.

Yet what about the desires of the males, who are inscribed in those theorizations of figure as their implied authors? Is the attitude of these male rhetoricians coeval with the attitude of the authoritative speaker of Donne's elegy, the proficient lover who knows what to say, knows what to do, and is all too eager to "teach" (line 46) his mistress, provided she accept the condition of having no "more covering than a man" (line 47)? What is the attitude toward the female body of the Renaissance rhetoricians who articulate definitions of figure implying a scenario of an unveiling of a seductive feminine body? Is this an attitude of a domineering mastery, like the attitude of the speaker in Donne's Elegy 19? Is this attitude an instance of "phallic desire," a desire which is an "obstacle to *jouissance*" because of its solipsism, its insistence on the impossible One and attendant disavowal of the separateness of the object as not One and not-All, an attitude coeval with the non-recognition of the subjectivity of the other (Lacan, *Seminar XX*, p. 13)?

An examination of the early modern rhetoricians' inscription of their own subjectivity into their theorizations of figure shows they are far from being solipsistic and phallic, like the speaker of Donne's elegy who does not recognize his mistress as subject. Instead, the subjectivity of the seductive feminine other with which early modern rhetoricians transcode figure is often the object of their epistemological and erotic yearnings.

The theorizations of figure in Dudley Fenner's *Artes of Logike and Rhetorike* and Abraham Fraunce's *Arcadian Rhetorike* are cases in point. Fenner theorizes figure as a "garnishing of speech," in terms of a gastronomic category denoting the addition of taste-enhancing substances to food so as to make it more savory, more pleasant to the *gargouille* (Old French for "throat"). Fenner theorizes figure by means of a gustatory addition hailing the oral drive. In doing so, he underscores the function of the categories of rhetoric as oral objects, substitutes for the primal oral object, the maternal breast (see my previous chapter). No less significantly, Fenner suggests that in order for a rhetorical category to function as a substitute oral object, it is not enough, as Kristeva was to argue, for it to be a "linguistic signifier" (*Powers of Horror*, p. 41). In order to function as a substitute oral object, a rhetorical category must be a signifier whose nature, limited to its structure, be alluring, tempting with a promise of a pleasure to come.

Similarly to Fenner, Abraham Fraunce theorizes figure in terms of an addition rendering a substance seductive. Using a term derived from a Middle Dutch word, *"dekken,"* meaning "to cover," Fraunce describes figure as a "decking" of speech (*Arcadian Rhetorike*, sig. B9). "Decking," however, involves more than a veiling or covering of an object. "Decking" involves a covering serving as a decoration increasing the beauty and allure of the veiled object. In this case, the represented lure is not of the oral but of the scopic drive, like the "embellish[ing]," the attempt to approximate the condition of beauty which John of Salisbury, a twelfth-century precursor of Fenner and Fraunce, associates with figure in his *Metalogicon* (p. 53). In all three cases, figure is theorized as an addition to an already complete substance. In all three cases, figure is theorized as a supplement: the adding of a "surplus" or "plenitude" in order to "enrich...another plenitude" (Derrida, *Of Grammatology*, p. 144).

The category of decking Fraunce uses to theorize figure and its antecedent, embellishing, in John of Salisbury's treatise, is a supplement of a particular type, a supplement luring the scopic drive with its beauty. The supplement theorized by Fraunce is phonically and conceptually aligned with another veil/supplement used to theorize figure in Renaissance rhetoric: *decorating*. In Charles Butler's *Oratoriae Libri Duo* (1633), figure is theorized as a form of *"decoris"* (decoration) (unpaginated), and in John Prideaux's *Hypomenmata logica, rhetorica, metaphysica, pneumatica, ethica, politica, oeconomiae* (1682), figure is similarly said to decorate sentences (*"decorant sententiae"*) (unpaginated). In these two texts, the category of figure is conceptually aligned with the aesthetic supplement Derrida calls *parergon*. For Derrida, the *parergon* or aesthetic supplement is an "exteriority" of the artwork also intervening in the inside of the artwork "to the extent...the inside is lacking" (*The Truth in Painting*, pp. 53–77).

In Vaughan's *The Golden Grove* (1600), the parergonality accruing to figure in other Renaissance theorizations is ascribed to the concept of rhetoric itself. Rhetoric is defined as figure and as parergon. Vaughan conceptualizes rhetoric in opposition to "Logick," the truth-function of speech, which he images as a "bare picture" with "simple draghts [*sic*], which serve to furnish it in respect of ech [*sic*] part and lineament thereof" (unpaginated). Logic is theorized here as the *ergon* of a picture, the semiotic infrastructure of lines and differentiating contours enabling the picture to function as representation. Rhetoric, in contrast, is conceptualized as what gives this infrastructure "shap[e]," the English equivalent of *skhema*, the Greek synonym of the Latinate "figure" featuring in Sherry's *Treatise of Schemes and Tropes*. In Vaughan's treatise, rhetoric is rendered conceptually co-extensive with the category of figure.

This "shape" or figure is theorized in Vaughan's text in parergonal terms. This "shape" is what renders the picture "enriched" (ibid.). It adds to the picture something which increases the picture's economic value. This shape, according to Vaughan, also adds to the picture's aesthetic value. It makes the picture "fair" (ibid.). This added aesthetic value increases the picture's appeal to the look, its visual seductiveness. The aesthetic supplementation or parergonality which Vaughan claims rhetoric-as-figure provides is underscored by his theorization of rhetoric-as-figure as ensuring the picture's being "well-varnished," possessing a coating which while increasing its beauty belongs to its surface, not its contents. Conflated with the category of figure, rhetoric in Vaughan's text is theorized as the external varnish of the work of art. This is the "additive" to the artwork nevertheless "rivet[ed]…to the…interior of the [artwork]" Derrida calls *parergon* (*The Truth in Painting*, pp. 56–59).

Vaughan theorizes figure as an additive to an object which makes the object alluring to the look because of the dazzle of a "varnish" rendering the object "enriched," more precious. Butler and Prideaux too call attention to the dazzle of the *parergon* with which they transcode the category of figure. The concept of "decoration" in reference to which they theorize figure derives from the Latin root *decus*, brightness. Vaughan, Butler, and Prideaux theorize figure as a *parergon* luring the scopic drive. What lures the scopic drive in their theorizations of figure is a dazzle which signifies richness. This dazzle tantalizes with a promise of the further richness of the *ergon* or substance it veils. The *parergons* with which Vaughan, Butler, and Prideaux transcode the category of figure are conceptually and functionally coeval with the category Lacan, following Plato's *Symposium*, theorizes as the object-cause of desire in his eighth seminar: the *agalma*.

The Greek term *agalma*, which features prominently in Plato's famous dialogue on Eros, carries phonic and etymological resonances of *aglaia* (brightness and splendor), *agallomai* (intense joy), and *a gelao* (laughter) (Henrion, p. 12). Like the decorations and the resplendent varnish with which Butler, Prideaux, and Vaughan transcode the category of figure, *agalma* in its archaic deployment signifies a "radiance" or "brilliance" (Henrion, p. 41) suggesting the "richness" (ibid., pp. 17, 28) of a "precious object" (ibid., pp. 28, 39, 40) beyond it. *Agalma* has the "charm of a seductive look" (ibid., p. 41) tantalizing with a promise of *jouissance*. *Agalma* is what sets in motion the scopic drive as "anterior to the look unveiling the object" (ibid., p. 96), the dazzling surface of physical beauty as the "point of attraction" of the look of a desiring other (ibid., pp. 97, 105).

The desiring look is at the psychic core of one of the most archaic expressions of the trajectory of the scopic drive, the myth of Apollo's love for Daphne. In Ovid's fictionalization of this myth, Apollo's desire for Daphne is described in scopic terms:

> His eyes praised all they saw — her lips, her fingers,
> Her hands, her naked arms from write to shoulder;
> And what they did not see they thought the best. (p. 45)

Apollo does "not see" beyond the dazzling surface of Daphne's physical beauty, yet believes what he does not see is "better still" (ibid.). What is the seductive category beyond the scopic drive luring Apollo to believe it is "better still" than what is exposed to the look? What does the look of the desiring other seek beyond the dazzling veil of the *agalma*, the "cause of desire" (Henrion, p. 136) with which Prideaux, Butler, Vaughan, and Fraunce transcode the aesthetic category of figure? Plato's *Symposium* is another formative and explicit archaic articulation of *agalma* as the cause of desire. In this dialogue, Alcibiades seeks to know what about Socrates "engenders his desire" (Lacan, *Seminar VIII*, p. 182). What is this "indefinable and precious" cause of desire (ibid.) Alcibiades seeks?

Lacan's answer describes what the subject seeks in the love object as what "the subject lacks" (ibid., p. 63), namely Being (Henrion, p. 152). The *agalmata* are those aspects of the love object captivating the subject's look, singling out the love object from all others and determining its value for the subject. This value of the love object consists in the promise of further *agalmata*, cyphers of Being, fragments of a primal *jouissance* and a forgotten archaic, cached within the object (Lacan, *Seminar VIII*, p. 179; Henrion, p. 215).

What Alcibiades seeks beyond the scintillating *agalmata* he perceives in Socrates is a promise of Being, of a return to a primal *jouissance*. This promise of *jouissance* engenders in Alcibiades a desire so powerful it "does not recognize any limits" (Lacan, *Seminar VIII*, p. 187). This desire "braves interdictions" and "stops at nothing" (Henrion, p. 141) in its efforts to "make [the object] make love" (Lacan, *Seminar VIII*, p. 199).

The desire of the structure manifested by Alcibiades is not reductive, possessive, or covetous (Henrion, p. 125). Desire of this structure does not deny the subjectivity of the other, like the desire of the speaker in Donne's Elegy 19. Instead, desire of this structure "takes the other as a subject and not as an object," and desperately seeks "the *jouissance* or the perfection of the other" (ibid., p. 214), which become coextensive with those the subject seeks for himself or herself. The *agalmata* conceptualized by Ovid, Plato, and Lacan are causes of an intense desire propelling the desiring subject to "go...as far as s/he can along the path of *jouissance*"

(Lacan, *Écrits*, p. 323), so as to uncover, within the other, a primordial *jouissance*. In Lacan's terms, *agalmata* are catalysts of perversion.

Transcoding the category of figure with *agalmata*, Renaissance rhetoricians such as Fraunce, Prideaux, Butler, and Vaughan inscribe within this category their own desires as perversions. The aesthetic category of figure in Renaissance rhetoric is thereby aligned with the psychic structure of perversion in two complementary ways. (1) Figure is theorized as a seductive female body, an incarnation of the Primordial Maiden Anadyomene, the archetypal object of all desire, whose existence is co-extensive with its seductiveness since it seeks nothing but to allure others and serve as an instrument of their *jouissance*. (2) Figure is theorized as an *agalma*, a dazzling veil luring the scopic drive with the promise of a pleasure inherent in the object it veils and setting in motion a trajectory of perversion wherein others seek to make themselves instruments of the *jouissance* of this object. Theorizing figure as *agalma*, Renaissance rhetoricians imagine it in relation to a female subject who makes herself an instrument of the *jouissance* of others, and they imagine figure in relation to a subject who elicits in others a desire to serve as instruments of her/his *jouissance*.

The *jouissance* perversion seeks is never completely attainable. The *agalma* qua veil does not give way to a view of the primordial object of maternal incest. The subject's erotematic demand for Being beyond the *agalma* receives no response. Instead, the subject's erotematic-erotic demand for the beyond of the *agalma* functions in the same way as the narratologically marginal but psychologically and philosophically crucial interchange opening Shakespeare's *Hamlet*:

> Barnardo: Who's there?
> Francisco: Nay, answer me. Stand and unfold yourself. (Act 1, scene1, lines 1–2)

Like Barnardo's question, the demand for the other's *jouissance* structuring perversion rebounds upon its subject in inverted form, demanding that the subject confront and "unfold" her/his own desire. This demand of the subject to unfold desire, not Being, "institutes subjectivity" (Henrion, p. 131). What is revealed within the other is not the Being seemingly veiled yet promised by the *agalma* with which Renaissance rhetoricians transcode the category of figure, but the "want-to-be" (Lacan, *Écrits*, p. 259), the lack coextensive with desire.

The theorization of figure as *agalma* by several early modern rhetoricians aligns this category with the "want-to-be" subtending subjectivity as desire. Figure is aligned with desire even more forcefully because of its more general theorization in terms of the aesthetic category of the *parergon* and the grammatological category of the supplement. The *parergon* is a dazzling extra appended to the artwork, making the artwork alluring. The *parergon* functions isomorphically with the way in which the psycho-aesthetic category of the *agalma* makes one subject seductive for another. Yet the ability of the *parergon* to lure the look to an artwork or *ergon* is, Derrida shows, a function of "an internal lack in the system to which it is added" (*Truth in Painting*, p. 57). What the viewer's look is "riveted" to by means of the *parergon* is not any aesthetic, ontological, or epistemological plenitude the artwork proffers any more than what the subject's look discovers in the other beyond the brilliance of *agalmata* is Being. Instead, the subject discovers the constitutive lack in the interior of the *ergon* (ibid., p. 59).

Similarly, the supplement with which Fraunce and Fenner transcode the category of figure by theorizing it as an additive "decking" or "garnishing" does not signal the plenitude of what it veils. Supplementation involves adding a "surplus" or "plenitude" in order to "enrich...another plenitude" (Derrida, *Of Grammatology*, p. 144). Yet the supplement "adds only to replace." The supplement is not "simply added to the positivity of presence" but "insinuates itself *in-the-place-of*" a putative part of presence (ibid., p. 145, Derrida's emphasis). Although posited as a mark of the "plenitude" of what is supplemented, the supplement exposes the "anterior default" or "emptiness" it would efface (ibid.). The supplement marks a void or originary lack at the heart of what would be represented as self-sufficient positivity.

The category of figure as theorized in Renaissance rhetoric reveals the deficiency of the ostensible plenitude to which it is appended even more clearly than the notion of writing, Derrida's example for supplementarity. Like the category of writing in Rousseau's *Essay on the Origin of Languages* as analyzed by Derrida, figure is theorized in the rhetorics of Fenner and Fraunce as a supplement to "speech." This theorization is symptomatic of the desire for transparent speech as a source of truth and authenticity. For Fenner and Fraunce, figure is a component of the discipline of rhetoric which includes speech and writing. For these rhetoricians, figure is a potential part of the speech it would supplement. The theorization of figure as supplementing the category to which it potentially belongs shows this category is not a plenitude. If figure supplements speech, one of the two mediums of language in which it can appear, then speech cannot be complete without it. In rhetorics of the Renaissance, figure, by definition a potential part of the speech it would supplement, is more clearly indicative of the incompleteness of speech than writing, to which speech is habitually opposed in Western philosophy.

Theorizations of figure in the texts of Fenner and Fraunce underscore the absence at the heart of speech, the impossibility of a fantasized "original, natural...language" speech stands for (Derrida, *Of Grammatology*, p. 56). In the cases in which the category of figure is theorized as a supplement as in the more particular instances in which it is theorized as *parergon* or *agalma*, the category of figure is aligned with the opening up of an empty space, the space of possibility, of desire as what is eternally about to happen.

Theorizations of figure in Renaissance rhetoric fall into three groups. (1) In the treatises of Sherry, Puttenham, Phillips, and Smith, figure is aligned with the Eleusinian mysteries, in particular with the omphalic, homoerotic, and incestuous scenario of the Primordial Maiden Anadyomene, the archetypal object of desire, rising from the waves. (2) In the majority of cases of theorizations of figure in Renaissance rhetoric, this archetypal object remains hidden, obliquely referenced by the fetishes of ornament, clothing, and cosmetic color veiling archetypal femininity yet enabling a woman to access, appropriate, and deploy this femininity in a structure of perversion, as a means for the *jouissance* of the others it seduces. (3) In a number of cases, figure is theorized in Renaissance rhetoric as a supplement, *parergon*, or *agalma*, an additive functioning as the trace of the desire of the theorizer as perversion.

In all three cases, the femininity inscribed into the category of figure is different from the femininity inscribed into the primal substance of semiosis. While the primal substance of semiosis is transcoded by Renaissance rhetoricians with the archaic mother as alluring yet frightening, figure is associated only with the alluring and seductive aspects of femininity. The maternal is inscribed in Renaissance theorizations of figure not as the imaginary mother, the devouring mother resisting separation who is at the root of anxiety, but as the symbolic (m)Other, the prototype of all objects of desire, as inscribed in the Eleusinian image of Aphrodite Anadyomene, referred to in an ancient hymn as a *schema* or figure.

The originary, fundamental eroticism of the symbolic m(O)ther informs early modern theorizations of figure in terms of the fetishistic veils of clothes, ornaments, and cosmetics serving as substitute placenta and as omphalic means, for a woman, of accessing archaic femininity and deploying it seductively to the point of perversion, to the point of making femininity into an instrument for the *jouissance* of the seduced. This predominant theorization of figure as the prototypical female object of desire, the prototypical seductress who deploys her femininity as perversion, resonates in those theorizations of figure as *agalma*, which bespeak the perversion not of the seductress but of those whom she seduces, those in whom the dazzle of her visual allure generates a drive to make of themselves servants of her *jouissance*.

The *jouissance* of the seductress seemingly promised beyond the veil, one of whose names in classical Greek is *schema,* is never given. Instead, the theorizations of figure as *agalma*, and more generally, its theorizations as *parergon* and supplement reveal not the *jouissance* of the other but the lack in the other to which the demand for love, originating in the subject's own constitutive lack, is addressed. This lack determines the subject's relation to the love object as a relation of an impossible demand, an *erotema* instituting the subject as *erômenos*: lover and/as questioner (Lacan, *Seminar VIII*, p. 139; Henrion p. 195). In all cases, the aesthetic category of figure in Renaissance rhetoric is conceptually aligned with eroticism, especially feminine eroticism, in its positive, seductive aspect of the want-to-be, the intersubjective space of intention toward a primal *jouissance* incarnated in the archaic image of the Primordial Maiden. Given the intensity of the perversion figure is conceptualized as both embodying and generating, in this intersubjective space one can, like Alcibiades in Plato's *Symposium*, go as far as it is possible to go along the path of *jouissance*.

CHAPTER THREE

Displacement as Detour:
Tropology, the Tropics, and the Troubadors

The want-to-be, the constitutive lack in self and other is, in the last analysis, the structure subtending the theorization of the aesthetic category of figure in Renaissance rhetoric. Confrontation with this want-to-be is no easy matter. This confrontation is the point of emergence of anxiety. Anxiety surges, as Freud and Kristeva put it, from the experience of birth, from the constitutive fall from the placental. Anxiety, Freud comments in *Symptoms, Inhibitions, and Anxiety*, "is modeled upon the process of birth," and surges whenever the subject confronts a similar prospective loss of an object of need (p. 63). In *Powers of Horror,* Kristeva describes "the good maternal object that is wanting" as the fundamental cause of anxiety (p. 45). Anxiety "surges as a pure apprehension of the desire of the other" (Conté, p. 13). Anxiety is generated at the moment the desire of the other reveals itself as stemming from and addressed to the lack in the beyond of the phenomenal and virtual veils by means of which subject and object adorn and reveal themselves to one another. The emergence of anxiety is contemporaneous with the apprehension of the lack beyond fetishistic veils, the psychically significant objects with which Renaissance rhetoricians ubiquitously and overdeterminately transcode the aesthetic category of figure.

The desire inscribed into the category of figure takes the extreme, non-questioning form of perversion, in which the subject strives to make those veils into active gifts, instruments of the object's *jouissance*. The desire inscribed into the category of figure, in other words, goes as far as it is possible to go along the path of *jouissance* (Lacan, *Écrits*, p. 323). Because the type of desire inscribed into the category of figure has the structure of perversion, it comes all the closer to a confrontation with the lack which drives yet hails it. Desire of this structure comes as close as it is possible to come to the point of emergence of anxiety.

Deployments of femininity in Renaissance theorizations of aesthetic forms are related to anxiety. Early modern conceptualizations of the primal substance of semiosis often bring into play a menacing, abject deployment of femininity, the deployment of femininity as devouring maternality (see Chapter One above). Early modern rhetoricians conceptualize the category of figure in terms of a seductive deployment of femininity (see Chapter Two above). The aesthetic category of figure is theorized in terms of the archetypal object of desire, the Primordial Maiden of the Eleusinian mysteries. The seductiveness of the archetypal object of desire inscribed into the aesthetic category of figure is imagined as connected with the phenomenal veils adorning her, inscribed into the category of figure in its early modern theorizations. Adorned with veils, the archetypal object offers herself as a conduit to the *jouissance* of those she seduces and induces in them a desire to access her own *jouissance*, imagined to be cached beyond the veils. The postulation of figure in terms of a seductive deployment of femininity as archetypal object of desire, however, does not make the category of figure much less phobogenic than the primal substance of semiosis qua archaic mother. The theorization of figure in terms of the perversion related to the archetypal object of desire and to seduction too has anxiety as its psychic price.

The consequence of Renaissance rhetoricians' theorization of figure in terms of the structure of perversion is a confrontation with the lack or want structuring subjectivity and/as desire. This confrontation breeds anxiety. Most Renaissance rhetoricians deal with this anxiety by means of postulating and privileging another elocutionary category: trope. The category of trope too is marked by a structure of desire. The structure of desire involved in the category of trope as conceptualized in Renaissance rhetoric is phallic. What I call phallic desire is predicated upon the desubjectivation of the other. Far from striving, like perversion, for the *jouissance* of the other, phallic desire seals itself off from *jouissance*. What I call phallic desire is hence related to what Lacan paradoxically calls phallic *jouissance* and theorizes as "the obstacle owing to which man does not come" (*Seminar XX*, p. 7). Phallic desire replaces intersubjectivity with solipsism. The intersubjective relation of love is an "active gift...always directed, beyond imaginary captivation, toward the being of the loved subject" it transforms through transference (Lacan, *Seminar I*, p. 276). In phallic desire, the striving to offer an active gift to the other subtending love is replaced with the impulse to control and possess the other.

Early modern theorizations of the aesthetic category of trope seem to be symptoms of the impulse to control and master subtending phallic desire. These theorizations are structured by implicit narratives of forceful displacement and conquest, placed in a relation of conceptual exchange with a colonialist symbolic economy whose general equivalent is the idea of Europe as site of absolute presence, of Being. In many of these narratives, those who aggressively penetrate a zone once foreign to them proclaim themselves the hosts of the indigenous inhabitants of this zone. The indigenous inhabitants, in turn, are made guests, provisional presences in a domain they had considered their own.

The theorization of the category of figure in terms of the Primordial Maiden, the fetishized feminine subject/object of perversion, makes it conceptually possible to theorize the would-be privileged category of trope in terms of an aggressive foreign policy subtended by a phallic drive for the mastery of an other (and Other) whose subjectivity is denied. The deployment of the feminine within the category of figure as the Primordial Maiden, the primal and prototypical object of drive whose body is imagined as repeatedly penetrated, opens up a space of representation in which the would-be privileged complement of figure, the elocutionary category of "trope," is set up as a phallic drive for mastery triumphantly penetrating a conceptually feminized setting and subordinating this setting to its power. The purpose of the postulation of the tropological in terms of a conquistadorial, phallic drive is a foreclosure of the poetics of the unconscious running counter to the known laws of discursive ratiocination and an affirmation of the logic of general equivalency, the reign of the phallus.

The theorization of the category of trope in terms of a structure of phallic desire is part of an anxiety-induced attempt to foreclose the archaic femininity transcoded with the primal substance of semiosis. This attempt involves the partitioning of the primal substance of semiosis into the two categories of figure and trope. These two categories are organized in a hierarchical binarism, wherein trope is the privileged category. Renaissance rhetoricians unconsciously seek to inscribe the archaic and anxiety-inducing femininity transcoded with the primal substance of semiosis only in one of the binaries, the category of figure. The feminized category of figure is subordinated to its binary, trope. In their imaginary captations of the category of trope, Renaissance rhetoricians seek to repress the femininity they attribute to the substance of semiosis in its entirety. Instead, in these imaginary captations of trope early modern rhetoricians seek to find grounding in the conceptually paternal discourse of imperialism.

The unconscious purpose of the imaginary focus on the phallic categories of imperialism in the theorization of a linguistic category is to avoid recognition of femininity, especially maternalized femininity, in terms of which early modern rhetoricians imagine the substance of all linguistic categories.

Tropology is postulated as an imperial drive. Trope is imagined in terms of what Jean-Francois Lyotard calls a *dispositif* of conquest, a cultural impulse combining movement with economic and psychic expenditure whose aim is to turn a profit (p. 154). The category of trope is postulated as an imperial, phallic drive against the conceptual backdrop of the deployment of figure as a female body marked by perversion and hence ever-hospitable, ever-penetrable. This imaginary postulation of the category of trope as a phallic pulsion is not free of risk. The category of trope is imagined in terms of a drive for conquest and full mastery of an other, a drive which is an instance of the totalizing discourse of the master theorized by Lacan in *Seminar XVII* and *Seminar XX* (pp.16–17, 30–31).

Because this drive to mastery invested in early modern theorizations of trope is imagined as the penetration of a feminized space, the category of trope is phallic in another sense. The category of trope is phallic in the imaginary, Freudian sense of an isomorph of the penis. The category of figure is imagined as an ever-hospitable female body. The theorization of the category of trope as phallic in the imaginary and in the symbolic or structural senses makes it possible for the category of figure to sheath up the phallic pulsion transcoded with trope in the structural and imaginary senses as a contingent guest. Sheathed up within the category of figure imagined as the ever-penetrable body of the archetypal seductress, trope qua phallic drive is made to disappear. Because of the conceptual association of the category of figure with the penetrable, hosting body of the seductive Primordial Maiden, figure becomes the vanishing point of the phallicized category of trope.

The function of figure as vanishing point for the category of trope menacingly calls into question trope's assumption of the role of masterful host in the zone trope is imagined as penetrating. Renaissance rhetoricians attempt to theorize trope as an aggressive, colonizing hospitality in which the name of the indigenous host is erased by the name of the guest who proclaims himself host. This attempt is disabled, cancelled out, by the theorization of figure as the host of this tropological host, in whose permeable body the would-be host vanishes. The body of the guest who proclaims himself host in terms of which the category of trope is imagined manifests itself as disappearance at the moment which was to be a powerful assertion of its presence, its Being.

In Lacan's thinking, a moment of would-be appearance manifesting itself as a fading, vanishing, or disappearance is theorized as aphanisis (*Seminar XI*, p. 218). The vanishing of trope within figure is a moment of rhetorical aphanisis. This moment of aphanisis prevents tropology from becoming the stabilizing grid of elocution it was supposed to be in the psychic economy unconsciously driving the enterprise of Renaissance rhetoric. Because of the structural and imaginary sheathing up of the category of trope within the category of figure, trope becomes the anasemically, symptomatically telling faultline of elocution. The category of trope in early modern rhetoric is a metalinguistic site pointing to a vexed, fractured poetics of hospitality. The fractured hospitality anasemically inscribed into early modern theorizations of the category of trope ultimately points toward the imago or unconscious prototype of primal, feminine *jouissance* imagined as a condition in which boundaries between guest and host disappear. This imago of infinite feminine *jouissance* is the alluring deployment of the archaic mother Renaissance rhetoricians transcode with the primal substance of semiosis.

Derived from the Greek verb, *trepein* (to turn), the signifier "trope" hinges upon the notion of movement, generating narratives of displacement which set out "the tropological as inseparable from the topological" (Parker, *Literary Fat Ladies*, p. 37). Verbs from a vocabulary of travel, such as "transfer," "transport," or "draw" are featured in imaginary captations of trope in early modern rhetorical treatises. These verbs make the imaginary captations of trope into transpositional narratives in which words function as actants and significations function as settings. These transpositional narratives chart transitions between two significantly different settings. They inevitably bring into play deployments of hospitality which modify an agent's presence in a setting different from the one from which the agent had set out.

Hospitality is a psychic function "fixing and subtending primary narcissism" (Montrelay, p. 48). The hospitality of the type involved in primary narcissism dissolves receptivity of guest by host into cohesion (ibid.). The moment of cohesion, at which guest and host become a single substance (ibid., p. 152) offers a glimpse of archaic, feminine *jouissance* imagined as infinite (ibid., p. 54).

The predominant deployment of hospitality in Renaissance tropologies is of a different order. This deployment involves what Jean-Francois Lyotard calls "a *dispositif* of conquest" (p.154). This *dispositif* is predicated upon the violent conquistadorial imposition of the name of the guest as the name of the host, and the verbal-ideological transformation of the indigenous host into a "barbarian" fated to economic and cultural "despoilment and destruction" (ibid., p. 199).

The natives of America, William Rogers writes in *A Key into the Language of America* (1643), the earliest known attempt to provide a guide to the Amerindian language in English, are "Barbarians" (sig. A2). In so doing, Rogers represents the natives of America by means of a signifier denoting savagery and cultural-linguistic alterity. This signifier and its denotations are woven into the rhetorical category of barbarism, technically the use of a word from a foreign language. The cultural notion of the barbarian and the rhetorical category of barbarism have been associated with one another from as far back as Aristotle's *Politics* and his *Rhetoric*. Like the category of trope, the category of barbarism is unconsciously underlain by an intense xenophobia (Nye, pp. 75–81; Kristeva, *Strangers to Ourselves*, pp. 41–52).

Rogers represents alterity in culture and language as conceptually feminine. The "Peoples and Territories" of America, he writes, are a "Lump" (sig. A3), an amorphous substance. In *Symbolic Economies*, Goux traces the ubiquitous association, harking back to Aristotle's *Metaphysics*, between the amorphic and the maternal as inert matter awaiting the morphology or conceptually paternal pattern provided by the male (pp. 223, 232). Given this ubiquitous association of the amorphic and the maternal, the people and territories of America in Rogers's treatise are maternalized, and implicitly characterized as in need of the civilizing imprint of the European colonizers.

Rogers conceives of this colonizing imprint as phallic in the imaginary sense of an "image of the penis" (Lacan, *Écrits*, p. 319). This is suggested by Rogers's representation of the feminized "territories" and "Countries" of America as a domain of "secrets" into which the European writer-colonizer has "entered" (sig. A2). In 1595, Walter Raleigh described Guiana in similar sexualized terms. Guiana, Raleigh wrote, is "a country that hath yet her maydenhead never sackt" (quoted by Parker, *Literary Fat Ladies*, p. 140). In Raleigh's description of Guiana, in Rogers's description of America, and in similar early modern articulations cited by Parker, the new land is "gendered as female." The European colonizer is implicitly conceptualized as the male lover for whose penetration of her body she yearns (Parker, *Literary Fat Ladies*, pp. 140–141).

In Rogers's text, the imaginary phallicization of the colonizer is suggested by more than his representation as having "entered into" the "secrets" of America as female body. Rogers's imaginary phallicization of the colonizer is overdeteremined by his representation of the colonizer's entrance into the feminized geographical space of America and the language of its indigenous inhabitants by means of the phallic image of a "key" capable of "unlock[ing]" the precious "Rarities" this space and this language proffer (sig. A2). Rogers represents the displacement of European colonizers to America and the consequent political, economic, and cultural-linguistic colonization of America in terms of a sexualized narrative of phallic penetration and possession. An analysis of the theorizations of the aesthetic category of trope in treatises on rhetoric of the same period shows they too are based on just such a narrative.

Within the rhetorical tradition, the phallic, colonialist narratives subtending Renaissance tropologies look back to the founding gesture of imperial tropology in which the communion of guest and host is foreclosed and re-written as the conquest of the guest by the host. This founding gesture of imperial tropology occurs in Quintilian's *Institutio oratoria*, where trope is theorized as the "moving about" (*mutatio*) of a word from its "proper" meaning to "another" (*aliam*) (bk. 8, sec. 6, line 1).

Harking back to Quintilian's formative theorization of trope as movement from the proper to the alien, the narratives subtending Renaissance tropologies are predicated upon an opposition between a setting of departure and a setting of arrival. The setting of departure is commonly defined as an intrinsic attribute of the word-actant, and the setting of arrival is commonly identified only by its otherness to this actant. Thomas Farnaby's theorization of trope in *Index Rhetoricus* (1625) well demonstrates the opposition between the settings of departure and arrival structuring early modern tropologies. Farnaby conceptualizes trope as a *"deflectunt"* (deflection) of a word from a signification *"genuina"* (genuine) to it to a signification described as *"aliena,"* alien, the locus of alterity (p. 10). The tropological narrative in Farnaby's *Index Rhetoricus* and similar narratives in other early modern theorizations of trope may be seen as unconsciously inscribed with discourses of power which articulate ethnic difference as a pretext for domination while anxiously calling domination into question, discourses bespeaking a sense of the precariousness of the power of the colonial guest who is self-proclaimed a host and a master.

The reverberation, in Renaissance tropologies, of the colonialist trajectory in which the European guest in the New World becomes a host to its indigenous inhabitants who had received him, is in part an effect of the kinetic verbs chosen to theorize the aesthetic category of trope. Such verbs function as symptoms of the process of displacement involved in colonial encounters. They symptomatically point to the mutual othering such encounters entail. Richard Sherry's translation of Quintilian's theorization of trope as involving "a movynge and changynge of a worde and sentence" in the *Treatise of Schemes and Tropes* (unpaginated) is a case in point. John Smith's similar theorization of trope as the use of a word in a "changed signification" (p. 2) is another.

"Moving" and "changing" are an English rendering of the Latin verb *muto* featured in Quintilian's theorization of trope. The categories of "movement and change" are symptomatic of historical-psychic effects bound up with the rise of early modern capitalism. Jean-Christophe Agnew diagnoses these effects, noticeable in an increasing circulation of money and commodities and an increasingly less stable subjective identity, as liquidity effects (pp. 9–14).

This sense of mobility and change in sixteenth-century England was internal yet exceeded national boundaries. The rise of mercantile capitalism with which the practice of colonialism was closely bound (Stratton, p. 142) caused national boundaries to be more and more often crossed in the context of trade. Economic texts of the sixteenth century mournfully represent trade as a practice of depletion. In the sermon on *Trade and Usury* (1524), Martin Luther complains about foreign trade. Such trade, he writes, "brings from Calcutta and India and such places wares like costly silks, articles of gold, and spices…which drain away the money of land people" (p. 246). In *An Alarvm Against Vsurers* (1584), Thomas Lodge articulates a similar complaint. Merchants, he writes, "bring in store of wealth from forrein Nations" and this advances "publyke commoditie." Yet, Lodge continues, "such are their domesticall practice…[they] eate our English Gentrie out of house and home" (p. 13).

These early modern economic texts accentuate the national and geographic borders across which early modern trade operated. They speak of the geographic movement involved in early modern mercantile capitalism. Luther and Lodge articulate an anxiety with regard to the movements of border crossings involved in trade. This anxiety has to do with the second operation in terms of which Sherry and Smith theorize the aesthetic category of trope: change.

In the context of early modern colonial trade, national borders were crossed when merchants set out to the colonies, and when goods from the colonies were imported into Europe. The importation of goods from the colonies, Luther and Lodge fear, involves perilous and potentially uncontrollable change. This feared change is an economic change, a change in monetary status. The allure of goods imported from the colonies, Luther and Lodge anxiously imagine, is powerful enough to entice residents of the colonial center into spending much money, imagined by Luther in liquefying terms accentuating the unpredictability of its circulation in the context of trade.

The anxiety of uncontrollable monetary loss as a result of confrontation of Europeans with alluring goods imported from the colonies articulated by the early modern economic texts of Luther and Lodge is symptomatic of a deeper anxiety. Psychically, goods imported from the colonies function as cyphers of the colonial Other. Their allure is the seductive appeal of the exotic. The feared unpredictable economic effect of the appeal of exotic goods to European "gentry" is a correlative of the psychic effect of the appeal of the colonial Other associated with those goods in the European imaginary.

The allure of the colonial Other, Lodge and Luther fear, might lead to emotional upheaval, to the loss of control over libidinal affect in the colonialist psyche, to unpredictable libidinal changes within this psyche. In the texts of Luther and Lodge, this fear of the loss of control over the libidinal affect of the colonizers is registered as a fear of loss of Europe's privileged economic status, of control over European money, which becomes transcoded with libidinal affect. The privileged economic status of Europe with respect to the colonies is a function of Europe's political supremacy over the colonies. The anxiety of economic and psychic loss articulated by Lodge and Luther is embroiled with the colonialist anxiety of the loss of European political power over the colonies. Because the privileged status of Europe involves phallic empowerment, the anxiety of loss these early modern economic texts articulate is an anxiety of symbolic castration. In the early modern economic texts of Luther and Lodge, the geographic movement involved in mercantile capitalism is feared to have uncontrollable economic, psychic, and political changes as its effects. In these texts, the categories of movement and change in terms of which Sherry theorizes trope are bound up in an uneasy, anxiously imagined dialectic of master and slave, European and colonial Other.

The functions of movement and change in relation to which Sherry theorizes the aesthetic category of trope are implicated in colonialism in a constitutive, structural sense too. In contravention of the economic and political anxieties of early modern writers like Luther and Lodge, mercantile transactions with the colonies did not deplete European economic and political power. Trade with the colonies impoverished the inhabitants of the colonies, "changyng" them, in terms of Sherry's tropology, from self-sovereign subjects to colonized subalterns.

Sherry's theorization of trope as the "movynge and changynge" of words is bound up, in the imaginary register and in the symbolic register, with the symbolic economy of mercantile capitalism. This symbolic economy is premised on the constant border-crossing motions of trade (Stratton, p. 144) and the social and economic changes these motions entail. Most notable of the social and economic changes entailed by early modern colonialism were the "increased accumulation, growth [and] development" of the European powers and the concomitant depletion of the people of the New World (Lyotard, p. 154).

Within the early modern rhetorical tradition, the symbolic economy of mercantile capitalism is articulated most clearly in the tropology of the Port Royal *Rhetoric*, whose English version was published in 1676. In this rhetorical treatise, tropes are described as "words transported from their proper significations" (p. 71). In this case, the tropological verb is "transport." This verb is used in relation to the border-crossings involved in early modern mercantile capitalism. In the *Basilicon Doron* (1599), King James complains: "Merchants...transport from vs things necessary; bringing back sometimes vnnecessary things and at other times nothing at all" (p. 89).

The political stakes of the transportation involved in early modern mercantile capitalism to which King James alludes is exposed in an articulation of the most famous of the explorers whose ventures made early modern mercantile capitalism possible. In one of his letters to his agent, Columbus uses the same verb to speak of the transportation by sea of goods necessary "for the colonization of the country" (quoted by Greenblatt, *Marvelous Possessions*, p. 71). In the Port Royal tropology, the tropological verb ("transport") is lexically allied with Europe's superior technologies of maritime transportation, which were among the enabling conditions of colonialist practice, and with the mercantile uses to which these technologies were put.

This lexical alliance between the verb used to theorize the aesthetic category of trope in the Port Royal *Rhetoric* and a verb which subtends representations of early modern colonialist ventures makes it possible to see these ventures as culturally symptomatic, a part of the political unconscious of the Port Royal tropology. This tropology can be seen as a cultural product, inevitably, yet not necessarily consciously, "reorganiz[ing]" ideological content at its cultural backdrop. In Frederic Jameson's terms, this ideological content is part of the "political unconscious" of early modern theorizations of trope, an "absent cause, which cannot [be]...directly or immediately conceptualize[d]" by their articulators, who in this case are early modern rhetoricians (p. 82).

Because "transport" is a signifier from the vocabulary of trade, this verb may be seen as anasemically indexing the economic dimension of the colonialist narrative constituting part of the political unconscious of the aesthetic category of trope. The economic dimension of colonialism involves the "economic myth" of "limitless gold, the infinite surplus of the periphery" which explorers and traders would transport back to Europe (Stratton, p. 167). The aesthetic category of trope in the Port Royal *Rhetoric* is implicitly aligned with the category of gold, itself "deeply inscribed in the practice of exploration" (Stratton, pp. 167–168). This transcoding of the categories of trope and gold allows for the explicitly economic representation of the potential hazards of troping:

[as] the ill use of a man's wealth, is the destruction of his Estate, so the ill choice of Tropes occasions a multitude of faults in discourse. (p. 82)

Elevated to the status of gold, the "regulatory element among commodities" (Goux, *Symbolic Economies*, p. 31), trope becomes transcodable with the phallus as general equivalent of objects of drive. Like all elevations of a signifier to the rank of general equivalency, this transcoding of trope, gold, and phallus has a perilous potency. The general equivalent of gold is economically empowering, the source of "wealth." For the same reason, the general equivalent of gold is the source of an anxiety of impoverishment, of the "destruction" of an "Estate." In the context of general equivalency evoked by the representation of trope in the Port Royal *Rhetoric*, this destruction is economically impoverishing and symbolically castrative. Given the isomorphism of the general equivalents of gold and the phallus (Goux, *Symbolic Economies*, pp. 21–34), the loss of wealth implies the dissolution of privileged phallic status.

Castration is involved in the Port Royal theorization of trope even in the literal, Freudian sense. The denotations of the verb "use" which is featured in this theorization are economic and sexual (Shell, *Money, Language and Thought*, p. 59, n. 24). The sexual denotation of "use" inflects the loss implicated in the Port Royal tropology toward the loss of sexual potency. In the Port Royal tropology, the "ill use of tropes" is transcoded with loss in the economic and sexual senses, and with loss on the level of the phallus function, loss in the symbolic register. Phallus function, gold, and sexual potency are general equivalents in their respective spheres. In the Port Royal *Rhetoric*, these general equivalents are implicitly transcoded with the aesthetic category of trope. The theorization of trope in terms of a narrative of "transport" conceptually aligns it with the colonialist general equivalent of Europe as site of plenitude and Being. The function of general equivalents, Goux writes, is to stabilize the part-objects gravitating to them (*Symbolic Economies*, p. 46). In the imagining of the "ill use of Tropes" which is part of the Port Royal tropology, the general equivalents transcoded with the aesthetic category of trope are destabilized, if not dissolved.

In the Port Royal *Rhetoric*, the "ill use of Tropes" is implicitly theorized as decapitated language, dismembered into a "multitude of faults." Symbolic castration turns "ill used" tropes into dysfunctional part-objects dislodged from the general equivalent which would have stabilized them. Because in the Port Royal *Rhetoric*, trope is theorized in terms of the colonialist scenario in which Europe or European culture function as general equivalents, the dissolution of general equivalents in the theorization of the "ill use of Tropes" in this treatise involves an undoing of the scenario of colonization.

In the Port Royal tropology, colonialism as a capitalist practice is bound up with a specter of its violent disintegration. In the context of such disintegration of a colonialist scenario, those Others who are turned in the context of the colonial situation into unwelcome guests in the spaces they had inhabited would hound their conquerors, who had proclaimed themselves hosts within those spaces. The Port Royal tropology symptomatically indexes the anxiety of decolonization plaguing the colonialist psyche, the anxiety diagnosed in other contexts by Franz Fanon (*Wretched of the Earth*, p. 43), and Julia Kristeva (*Strangers to Ourselves*, p. 20).

Most early modern tropologies attempt to deal with the specter of self-destruction raised by the intoxicating revenues of colonization. They do so by recourse to a discursive strategy which appears in rhetorical texts as early as the *Institutio oratoria*. This strategy, an instance of repression, involves the postulation of an Other, projecting violence onto the Other and consequently justifying the Other's subjection to violence (Folena, pp. 220–232).

Some early modern rhetoricians pursue this strategy only to the point of postulating the colonial Other within the discourse of tropology. Thomas Wilson's *Arte of Rhetorique* of 1560 (p. 197) and Henry Peacham's *Garden of Eloquence* of 1577 (unpaginated), describe trope as an "alteration of a word." Linking trope with the category of alteration, Wilson and Peacham implicate this aesthetic category within an act of cultural "making strange" characteristic of Europe's interactions with its Others (Chabani-Manganyi,

p. 52). This cultural "making strange" generates a fracture between a European self and a colonial subaltern (Stratton, p. 142). The theorization of trope as alteration in the treatises of Wilson and Peacham inscribes this psychic fracture between European and Other into the aesthetic category of trope.

The theorizations of trope in Dudley Fenner's *Artes of Logike and Rhetorike* of 1588 (p. 2), John Smith's *Mysterie of Rhetorike Unvail'd* of 1657 (p. 4), and Thomas Hobbes's *Art of Rhetoric* of 1681 (p. 148) assume the same fracture between a European self and a colonial subaltern who is identified with violence and made the object of violence. Fenner, Smith, and Hobbes theorize trope as an act in which a word is "drawn" from one signification to another. The operation of "drawing" Fenner, Smith, and Hobbes inscribe into the aesthetic category of trope involves the displacement of an object or body by a force over which this object or body has no control. Semantically, "drawing" is linked with the practice of drawing and quartering, the violence of disemboweling and execution. Fenner, Smith, and Hobbes theorize trope in terms of a signifier structurally and semantically embroiled with violence.

The violence implicit in the two senses of the signifier "drawing," dislocation and mutilation, was unquestionably part of early modern colonialist practice. These two senses of "drawing" are articulated in the *Requerimiento*, the Spanish colonial proclamation of 1513. This document warns newly encountered peoples they should accept the authority of the European colonizers or else be displaced from their homes to serve as "slaves" and suffer "mischief and damage," signifiers whose vagueness intensifies the threat of violence, possibly leading to "death," which they were designed to insinuate. This document, Stephen Greenblatt writes, involves a "process of mimetic doubling and projection — a representation of the natives as displaced European self-representation [which] does not lead to an identification with the other but to a ruthless will to possess" (*Marvelous Possessions*, p. 98).

Colonizers, however, characteristically (mis)represented their culture as a benefactor who saves the subalterns from their own violence, or as Fanon puts it, as "a mother who unceasingly restrains her fundamentally perverse offspring from...giving free reign to its evil instincts" (*Wretched of the Earth*, p. 266). The violence of colonization is concealed under a mask of beneficence.

Significantly, the need for such concealment is articulated in early modern tropologies, frequently in conjunction with narrativizations of trope as "drawing" which bring the dialectic of otherness and violence into play. Fenner (sig. C2) and Hobbes (p. 138), who theorize trope as a word "drawn" from one signification to another, require the submerging of the violence involved in the drawing they associate with the rhetorical operation of troping. In this rhetorical operation, they instruct, the word should "seem rather to be ledde by the hande to another signification, then to be driven by force into the same" (Fenner, sig. C2; Hobbes, p. 138). The use of "force" involved in the act of drawing is openly acknowledged, but what Hobbes and Fenner are interested in is the act's not "seeming" coercive. They dictate an imaginary captation of this act. They would like, Fenner and Hobbes imply, for the violent act of "drawing" they inscribe into the category of trope to be represented as a beneficent act of guiding in which the hierarchical tension between leader and led is mitigated by the image of their holding hands.

This mitigating image of manual contact between leader and led, master and slave, appears in the advice, transcribed around 1575, for the rounding up of Indians who are to be sold into slavery by Hernando de Escalante Fontaneda, a Spanish interpreter, who advised his countrymen to "let the Indians be taken in hand gently, inviting them to peace" and then "sell them among the Islands" (quoted by Greenblatt, *Marvelous Possessions*, p. 98). In the rhetorical vocabulary of tropology as in the vocabulary generated by colonialist practice with which early modern tropology is conceptually allied, the violence of dislocation is occluded by an image of manual bonding.

Whatever ambivalence this image leaves as to the degree of violence involved in the act of displacement it represents, this ambivalence is done away with in Abraham Fraunce's tropology, which requires of the displaced word to "seeme rather willinglie ledd, than driuen by force to [an]other signification" (*Arcadian Rhetorike* [1588], sig. A3). Explicitly demanding the glossing over of the violence of displacement, Fraunce requires for the displacement to be represented not as an act of coercion in which an actant is "driuen by force" from one location to another, but as an act of benevolence extreme to the point of making the displaced actant "willing" to go along with it. The key word in Fraunce's theorization of trope is "seeme," the mark of the imaginary register, which in this case is consciously used to produce the misrecognition to which deployments of the imaginary are all too prone. In Fraunce's theorization of trope, Eric Cheyfitz correctly observes,

> the skilled...rhetorician, like the skilled overseer with a slave, must use force in transporting a word from its proper...place, but conceals that

force, or tries to, under the semblance of the word's willingness to give up its property in itself. (p. 37)

Postulating the cooperation of the displaced as an ideal of representation, Fraunce taps into one of the most deep-seated fantasies of colonialism in all of its historical phases: the fantasy of "convinc[ing] the natives [it] came to lighten their darkness" (Fanon, *Wretched of the Earth*, p. 266). Colonizers, Fanon observes, have always sought to convince the colonized they should be willing to go along with the programs of their colonizers, since they would otherwise "at once fall back into barbarism, degradation, and bestiality" (ibid.).

The verbs narrativizing Renaissance theorizations of trope are sites of cultural exchange where the vocabulary of rhetoric crosses with the vocabulary of colonialism. The tropological plot of a word's displacement from one signification to another intersects with and is contaminated by the colonial plot of a voyage from Europe to the New World and back. Not all tropological verbs cover the two parts of this plot, the setting out of discoverers, merchants, and settlers from Europe to the New World, and the dispatching of bodies appropriated in the New World to Europe. "Alteration," suggests the Othering or ideological defamiliarization of an actant. "Drawing" suggests the brutal dislocation of the colonial Other, or, more accurately, of the particular others standing in for this Other. These two tropological verbs focus on the second part of the colonial plot, which involves the imaginary transformation of the inhabitants of the New World into Europe's Others and their consequent subjection to brutality and exile. "Transfer" and "transport" evoke the change with respect to location underlying the two parts of the colonial plot. These verbs underscore the psycho-cultural and economic co-implication of colonizer and colonized engendered by Europe's encounter with the New World.

Economically, the New World provided a source of goods which helped European trade flourish. The New World colonies, in turn, became dependent on the colonizing powers. This dependency was a result of the "direct conquest and subjugation" of the colonized and of the colonized people's "acquiescence with the imperial power...in return for protection" (Mellor, p. 159). On the psycho-cultural level, the conceptual fracture distinguishing the European colonizer from the colonial Other bound colonizer and colonized in a relation of center and margins, in which the margins signified what the center represses (Shields, p. 276). Placed on the margins of early modern Europe's coded geography, colonial Others came to signify, in the European imaginary, what Europe repressed. The colonial Other became the indirect determinant of European identity.

The repressed famously returns. The psychic price of the imaginary and symbolic suppression and material subjection of the colonial Others is the phobogenic image of the inversion of this subjection, in which those Others hound their conquerors. Colonization generates and depends on the anxiety of its own deconstruction. In early modern rhetoric, this "settler anxiety," to borrow Fanon's term, is part of the political unconscious of tropology. This settler anxiety plaguing Renaissance tropologies is symptomatically registered in the semiotic instability of the topographizing signifiers, such as "proper," "first," "natural," or "original," between which the displacement structuring the theorizations of trope is said to take place. Qualified and described, however minimalistically, these signifiers take on the significance of "places": locations with "a distinctive internal structure to which meaning is attributed" (Pocock, p. 17) and with which attitudes and values are associated.

These places are implied to be different from one another. One is conceptualized as an attribute of the word-actant; it is the word-actant's "proper," "first," or "natural" setting. The other place is in most cases described only in terms of its alterity. This difference between the two limiting settings of tropology is a *différance*. Like Derrida's category of *différance*, the difference between the limiting sites of tropology in Renaissance rhetoric involves the deferral not of the destination, which is always a "present possibility," but of the setting of departure, which once departed from remains "determined outside any teleological or eschatological horizon" (Derrida, *Writing and Difference*, p. 203). In the context of *différance.*, the setting of departure inscribed into Renaissance tropologies would be endlessly displaced from its presence as point of departure, even were it to be returned to at a different time.

None of the different representations of the limiting sites of tropology can be univocally fixed to either side of the geographical division between center and margins, Europe and the New World, which underpins the early modern colonial imaginary. In the indeterminacy of the interpretations they generate, these representations anasemically and unconsciously articulate the potential deconstruction of European hegemony over the New World, the realization of what Fanon describes as the native's envious dreams of repossession (*Wretched of the Earth*, p. 39). This specter of deconstruction is inscribed in the colonialist practice whose constituting discourse the early modern theorizations of trope echo yet turn on its head.

The most common undecidable signifier of the setting of departure in Renaissance theorizations of trope is "proper" (Fenner, sig. C2; Hobbes, p. 138; Wilson, p. 94; Lamy, p. 38). This signifier is the closest to the Latin sources of Renaissance rhetoric. In those cases in Renaissance theorizations of trope wherein a setting of departure is labeled "proper" to the word-actant, as in Quintilian's *Institutio oratoria*, the conjunction of "proper" with a verb denoting displacement reveals the association between the word-actant and the category of property.

The association of the word-actant in early modern theorizations of trope with property is reinforced in the conceptualization of trope in Richard Sherry's *Treatise of Schemes and Tropes*. In Sherry's first treatise, the setting of departure is designated as the word-actant's "owne" (unpaginated). In the early modern colonial context at the backdrop of early modern tropologies, property relations often took the form of the annihilation of the indigenous peoples' relation to their land and their expropriation (Marx, *Capital*, vol. 1, pp. 716–724; Greenblatt, *Marvelous Possessions*, p. 169; Cheyfitz, p. 59).

In this context, the displacement from property informing the theorization of trope signals the exclusion of the colonial Other from the capitalist discourse of ownership and possession. This exclusion sanctioned the deportation of Othered others, inscribed into the tropological verbs "transfer," "transport," and, more radically, "draw." This exclusion had a linguistic correlative: the erasure of the indigenous appellations of colonized property and their supplanting by European proper names (Campbell, pp. 202–203; Pratt, p. 33; Greenblatt, *Marvelous Possessions*, p. 83). This linguistic correlative too is referenced by early theorizations of trope as a departure from the "proper."

The tropological theorization of the "proper" intersects with the appropriation of native land and the erasure of native place-names characterizing early modern colonialism. This theorization also conceptually intersects with the philosophical notion of "property" as an attribute of identity. This philosophical notion harks back to Aristotle's *Topics*, where the "property" of an entity is conceptualized as what "does not indicate [its] essence...but yet belongs to [it] alone, and is predicated inconvertibly of it" (bk. 1, ch. 5, sections 17–19). Combined with the notion of place as it is in early modern theorizations of trope by virtue of spatializing verbs such as "transfer," "transport," or "drawing," the "proper" signifies the location in relation to which selfhood is defined. For the European colonizers, this "proper" site of self-definition was Europe as privileged signifier. The "proper" site of departure in early modern tropologies allows itself to be read as the property of which indigenous inhabitants of the New World are dispossessed, and as the national property of European states from which colonizers set out toward the property they colonized.

Roland Barthes reads in this way. According to Barthes, the field of elocution, in which words are said to be "transported, strayed, deviated from their normal, familiar habitat," rests on the opposition "proper/figured," which is inseparable from the opposition "national/foreign" ("The Old Rhetoric," p. 88). Cheyfitz reads in a similar fashion when he observes how in "the way Westerners think about language…the proper becomes the national, or normal" (p. 36). The departure from a "proper" place in early modern tropologies intersects with a type of negation characterizing colonialist discourse. Colonialist discourse negates the natives' rights of property and the proper names natives had given their property. At the same time, the departure from the "proper" in early modern tropologies intersects with the representation, within colonialist discourse, of the egress from national territory as a property of the national identity in whose name colonizers set out to the New World.

The early modern tropologies which feature the departure from the "proper" may be seen as symptomatically pointing to two colonialist trajectories included in their political unconscious: the voyage of Europeans to the New World, in which the Europeans initially function as guests in the lands whose threshold they cross, and the forced migration of the peoples of the New World from their colonized lands in which they have come to be the unwelcome guests, whether to serve as slaves in Europe or European colonies or to go into unspecified exile. These tropologies obliquely, anasemically suggest the uneasy political, economic, and psychic interdependence of these two trajectories and the possible decolonizing displacement of one by the other, which is the nightmare unconsciously haunting the colonialist enterprise.

The signifier "first," featuring as a site of departure in the tropologies of Fenner and Hobbes (sig. C2; p. 38), suffers from comparable instabilities. This signifier implicitly links the tropological setting of departure with notions of the New World as the Garden of Eden, the primal setting of human history as constructed in the Scriptures, the site where a "lost childhood" could be recovered (Kolodny, pp. 17–21). Early modern manifestations of the notion of the New World as paradise include Columbus's claim he had discovered the "earthly paradise" (*Diary*, quoted by Campbell, p. 175). This use of a term from biblical myth to name a geographical location empirically designated as being at "a distance of twenty-six leagues from the equator" (ibid.), loads this location with connotations accruing to what was conceived as the primal scene of humanity. This location is emplotted as the first, rather than most recent, site of history (Campbell, pp. 175–177, 223).

The tropological emplotment of this Edenic site as point of departure, for all the hypocritical nostalgia for a lost European innocence it involves, is an affirmation of European power. If Europe is the epitome of post-lapsarian history, while the New World is the earthly paradise, then the explorer who sets out from Europe to the New World and appropriates it for European powers is a savior figure who, as Milton was to say of Christ, "regain[s] the blissful seat" (*Paradise Lost*, bk. 1, line 5). Columbus conceived of himself as a Christ figure, signing his letters, after the discovery, "Christoferens" (Christ-bearer). This signature indexes Columbus's sense of himself as a "conveyor...figure, bringing the faith of Europe to the new land" (Parker, *Literary Fat Ladies*, p. 143). Implicit in the signature "Christoferens" is a sense of the European discoverer's restoring the discovered land to Europe not as new but as a site of a paradise lost long before. This sense of the New World as a paradisal first place resonates in the specification of the setting of departure in early modern tropologies as "first."

The colonialist imagining of the New World as paradise and of its European discoverer as a Christ figure emplot the European appropriation of the New World as a re-enactment of the New Testament story of the reinstallment of humanity in paradise. In the New Testament story as refashioned by Milton in a cultural context of early modern colonialism, the heavenly paradise to which the Son restores humanity is no more empty, eagerly anticipating the arrival of its rightful possessor, than the New World was upon the arrival of European voyagers. In Milton's text, the Edenic site is occupied by Satan, the "thief of Paradise," who gained possession of paradise by supplanting the first Adam, and who must be vanquished to make room for the lawful possessor (*Paradise Regained*, bk. 4, lines 604–607). The New Testament myth of the restoration of paradise enabled European colonizers to inject transcendental values into their acts of land annexation and to morally justify the expropriation and exile of the occupants of these lands.

Summoned from the cultural unconscious to raise Columbus from the status of an admiral in the Spanish fleet, bearing the military, economic, and technological power of Europe, to the status of a transcendental Savior, the myth of the New World as paradise provided the adequate narrative for Europe's vision of the colonial Other as posing the ultimate threat to its bliss in the newly discovered paradise. The myth of the New World as paradise made it possible to imagine the colonial Other as an entity which should be driven out of this "Paradise." Renaissance theorizations of trope are informed by a Christian vocabulary of a paradise lost and regained. In the context of this vocabulary, the "first" setting from which the word-actant is said to be displaced in Renaissance theorizations of trope may be read as informed by the notion of the native as, like Milton's Satan, a "thief of paradise" who must be made to vacate this privileged and archaic property.

Yet the term "first" does not univocally reference the paradisal New World, imagined to be inhabited not by owners whose receptive, communal hospitality the Europeans must count on, but by usurpers who must be driven out by the Europeans, self-proclaimed hosts of this paradisal site and hosts to all present within its bounds. At the same time, "first" is a signifier of the precedence and privilege which European colonizers attributed to themselves and which enabled their psycho-semiotic manoeuvre of transforming their hosts into their guests. The notion of primacy as privilege harks back to the creation story in Genesis, where Adam's temporal precedence to Eve justifies her subordination to him (Parker, *Literary Fat Ladies*, pp. 178–180).

The signifier "first" in early modern tropologies is radically unstable. This signifier symptomatically invokes Europe as the first station of the journey to the New World, venerated by official agents such as Columbus or Drake and deplored by persecuted Puritans. At the same time, the signifier "first" symptomatically invokes the New World as a reincarnation of a biblical primal scene, as a paradise regained or a New Jerusalem, whose occupants, reproduced by the colonial imaginary as unwanted guests, must be evacuated to make room for the return of the lawful possessor. The instability of the signifier "first" in early modern tropologies underscores the inextricability of colonization and dislocation within the early modern colonialist imaginary. The early modern colonialist imaginary may be seen to function as the political unconscious of early modern tropologies.

The inextricability of colonization and dislocation, of hosting a guest and dispelling him, may be seen to unconsciously underlie Renaissance theorizations of trope as the displacement of a signifier from its "natural" signification too. In *The Arcadian Rhetorike*, Fraunce theorizes trope as a "word turned from his naturall signification, to some other" (sig. A2). In *The Garden of Eloquence*, Henry Peacham theorizes this category as "the alteration of a word from the...natural signification to another" (unpaginated). In the same vein, the Port Royal rhetoricians theorize trope as involving words "applied to other things than what they naturally mean" (p. 71). In all these instances, the aesthetic category of trope is theorized as involving a journey away from the "natural," which in sixteenth-century England was often associated "with the instinctive, the savage, the uncivil, the ignorant" (Attridge, p. 26). These are some of the negative qualities which Europeans attributed to inhabitants of the New World, who could thus be fantasized as needing the hosting of their colonizers in order to be civilized. The same negative qualities are attributed to the inhabitants of the New World in the rhetorical myth of the orator as civilizer.

However, "nature" in Renaissance vocabulary does not signify in a stable way, tending to slip from the referencing of the untamed and disorderly to a referencing of order and decorum. Normative heterosexuality, for example, was described as "natural" in opposition to denounced forms of intercourse such as sodomy, described as "unnatural lechery" (quoted in Goldberg, *Sodometries*, pp. 180, 187). In the Port Royal tropology, the sense of "natural" as normative is accentuated in the prefacing of the theorization of tropes as words "applied to other things than what they naturally mean" by their description as words "which Custom has applied to another subject" (p. 71). Signification, in this case, is defined as a product of "Custom" or regulating cultural convention, and this convention, in the next sentence, is described as "natural." The departure from the "natural" referenced in Renaissance tropologies conceptually intersects with the chauvinistic self-representations of European colonialists as agents anchored in a "natural" ideological code of unquestioned truth and value which they carry into the New World. The chauvinistic self-representations of European colonialists include the fantasized transferal of this "natural" code to the uncivilized inhabitants of the New World whose lack of civility is referenced by the same term, "natural." In this fantasy, "natural" and "unnatural," normative and deviant, civilized and savage, (un)easily change places, underscoring the conceptual and psychic dependency of the European self on the colonial Other whose host it proclaims itself to be, and the perpetual possibility of the collapsing of one into the other.

The theorizations of the aesthetic category of trope in Renaissance rhetoric unconsciously index the two trajectories of the colonialist project. (1) One trajectory of the colonialist project indexed by early modern tropologies is the imperial, possessive, phallic movement of discovery and conquest which explorers and settlers carried out from the ontological center of Europe to the margins of its coded geography. (2) The other trajectory of the early modern colonialist project equally indexed by early modern tropologies is the cultural and economical expropriation of the inhabitants of the margins, carried out under the guise of "civilizing," with which the movement of European discovery and conquest was psychically, conceptually, and historically allied. Renaissance tropologies invoke both these colonialist trajectories, structurally and semantically. At the same time, in their use of duplicitous signifiers, attributable to valorized center and debased periphery, to represent the settings of departure of these trajectories, Renaissance tropologies deconstruct the hierarchy of center and margins on which the colonialist enterprise depends.

The colonialism inscribed into the category of trope is an anxious one, haunted by specters of its downfall. Produced at the beginnings of colonialism, Renaissance theorizations of trope unconsciously reflect Europe's sense of supremacy over the colonial periphery, and register a deep-seated anxiety of the periphery's usurping the power of the center. Theorizations of the aesthetic category of trope in Renaissance treatises on rhetoric allow the colonized margins to be glimpsed through the reading of these settings as Europe, and the attributes of Europe to show through the reading of these settings as the New World. Because they generate these two narratives, early modern theorizations of trope obliquely and unintentionally yet significantly expose the imaginary differentiation between civilized and savage, European and native, on which colonialism relied to justify its acts of domination, as radically unstable. Early modern theorizations of trope show how these two narratives always threaten to dissolve one into the other. These theorizations of trope ultimately disable the partitioning topography of an imperial tropology relying on the concept of colonizing hospitality, on the *dispositif* of conquest leading to "the destruction and exhaustion" of colonized lands (Lyotard, p. 200).

Early modern theorizations of the aesthetic category of trope repeatedly relate an elocutionary category to a narrative of often forced displacement and to two senses of the term "tropical." Early modern tropologies invoke the tropical in the general geographical sense of the zone between the tropics which was the destination of so many colonialist displacements. At the same time, early modern tropologies invoke the tropical in the cultural sense of the exotic place on the margins of coded geography with which the colonial space came to be identified in Eurocentric discourse. Theorizations of trope are narrativized to tell the same kinds of stories early modern European travelers, explorers, colonizers, playwrights, and poets told about "the strange regions of the world known as the 'tropics'" (Said, p. xii).

The analysis of the conceptualization of the aesthetic category of trope in the Renaissance suggests the collusion of writing and travel, especially the travel connected with colonization, is far more intimate than has hitherto been suggested by theorists who have remarked upon it. It is not only that writing and travel are structurally parallel, bringing the subject into contact with a novel (tangible or imagined) place (Jafari and Gardner, p. 31). It is not only that writing and travel are philosophically parallel, commonly informed by "the decision of Western metaphysics to privilege presence over absence, voice over writing, and hence the near over the far" (Van den Abeele, p. xx). It is not even only that, as Jon Stratton argues, writing, as "the representational site of knowledge, provides the space within which travel occurs" (p. 56). Instead, Eurocentric writing of the Renaissance has been able to conceptually provide and mark out this space, allowing travel to take place and spawn representations of alterity which were instrumental to the "attempt to fix and limit otherness" (Stratton, p. 73), because one of the most privileged components of European theory of writing, the concept of trope, was from its inception inscribed with the notions of travel and of Otherness.

The story of displacement from a privileged site of presence to a foreign land or back is written in colonialist narratives and into a privileged component of the theory of the language in which such narratives were written. If writing produced in early modern Europe has provided a model for travel and marked out the space in which travel could occur (Stratton, p. 56), this is because the notion of travel was already placed in a relation of conceptual exchange with tropology, which was one of the seminal components of rhetoric as a theory of writing (and of speech). Tropology is inextricably intertwined with economic, geographic, exploratory, ethnographic, pedagogic, and administrative vocabularies related to politically-significant displacements. Tropology provides a blueprint for and an ideological reinforcement to colonialist ventures into the tropical.

Tropology, as Derrida puts it, "is inevitable" (*On the Name*, p. 94). Tropology is all the more necessary in the context of the early modern aesthetics of rhetoric, unconsciously motivated by a drive to foreclose (and, dialectically, to approximate) a vision of the primal substance of semiosis as a site of primal narcissism in which all identity is oceanically diffused. No less inevitable, it seems, is the subliminal contamination of tropology by a colonialist logic produced by the topological partitionings structuring tropology, a logic which brings out the unconscious alliance of trope with a penetrative, phallic, conquistadorial pulsion, transcodable with the colonialist *dispositif* of conquest.

Yet early modern tropology has more to it than the conceptual alliance with a political unconscious involving the narratives of the colonization of the tropics and the conceptual structures granting Europe ontological privilege which underpin these narratives. Viewed from a limiting historicist perspective responding to the imperative to "always historicize" (Jameson, p. 9), seeking to relate texts to their political unconscious and to trace the ways in which they unconsciously "reorganize" the ideological "subtext" manifesting itself in their symptomatology (Jameson, p. 82), Renaissance tropologies appear to be cultural symptoms which bear an unconsciously produced inscription of an episteme of domination in which a guest proclaims himself a host.

The idea of receptivity, crucial to the identity of the host, entails the reversibility of the roles of guest and host, the possibility of the host's "receiving hospitality from the guest to whom he thinks he is giving hospitality" (Derrida, *Aporias*, p. 10). Similarly, the condition of being a "guest" always already implies the possibility of usurping the property of one's host. This possibility may be seen to be anasemically inscribed in the brisuric structure of imperial theorizations of trope in early modern rhetoric, whose constant slippage between imperial center and colony as limiting sites of tropology indexes the unconscious anxiety of these sites' being interchangeable. Predicated upon the distinction between center and margins, a centrist coded geography involves the specter of its own dissolution, its fall into s(e)am-less sameness, into a ex-centrist economy whose categories may always be reversed, enabling a subdued guest to assume the position of a dominating host.

The slippage from colonization to decolonization traceable in early modern tropologies is not only a function of history, not only a cultural symptom indicative of the postulation of Europe, in the early modern collective imaginary, as a "body of capitalization endowed with the properties of the *jouissance*...which capital requires" (Lyotard, p. 196). This slippage is much more a function of the irreducibly double, brisuric conceptual structure of the guest/host relation consistently used to theorize tropes in early modern treatises on the aesthetics of rhetoric. The anticolonial contaminations or reversals of domination whose specter haunts the tropologies of such early modern rhetoricians as Abraham Fraunce and Bernard Lamy are effects of the constitutively indeterminate structure of the category of hospitality. They are conceptual effects, existing irrespectively and independently of contingent historical manifestations of communality and conquest.

The exchangeability and instability of the positions of guest and host, and the brisuric structure of the symbology of hospitality, unsettle the rhetorical discourse on trope, the category produced as the cornerstone of the symbolic economy seeking, albeit dialectically, ambivalently so, to stabilize, through definition and differentiation, a phobogenic vision of the primal substance of language as oceanic and diffuse. The category of the guest, reversible into the category of the host, is destabilizing. The guest carries the threshold between a here and an elsewhere of his or her home. The guest is a liminary, whose in-betweenness involves a potential for subversion. This is a potential to destabilize the containment of the categories between which he or she is poised, to rupture them and make them flow into one another and become "no longer simply identifiable and to that extent no longer determinable" (Derrida, *Aporias*, p. 7).

Like the early modern European travelers to the New World transcodable with the word-actants of early modern tropologies, the guest, to whom Derrida refers as the *"arrivant,"* has the constitutive potential of turning into a colonizer through the invagination of the threshold on which he stands. This potentiality of the *arrivant*, Derrida says, troubles the host "enough to call into question, to the point of annihilating or rendering indeterminate, all the distinctive signs of a prior identity, beginning with the very border that delineated a legitimate home" and proceeding through larger structures of racial and cultural identity (*Aporias*, p. 34).

The use of the structure of the *arrivant* to theorize the rhetorical category of trope in Renaissance treatises on the aesthetics of rhetoric troubles the historically particular configurations of guest/host relations unconsciously registered in Renaissance tropologies. The use of this structure causes the specters of miscegenation and decolonization to haunt the colonialist tropologies of Renaissance rhetoricians. The recourse to the structure of the *arrivant* troubles the category of trope early modern rhetorical texts seek to posit as a signifier stabilizing a differentiated symbolic economy of linguistic forms produced through a hierarchizing partitioning of a substance of semiosis imagined as oceanic and non-differentiated. The use of the category of the *arrivant* in theorizations of trope destabilizes the status of trope as a would-be stabilizing master category.

The symbolic economy of Renaissance elocution is generated in an attempt to stabilize and control the primal substance of semiosis, imagined in maternalized terms of oceanic diffusion. The category of trope is imagined in phallic terms of mastery and colonization. The function of the category of trope in the symbolic economy of elocution is supposed to be the mastery and control of the primal substance of semiosis qua maternalized oceanic dissolution. Yet the inscription of the deconstructing category of the *arrivant* into early modern theorizations of trope makes it impossible for those theorizations to perform the stabilizing function they are supposed to perform. The category of the *arrivant* deconstructs the category of trope within which it is inscribed. Subversively operating within the would-be stabilizing category of trope, the category of the *arrivant* signals the possible destabilization and dissolution of the edifice of elocution into oceanic diffusion. The subversive, deconstructing operation of the category of the *arrivant* within the category of trope makes it ultimately impossible for the category of trope to fulfill the psychic function of foreclosing the infinite, archaic femininity transcoded with the primal substance of semiosis.

The conceptual and psychic consequence of the deconstruction of the would-be masterful, stabilizing, and phallic category of trope by the category of the *arrivant* is the unsettling possibility of the dissolution of the symbolic economy of elocution into oceanic diffusion. This deconstruction has another significant psychic consequence. The attitude of Renaissance rhetoricians to the primal substance of semiosis qua archaic maternality is dialectical (see Chapter One above). Renaissance rhetoricians relate to this substance in repulsion born of an anxiety of an inundation and dissolution of subjectivity as separation. They inseparably relate to this substance as the origin of all *jouissance* to which they yearn to return. This yearning is symptomatically registered within the symbolic economy of elocution in the theorization of aesthetic categories such as asyndeton, climax, apostrophe, and syncope (see Chapter One above). In the fifth and sixth chapters of this book, I show in more detailed fashion how the yearning for the archaic is symptomatically registered in early modern theorizations of simile in relation to the psychic categories of the symbolic mother, the object-cause of desire, the polymorphic libido, primal *jouissance*, and the orgasmic. My fourth chapter shows how the yearning for origin is inscribed in the inevitable deconstruction of the would-be phallic and ontological category of metaphor.

The deconstruction of the category of trope by the category of the *arrivant* functions in a similar way. This deconstruction of an aesthetic category whose function would have been the repression and stabilization of a substance of origin imagined as diffuse and unpredictable is a symptom of the yearning to revisit this archaic substance. The alluring danger inherent in the shuttling, liminal image of the *arrivant* subtending early modern tropologies is the danger of the disappearance of the differentiating Names of elocutionary vocabulary and the consequent relapse of language into an imagined infinite, archaic One-ness of primal, "intra-uterine" narcissism (Montrelay, p. 154). Such inevitably imagined yet impossible primary narcissism is coeval with a hospitality within which the boundaries between guest and host disappear. This hospitality of the infinite is the psychic function from which early modern rhetoric would have rescued language and to which early modern rhetoric is irresistibly allured to return.

The theorization of trope in early modern treatises on rhetoric includes other symptoms of the yearning for the imagined infinitude of archaic maternality, a yearning simultaneous with the anxiety of this maternality, and as intense as this anxiety. Early modern theorizations of trope are narrativized by verbs from a vocabulary of travel such as "moving" and "transporting." These verbs are part of the vocabulary of early modern mercantile capitalism and colonialism. At the same time, these verbs reference the structure of the displacement of people and commodities underpinning the economic and political operations of mercantile capitalism and colonialism. Other verbs narrativizing the aesthetic category of trope, "changing" and "altering," invoke the psycho-political operations of mutual othering involved in colonial encounters. The verb "drawing," used to narrativize the category of trope in the rhetorical theory of Fenner, Smith, and Hobbes, indexes the violence involved in colonial encounters.

The verbs used to theorize the category of trope in early modern rhetoric are all kinetic verbs. Because these verbs are kinetic, they are, in Bataille's terms, constitutively and conceptually erotic. Some of these verbs are semantically and lexically erotic. The signifier "moving" featuring in the tropologies of Sherry and Smith is eponymous with one of the functions traditionally ascribed to rhetoric at large since Cicero: *movere*, the production of affect. "The moving of the audience, the manipulation of *pathos*, is [a] main preoccupation of Renaissance rhetoric" (Rebhorn, p. 84). The formulations of several Renaissance thinkers on language indicate their conception of *movere* is distinctly amatory, connected with Eros. The rhetorician's aim, Puttenham writes, is to make the "heart...most affectionatly bent" (p. 5). Samuel Daniel too speaks of the ability of language to "stir...the heart" (p. 10).

Another verb used to narrativize the category of trope in its Renaissance theorizations, "drawing," is even more constitutively eroticized. The verb

156   Fetishization/Colonization: The Brisuric Binarism of Elocution

"to draw" is erotic in semantic and structural terms. This verb references attraction. The Latin equivalent of "drawing," *ducere*, is the root of the fundamentally erotic function of *se-ducere*, seduction. Inscribed in the tropologies of Fenner and Hobbes, who use the verb "drawing," is the sense and the structure of the erotic operation of seduction, more overdeterminately inscribed into the binary of trope, the rhetorical category of figure. The unconscious motivation for the postulation of the category of trope in terms of a phallic drive for mastery and conquest is the control of the seductive deployment of archaic femininity ascribed to the category of figure. But far from controlling the seductive eroticism inscribed into the category of figure, the tropologies of Fenner and Hobbes ultimately repeat this seductiveness.

The Latin verb "*deflectunt*" (to deflect) used to narrativize the aesthetic category of trope in Farnaby's *Index Rhetoricus* is the closest in structure to the psychic operation of seduction. Etymologically, "*de-flectunt*" is an alteration of route, an operation whose structure is identical with the structure of *se-ducere*, leading aside. In Farnaby's rhetorical text the would-be phallic category of trope deconstructs into the aesthetic category of figure qua seductiveness instead of controlling this category.

For all their imbrications with historically-specific deployments of the early modern economic and political imaginary, early modern tropologies gesture beyond the historical, the economic, and the political. Beyond the contingencies and vicissitudes of the factual and its imaginary captations, early modern tropologies gesture toward the psychic real, the real of the structures of the unconscious.

The most fundamental structure of the unconscious, the structure installing subjectivity, is, Lacan teaches, "the desire of the Other's desire" (*Seminar XI*, p. 235). The desire of the Other's desire is the yearning to hail the desire of the other as Other, to seduce. The erotic operation of seduction is ultimately inscribed into the category of trope in its early modern theorizations, just as this operation is inscribed into the category of figure, which early modern rhetoricians unconsciously, and anxiously, seek to produce as the debased binary of trope. Ostensibly opposed, trope and figure are inscriptions of eroticism within the symbolic as the register not only of law but primarily of desire.

For all their imbrication with phallic vocabularies and phallic structures, early modern tropologies gesture beyond the solipsism and de-subjectivation of the other as generalized Other to an attempt to engage the erotic attention of a unique and irreplaceable other. Even the elocutionary category most closely allied in structural and semantic terms with the totalizing discourse of the master ultimately does not and cannot escape the nexus of love and language, of eroticism and rhetoricity.

The cathexis of the exterior, the factual, and the contingent is symptomatic of an attempted foreclosure of the real of the psychic and/as the erotic, of the structures of the unconscious. In its imaginary and structural alliances with the vocabularies and trajectories of early modern capitalism and colonialism, the category of trope manifests intense cathexis of the exterior and factual. Yet even this category, the most invested of all elocutionary categories as theorized in early modern rhetoric books in the exterior, the factual, and the contingent, gestures toward the fundamental psychic functions of intersubjective eroticism and of nostalgia for the archaic within the symbolic.

The tropologies of early modern rhetoricians such as Abraham Fraunce, Henry Peacham, Richard Sherry, and Thomas Hobbes cannot be described only as unconscious reflections or inscriptions of a cultural "subtext" of colonial practice and its attendant anxieties. Two factors encourage us to read early modern tropologies as more than records of a phallic drive for mastery and colonization. (1) First of these is the implication of early modern tropologies in a constitutively deconstructive guest/host symbology, and the constant slippage of guest into host within this symbology. This slippage gestures toward a structure of communal, not colonizing, hospitality, the hospitality coeval with primal narcissism and with the momentary seizure of archaic feminine *jouissance* described by Montrelay. (2) The second factor encouraging us to read early modern tropologies as more than phallic pulsions is the simultaneous function of verbs narrativizing theorizations of trope as records of a will to dominate and of a yearning to seduce.

These two factors in early modern theorizations of trope clarify a ceaseless motion of "setting up and wiping out" characterizing libidinal economies (Lyotard, p. 101). In the case of the libidinal economy of early modern theorizations of trope, this ceaseless motion involves the setting up of structures of colonization and their wiping out by structures of infinite, communal hospitality and of seduction. The aesthetic category of trope as theorized in the Renaissance involves what Derrida calls a "strange topography of edges" (*Aporias*, p. 45) leading to its own fraying, its own de-circumscription, its own inevitable attraction to the archaic femininity it seeks to foreclose yet recuperate.

The theorization of the aesthetic category of trope in Renaissance rhetoric is predicated on a constitutively indeterminate symbology of hospitality hinging on the distinction between the categories of host and guest or stranger. Host and guest, Montrelay writes in her psychoanalysis of the category of communal hospitality, inevitably "fuse," at the moment of their encounter, to momentarily form "attributes of the same substance" (p. 48). The psychically inevitable fusion of guest and host in the structure of communal hospitality points, beyond history, to an imago of an alluring archaic. This imagined archaic is the site of a primal narcissism and of a *jouissance* (Montrelay, p. 54) for which even the phallocentric regimes of rhetoric can never stop yearning, even as they repress and disavow this yearning.

The contingent contextualization of early modern tropologies as traces of an early modern capitalist-colonialist imaginary is reached by means of a hermeneutic regarding them as unconsciously generated symptoms of an ideology-saturated cultural context in which they are produced. This historical contextualization is rendered insufficient by the two psychic structures implicated in early modern theorizations of trope: the structure of communal hospitality, and the structure of seduction. The structures of communal hospitality and of seduction structurally and semantically implicated in early modern theorizations of trope are not solipsistic. Unlike the drive for phallic mastery subtending early modern theorizations of trope, the psychic structures of communal hospitality and of seduction implicated in these theorizations do not attempt to ignore the subjectivity of the other. Communal hospitality and seduction are intersubjective structures. Their point of beginning is the separateness of subjects, who draw closer to one another in the case of seduction, or momentarily glimpse an archaic infinitude in the case of a communal hospitality coeval with primary narcissism as theorized by Montrelay. The shattering emergence of these intersubjective structures within theorizations of an aesthetic category predicated on colonization and desubjectivation is a trace of the repressive damage of desubjectivation.

Although it is possible to trace historically contingent connections between early modern tropologies and their cultural contexts, these tropologies ultimately gesture toward an unconscious source deeper than the variable instances of the "political unconscious" to which they can be shown to indirectly, symptomatically relate.

The most important unconscious source Renaissance tropologies implicitly betray in their textual symptomatology is not political but psychological. Renaissance theorizations of trope have a psychic source deeper than their historical and political source. The psychic source of Renaissance tropologies is an imago functioning as their hidden kernel and dictating their explicit configurations. This is the imago of oceanic

Oneness, of primal narcissism. Renaissance rhetoricians unconsciously attempt to sidestep this imago by means of the privileged elocutionary category of trope. At the same time, Renaissance rhetoricians nostalgically yearn for this oceanic Oneness imagined to have existed and to have been traumatically lost with the advent of the separating scissions of grammatical and rhetorical classifications. What the (psycho)-analysis of Renaissance tropologies most significantly proffers is not knowledge of their embededness in the historically contingent episteme of colonialism, but a sense of their nostalgic, unconscious appeal to a cosmic Oneness, through the structures of seduction and of communal hospitality which momentarily glimpses the infinite.

The alliance of the category of trope in Renaissance rhetoric with the category of the tropics turns out to provide little guarantee for the attainment of the repressive psychic objective underlying the postulation of the category of trope. This objective is allaying the anxiety generated by the transcoding of the primal substance of semiosis with the archaic maternal body imagined as abject and devouring at the same time as it is the underlying model for all of the subject's prospective objects of desire. This anxiety of the abject and devouring aspect of the maternal body is not completely allayed by the postulation of the elocutionary category of figure, transcoded with the seductive aspects of archaic maternality, with an alluring femininity marked by perversion. The confrontation with desire as perversion wherein the subject offers herself as an instrument for the *jouissance* of the other is a cause of anxiety. Leading the other to a moment of "pure apprehension of the [subject's] desire," perversion places the other in a situation wherein s/he "does not know what s/he is as an object for [this subject]," a situation generative of anxiety (Conté, p. 13).

The attempt to allay this anxiety, the product of intersubjective perversion, by postulating, in the theorization of the aesthetic category of trope, a relation of phallic desire wherein the subjectivity of one of the partners is denied, fails necessarily and constitutively. The deconstruction of this relation of a phallic desire for domination finds its expression in narratives transcodable with those of colonization by a guest-host symbology. Because this guest-host symbology is by definition radically unstable, this symbology makes it impossible to deny the subjectivity of the colonized as the guest of the European colonizer who proclaims himself a host. The brisuric structure of the signifieds referencing the limiting sites of the trajectory of displacement subtending Renaissance tropologies demonstrates all too well how the self-proclaimed colonial host is always in the process of slippage into the position of the guest in the colonial space, the position enabling the colonizer to declare himself a host in the first place.

Theorizations of the aesthetic category of trope in Renaissance rhetoric ultimately exacerbate rather than allay anxiety on two counts. (1) Structurally and conceptually crossing with the vocabulary of early modern colonialism, theorizations of trope in early modern rhetoric are inevitably bound up with anxieties of decolonization. The political structure of decolonization is psychically significant. The specter of decolonization haunting Renaissance tropologies is a trace of the ultimate impossibility of desubjectivation, of the denial of the subjectivity of the colonial other imagined as low-Other, on which the colonial imaginary relies. The specter of decolonization haunting Renaissance tropologies indicates the inevitability of the encounter with the subjectivity and hence the desire of the other. The theorization of the aesthetic category of figure in terms of a structure of perversion wherein the subject seeks to become an instrument for the *jouissance* of another subject and goes as far as it is possible to go along the path of *jouissance* entails yet another encounter with the desire of the other. This encounter too is inducive of anxiety because it is an encounter with the lack structuring the subjectivity of both self and other, beyond all phenomenal and virtual veils, and beyond imaginary captations of the other, whether as scintillating object of desire and perversion, or as a debased subaltern. (2) The constitutive dissolution of the categories of guest and host subtending Renaissance tropologies into one another, a dissolution which erases differences, is in itself directly inducive of the anxiety of dissolution bound up with the category of archaic maternity, the primary anxiety informing the early modern rhetorical enterprise. Because the archaic mother is the primal object, the anxiety accruing to the primal substance of semiosis qua archaic maternality too is the result of a confrontation with desire.

All three programmatic categories of Renaissance rhetoric: the primal substance of semiosis, figure, and trope are bound up with anxiety. The cause of the anxiety symptomatically surging in early modern theorizations of all three programmatic rhetorical categories is confrontation with an Other, whether as colonial subaltern, as a seductress, or as the archaic mother, the primordial Other beyond the deployments of subjectivity, including those of subaltern or seductress. Like early modern theorizations of the categories of the primal substance of semiosis and of figure, early modern theorizations of trope confirm Lacan's theorization of anxiety as arising from a moment of confrontation with the Other wherein the subject does not know what s/he is for this Other (*Seminar X*, quoted by Evans, p. 12).

The postulation of the category of trope fails to allay the anxiety of archaic femininity qua primordial Other driving the early modern rhetorical enterprise. Nor can it erase the inextricable underside of this anxiety: the intense longing to revisit archaic femininity. This desire is indexed, as I demonstrated above, in the structural and semantic alliance of verbs used to narrativize tropes in early modern rhetorical treatises with operations of seduction besides operations of colonization. The semiotics of the signifier "trope" itself index the dialectical relation of irresistible seduction by and anxiety-induced repulsion from archaic femininity.

The tropological is aligned with the topological. This alignment of trope and topos is phonic and paronomastic. Because early modern theorizations of trope proceed by means of scenarios of the conquest of place, the alignment of trope and topos is narrative too. In the tradition stemming from Aristotle's *Topics*, the topological has been a basic component of logical argument. The category of topos partakes of logocentrism. Heidegger has made clear how in the Western philosophical tradition harking back to Aristotle and Plato, the topological has everything to do with the logical and with the ontological. In philosophy, Heidegger says, "place" has the sense of "the dimension in which Being can unfold itself" (*The Question of Being*, p. 26). This notion of place as a reassuring mainstay of onto-logy, logocentrism, and rational, conscious control resonates in Wilson's disavowing reference, at the end of his *Arte of Rhetorique*, to the "safe ground," the refuge from the oceanic which the symbolic economy of Renaissance rhetoric purportedly affords.

Paronomastically, narratively, and conceptually, the category of trope is aligned with the reassuring phallic possession of stabilizing "safe ground." Etymologically, however, the signifier "trope" derives not from the Greek noun "topos" but from the Greek verb *trepein* (to turn). This Greek verb suggests movement toward a place. Yet the movement suggested by this verb is not a movement of flight toward the reassuring ground of possessed place from the simultaneously alluring and frightening psychic substance of archaic femininity qua object-cause of all desire. The movement suggested by the Greek verb *trepein*, to turn, from which the signifier "trope" derives is a movement of a (re)-turn

Etymologically indexing a movement of re-turn, the signifier "trope" semantically colludes with the Latin *verto* (the act of turning). This Latin signifier is the grammatical source of the signifier "verse," the name of an aesthetic category tapping the sensuous, unconscious dimension of language, the dimension early modern rhetoricians transcode with the primal substance of semiosis qua archaic femininity. Verse, with which trope is semiotically allied, "commemorates [language's] own inaccessible origin" (Agamben, *Language and Death*, p. 78). The category of verse with which trope colludes etymologically and semantically is the conceptual re-verse of the category of prose, derived from the Latin *prorsus*, to proceed directly (ibid.). Prose, as Giorgio Agamben has shown, is the medium of rational, logocentric argumentation constituted by Aristotelian *topoi*, the secure "places" featured in early modern narrativizations of troping as conquest.

The alignment of the category of trope with the colonizing, phallic hyper-rationality of prosaic, topical argumentation and, dialectically, with the seductive sensuality of verse, is evident in the phonic and etymological proximity between the signifier "trope" and the name of an influential school of composers of amatory verse, the twelfth-century Provençal troubadors (Agamben, *Language and Death*, p. 67). The signifier "troubadors" names the poets for whom "the event of language [was] above all an amorous experience" (ibid., p. 68). The affinity between the aesthetic category of trope and the function of the troubador accentuates the psychic dimension of re-turn to origin implicit in the sense of troping as turning. The etymology of the signifier "troubador" combines the originally Greek *trepein* (to turn) with the Provençal *trobar* (to find). This combination indexes an impulse whose structure is not the structure of linear conquest subtending phallic desire and the logocentric categories of argumentation and prose. The impulse indexed by the combination of *trepein* (to turn) and *trobar* (to find) in the names of the troubadors has the structure of re-versal. This is a structure of a striving to re-turn, the structure of the impulse to re-trieve, find again, an impulse resulting from the seduction implicated in early modern theorizations of trope. The object of the troubadors' desire in language is the amatory, sensuous dimension of language.

Like the troubadors, early modern thinkers on language are irresistibly attracted to the amatory and sensuous dimension of language. The amatory and sensuous dimension of language early modern thinkers of language nostalgically yearn for is inextricably connected with their imaginary captation of the primal substance of semiosis as the archaic mother, the object-cause of all amorous attachments. The phonic, etymological, and structural resonance of the category of the troubador within the aesthetic category of trope inflects the desire to re-turn or retrieve informing this aesthetic category as the desire to revisit archaic femininity. This desire to revisit the archaic, Lacan was to say, "establishes the orientation of the human subject to the object" (*Seminar VII*, p. 58). This orientation of a seduced re-turning inscribed into the category of trope is nothing less than eroticism, authentically expressed in verse of amatory yearning such as the verse of the troubadors.

The attempt to institute the category of trope as the stabilizing binary of figure fails to allay the anxiety of confrontation with archaic femininity generated by the reinscription of femininity attributed to the primal substance of semiosis as the subject/object of perversion. The signifier "trope" itself is semiotically split between the articulation of a linear drive for hyper-rational, phallic control of "safe ground" and of a non-linear impulse to re-turn to archaic femininity. If archaic femininity predominates in theorizations of figure and in theorizations of trope then the trope/figure binarism as a whole fails to work as an opposition, let alone a hierarchical opposition.

The necessary, constitutive failure of Renaissance rhetorical theory to produce a psychic and conceptual grid of control over the archaic femininity transcoded with the primal substance of semiosis is indicative of the powerful seductive allure of archaic femininity. This failure taints the subdivisions of tropes and figures. The necessary failure of this attempt at rational control over the substance of semiosis tells us something more about the psychological attitude of Renaissance rhetoricians toward this substance. The constitutive failure of the category of trope to stabilize the primal substance of semiosis inflects the attitude of Renaissance rhetoricians toward this substance as, in the last analysis, neither rational nor conscious but as most fundamentally erotic. This erotic attitude is evident in the deconstruction, within the discourse on tropes, of the privileged *dispositif* of colonial conquest into its feared inversion, which leads to a psychic confrontation with the subjectivity and hence desire of the colonial Other. The deconstruction of the category of trope uncannily adumbrates the inescapable falling into contradiction of the attempt to mobilize the imaginary captations of tropes for a conquest or control of the fluctuations of desire associated with the concept of figure. Theorizations of the various forms of elocution early modern rhetoricians endeavor to neatly parcel out between the two would-be polarized components of the libidinalized symbolic economy of rhetoric too are symptoms of the fundamentally erotic attitude of Renaissance rhetoricians toward language. In the following section of this book, I explore the imaginary captations and inscriptions of desire in the most conceptually significant subdivision of Renaissance elocution. This subdivision is the impaired pair consisting of the trope of metaphor, theorized as the general equivalent of early modern elocution, and the figure of simile, theorized in early modern rhetoric as metaphor's debased binary.

PART THREE
*Impaired Pair:
Metaphoric Denial, Similaic Desire*

CHAPTER FOUR

Master Trope/Trope of Mastery?
Metaphor, Ontology, and Phallic Masculinity

> Each time a rhetoric defines metaphor, not only is a philosophy implied, but a conceptual network in which philosophy itself has been constituted
>
> — Derrida, "White Mythology: Metaphor the Text of Philosophy"

Like all intellectual enterprises valorizing the extrinsic as the result of the abreaction of a desire foreclosed and feared, rhetorical theory of the Renaissance would seem to be subtended by a search for small and reassuring definiteness. Much like contemporary new historicism which has all but ignored this theory and consistently, phobically resisted the kind of psychoanalytical reading it insists on, Renaissance rhetorical theory would seem to psychologically rest on a cathexis of the rational and conscious "safe ground" Wilson speaks of at the end of his treatise. The cathexis of groundedness in Renaissance rhetorical theory is undergirded by a wish to circumvent anxiety-inducing confrontations with two interrelated psychic structures. (1) First of these is the archaic femininity inscribed into the primal substance of semiosis. (2) The second psychic structure indexed by the cathexis of the definite in the rhetorical theory of the Renaissance is the desire of the other intensified, through perversion, to the point of maximum incandescence, maximum approximation to *jouissance*, the structure of desire inscribed into the elocutionary category of figure. The unconscious wish to circumvent confrontation with the archaic and with the desire of the other is symptomatically manifest in Renaissance rhetoric's attempt to partition, classify and thereby control the primal substance of semiosis. This unconscious wish is symptomatically manifest in the postulation of the category of trope in terms of a possessive, phallic drive for conquest, of an "Eros [tranformed into]...a means of destruction" (Lyotard, p. 200). The unconscious wish to circumvent the archaic and the confrontation with the desire of the other, a wish generating Renaissance rhetoricians' cathexis of the definite, is best manifested in those rhetoricians' theorization of the aesthetic category most privileged among the conceptually phallicized tropes: metaphor.

Why, of the many dozen elocutionary forms theorized in Renaissance treatises on the aesthetics of language, is metaphor chosen for such idealization and privileging? What about metaphor as theorized by Renaissance rhetoricians appeals to the anxiety-generated drive for definiteness, the drive subtending the theorization of the aesthetic category of trope in terms of a structure of phallic desire and allowing trope to be consistently privileged in metalinguistic treatises of the Renaissance? A philosophically-inflected psychoanalysis of the formal and conceptual properties of metaphor as theorized in Renaissance treatises on the philosophy of language exposes its idealization and privileging, albeit ultimately deconstructed, as having everything to do with two factors. (1) First of these is the phallic masculinity inscribed into the category of metaphor. (2) The second factor accounting for the privileging of metaphor in early modern rhetorical theory is its relationship to the category of the ontological, of presence and Being.

Renaissance rhetoricians and other theoreticians of language habitually theorize metaphor in terms of the semantic operation it performs. In *The English Expositor* (1616), John Bullokar theorizes this semantic operation as the "changing" of the "sense" or signification of a given signifier (unpaginated). Yet ever since Aristotle's formative theorization of metaphor in the third book of his *Rhetoric*, metaphor has been known through a constitutive formal property. This formal property constituting metaphor is the "particular" by means of which it couples a given signifier with another, semantically different signifier. This particular is metaphor's copula (Aristotle, *Rhetoric*, p. 218).

Semantically-oriented theorizations of metaphor predominating in Renaissance treatises on rhetoric describe the operation performed by metaphor as "changing" the signification of a given signifier into the signification of another signifier with which it is coupled. As a result of this rhetorical changing, the signification of the signifiers coupled in a metaphor becomes momentarily identical. This makes the nature of the metaphoric copula of which Aristotle speaks eminently clear. The metaphoric copula identifies or equates the two signifiers in question.

The metaphoric copula is an equating signifier such as "is," "are," or "am." These signifiers are derivatives, in the present tense and indicative mood, of the verb "to be."

Examples of metaphors provided by Renaissance rhetoricians foreground the predication of metaphor on the equating copula. Peacham's examples in *The Garden of Eloquence* include "Thy word *is* a Launterne unto my feete" (sig. C2). The examples Joshua Poole supplies in *Practical Rhetorick* (1663) include "Self-love *is* a meer Suffoenus," "Self-love *is* blind beyond belief" (p. 40), "They *are* Ropes of sand, Towers of Lamia, Old-wives Tales, vain Dreams" (p. 48), and "The breath of honour *is* the Zephyrus, the Favonius of the Arts" (p. 70). John Smith's examples include "You *are* the most excellent star that shines in the bright Element of beauty," "Drops of dew *are* pearls," "Flowers in the medowes *are* stars, and "The murmuring of waters *is* musick" (p. 11). Thomas Blount's examples of metaphors include "little Birds *are* Angels of the Forrests," "Whales *are* living Rocks," and "The Sea *is* a moving Earth" (p. 1, emphases mine).

In "his dame the common sinck of euery rakehels filthinesse," the example of "Metaphora" provided in Angel Day's *English Secretoire* of 1586, the copula "is" is ellipted from the surface structure, and implied by the logical relation of equivalence grammatically created between the "dame" and the "common sinck" (p. 74). The same is true of examples of metaphor furnished by Puttenham, including "His head a source of grauitie and sence, / His memory a shop of ciuill arte: / His tongue a stream of figured eloquence" (p. 149).

The signifier "is" and its correlates "am" and "are," structuring the metaphoric copula in the examples provided by Renaissance rhetoricians, receives particular, and philosophically significant, theorization in early modern treatises on grammar and logic. Expounding the use of this signifier in the "Italian tongue," John Florio describes its "tence" as "present" and "definitiue" (p. 645). R[alph] R[obinson] in *The English Grammar* (1641) (p. 59), Richard Busby in *A Short Institution of Grammar* (1647) (p. 13), and Jeremiah Wharton in *English Grammar* (1654) (p. 43) describe the signifier "is" as "speak[ing] of the time that now *is*" (emphases mine).

Martin Heidegger would theorize the time of which these Renaissance grammarians speak in relation to the copula "is" as the persistent "now of the present world" in which Being is absorbed (*The Concept of Time*, p. 16E). The present, Heidegger writes, "in making present, says pre-eminently Now! Now!" (*Being and Time*, p. 459). The "essence" of Being, Heidegger says, "lies in its 'to be,'" the verb subtending the metaphoric copula (ibid., p. 67). Lacan offers a similar observation, a-propos of the copula "to be." "Ontology," Lacan says, is "what is highlighted in language [in] the use of the copula, isolating it as a signifier" (*Seminar XX*, p. 31).

In *The English Accidence* of 1646, Joshua Poole repeats the theorization of the present tense in relation to the copula "is" (sig. A4, p. 10), and defines the "signes" of the present tense as "am, art, is, are" (p. 10). These are the signifiers of the metaphoric copula, the signifiers Heidegger would theorize as providing "an authentic assertion of Being" (*The Concept of Time*, p. 6E). Early in his treatise on grammar, Poole makes an observation regarding the signifier "is," used by other early modern theoreticians of language to exemplify the metaphoric copula. "Is," Poole says, "signifies to bee" (sig. A4).

Early modern theoreticians of language were aware of the copulaic rhetorical function of the signifier "is" even when conceptualizing it in the context of grammar as a manifestation of the present tense of the verb "to be." This is made evident in Christopher Cooper's *Grammatica Linguae Anglicanae* (1685). In Cooper's treatise, the signifier "is" is referred-to in the course of the discussion of the *"Temporibus"* (temporality) of verbs as an instance of *"Copulae"* (p. 146). Joseph Aickin's *English Grammar* (1693) provides similar evidence. In this treatise, the signifier "is" is referred-to as one of the "Copulas" (p. 12).

Aickin's treatise further underscores the conceptual connection between the present tense of the metaphoric copula and the category of Being. Aickin theorizes the present tense as "the present Instance in which we speak" (p. 10). This formulation accentuates the implication of the present tense in the state of "being present" which, Heidegger would say, has been the meaning of Being "since the early days of the Greek world" (*The Question of Being*, pp. 77, 63).

For Aickin, the present tense has an additional significance. It signifies "the Theme" (p. 10). The signifier "theme" denotes a foundational meaning-unit of language. This denotation of the signifier "theme" is related to its etymological derivation from a Greek root, *tithemi*, signifying "place." According to Heidegger, the ontological meaning of the category of place "precedes [its] political, social, or economic" significance ("An Ontological Consideration of 'Place,'" *The Question of Being*, p. 26). Ontologically, for Heidegger, "place" is a dimension "in which being can unfold and manifest its Being" (ibid.).

The tense of the metaphoric copula, the theorizations of Florio, Robinson, Busby, Wharton, Poole, and Aikin imply, is the tense of "what now is." This is the tense of the temporal present ("now") and of ontological presence ("is"). Ontological presence is what Florio calls the "definitiue"

(p. 645). The present tense, as Busby puts it, "signifies...beeing" (p. 11). In Wharton's terms, the present tense "betokeneth...beeing" (p. 42). In the grammatical treatises of Busby and Wharton, the present tense subtending the metaphoric copula is theorized in terms dependent on the ontologicality of this copula, its denotation of "to be," which makes it an articulator of Being, of the ontological.

The theorization of the tense of the metaphoric copula in Renaissance treatises on grammar aligns it with the philosophical category of presence, of the definite and the ontological, or in short, with the category of Being. Long before thinkers like Heidegger, Derrida, Lacan, or Jean-Luc Nancy were to write of the ontologicality of this copula, Renaissance theoreticians of language realized this copula was "the unique 'form' and the unique 'fundament' of Being" (Nancy, *Birth to Presence*, p. 2).

The theorization of the mood of the metaphoric copula in Renaissance treatises on grammar reinforces its alignment with Being. This mood, Florio states, may be characterized as "Indicatiue" and as "Demonstratiue" (p. 645). In *Speech and Phenomena*, Derrida theorizes the category of the indicative as assuming the possibility of reference (pp. 21, 27–29). The category of the demonstrative too is inflected toward referentiality. In Heidegger's terms, the categories of indication and demonstration in relation to which Florio conceptualizes the mood of the metaphoric copula are instances in which language becomes "a form of gesture," toward what is "ready-at-hand," conclusively there (*Being and Time*, pp. 108–114). The categories of demonstration and indication involve the possibility of a direct pointing, a direct, and graphically phallic, ostension to a conclusively, definitively given object. Such direct pointing is a grammatical manifestation of the image of the authoritatively ostended finger authors of Renaissance schoolbooks habitually used in the margins of their texts to point out pertinent rules, instances of the Law of the Father (see Wharton, p. 20; Ascham, p. 27).

R[obinson] emphasizes the definitiveness associated with the indicative mood. In his terms, the indicative mood, on which the metaphoric copula is predicated, "doth determine a thing" (p. 57). For R[obinson], the indicative mood articulates the determinate, unquestionable presence of an object. Heidegger would philosophize such unquestionable presence as the attribute of an object's being "determinable and [hence] representable," as what assures the appearance of Being (*The Question of Being*, p. 57).

In Busby's terms, the indicative mood on which the metaphoric copula is predicated "plainly affirmeth...a thing" (p. 12). In *The English Accidence*,

Joshua Poole too theorizes the indicative mood in relation to the category of a "thing" (p. 10). Like Poole, Heidegger would align the category of a "thing" with the metaphoric copula. Heidegger glosses the category of a "thing" in terms of the metaphoric copula as "anything that in any way is" (*On the Way to Language*, p. 62).

Poole's theorization of the indicative mood on which the metaphoric copula is predicated is aligned with ontology, with the category of Being, in another way. The indicative mood, Poole says, "saith plainly a thing doth...bee" (*English Accidence*, p. 10). For Poole, the indicative mood asserts the Being of a thing. The indicative mood, related by Poole to the category of a "thing," performs the ontological function Heidegger too would attribute to this category, the function of "giv[ing] Being" (*On the Way to Language*, p. 88). Early modern theorizations of the mood of the metaphoric copula already imply what Derrida was to observe concerning this copula, namely, its being the site "where the signification 'Being' is produced" ("The Supplement of Copula," *Margins of Philosophy*, p. 183), whose absence, therefore, is "absence itself" (ibid., p. 201).

The metaphoric copula as theorized in Renaissance treatises on grammar is strongly aligned with the category of Being, of the ontological as what is determinately, definitively given, what makes definite, phallic, referential ostension possible. This copula is inscribed with categoricity at its highest. The metaphoric copula is marked by a maximal degree of assertion, never attained, for example, by the optative, potential, or subjunctive mood.

The subjunctive mood "wisheth, prayeth, or desireth" (Poole, *Accidence*, p. 10). This mood is not predicated on Being but on the absence of Being, the absence Heidegger would philosophize as structuring existence as a ceaseless in-tension toward Being, (Heidegger, *Poetry, Language, Thought*, p. 4). The optative mood as theorized in early modern grammar treatises is what Lacan would call the "want-to-be," the lack of Being subtending subjectivity as desire. Desire, Lacan observes in *Seminar II*, "is a relation of being to lack. This lack is the lack of being properly speaking" (p. 223).

The indicative mood subtending the ontological copula of metaphor, as conceptualized by early modern theoreticians of language, articulates Being, not the lack of Being. The indicative mood in its early modern theorizations involves a disavowal of the optative as the mood in which, as Guy Miege puts it in *The English Grammar* (1688), "we make wishes" (p. 54). The optative mood as conceptualized by Miege is expressive of what Heidegger would call "the potentiality-for-Being" (*Being and Time*, p. 458), the potentiality structuring the erotic. This constitutively erotic potentiality is absent from early modern theorizations of the indicative.

The metaphoric copula linked with the indicative, not the optative mood brackets what Heidegger would philosophize as the constitutive "concealment of Being," its being what can only ever be proleptically grasped ahead (*The Question of Being*, p. 89). The metaphoric copula as conceptualized by early modern grammarians is predicated on a refusal to recognize what Stephen Whitworth theorizes as the impossibility of seizing definitively, ontologically ("Far from Being," p.168). The conceptual and psychic consequence of this impossibility is the existential inescapability of the erotic. The metaphoric copula as theorized by early modern grammarians involves a denial of this inescapability, an unconscious refusal to realize the way in which desire (and hence potentiality and lack) "achieve...the primitive structuration of the human world" (Lacan, *Seminar II*, p. 224). Theorizations of the metaphoric copula in early modern grammar treatises are driven by a wish to replace the erotic with the axiomatic.

The axiomatic is the unquestioned, a logical category predicated on the suspension of the structure of the question. In early modern rhetoric, the question form is theorized as the "erotema." In early modern grammar theory, the question mark is theorized as "erotesis." Early modern rhetoricians relate the form of the question to the intersubjective category of the demand and to the psychic structure of the erotic. Like Plato in his *Symposium*, and like Lacan, early modern thinkers on language transcode erotema and erotesis with the erotic (see below). Given the conceptual association of the erotema or question with the erotic in early modern language theory, theorizations of the metaphoric copula in terms of an axiomatic suspension of questioning are implicated in a psychic dynamic of the suspension of eroticism.

The suspension of the category of the question in early modern theorizations of the indicative mood subtending the metaphoric copula has a logical consequence too. This suspension places the metaphoric copula in the conceptual domain of the unquestioned absolutes of cognition, of what Derrida calls the "logical a-priori of language" (*Speech and Phenomena*, p. 8).

For Renaissance theoreticians of language, the signifier "is" constituting the metaphoric copula has everything to do with the indicative, the ontological, and the logical. For these theoreticians, the metaphoric copula has everything to do with the essence of logicality. This is evident in the treatment of the metaphoric copula in Abraham Fraunce's *Lawier's Logike* (1588). Fraunce was an avowed lover of the pastoral poetics of eroticism. He translated instances of pastoral texts and made other such instances the declared source of his *exempla* in *The Arcadian Rhetorike* (1588) and *The Shepheardes Logike* (1585). In *The Name of the Ancients*, "Far from Being," and "Passing for Mean," Stephen Whitworth has brilliantly demonstrated the centrality of the similaic, of the function of likeness, in early modern pastoral poetics. In responding to the allure of the polymorphic eroticism pastoral thematizes, Fraunce implicitly recognized the centrality of the similaic in these poetics. In *The Arcadian Rhetorike*, a rhetorical treatise flaunting its conceptual alliance with pastoral, Fraunce articulates his appreciation of the centrality of the similaic function in language and of rhetoric's attempt to deny this centrality. Unlike poetry, Fraunce says, rhetoric is "alwaies *vnlike* it selfe" (unpaginated, emphasis mine).

Although repeatedly attracted to pastoral, Fraunce is aware of the risks involved in the allure of the polymorphic eroticism structuring the aesthetics of this genre. Fraunce's *Lawier's Logike* avows its affiliation with logic, the discipline of the definite. Many of Fraunce's examples in this treatise on logic, however, come from Spenser's pastoral poetics, where "lincks of loue" passionately yearned for (*Shepheardes Calender*, Eclogue 6, line 34), all too often remain hopelessly unrequited, less than definite. The non-definiteness in love sung in the pastoral examples brought into Fraunce's treatise on logic has a formal trace, the trace of a semantic instability threatening to unsettle logical definiteness. Fraunce is aware of the formal and psychological threat entailed by the introduction of the pastoral into the logical. He speaks of this threat as the threat of "inconstancy...in words" (unpaginated).

Fraunce recognizes the impossibility of removing the threat of the non-definite and hence erotic of which he speaks. For Fraunce, the words, the semantemes of language, are constitutively less than definite. This is implied in Fraunce's imagining of words, of the semantemes of language, in relation to Horace's conventional pastoral image of "leaues" (unpaginated). Words qua leaves, Fraunce imagines, "spring before Summer" (unpaginated). They are intensely kinetic and hence constitutively erotic. For Fraunce, words qua leaves "fall before Winter" (unpaginated). They are subject to an inevitable loss. They leave, vanish, disappear. The vanishing of pastoralized leaves in Fraunce's imaginary captation of words makes words into reflections of the aphanisis, the dis-appearance of erotic objects who populate pastoral texts.

Seeking to circumvent this risk of the pastoral and/as the similaic, Fraunce composed a treatise responding to the allure not of the erotic but of the axiomatic, of "constant and philosophicall...lawe" immune to the risks of "inconstancie," of indeterminacy and aphanisis (unpaginated). In the theorization of this reassuring "lawe" seeking to escape the allure of past-orality, what predominates for Fraunce, thematically and conceptually, is the "is" function subtending the copula of metaphor.

Fraunce's stated concern in *The Lawier's Logike* is to establish principles of thinking providing "certayne knowledge" (p. 5), knowledge of an order avoiding an aphanistic fall of the type he aligns with words qua pastoralized leaves. He seeks knowledge of a type which would not involve "falling...headlong into diuers delusions and...conceipts" (ibid.). Fraunce seeks a type of certain, definite knowledge avoiding the risks entailed by indulgence in ludic imaginings and conceived fantasies. He seeks a kind of knowledge not dependent on the articulation of conceived ludic fantasies in rhetorical conceits. In "Far from Being," Stephen Whitworth has shown how in early modern thinking of the linguistic and/as the psychic, non-metaphorical conceits constitute "a type of writing...best described as unconscious" (p. 157), a kind of writing aligned with fantasy and dream, the writing of pastoral. The risks Fraunce seeks to avoid in his theorizations of the language of logic and the law are the risks of the "pleasurable shattering" (ibid., p. 158) involved in falling into the unconscious pastoral thematizes through its verses and institutes in its rhetorical conceits.

What logic proffers, according to Fraunce, is the reverse of this frightening yet, as his translated pastorals and pastoralized treatises on logic and rhetoric well demonstrate, alluring fall into the unconscious. For Fraunce, logic proffers a "firme [and] constant" cognition (*Lawier's Logike*, p. 8). Cognition of this type is definitely, statically fixed. It poses no risk of ever being "inconstan[t]" like the archaic, pastoral Horatian image of leaving leaves anxiously invoked by Fraunce in the beginning of his treatise on logic as what he wishes to avoid. The "certeine and immutable" cognition Fraunce seeks is non-changeable, not even potentially running the risk of aphanisis.

The logical category which most reassures Fraunce of the circumvention of the risks of aphanisis inseparable from the allure of pastoral poetics is the category most intimately allied with the metaphoric copula: the axiom. Like the metaphoric copula as theorized by early modern grammarians, the axiom, as theorized by Fraunce, has everything to do with the category of Being. Fraunce theorizes the axiom as a statement by means of which we "iudge" something "eyther to bee or not to bee" (ibid., p. 87).

In Fraunce's theorization, what grants the axiom the ability to perform the ontological judgment of "to bee or not to bee" is its structural predication on a "bande" (ibid., p. 86) or copula. Fraunce describes this copula as the "affirmatiue" (p. 88). He provides the following *exempla* for the axiom: "Plato *is* a learned disputer" (ibid., p. 87), "A man *is* apt to laugh, A man *is* reasonable...Logike *is* an Arte of reasoning" (ibid., p. 89, emphases mine). In all these *exempla,* the affirmative copula of the axiom is identical to the metaphoric copula.

The reverse of the affirmative, the negative, Fraunce explains, cannot ever be axiomatic since it "doth but deprive and take away" (ibid., p. 88). The negative, for Fraunce, is aligned with the loss he associates with leav-ing, with lack. In Lacanian terms, lack subtends the erotic. What Fraunce seeks to flee in *The Lawiers Logike* is the negativity of Eros, of desire. He seeks to flee the falling and leaving structurally and thematically constitutive of the eroticized poetics of pastoral to which, his use of the pastoral images of falling leaves and of pastoral *exempla* suggest, he remains irresistibly drawn.

Fraunce's affirmative axiomatic copula involves the negation of negativity. The axiomatic copula as he theorizes it is inscribed with the negation of the eroticism structurally and conceptually aligned with negativity. Fraunce's axiomatic copula is inscribed with the denial of desire. The axiomatic copula or "bande" can only be, for Fraunce, a copula bound up with the refusal to recognize the negativity and lack structuring desire. Fraunce's axiomatic copula can only be a function of absolute, totalizing affirmation. The signifier articulating such totalizing affirmation, Fraunce's *exempla* of the axiomatic copula indicate, is the ontological "is," or its parallels "are" and "am," the copulas subtending the aesthetic category of metaphor.

The metaphoric copula is implicated in Fraunce's theorization of the axiomatic in other ways. This copula is invoked in Fraunce's articulation of the logical rule of *"vniuersaliter primum"* (p. 89). According to this rule of logic, as theorized by Fraunce, the signifiers "ioyned together" in the axiom must have a particular logical relationship between them. They must be "equall" to one another (ibid.). Elsewhere in his treatise on logic, Fraunce theorizes the logical function of the "Aequall," which he considers the substrate of the axiomatic copula, as the function of "same[ness]" (p. 75). The relation between the signifiers coupled in the axiom, as theorized by Fraunce, is identical with the relation theorized by Renaissance rhetoricians as obtaining between the signifiers coupled in a metaphor.

Theorizations of metaphor in early modern treatises on rhetoric foreground the function of making two signifiers same, equal, one, attributed to the axiom in Fraunce's *Lawier's Logike*. In Dudley Fenner's *Artes of Logike and Rhetorike* (1588), "the excellence and finesse of [metaphor]" is said to be "most excellent, when shut up in *one* [word]" (unpaginated, emphasis mine). In John Newton's *Introduction to the Art of Rhetoric* (1671), metaphor is theorized as an aesthetic form "by which we express ourselves by *a* word" (p. 1, emphasis mine). Puttenham too mentions metaphor among the categories of elocution based on unitary "single words" (p. 148). In *The Arcadian Rhetorike*, Fraunce describes metaphor's "excellencie" as "singular" (sig. B3). The alliance of metaphor with the category of the One appears in a later treatise, Daniel Turner's *Abstract of English Grammar and Rhetoric* (1741). In Turner's treatise, metaphor is theorized as "the putting of *one* word for another" (p. 45, emphasis mine). The categories of metaphor and of the axiom are theorized by early modern thinkers on language as the semiotic production of a One.

Modern thinkers emphasize the relationship of the One with the totality of a closed circuit. Jean-Luc Nancy diagnoses the fantasy of unicity as involving a solipsistic illusion, the illusion of the presence of the "I" to itself as self-same (*The Birth to Presence*, p. 3). The functions of unicity and sameness early modern thinkers inscribe into the metaphoric copula are conceptually aligned with solipsistic totalization. For Lacan, totalization is the hallmark of the discourse of the master. This discourse is predicated on a non-recognition of plurality. It "masks the division of the subject" (*Seminar XVII*, p. 118). Another aspect of totalizing unicity is its alignment with the phallic. The fantasy of totalizing, "universal" (rather than momentary) "fusion," Lacan would say, is the phallic fantasy *par excellence* (*Seminar XX*, pp. 7, 10). The fantasy of "unicity," Luce Irigaray too remarks, is the mark of "the reign of the phallus" (*This Sex*, p. 26). In not recognizing plurality and division in subjectivity, the totalizing and solipsistic discourse of the master with which metaphor in its early modern theorizations is allied is embroiled with what I call phallic desire, desire predicated on the desubjectivation of the other, on the production of the other as low-Other.

The relation of sameness Fraunce inscribes into the axiomatic copula is a relation which does not and cannot recognize the constitutive separateness of signifiers and of subjects who share with signifiers a differential structure. The separateness denied in the axiomatic copula as theorized by Fraunce is the condition of a meaningful joining in which subjects or signifiers retain their difference yet are transferentially transformed. For Lacan, in transference, speech, as joint of the emergence of desire (*Seminar II*, p. 234), "links [two] subjects together into [a] pact which transforms them" (*Seminar I*, p. 108).

The work of "linking" presupposes separation. The copula of transference, in Montrelay's terms, maintains the condition of separation (*se séparer*), so as to allow for a pairing coeval with a comparing and adornment of one's self (*se parer*) with the other (p. 151). The copula of transference is what the equating copula of the axiom, as theorized by Fraunce, is not. In equating, the copula of the axiom structuring the aesthetic category of metaphor is "gulped down" (Derrida, *Glas*, p. 66). In equating, the axiomatic-metaphoric copula is "properly consum(mated)" (ibid.), to produce a s(e)amless, continuous sameness. In producing absolute sameness, the axiomatic-metaphoric copula forecloses transference and consumes, annihilates, destroys the couple or pair.

In the condition of subjectivity as separation and hence desire Oneness is an impossibility. The constitutively differential structure of the signifier, and of the subject as a "discontinuity in the real" verified by a "cut in the signifying chain" (Lacan, *Écrits*, p. 299), confirms scission. Within the condition of intrasubjective and intersubjective scission, "the One...no sooner thought, stops being unique" and is at least double (Jabès, *Unsuspected Subversion*, p. 21). The One cannot be thought. It can only ever be misrecognized in an imaginary captation of universal fusion. The price of this imaginary captation is the imagining subject's alienation from the schisms and fragments structuring the unconscious and the truth of desire. Another price of this imaginary captation is the denial of the subjectivity of the other. This denial precludes transference.

The Oneness and sameness Fraunce inscribes into the axiomatic-metaphoric copula is implicated in a structure of desire reversing the structure of perversion he and other Renaissance rhetoricians inscribe into the aesthetic category of figure. In the structure of desire Fraunce inscribes into the axiomatic-metaphoric copula, the subject does not transform herself into an instrument for the *jouissance* of the other. Instead, the subject de-subjectifies the other, makes the other into an Other object of her solipsistic pleasure in psychic or sexual possession and control. In Levinas's terms, the structure of desire inscribed into the axiomatic-metaphoric copula in Fraunce's theorization involves "transmuting the alterity," the uniqueness of the other "in the universal immanence of the Same" (*Basic Philosophical Writings*, p. 11). This solipsistic, egocentric structure of desire as possession and control of the other as object or low-Other is, I suggested in the previous chapter, aligned with phallic desire and phallic *jouissance*.

In *The Lawier's Logike*, Fraunce theorizes the axiomatic copula as conceptually ontological and, inseparably, conceptually phallic, aligned with the phallus in its repressive deployment as a powerful, privileged signifier seeking to legislate the advent of desire. Even more pervasively, Fraunce aligns the axiomatic copula with a structure of phallic desire, a structure de-subjectifying the other and making the other an enslaved object. In phallic desire, the other is made an instrument used to fulfill the subject's phallic fantasy of totalizing control. Phallic desire is predicated on the subject's refusal to recognize completion as "the kiss of death" (Jabès, *From the Book to the Book*, p. 140). Forgetting what Levinas calls "the resistance of the other to the Same" (*Basic Philosophical Writings*, p. 14), the subject trapped in phallic desire insistently misrecognizes completion as an alluring fantasy of the presumed fulfillments of the Same, of s(e)amless identity, of universal fusion.

The axiomatic copula predicated on the relation of sameness is formally identical with the metaphoric copula. The inscription of sameness into the axiomatic-metaphoric copula indicates the extent to which the ontologicality of this copula has a phallic inflection. This phallic inflection, I argue below, is inscribed overdeterminately, albeit unstably, into early modern theorizations of the aesthetic category of metaphor, and into Fraunce's own theorization of the axiomatic copula in *The Lawier's Logike*.

The term axiom, Fraunce writes in *The Lawier's Logike*, derives from the "Greeke woorde" *axios*, which "signifieth dignitie, authoritie" (p. 87). The etymology of the axiomatic as Fraunce construes it has to do with a status of elevation and privilege inseparable from the right to "iudge" (ibid.) and to exercise power. This right to rule is attributed to the phallus as a privileged signifier, "elevat[ed]," in the symbolic, "to the place of centralized standard of objects of drive" (Goux, *Symbolic Economies*, p. 3). Fraunce's phallicization of the ontological axiomatic-metaphoric copula is evident in his description of this "affirmatiue" copula as providing "certein" knowledge (*Lawier's Logike*, p. 88). Fraunce theorizes the metaphoric copula as proffering knowledge of the same "certaine and immutable," unquestioned, categorical order he believes logic as a whole can provide (ibid., p. 8).

For Fraunce, logic is a locus of regulatory "framing" (ibid., sig. B2), and of "ordering and disposing" (ibid., p. 6). The category of "disposing" with which Fraunce aligns logic has a conceptual affinity with the early modern "gynecological conception of the male as 'disposing' the female in generation" (Parker, *Literary Fat Ladies*, p. 116). In the Aristotelian tradition of thought, the "masculine principle of generation" is the category of the phallus (Goux, "The Phallus," p. 46). The misrecognition of knowledge as immutable, an attitude Fraunce attributes to the axiomatic, is an attribute of what Lacan calls the discourse of the master (*Seminar XVII*, p. 23), a master signifier or system of signifiers authoritatively and authoritarianly "representing a subject for all other signifiers" (ibid., p. 31). Because the discourse of the master as theorized by Lacan occupies a privileged position with respect to other signifiers, it functions, in Goux's terms, as a general equivalent. The discourse of the master is isomorphic with "the centralized standard of objects of drive," the phallus (Goux, *Symbolic Economies*, p. 3). Certain knowledge of the type Fraunce transcodes with the logical category of the axiom and with the system of logic in its entirety is of the order of the phallic.

Fraunce believes axioms and the system of logic of which axioms are the conceptual kernel can provide certain, categorical knowledge. Knowledge of this type is inflected as phallic by his imaginary captation of the epistemological effects of the axiomatic copula. This copula, Fraunce writes, "dooth...imprint" categorical, axiomatic knowledge "in man's minde" (p. 8). Fraunce imagines the axiomatic copula as being of the order of what "imprint[s]," what bestows an imprint or definite form on the substance of "man's minde[s]." In Goux's terms, Fraunce imagines the axiomatic copula as what bestows conceptually paterial, phallic pattern on inert, conceptually maternal matter and numismatically coins this matter (*Symbolic Economies*, p. 222).

Fraunce's numismatic theorization of the axiomatic copula aligns it with Peacham's theorization of the aesthetic category of metaphor whose copula is formally identical with the axiomatic copula. Metaphors, Peacham writes in *The Garden of Eloquence* (1577), "leave...a firme impression in the memory...they are as seals upon soft wax, or as deep stamps in long lasting mettall" (unpaginated). Here metaphor is theorized by means of the image of imprinting a pattern on a material ingot. In Peacham's theorization of metaphor, the vocabulary of elocution is crossed with the vocabularies of numismatics and of sexual difference. The difference between the stamp and the stamped, form and formed, implicit in Peacham's numismatic theorization of metaphor and Fraunce's numismatic theorization of the axiomatic-qua-metaphoric copula is based on what Jean-Joseph Goux diagnoses as "the inaugural opposition of metaphysics." This is the opposition between pattern and material, *pater* and *mater*, male and female ("The Phallus," p. 46). In the context of this opposition, "the male is associated with the transmission of a pattern, a model," while the female "is merged with what is other in relation to constant ideal form:...with amorphous, transitory, inessential material" (Goux, *Symbolic Economies*, p. 222). The signifier organizing this formative opposition is the phallus (Goux, "The Phallus," p. 46), the signifier supposed to rule over "objects of drive" (Goux, *Symbolic Economies*, p. 20).

The phallicization of metaphor evident in Peacham's numismatic theorization is borne out by the sexually-inflected theorization of this aesthetic category in Thomas Hobbes's *Art of Rhetoric* (1681). "Metaphors please," Hobbes writes, "for they beget in us by the Genus" (sig. A2). Hobbes theorizes metaphor as a procreative force, whose role, like the role of the patriarchs represented in biblical chronicles, is to perpetuate the "Genus" to which he belongs. In biblical chronologies such as "Terah begat Abram, Nahor and Haran...and Haran begat Lot" (Genesis 11:27), the function of "begetting" (הולדה) which the Vulgate had translated more accurately as one male's becoming the *"patrem"* (father) of the next, is to perpetuate the patrilineal chain of sons, to replicate the genus of male heirs, to ensure filiation. In Hobbes's theorization of metaphor, this patriarchal role of the father to perpetuate his seed by putting forth male offspring is designated as a source of metaphor's ability to "please." In a later treatise, John Milner's *Rhetoric* (1736), too, metaphor is associated with male procreation. Milner describes metaphor as endowed with the ability to "give life" (p. 16). Like Hobbes, Milner makes the masculinization of metaphor a source of its value. Milner transcodes metaphor's ability to "give life" with its aesthetic value, its ability to bestow "beauty" on "the meanest subject" (ibid.). Abraham Fraunce aligns metaphor with the generational qua erectional too. He theorizes metaphor as a linguistic means of bestowing "life and action" and as "loftie" (*Arcadian Rhetorike*, unpaginated).

The alignment of metaphor with a phallic masculinity giving pleasure and ensuring procreation in the early modern treatises of Hobbes and Fraunce finds an echo in the writing of a contemporary theorist of language, Georges Bataille. Bataille observes a conceptual connection, of which his early modern predecessors were aware, between "the copula of terms" and the "copulation of bodies." This observation is followed by an assertion according to which the metaphorical phrase "I AM THE SUN" results in an "integral erection" ("The Solar Anus," *Visions of Excess*, p. 5). For Bataille as for Hobbes, the copula of metaphor has everything to do with the erectional male organ of copulation. Bataille aligns metaphor with phallic masculinity in the register of the real qua speaking body. Hobbes's more extensive theorization aligns this copula with phallic masculinity in the registers of the real and the symbolic as locus of the law. Hobbes's imaginary captation of metaphor aligns metaphor with the phallus as a master signifier of a patrilineal ideology and with the anatomical point of reference of the phallus in the male body.

In all registers, metaphor in Hobbes's theorization is aligned with a phallic masculinity as a source of life, of pleasure, of value. Inversely put, this theorization aligns the phallus with the rhetorical form of metaphor. The in-forming copula of metaphor ("is"), the examples of metaphor provided by early modern rhetoricians make evident, is the logical copula *par excellence*, the copula of the logical category theorized as articulating the most categorical assertion, the axiom. The alignment of the metaphoric copula, phallic masculinity, and logicality in Hobbes's theorization of metaphor confirms Lacan's insight, in "The Signification of the Phallus," concerning the conceptual connection between "the phallus as privileged signifier" and "the (logical) copula" (*Écrits*, p. 287).

The logical copula, Lacan observes in the same essay, is aligned with the phallus "in the literal (typographical) sense of the term" (ibid.). In theorizations of language of the English Renaissance, this alignment is perhaps better evident than in Lacan's native French. In these theorizations, the first character of the logical/metaphoric copula is "i" (or "I"). This character is (typo)graphically reminiscent of the male sexual organ as an anatomical point of reference for the phallus as master signifier (Lacan, *Écrits*, p. 232).

Early modern theorizations of the character "i" confirm its phallic inflection. In Joseph Aickin's *English Grammar*, the rule provided for the pronunciation of this character involves the injunction to move the tongue "fiercely" to the palate (p. 8). This is an injunction to force, to phallic power. Similar injunctions do not appear in the rules for the pronunciation of other vowels. In the pronunciation of "a," Aickin recommends, the "mouth" should be "open," receptive and hence conceptually feminine (ibid.). The recommended pronunciation of "o" with the "lips drawn round" invokes a similar graphic image of conceptually feminine penetrability and receptivity.

John Busby's *Short Institution of Grammar* and Ben Jonson's *English Grammar* (1640) foreground another phallicizing attribute of the character "I" in the upper case. "I" is a "numericall letter" (Jonson, p. 35). The numerical value of "I" is "*Unum*" (one) (Busby, p. 1). "I" becomes conceptually aligned with the philosophical concept of the One of universal fusion. In Fraunce's *Lawier's Logike*, the category of the One is inscribed into the equating copula of the axiom. This copula is identical with the copula of metaphor as it appears in the *exempla* of rhetoricians such as Puttenham, Peacham, and Blount. The copula of metaphor is graphically and conceptually aligned with the category of the phallic, and inseparably, with the category of the totalizing One.

The phallic inflection of the typo-graphical character "i" inaugurating the metaphoric copula in English is evident in early modern theorizations of its graphic inversion, the exclamation mark "!," or, as Renaissance theoreticians were wont to call it, "ecphonesis." The signifier "ecphonesis" derives from the Greek prefix *ec* (outside or beyond) and *phoneo* (speech). Etymologically, this signifier denotes what is outside phonesis or speech. The conceptualization of the exclamation mark as outside speech anticipates Theodore Adorno's theorization of exclamation marks as "gestures of authority with which the writer tries to impose an emphasis external to the matter itself" (pp. 92–93). For Adorno, the exclamation mark appeals to the modality of absolute assertion, of the axiomatic, the modality subtending the theorization of the copula "is" in Fraunce's *Lawier's Logike*.

For Renaissance theoreticians of language, the exclamation was, as Adorno was to diagnose, aligned with authority, with the law embodied by the Name of the Father and with the phallus as the master signifier to which the law gravitates. This is evident in Wharton's theorization of ecphonesis in erectile terms, as a particle which "raiseth the tone" and "always requireth a louder sound" (p. 86). The loud sound with which Wharton associates ecphonesis is a trace of what Adorno calls an "incursion of subjective will" (p. 93). This is a phallic psychic manoeuvre akin to the discourse of the master as theorized by Lacan, wherein one subject, assuming the position of mastery and authority, presumes a totalizing representation of truth, thereby negating the right to representation of other subjects and in effect de-subjectifying them.

For Adorno, the phallic authoritarianism of ecphonesis is manifest aurally, in the tone in which it is spoken. This authoritarianism is manifest visually too. The exclamation mark, Adorno observes, "looks like an index finger raised in warning" (p. 91), a gesture bespeaking threatening power. This gesture is graphically phallic. This gesture is the verticalization, and hence erection, of the authoritative gesture of ostension. The graphic trace of this authoritative gesture, the pointing finger, often appears in the margins of early modern schoolbooks, articulations of the symbolic in its repressive function. The grammatical embodiment of this gesture of ostension is the indicative mood, the mood subtending the metaphoric copula.

In Adorno's theorization of the exclamation mark, in early modern theorizations of ecphonesis, and in Hobbes's theorization of metaphor as begetting, the linguistic is conceptualized by means of erectional images. Early modern theorizations of ecphonesis and Hobbes's theorization of metaphor bear out Phillipe Lacoue-Labarthe's observation concerning the ubiquitous connections made in the western philosophical tradition between categories of writing and those of "engenderment...procreation, [and] insemination" (*Typography*, pp. 127–128). The philosophical function of these connections, Lacoue-Labarthe observes, is "assuring the schematization of chaos through its organization" (ibid., p. 179), an observation supported by the findings of this book regarding the drive for control over a primal substance of semiosis phobically imagined to be chaotic and unpredictable.

Early modern theorizations of the linguistic categories of ecphonesis and of metaphor, whose English copula starts with "i," the graphic inverse of ecphonesis, are phallic categories aligned with images of insemination. The phallic categories of metaphor and ecphonesis in their early modern theorizations are caught up in an attempt to stabilize a primal substance of semiosis imagined in maternalized terms of unpredictable diffusion.

Ecphonesis is connected with the metaphoric copula graphically, by virtue of its being the inversion of the first character of this copula in its English version, which like ecphonesis typographically manifests phallic ostension. Early modern grammarians connect ecphonesis with the metaphoric copula conceptually, via a similar alignment with the indicative mood subtending the theorization of the metaphoric copula. Early modern logicians such as Fraunce align ecphonesis with the axiomatic, categorical modality subtending the theorizations of the metaphoric copula.

Ecphonesis as conceptualized by early modern theoreticians of language is connected with the phallus as master signifier, and with phallic desire as a psychic structure wherein the subject constructs herself as a fully authoritative master. This psychic construction involves the negation of the subjectivity of the other and a concomitant imaginary inflation of the subject's ego to the point of an illusory self-sufficiency which is nothing more than a dangerous solipsism. Ecphonesis, writes Guy Miege, occurs, like the period or full stop with which Jeremiah Wharton too aligns ecphonesis (p. 86), "when the Sense is full" (p. 123), when an articulation is judged to be complete, sufficient unto itself. This is a judgment structurally coextensive with the subject's misrecognition of her psychic self-sufficiency within the economy of phallic desire, an economy obstructing *jouissance*. Because it involves the de-subjectivation of the other, the economy of phallic desire precludes a transferential, intersubjective erotic economy. In a transferential erotic economy made impossible by phallic desire, two subjects, recognizing their incompleteness, address to one another demands which could only ever be partially, fragmentarily fulfilled (Lacan, *Écrits*, pp. 263, 265, 311), demands whose partial fulfillment is what constitutes desire qua eroticism.

Long before Lacan, early modern rhetoricians implicitly recognized the connection between demand (rather than satisfaction) and eroticism. They recognized this connection when they theorized the rhetorical form of the demand as the erotema (see Chapter One above), and the typographical character of the question mark, the diametrical opposite of ecphonesis, as "erotesis" (for instance, Wharton, p. 86). In early modern theorizations of language, ecphonesis, typographically the inverted reflection of the character "i" inaugurating the metaphoric copula in the English language, is not aligned with the erotic and/as transferential (Lacan, *Seminar I*, pp. 108–112). Ecphonesis is aligned with the economy of phallic desire, an economy whose point of reference is not the other but the ego, misrecognized, in an imaginary captation, as possessing self-sufficiency and omnipotence.

"I," the English signifier for the ego, is yet another typographical mark of the One and the phallus. The phallically aggressive inflection of the character "I" is accentuated in Ben Jonson's choice to theorize it as a "letter of double power" and as the binary opposite of the character "O," which he describes as marked by "change and uncertainty," by a castrative epistemological indefiniteness (*English Grammar*, p. 39).

Via its typographical link with ecphonesis as conceptualized by early modern theoreticians of language, the metaphoric copula is aligned with the phallus. Via this typographical link with ecphonesis, the metaphoric copula is aligned with phallic desire, and with the imaginary captation of the ego as a self-sufficient and omnipotent "I," self-present to itself as what Hegel calls a "pure self-contained unity" (*Logic*, p. 168). The relation of the metaphoric to self-presence and phallic desire is confirmed and overdetermined by the phonic resonance within its first syllable of the Latin first-person possessive "*me*." In Latin, "*me*" designates the self's sovereignty over itself and over whatever it comes to designate as its owned objects, rather than co-subjects with whom a transferential relation is possible.

For early modern rhetoricians, the category of metaphor is aligned with the "I" as the typographical mark of the phallus, the numerical inscription of the One, and the hubristically inflated ego. This is manifest in Abraham Fraunce's theorization of metaphor in *The Arcadian Rhetorike* in terms of a homophone of the "I," the eye, the sensory organ in relation to which Thomas Blount and John Hoskyns too theorize metaphor (Blount, p. 2; Hoskyns, p. 8). Metaphor, Fraunce writes in his rhetorical treatise, is at its best "if it be applied to the sense, & among the senses chiefly to the eie, which is the quickest of all the senses" (sig. B2). Fraunce aligns metaphor with the eye as the most privileged of senses. This is evidenced in his reference to metaphor by means of a superlative ("quickest") and by means of an image of rulership, the "chief" or monarch form isomorphic with the functions of father and phallus (Goux, *Symbolic Economies*, p. 21). In the *Treatise of Schemes and Tropes* (1550), Richard Sherry too writes of metaphor in terms of the visual, as the trope "shew[ing] the thyng before oure eyes mo[st] euidently" (unpaginated). Fraunce and Sherry theorize metaphor in relation to the visual in what Levinas would describe as its totalizing, phallic deployment as the universally totalizing "mastering grasp of [Being]" (*Outside the Subject*, p. 115).

The description of the eye as the sensory organ closest to the mind, to reason and logos, was a Renaissance commonplace. This commonplace transcoding of the ocular and visual with the rational, the logical, the understandable, or, as Shakespeare's Othello would have it, with the conclusively provable, has significant conceptual consequences. This transcoding creates an opposition between the visual and the oral/aural, the sensory functions early modern rhetoricians and writers of pastoral align with primal, past-oral pleasures connected with archaic maternality (see Chapter One above).

Fraunce was a translator of the pastorals of Virgil and Tasso and a lover of pastoral poetry. This is well-evident in the references to shepherds and to Arcadia in the titles of his treatises on logic and rhetoric (see Chapter One above). In aligning metaphor with the eye, Fraunce was following a theorization of one of the writers of pastoral he cherished, Sir Philip Sidney, whose *Arcadia* (1580) is the source of many of Fraunce's examples for rhetorical categories. In *The Defense of Poesy* (1581), Sidney, assuming a pedagogical as much as, and perhaps more than, a pastoral stance, describes the function of poetry as a whole as the providing of "delight" in addition to teaching (p. 217). In the dedication to his translations of Tasso's pastorals, Fraunce too makes the production of delight the principal end of poetry. In Sidney's theorization, as Stephen Whitworth has brilliantly argued in "Far from Being" (p. 160), the pedagogical thrust of poetry, its appeal to the rational, conscious mind rather than to the delights accessing the unconscious, is said to be achieved by means of "speak[ing] metaphorically" (Sidney, *Defense*, p. 217). Sidney elides the pedagogical function of speaking metaphorically with the function of "speaking pictures" (ibid.), of making an object or idea "be seen by the eyes of the mind" (ibid., p. 215). Fraunce's alignment of metaphor with the eye taps into a similar alignment in the *Defense* of Sidney, one of his avowed masters. In Sidney's *Defense*, metaphor and the eye are aligned with the understanding, and with the rational mind to which the teaching function of poetry appeals. The delighting function of poetry does not appeal to the rational mind. The delighting function of poetry appeals to the unconscious. The alignment of metaphor with the eye, with the rational mind, and with the teaching function of poetry, opposes metaphor to the unconscious. Metaphor becomes associated with the repression, if not the total foreclosure, of unconscious, past-oral delights by the hubristic fixation on the homophone of the eye and the "I" as consciously apprehended ego, "an irreducible kernel of self-constitution" (Nancy, *Birth to Presence*, p. 9).

The alignment of metaphor in early modern theorizations of language with categories providing a reassuring sense of groundedness, definiteness, categoricity, identity, presence, and Being, and the transcoding of metaphor with the phallus, enable a significant semiotic operation to be performed with regard to metaphor. This alignment sets metaphor apart from other aesthetic categories conceptualized in treatises on rhetoric. Unlike metaphor, these other rhetorical categories are not theorized in terms of an absolute ontological plenitude and absolute epistemic certainty. Unlike metaphor, they are not theorized as isomorphs of the phallus as master signifier and the erectile penis as the anatomical point of reference of the phallus. Rhetorical categories other than metaphor are not aligned with life-granting sexual potency and political power.

The alignment of metaphor with the phallus, with presence, with Being, foregrounds the ontological, epistemological, and sexual-political lack of other aesthetic categories with respect to metaphor. The alignment of metaphor with the phallus and with Being necessarily makes metaphor function as a standard of value in relation to the other aesthetic categories constituting the set of rhetorical forms of which it is a part. In *Symbolic Economies*, Jean-Joseph Goux defines the standard of a symbolic "set" as a signifier of this set which becomes prioritized, hegemonic, invested with a "privileged representativeness and even with a monopoly on representativeness within the...set" (p. 10). Goux calls this privileged signifier a "general equivalent" (ibid.). In Goux's terms, metaphor functions as the "general equivalent" for other forms of elocution. Metaphor in Renaissance rhetoric is isomorphic with gold in the economic sphere and with the phallus, the master signifier with which Renaissance rhetoricians transcode metaphor, in the sphere of the objects of drive.

According to Goux, a general equivalent's "accession to power" is "accompanied by excommunication." "The sovereign element, as universal equivalent," Goux continues, "itself has no equivalent; it is out of the ordinary, placed for this reason outside the community it governs. It is cut out, subtracted, withdrawn. It legislates as an exception" (*Symbolic Economies*, p. 31).

Early modern rhetoricians conceived of metaphor as the general equivalent of elocution, the elocutionary form "economizing all the others" (Derrida, "White Mythology," *Margins of Philosophy*, p. 221). This is evident in the superlative expressions they attach to metaphor, expressions representing metaphor as a measure and standard of value for other elocutionary forms. John Spenser describes metaphor as the "most suitable for the Orator" (*A Storehouse of Similes* [1658], p. 3). In *The Arcadian Rhetorike*, Abraham Fraunce singles metaphor out as the "most excellent" form of elocution (sig. B1). In *The Arte of English Poesie* (1589), Puttenham speaks of metaphor as the "most commendable" of elocutionary forms (p. 150). In all three of these cases, metaphor is theorized in terms of a category of value ("most") glossed by William Walker as expressing the "*Summum*" or "maxim[al]" (p. 63). In the same spirit, Sturmius praises metaphor as the linguistic activity in which "an imitator may mo[st] glorie" (p. 38). No other trope or figure, Sherry writes in *The Treatise of Schemes and Tropes*, "persuadeth more effecteouslye...none moweth more mightily the affecions, none maketh the oracion more goodlye" (unpaginated). No other trope, John Smith writes, is "more excellent and...beautiful" (p. 9). In all these cases, metaphor is represented in relation to other members of the set of elocutionary forms of which it is a part. In all of them, its value is found to exceed the value of all other forms. Metaphor is theorized in early modern treatises on the aesthetics of rhetoric in accordance with the excommunicating logic of the general equivalent, the logic wherein exclusion and transcendence are the consequences of investments of value and sovereignty in a particular member of a symbolic set.

The logic of general equivalence informing early modern theorizations of metaphor has everything to do with another general equivalent, phallic masculinity. This is evident in the erectile imagery in which metaphor's general equivalence is stated, the same imagery allowing the penis to become the anatomical reference point for the phallus as master signifier (Goux, *Symbolic Economies*, p. 28; Lacan, *Écrits*, p. 287). Quoting Longinus, Thomas Blount describes metaphors as being "of excellent use," and "much conducing to *height* in eloquence." Blount declares it "unfit" for metaphor to be "lower than the Heaven," the supreme level of the cosmological hierarchy (*The Academie of Eloquence* [1654], p. 2, emphasis mine).

In many early modern treatises on the aesthetic of rhetoric, the evaluative precedence granted metaphor by the superlatives cited above is accompanied by a sequential precedence. Hoskyns, Blount, Wilson, Smith, Puttenham, and Sherry pour lavish praise upon metaphor, and choose it to open their elaborate taxonomies of many dozens of forms of elocution. Fraunce, in *The Arcadian Rhetorike*, opens his taxonomy of forms of elocution with metaphor. In Renaissance treatises on the aesthetics of rhetoric, metaphor almost invariably comes first, evaluatively, sequentially, or both. The economic-philosophical repercussions of this temporal priority granted metaphor are made explicit in Peacham's *Garden of Eloquence*, where the choice to place metaphor first among nearly two hundred linguistic forms is glossed by the author's exposition of the principle of temporal "order":

> an apt and meete placing of words among themselves...when the *worthiest* word is set *first*...as we say me [sic] and women; Sunne and Mone...the King and his Nobles...And not Women and men, Mone and Sunne...the Nobles and the King...which in common speech is foolish. (sig. N2, emphases mine)

In *The Arte of Rhetorique* (1560), Wilson expounds a similar principle. In the order of speech, he maintains, "the *worthier* is preferred, and *set before*. As a man is sette before a woman" (p. 234, emphases mine). This acknowledged association of precedence in syntactic sequence with "worth" and the specific privileges of men and kings indicates the complicity of Peacham's and Wilson's placing of metaphor with the logic of patriarchy. Within the logic of patriarchy, priority in temporal structure "has hierarchical superiority as its con-sequence or result" (Parker, *Literary Fat Ladies*, p. 179). This patriarchal logic is at work in the readings of the Genesis myth of creation by humanist theologians, in which the coming first of the male is taken as an index to his superiority (ibid.). By the force of this logic of order, Peacham implies, the conceptual privilege of other primates (or, in modern parlance, general equivalents) should be defined. In the Renaissance treatises of Peacham and Wilson, metaphor is theorized as the primate of tropes, isomorphic and transcodable with other privileged categories such as the sun, the king, and the male. In this context, placing metaphor first among tropes puts it in line with categories endowed with the utmost social and political power, the categories of monarch form, father, and phallus, the general equivalents of which Goux was to speak (*Symbolic Economies*, p. 13).

The transcodability of general equivalents Goux points out is at work in early modern theorizations of metaphor. This is evident, for example, in Sherry's description of metaphor as the "cheyf" virtue of speech (*Schemes and Tropes*, unpaginated). Sherry theorizes metaphor as masculine and as an isomorph of the monarch form, a homologue of the phallus. John Smith similarly theorizes metaphor as tending to "majesty" (p. 9).

The transcodability of metaphor with general equivalents is yet more evident in Ramist treatises, such as Fraunce's *Arcadian Rhetorike* and Fenner's *Artes of Logike and Rhetorike*. Peter Ramus (d. 1572) subjected rhetoric to a logocentric systematization, imposing upon it "definitions and divisions leading to still further definitions and divisions, until every last particle of matter had been dissected and disposed of" (Ong, *Orality and Literacy*, p. 134). One of the results of this logocentric, paterialist systematization of rhetorical "matter" was the reduction of the long list of tropes and figures featured in figurist rhetorics to the four "master tropes": metaphor, metonymy, synecdoche, and irony. In Ramist treatises, in accordance with the logocentric principles of Peter Ramus (Joseph, pp. 35–36), metaphor is theorized as a "master trope" and thus aligned with the position of mastery, of authority.

In early modern treatises on language, the position of mastery inscribed into metaphor as "master trope" is ascribed to the teacher, referenced in the title of Roger Ascham's influential pedagogical tract of 1570, *The Scholemaster*. The early modern schoolmaster is the teacher of the precepts of the symbolic as formulated in the disciplines of grammar, logic, and rhetoric. At the beginning and at the end of his *English Grammar*, Joseph Aickin describes the schoolmaster as the representative, for his "scholars," of the "father" (pp. 1, 35). In Sherry's translation of Erasmus's tract on education, which he appended to his *Treatise of Schemes and Tropes*, the schoolmaster is described as being the embodiment of the "office" and "name of the father," of paternity as law (unpaginated). The theorization of metaphor as "master trope" aligns it with the function of the pedagogical master, whose role is conceived of in early modern texts as the mediation of the law of the Father as unquestioned totalization such as Lacan would theorize as the discourse of the master.

Master Trope/Trope of Mastery? 191

The theorization of metaphor as master-trope explicitly articulates its conceptual alignment with what Lacan was to theorize as the totalizing, would-be omniscient "discourse of the master" implicit in early modern transcodings of the metaphoric copula with the totalizing One (see above). The theorization of metaphor as privileged "master trope" within the early modern logocentric Ramist revision of rhetoric anticipates by four centuries Lacan's insight into the linguistic underpinnings of the discourse of the master. This discourse involves a solipsistic focus on the Being of the master to the exclusion of the recognition of the desire of the other. This solipsistic focus is undergirded by a linguistic structure. Lacan transcribes "master" (*maître*) as "*m'être*" (my Being) so as to foreground the predication of the discourse of the master on "the verb 'to be' [*être*]" (*Seminar XX*, p. 31).

Metaphor in early modern aesthetic theory is aligned with mastery, with the phallus as signifier of this mastery, and even more so with the colonizing structure of phallic desire. This conceptual alignment is a function of the Ramist theorization of metaphor as "master trope," of metaphor's isomorphism with the general equivalent of the monarch form, and of the transcoding of the metaphoric copula with the de-subjectifying, solipsistic category of the One who cannot and does not recognize the desire of the other. The alignment of metaphor with the phallic is also a function of the classification of metaphor in the taxonomy of elocutionary forms. Metaphor, so almost all Renaissance rhetoricians agree, is not a figure but a trope.

All rhetorical treatises cited in this book which split elocution into tropes and figures classify metaphor as a trope. This is the case in Sherry's *Treatise of Schemes and Tropes* (unpaginated); Wilson's *Arte of Rhetorique* (p.197); Fraunce's *Arcadian Rhetorike* (p. 4); Otho Casman's *Rhetoricae Tropologiae* (1600) (unpaginated); Soario Cypriano's *De Arte Rhetorica* (1612) (p. 125); Hoskyns's *Directions for Speech and Style* (p. 8); Charles Butler's *Rhetoricae Libri Duo* (1629) (sig. B2); Gerard Vossius's, *Rhetorices Contractae* (1640) (p. xxii); Joanne de Kerhuel's *Idea Eloquentiae Rhetoricae* (1673) (p. 18); Blount's *Academie of Eloquence* (p. 1); the Port Royal *Rhetoric* (p. 75); and John Prideaux's *Hypomenmata Logica, Metaphysica, Pneumatica, Ethica, Politica, Oeconomiae* (1682) (p. 104). I am not aware of any rhetorical treatise making the trope/figure distinction, in the Renaissance or any other epoch, where metaphor is classified as a figure.

Metaphor is classified as a trope, a category whose theorization in Renaissance rhetoric attempts to circumvent the anxiety attendant upon the confrontation with the desire of the other by investing this category with a structure of phallic desire wherein the desire of the other is solipsistically ignored. This theorization of metaphor in a way which attempts to sidestep the desire of the other in its most extreme form of perversion, inscribed into the aesthetic category of figure, underscores and increases the conceptual alignment of metaphor with the discourse of the master. This classification of metaphor as a trope, a category psychically aligned with the totalizing discourse of the master and the blindness to the other associates metaphor with the *"dispositif* of conquest" (Lyotard, p. 154): the practice of enforced psycho-political mastery whose precipitate is the de-subjectifying enslavement of the colonial other and its production as a generalized low-Other.

The raising of metaphor to the status of mastery and general equivalence in Renaissance rhetoric, however, is a function not only of its classification as trope and its Ramist theorization as "master trope." Metaphor is associated with trope much more strongly than the other forms of elocution usually classified under the same category. Apart from metonymy, synecdoche, and irony, listed as tropes in Ramist and post-Ramist rhetorics, pre-Ramist or non-Ramist treatises list hyperbole (Butler, p. 3; de Kerhuel, p. 23; Prideaux, p. 104; Joannes Alstendius, *Rhetorica* [1616], p. 33), metalepsis (Vossius, p. iv; de Kerhuel, p. 23), and allegory (Butler, sig. B; Vossius, p. iv; de Kerhuel, p. 23). De Kerhuel's list of tropes includes antonomasia, onomatopeia (p.18), periphrasis, and hyperbaton (p. 23). Many treatises list catachresis as a trope, a complex classification I analyze in Chapter Six below.

Theorizations of metaphor (but not of other tropes) are close to the displacement narrative subtending the theorization of trope, at times to the point of overlap. The word "metaphor" itself encapsulates this narrative, since it derives from the Greek root *metaphorein*, meaning to "carry across." Repeating the story of a transition from one habitat to another brought into play in the theorization of trope, theorizations of metaphor in early modern rhetoric are predicated upon a geography of partition. Metaphor, Thomas Wilson writes in his *Arte of Rhetorique*, "is an alteration of a word from the proper and natural meaning to one that is not proper" (p. 194), echoing, with the sole difference of adding the qualifier "natural" to the metaphorized word, the structure and the vocabulary of his definition of trope as the "alteration of a word from the proper signification to one that is not proper" (ibid.). Repeating most of the vocabulary and the narrative structure of Wilson's definition, Peacham defines metaphor as "a word translated from its proper and natural signification to another" (sig. B2), deviating from his definition of trope as "an alteration of a word or sentence from the proper signification to another" only in the narrativizing verb. Richard Sherry's definition of metaphor in *The Treatise of Schemes and Tropes* as "a word translated from the thynge it properlye signifieth, vnto another" similarly approximates his definition of trope as "the moving and changing of a word or sentence from their own signification to another" (unpaginated), deviating from it only in the choice of the Latin term for metaphor as the narrativizing verb.

Like the theorizations of trope with which they virtually coincide, all these Renaissance theorizations of metaphor encapsulate a narrative of displacement or movement from...to..., in which significations function as settings and words or sentences function as protagonists or actants. Renaissance theorizations of metaphor are undergirded by the same structure of a voyage, of a movement between geographical locations, characterizing theorizations of the category of trope under which they are classified. Like definitions of trope which they approach or duplicate, these theorizations of metaphor as displacement are symptoms of the co-implication of writing and colonization (Stratton, pp. 45–91; Van den Abeele, pp. xiii-xxx). This co-implication of writing and colonization is predicated upon an isomorphism. Writing is informed by a thwarted yearning for referential definiteness, a yearning informing early modern theorizations of the metaphoric copula. Colonization too is informed by a thwarted yearning for elusive definiteness, imagined to be attainable in the control of the colonial Other (Stratton, p. 73).

Early modern theorizations of metaphor are imbricated in the conceptual interface of writing and travel more closely than the theorizations of the category of trope in which they are included. Theorizations of metaphor such as those in Sherry's *Treatise on Schemes and Tropes* and Peacham's *Garden of Eloquence* opt for a narrativizing verb hardly ever used in early modern theorizations of trope. This verb is not to alter, nor to move, nor to transport, nor any other common tropological verb, but to "translate." This term derives from metaphor's Latin name, *translatio*.

Metaphor is theorized as "translation" in Sherry's *Treatise of Schemes and Tropes* (p. 40); Peacham's *Garden of Eloquence* (sig. B2); Jacobus Izelgrinus's *Rethorica Nova* (ca. 1457) (p. 35); Erasmus's *De Copia* (p. 333); Bartolomeo Cavalcanti's *La Retorica* (1559) (p. 253); Peter Guntherus's *De Arte Rhetorica Libri Duo* (1568) (p. 27); Otho Casman's *Rhetoricae Tropologiae* (1600) (p. 125); Soario Cypriano's *De Arte Rhetorica* (1612) (p.125); Gerard Vossius's *Rhetorices Contractae* (1640) (p. xxii); and Thomas Blount's

Academie of Eloquence (1664) (p. 1). Girolamo Mascher states in *Il Fiore Della Retorica* (1560): *"La Translatione [e] altrimente detta Metaphora"* (translation is otherwise called metaphor) (p. 181). In *The Arte of Rhetorique*, Wilson refers to the *exempla* he provides for the form he had defined as "metaphor" as "translations" (pp. 198–199). In Robert Cawdray's *Storehovse or Treasvrie of Similies* (1600) "Metaphors" and "Translations" are positioned as apposites (sig. A4). In Ben Jonson's *Timber* (1641) translation and metaphor are used as synonyms (p. 133). Joanne de Kerhuel asserts: *"metaphora autem sive translatio est mutatio sigificationis"* (a metaphor, otherwise called translation, is a change in signification) (p. 18). John Florio glosses metaphor as "translation" (p. 311) and translation as "metaphor" (p. 575).

Translation involves a semiotic operation often aspiring to the oppressive imposition of a "final, conclusive, decisive" meaning on the translated text, an imposition denying the alterity of the text's nucleus of specificity which does not lend itself to translation (Benjamin, "Task of the Translator," *Illuminations*, p. 75). The denial of Otherness involved in translation is isomorphic with what is at stake in colonial encounters (Cheyfitz, pp. xix, 43, 104; Niranjana, pp. 1–3, 11). Translation is "based on…a certain foreign policy" (Cheyfitz, p. 37). Translation encapsulates the conceptual interface between semiotic metamorphosis and political dislocation equally at work in early modern theorizations of metaphor and of trope.

Occasionally, the violence of colonialist dislocation inscribed into the rhetorical form of metaphor/translation is articulated explicitly. In Florio's introduction to Montaigne's *Essays* (1603), translation is described as usurpation (p. xxi), the forceful seizing of power whose psychic substrate is the non-recognition to the point of annihilation of the political rights of the usurped monarch. In Joachimus Camerarius's *Elementa Rhetoricae* (1540), metaphor, identified as *"translationim,"* is described as *"significatione hoc loco usurpatur"* (usurping the place of signification) (p. 129).

In Nicolas Caussin's *De Eloquentia sacra et humana* (1630), metaphor is represented as "the transfer of a certain word usurped [*usurpata*] from its proper referent to an improper one" (p 401). In *The Emperor of Men's Minds*, Wayne Rebhorn discusses Caussin's representation of metaphor as usurpation as betraying a "nervousness" about the "impropriety" of the form (p. 237). The anxiety Rebhorn describes is well-diagnosed; its dynamics are not. The representation of metaphor as a conqueror, a phallic hero, even when it is carried out in the morally ambivalent terms of "usurpation," is not the cause of rhetorical anxiety but an attempt to allay it.

The conceptual locus of the inscription of the colonial Other is the register of the symbolic, of structure. Yet in most cases, in early modern Europe the imperialist inscription, through translation, of the colonial Other as a slave with respect to the discourse of the European master was accompanied by a self-righteous imaginary captation. This imaginary captation disguises the de-subjectivation of the colonial Other as "a humanizing activity, a passport or transport into the fully human of the native speaker's tongue" (Cheyfitz, p. 103). Given this imaginary captation of colonialist translation as a "humanizing activity," the aesthetic category of metaphor-as-translation becomes conceptually intertwined with "the process of what the West typically calls 'civilization': an evolutionary process in which the mute or practically mute (those whose speech is poverty stricken) learn first to speak and then to speak eloquently" (ibid., pp. 119–120). The aesthetic category of metaphor as theorized in early modern rhetoric becomes charged with the self-righteous, guilt-eliding imaginary captation of colonialist aggression, predicated upon a structure of solipsistic phallic desire wherein the desire and subjectivity of the colonial Other are denied, as a beneficence toward the Other.

This imaginary captation of metaphor-as-translation as a benefactor of the colonial Other rather than its enslaving master intersects with a ubiquitous *topos* in early modern rhetorical theory. This is the narrative of the orator as the first civilizer. The earliest known, and most influential, articulations of this myth are in Cicero's *De oratore* (bk. 1, sec. 8, line 33) and *De inventione* (bk. 1, sec. 2, line 2). The many examples in early modern rhetoric include the texts of Andrea Ugo of Sienna, who in 1421 described eloquence as having "led savage humanity from a savage and bestial existence to civilized culture," and of Andrea Brenta of Padua, who in 1480 described "primitive men" as having led "brutish and lawless lives in the fields until eloquence brought them together and converted barbaric violence into humanity and culture" (quoted by Greenblatt, *Learning to Curse*, p. 20).

In Puttenham's articulation of the myth in *The Arte of English Poesie*, "Poesie" is described as "th'original cause and occasion of their first assemblies, when before the people remained in the woods and mountains, vagrant and dispersed like the wild beasts, lawless and naked, or verie ill clad, and of all and necessarie prouision for harbour or sustenance vtterly vnfurnished: so little differed for their maner of life, from the brute beasts of the field" (pp. 3–4). Puttenham's version of the myth of the orator as civilizer is predicated on the opposition between the naked, which he later associates with "the sauage and vncivill" (p. 10), and the clothed. This opposition between the naked and the clothed transcodes with Puttenham's distinction between the language of the "American...& the Canniball," and European "Poesie" (ibid.). This transcoding of the opposition between the naked savage and the clothed European with the opposition between the language of the colonial Other and the precepts of rhetoric within Puttenham's retelling of the myth of the first orator underscores the imbrication of his version of the myth of the origin of rhetoric with the imaginary captation of colonization as civilization.

In this ubiquitous myth, the orator mediates the exchange of savagery for civility. In his *Leviathan* (1681), Hobbes famously theorizes the savagery fictionalized by Puttenham and other articulators of this myth as the "State of Nature," eventually exchanged for the law of the body politic. In Hobbes's subsequent *Art of Rhetoric*, the body politic replacing the "State of Nature" is coextensive with the "Art of Speaking" (p. 13). Hobbes's conflation of rhetoric and the law is revealed in his choice to supplement his rhetoric with a legal excursus on the "Laws of England." In this excursus, Hobbes describes "Statute Laws" as necessary "for the preservation of all Mankind" which would otherwise fall back into a state of non-regulated violence, involving "envy, slaughter, and continual war" (pp. 9–10). This is the same state of "Primitive...Fighting" Hobbes associates with the absence of rhetoric (sig. A3). In Hobbes's thinking, rhetoric becomes transcoded with the law.

Hobbes's legological version of the myth of the first orator as civilizer is concerned with the imposition of law. The foregrounding of the law in Hobbes's version of the myth gives the process of civilizing described in this myth an inflection exceeding the colonialist parameters scholars of early modern culture have, albeit rightly, chosen to foreground (Parker, *Literary Fat Ladies*, p. 97; Greenblatt, *Learning to Curse*, pp. 20–21; Rebhorn, pp. 23–79). These parameters are limited to the register of the imaginary in which colonialist ideology is deployed and to the political and economic consequences of this deployment. The scholars who have foregrounded only the colonialist inflection of the myth of the first orator ignore the structural, symbolic substrate of this myth, and of the aesthetic category of metaphor-translation with which this myth conceptually intersects. This structural substrate of the myth of the first orator is beyond historical permutations. It involves the de-subjectivizing, pleasure-denying imposition of law. The "law" of rhetoric in question in the myth of the orator as civilizer is the law of the symbolic in its repressive deployment, of the Father.

The transcoding of rhetoric with the law of the Father in the myth of the first orator as civilizer is underscored in Wilson's version of this myth. In *The Arte of Rhetorique*, Wilson fictionalizes rhetoric as a better substitute, sanctioned by "God" (the Father) for the existential state of the "fall[en]...first Father" (pp. 41–42). This "first" archaic state Wilson imagines is the original, Paradisal, pre-rational, past-oral state conceptually, not temporally, preceding the legislating, prohibitive schizmatizations imposed upon the advent of paternal law. At its psychic roots, the myth of the first orator as civilizer is a myth of the attempted foreclosure of the archaic by the phallic.

In early modern rhetorical theory, the category of metaphor is closely aligned with ontologicality, with Being. Four other categories intersect and interpenetrate in early modern theorizations of metaphor. (1) First of these is the phallic and paternal myth of the primal orator as civilizer and purveyor of the law, of the symbolic in its repressive function. (2) The second conceptual category informing early modern theorizations of metaphor is usurpation as an instance of phallic desire denying the subjectivity and desire of the supplanted Other. (3) Taxonomically, early modern theorizations of metaphor are aligned with tropology as an elocutionary category conceptually subtended by a phallic desire whose manifestation is European possessiveness toward the tropical. (4) Etymologically and conceptually, metaphor is aligned with translation as the linguistic inscription of such possessiveness and drive for mastery.

The conceptual precipitate of the interpenetration of conceptual categories in early modern theorizations of metaphor is a rhetorical category strongly weighted toward ontologicality, categoricity, and presence, and toward a *"dispositif* of conquest" (Lyotard 154) subtended by a structure of phallic desire. The interpenetration of phallic categories involved in early modern theorizations of metaphor make metaphor more overdeterminately inflected toward a *dispositif* of conquest than trope, the category under which metaphor is generally classified. The categories of the phallus, the conqueror, the ruler or master, and the father as purveyor of the law, which are at work in early modern theorizations of metaphor are, in Goux's terms, general equivalents in the spheres of the sexual and libidinal, the political, and the familial. Transcoded with these categories, metaphor as theorized by the early modern rhetoricians is pushed toward general equivalency in elocution.

One other category pushes metaphor toward a general equivalency wherein it would have "an exclusive, exceptional place, an exemplary status" (Goux, *Symbolic Economies*, p. 31) among forms of elocution. This is the category of extraordinary wealth. In John Hoskyns's *Directions for Speech and Style* (1641), metaphor is conceptualized as "pleasant, because it enriches" (p. 8). Positing pleasure as a product of the accumulation of riches, Hoskyns theorizes metaphor as a conceptual analogue of gold as a substance "possess[ing] all pleasures in potentiality" (Marx, *Grundrisse*, p. 222): a conceptual analogue of a general equivalent. In Erasmus's *De copia*, metaphor, a form theorized by Erasmus as "fundamental to the literary exploitation of *copia*" (Cave, "Copia and Cornucopia," p. 54), is said to "contribute" to "richness in style" (p. 333). Metaphor thereby becomes aligned with the "golden river" in terms of which Erasmus conceptualizes *copia* in general (p. 295). More explicitly resorting to an excommunicating logic characteristic of general equivalency (Goux, *Symbolic Economies*, p. 31), in *The Arte of Rhetorique*, Thomas Wilson describes an oration as "wonderfullye enriched, when metaphors are gotte and applied to the matter" (p. 195). Wilson associates metaphor with a wealth rendered exceptional by the superlative used to characterize it. Similarly, for John Smith, metaphor is the "light and star of speech" because it "tends to richness" (p. 9). Smith simultaneously associates metaphor with economic abundance and with an image of a lucidity making the measurement of "speech" possible. This alignment of metaphor with a measure amounts to its implicit theorization as the standard or general equivalent of speech. Metaphor becomes the conceptual equivalent of maximized capital and hence of gold, a general equivalent in its own right, underwritten by the logic of over-valuation as excommunication. Metaphor is theorized as a general equivalent transcoded specifically with maximized capital whose measure or standard is gold.

Metaphor is phallicized, heroified, glorified, orified. It is theorized in a relation of conceptual equivalence to conqueror, colonizer, imprinter, and begetter and hence situated on a par with the general equivalents of phallus and father. Placed in a relation of conceptual equivalency with riches, metaphor is situated on a par with the general equivalent of gold. Traversing a range of general equivalents, given an extraordinary ranking in the hierarchy of aesthetic forms as first among the "master tropes," metaphor is the general equivalent of elocution. Or so early modern rhetoricians would have us believe.

Closer examination of the theorizations of metaphor in early modern treatises on rhetoric reveals their erecting metaphor as the general equivalent of elocution, an erecting made possible and necessary by the ontologicality inscribed into the metaphoric copula, as less than stable. Such closer examination reveals this theorization is, as Lacan was to remark of any attempt to produce ontology through the use of the equating copula, "a highly risky enterprise" (*Seminar XX*, p. 31).

Closer examination of early modern theorizations of metaphor reveals the investment in the enthroning of metaphor as the general equivalent of elocution as coming at the price of disrupting and destabilizing elocution. In the many early modern rhetorical treatises making the trope/figure distinction and classifying metaphor as a trope, the classifying category and one of its subdivisions coincide, structurally and sometimes semantically. The category used to classify metaphor (trope) encapsulates the same plot of displacement to which rhetoricians resort in order to theorize metaphor and ostensibly differentiate metaphor from the other components of the same taxonomic category. In *The Art of Speaking* (1676), Bernard Lamy self-consciously writes: "all Tropes are *Metaphors* or Translations...and yet...we give the name *Metaphor* to a particular Trope" (p. 75, emphases in the original). The relation between the aesthetic categories of trope and metaphor, initially asserted as taxonomic subordination, is leveled into an equivalence in a gesture of ill-logic known as a "strange loop" or "tangled hierarchy." This is the phenomenon occurring "whenever, by moving upwards (or downwards) through the levels of some hierarchical system, we find ourselves right back where we started" (Hofstadter, p. 10).

The strange loop involving definitions of metaphor and trope gives the lie to whatever presumptions Renaissance rhetoric may have had to logic and systematicity. Although rhetoric has been derided by philosophers ever since Plato for its illogicality, its capacity to incite, seduce, and deceive, Renaissance rhetoric had many presumptions to systematicity. These presumptions to systematicity are indexed by two factors. (1) First of these is the attempt of Renaissance rhetoricians to control the primal substance of semiosis imagined as archaic femininity by means of differentiation and systematization. (2) The second trace of the presumption of Renaissance rhetoricians to produce order and systematicity is the attempts to enthrone metaphor as a homologue of phallus and the father as purveyor of the law. Undermining logicality, the strange loop of trope and metaphor unsettles logos and its precipitates, the privileged signifiers or general equivalents in the numismatic chain including phallus, father, monarch, gold, and metaphor itself.

In early modern metalinguistic theory, metaphor is simultaneously the general equivalent of elocution, "a site of law" (Goux, *Symbolic Economies*, p. 38), and the site of the undoing of this law. Metaphor is the site where the centrism (logocentrism, phallocentrism) of rhetoric is at its most intense. The logocentrism and phallocentrism of rhetoric is in perpetual tension with the imaginary captation of the primal substance of semiosis in terms of the archaic mother, a captation inducive of anxiety and of fascination. The position of metaphor as general equivalent, a position of maximal logocentricity, is a position where the impulses militating against rhetoric's logocentricity are at their most powerful. The strange loop generated by the illogical meshing of theorizations of metaphor and of trope constitutes a faultline in the aesthetics of early modern rhetoric. Setting the rhetorical text against its avowed hierarchical logic, the strange loop involving trope and metaphor reveals an anasemic inscription, within the rhetorical text, of what the rhetorical text is fascinated with and seeks to repress.

The repressed returning to haunt rhetoric in the de-hierarchizing tangle of metaphor and trope is the imaginary captation of the primal substance of semiosis as archaic maternality, the imaginary captation rewritten in theorizations of figure as the seductive aspect of maternality, its deployment as the prototypical object of all desire. This imaginary captation is what early modern elocution strives to sidestep in its theorizations of the aesthetic categories of trope and figure. Renaissance rhetoricians attempt to gain control over the primordial Other, the potentially engulfing, oceanic archaic maternality they associate with the primal substance of semiosis, by rewriting this maternality, in the theorization of the aesthetic category of figure, as archetypal feminine seduction. Seduction leads to a confrontation with the desire of the other, not to control of the other as low-Other. Failing to achieve control over archaic femininity in the postulation of the category of figure, Renaissance rhetoricians attempt to keep this femininity in check by subordinating figure to trope, a category inscribed with a controlling, phallic desire manifest in the masculinized discourse of colonization and conquest.

Ultimately, however, the ability of the theorization of the aesthetic category of trope to counterbalance the archetypal seductive femininity associated with the aesthetic category of figure and to foreclose the archaic, potentially devouring maternality attributed to the primal substance of semiosis is undermined from within the section on tropes. I have shown in the third chapter of this book how the theorization of the classifying category of trope deconstructs, dissolving scenarios of colonization into scenarios of decolonization, barbarian invasion, and miscegenation. The signifier "trope" semiotically indexes both the "safe ground" of *topos* or place as logical and ontological sanctuary from the perils of oceanic femininity and the irresistible desire to re-turn (*trepein*) to archaic femininity. Within the category of trope, the theorization of metaphor, which is one of its sub-divisions, duplicates the structure of the level above it and brings the hierarchy of elocutionary forms tumbling down, tangling the containing level with what it contains. Metaphor, as Derrida says in a different context, "carries its death within itself" ("White Mythology," *Margins of Philosophy*, p. 271).

One indication of the dissolution of the general equivalency of the aesthetic category of metaphor in early modern rhetoric is the appearance, in its theorizations, of a register of borrowing, of economic scarcity, alongside the register of abundance, riches, gold. Metaphor, writes Thomas Blount, is a "neighbourly borrowing of a word" (sig. B). This formulation is repeated by John Smith (p. 9). The contribution of metaphor to the "richness of style" in Erasmus's *De copia* is not, after all, a function of its association with the "golden river" of *copia*, with the general equivalent regulating exchanges. Instead, this association is made possible by the functioning of metaphor as the agent of an economy of signification based upon the principle requiring lack to always be filled, requiring us to avoid a situation wherein "we...find ourselves with a concept for which there is no word available" (p. 335). Metaphor, as Girolamo Mascher puts it in *Il Fiore della Retorica*, exists "*per lo mancamente di parole*" (for the wanting of words) (p. 186). In Sherry's *Treatise of the Figures of Grammer and Rhetorike* (1555), metaphor is said to be generated when "there lacketh a proper worde" (fol. xxiii).

In the economy of impoverishment early modern rhetorics construct for their orified form, lack must always be made good, and it is made good by borrowing. What "forced us to borrow words translated," Thomas Wilson writes in his speculation on "The First Use of Tropes" in *The Arte of Rhetorique*, was "necessity" (p. 196). Metaphor, the category whose copula is theorized by early modern grammarians in reference to plenitude and Being, comes to be theorized by early modern rhetoricians in terms of the reverse of plenitude: scarcity and lack. Since the plenitude in question in early modern theorizations of the metaphoric copula is ontological plenitude, the plenitude of Being, the lack surfacing in early modern theorizations of metaphor as borrowing is implicitly inscribed as a lack of Being. This is the lack Lacan was to theorize as structuring subjectivity as desire (*Seminar II*, p. 223).

In early modern theorizations of metaphor, real privation, the absence of money or material goods, phenomenal objects in the register of the real, is transcoded with missing words, with holes in the signifying chain, with the lack of symbolic objects. According to Lacan, the second phase of the subject's gradual assumption of his/her constitutive ontological castration, the recognition of the lack instituting him/her as desiring subject, is privation, the confrontation with a real lack of a symbolic object (*Seminar IV*, p. 19). The association of real and symbolic lack in early modern theorizations of metaphor anticipates by centuries Lacan's theorization of privation.

While privation falls short of the subject's recognition of the castration enabling him/her to assume desire and allowing transferential eroticism to thrive, it is an important step on the way toward making such transferential eroticism possible. Privation permits the deprived subject to integrate into the sexual dialectic subtending human existence (Lacan, *Seminar IV*, p. 273). This is the dialectic wherein the subject's primal real object, the (m)Other, is constitutively barred by the imaginary father. This is the father imagined to be an omnipotent guarantor of universal order (ibid., p. 275). The imaginary father as theorized by Lacan is the father inscribed into the myth of the orator as civilizer intersecting with early modern theorizations of metaphor.

The inscription of the imaginary father into early modern theorizations of metaphor does not satisfyingly perform the psychic task it was supposed to perform. It does not shield the rhetorician and his audience from a confrontation with the desire of the Other inscribed into the category of figure, the desire reflecting the subject's own constitutive desire as lack of Being. Instead, the imaginary father reveals himself in the early modern theorizations of metaphor into which he is inscribed just as he does in the course of the personal history of the subject, as an agent of privation. The confrontation with privation is a psychic operation leading the subject to a confrontation with eroticizing ontological lack, the lack which the inscription of the imaginary father into the category of metaphor, and the ontologizations of the metaphoric copula with which this inscription is conceptually allied, are designed to circumvent.

In English treatises, the deconstruction of the economic general equivalency attributed to metaphor has phonic symptoms. The "or" constituting the last syllable of the name of metaphor signifies the Latin name for the economic general equivalent, gold, and disjunction, the simultaneous existence of separate alternatives which is the epistemological condition the equating copula of metaphor seeks to efface. The syllable "or" conceptually and phonically invokes the or-al, or the past-or-al, as the most archaic, polymorphic organization of the libido which encompasses all sexual alternatives, as the Renaissance pastorals thematizing these alternatives well demonstrate.

The other indication of the dissolution of the general equivalency of metaphor in Renaissance rhetoric is the appearance, in its theorizations, of the category of foreignness as a manifestation of unassimilable Otherness, alongside phallic, possessive, colonialist desire. In Lacan's terms, the Other is the locus of radical alterity "in which speech is constituted" (*Seminar III*, p. 274). This locus is first occupied by the mother, and is then particularized in specific objects, individual or collective, who come to embody Otherness for a given subject. Theorizations of trope in early modern rhetoric are predicated upon the attempt to allay the anxiety surging from the confrontation with the archetypal, seductive femininity qua perversion associated with the aesthetic category of figure by the subordination of femininity to a controlling phallic desire underpinning the heroicized colonialist narrative of movement between two cultural contexts. Theorizations of metaphor are structurally and semantically close to theorizations of trope, yet much less predicated on such an attempt to allay the anxiety of seductive femininity. Instead, in some early modern theorizations of metaphor, the colonialist narrative of phallic desire is supplemented by a counter-narrative whose protagonist is a constitutively de-phallicized low-Other.

The inscription of Otherness into the category of metaphor first appears in the third book of Aristotle's *Rhetoric*, where metaphor is theorized as the introduction of a "foreign" (*allotrios*) element into style (p. 209). Similarly, Cicero uses the image of the alien to theorize metaphor as a "word...put in a position not belonging to it as if it were its own place" (*in alieno tanquam in suo positum*" (*De oratore*, bk. 3, sec. 39, line 157). The theorization of metaphor as an Other persists in rhetorical treatises of the Renaissance. Erasmus, in *De copia*, theorizes metaphor as a word "outside its proper sphere" (p. 333), an "outside[r]" or Other. The Port Royal *Rhetoric* accentuates the Otherness of metaphor by theorizing it as "strange and remote" in relation to the "proper" word it would replace (p. 75). In these instances, metaphor is not theorized as a master of a given sphere. Metaphor is theorized as a stranger, outsider, alien, the embodiment, for the master, of alterity, Otherness.

Early modern theorists of language are clear as to what is to be done with linguistic qua national Otherness. Ben Jonson theorizes the Otherness accruing to "Strangers" as the "Rudenesse" and "Barbarisme" which linguistic theory is to efface by assimilation (*English Grammar*, sig. E), and William Walker theorizes Otherness even more phobically, as a "Disease" linguistic theory must "prevent or cure" (unpaginated). Such theorizations, harking back to the formative rhetorical theorizations of Aristotle and Cicero, destabilize and deconstruct the ubiquitous theorizations of metaphor as master and colonizer. They foreground the Other whose desire is what the colonizer's discourse of the master refuses to recognize. Ultimately, the Other "can...only be the Other sex" (Lacan, *Seminar XX*, p. 39), which, for both male and female subjects, is always woman. Woman, Lacan says, "becomes the Other for herself as she is this other for [man]" (*Écrits* [French edition], p. 732).

Renaissance rhetoricians place femininity at the origin of semiosis. They are irresistibly drawn to feminine origin. Simultaneously fearing feminine origin, they seek to control it by reinventing it as an eminently rational, logocentric theory. The theorization of metaphor as Other reinstitutes femininity within the would-be rational theory seeking to control and repress feminine origin. The inscription of Otherness into metaphor reinstitutes femininity within the aesthetic category whose early modern theorizations are most invested with the rational and phallic.

The reinstitution of ultimately feminine Otherness within the theorization of metaphor destabilizes the logicality, phallogicality, categoricity, and definiteness attributed to metaphor by early modern rhetoricians. The Other with whom Erasmus and the Port Royal rhetoricians associate metaphor is an entity whose presence is troublesome to the subject for whom it particularizes Otherness because it is "the presence of a lining" (Kristeva, *Strangers to Ourselves*, p. 4), of the unclear boundaries of the identity of subject. The Other is a reminder of the impossibility of ever fixing identity, whether collective or individual, of the ultimate impossibility of what Levinas calls "the peaceful and sovereign identification of the self with itself" (*Basic Philosophical Writings*, p. 150). The Other is reminder of the irreducible particularity of the Otherness always returning to haunt clear-cut and monolithic concepts of race, ethnicity, or individual identity. The stranger as Other, writes Kristeva, "is the hidden face" of identity. It what "wrecks [the] abode" of definiteness imaginary captations of identity seek (*Strangers to Ourselves*, p. 1), the definiteness early modern theorists of language are at pains to inscribe into the metaphoric copula.

Given the inscription into metaphor of general equivalence, early modern theorizations of this form include its overvaluation as a standard for the symbolic set of elocutionary forms. Given the inscription of

Otherness into metaphor, early modern theorizations of this form include defense mechanisms whose purpose is to police the unsettling presence of the Other within this set. Defense mechanisms deployed against the Other, Kristeva says, are designed to "expel" the Other "or at least, keep him in 'his' place" (*Strangers to Ourselves*, p. 20). Cicero was the first to have indicated the potential to destabilization inherent in metaphor as alien or Other when he cautioned:

> the metaphor ought to have an apologetic air, so as to look as if it had entered a place that does not belong to it with a proper introduction [*ut deducta esse in alienam locum*], not taken it by storm, and as if it had come with permission, not forced its way in [*non vi venisse videatur*]. (*De oratore*, bk. 3, sec. 41, line 165)

Cicero's demand of metaphor-as-Other to be "apologetic" and non-intrusive bespeaks an anxiety of the Other's overtaking the space of rhetoric. Cicero's phallic vocabulary of forceful entry and taking by force suggests this anxiety is an anxiety of the phallicization and empowerment of the Other. Yet the Other is constitutively lacking, castrated (Lefort, p. 18). The imaginary captation of metaphor as a phallic violator masks a deeper anxiety, namely, the anxiety of rhetorical theory being overtaken, inundated by the ultimately feminine, maternal, and oceanic Otherness it places at the origin of semiosis. This is the Otherness rhetorical theory always seeks to flee. Given this theory's attraction to origin, this Otherness is always all too able to return within it.

The anxiety of confrontation with Otherness as archaic, oceanic maternality Cicero inscribes into the aesthetic category of metaphor persists in the theorizations of his early modern followers. Like Cicero, Thomas Blount and John Hoskyns theorize metaphors as aesthetic entities prone to phallic intrusiveness, to being "too bold" (Blount, p. 2; Hoskyns, p. 8). The anxiety of metaphor in the theorizations of Blount and Hoskyns is ultimately more an anxiety of inundation, of the dissolution of individuating boundaries defining an entity as discrete, than an anxiety of this entity being conquered and overpowered. Metaphors, Blount and Hoskyns write, tend to "wander into the confines" and perilously "go beyond the signification of things," and so must be subjected to "rule." This tendency of metaphors as Others to "go beyond" boundaries or "confines," Hoskyns and Blount agree, is risky since it is telling of the failure of metaphors "to fix themselves upon one thing," to guarantee fixity, definiteness, and unicity. These are the attributes other early modern rhetoricians and grammarians are at pains to inscribe into the theorization of metaphor or of its copula. These are the attributes subtending the elevation of metaphor to the status of the general equivalent of elocution. The risks entailed by the boundary-crossing Blount and Hoskyns inscribe into the category of metaphor are the risks of losing the reassuring fixity of individuated, differentiated "thing[s]." These are the risks of inundation, of the collapsing of rhetoric into the oceanic substance imagined as its origin.

Blount indicates the inundation in question has to do with unpredictable, potentially uncontrollable affect. He describes the tendency of metaphors to transgress or go "beyond" as an expression of the "roving fancies of mens minds" (p. 2). The risk involved in the dissolution of rhetoric into the oceanic Hoskyns and Blount implicitly inscribe into the category of metaphor as Other is psychic. This is the risk of the loss of the boundaries of the ego and the consequent fall into unpredictably "roving fancies," the product of the unconscious. This risk is epistemological too. The risk entailed by the boundary-crossings inscribed into the category of metaphor by Blount and Hoskyns is the loss of the ability of direct ostension to a "thing" as a discrete "one." This is the loss of the ability to make the categorical assertion "this is," the loss of the ability to use the axiomatic copula of metaphor.

Hoskyns and Blount conceive of the loss of fixity they inscribe into the category of metaphor as Other as entailing the loss of the possibility of direct ostension other early modern theoreticians inscribe into the copula of metaphor. This is evident in their choice to theorize the risks of metaphor as Other in terms of the image of an "archer" who is aware "his bow will overcast or carry too short" and will make the arrow fail to fall, in precise ostension, "on the mark."

Metaphor as Other, in the early modern theorizations of Blount and Hoskyns, is a perilous category, entailing the risks of the loss of individuating boundaries, of fixity, of epistemological and psychic definiteness. These are the risks the logocentric and ontologizing theorizations of metaphor or the metaphoric copula by other early modern rhetoricians seek to sidestep. The theorizations of Blount and Hoskyns reveal the precariousness of the prevalent logocentric and ontologizing theorizations of metaphor. The theorizations of metaphor in the treatises of Blount and Hoskyns reveal the extent to which, as Stephen Whitworth has argued, all early modern rhetorical theory is driven by the anxiety of the fall into oceanic dissolution, and at the same time inextricably bound up with the fascination with this fall as a fortunate one, a return to the most archaic bliss, the bliss language tries to approximate in the poetics of pastoral.

Early modern theorizations of metaphor, for all their insistence on the ontological, the definite, the visual, the phallic, are ultimately irresistibly drawn back to the polymorphic domain of pastoral, the domain which would be barred by the phallus with which metaphor is so ubiquitously transcoded. This is evident in the symptomatic, anasemic eruptions of pastoral images within these theorizations. One example of such a pastoral image is Fraunce's ostensibly anxious Horatian reference to the "inconstancy" of "leaues" leaving before winter in the theorization of the category of definiteness inscribed into the metaphoric copula in *The Lawier's Logike*. Fraunce's anxiety of indeterminacy indexed by this Horatian image is belied by his overdetermined and consciously avowed attraction to pastoral poetics. This attraction is evident in the *exempla* from Spenser's *Sheapheardes Calender* in this treatise and in all of his other works as a theorist of language, and in his work as a translator of poetry.

Another example of a pastoral image within a theorization of metaphor is the choice of Blount and Hoskyns to theorize metaphor in terms of the pastoral image of a "flower" growing "in the garden of purpose" (Blount, p. 2; Hoskyns, p. 8). This is an image frequently used in Renaissance poetry to signify the ephemeral. For instance, in sonnet #79 of Spenser's *Amoretti*, "flowres" are used as an example for all things natural which "untimely fade" (line 14). In Shakespeare's sonnet #18, the "darling buds of May" (line 3), are cited among the components of a summer's day which are subject to "nature's changing course" (line 7).

Flowers as fictionalized by Spenser and Shakespeare are inconstant. They are characterized by the reverse of the constancy and definiteness inscribed into the metaphoric copula by early modern theorists such as Fraunce. The inconstancy of the flower embodies the erotic. The subtension of the inconstant qua non-definite by the erotematic is in dialectical tension with the categoricity of the ecphonetic associated with metaphor in early modern linguistic theory. Fraunce too uses the erotic and erotematic image of the flower, with its connotations of inconstancy and pastorality. Metaphor, he writes, is a trope of which none other is "more florishing" (*The Arcadian Rhetorike*, unpaginated).

Hoskyns was conscious of the pastoral connotations of the image of the flower he associates with the aesthetic category of metaphor theorized by so many of his peers in reference to the phallus whose function is to bar and close off the domain of pastoral. This becomes evident shortly after the theorization of metaphor in reference to the flower in his treatise. Metaphor, Hoskyns writes there, is "the best flower, growing most plentifully, in all of Arcadia" (p. 9). Hoskyns theorizes metaphor in terms of the image of the flower, a staple of the landscape of pastoral, and he localizes this landscape as Arcadia, the mythical locale of pastoral.

Hoskyns makes an effort to install the general equivalency of metaphor, which transcodes it with the phallus as general equivalent of the objects of drive by theorizing metaphor in terms of superlatives ("best," "most"). This effort to install the general equivalency of metaphor is deconstructed by the theorization of metaphor in terms of Arcadia, the irrevocably lost mythical space of pastoral, the poetic domain thematizing polymorphic forms of sexuality beyond the phallus.

The varied objects of the polymorphic libido deploying itself in the domain of pastoral are, like all objects of desire, encryptions of the archaic mother as primordial Other, the most primal addressee of erotic/erotematic demand, whose most archaic form is oral. In the domain of pastoral, none of these varied objects is barred by the Name/No of the Father. The domain of pastoral is erotically polymorphic. The domain of pastoral is conceptually maternal and oral, or better, past-oral.

Hoskyns was not alone among early modern rhetoricians whose theorization of metaphor as a phallic general equivalent, coeval with the Name of the Father, deconstructs into the category of the archaic mother who is the primal object of the oral drive. One century before Hoskyns's treatise was published, John Sturmius wrote, in the context of his theorization of metaphor, "nothing is more pleasant and acceptable to the ear than to hear one thing expressed in another" (*A Ritch Storehouse or Treasurie for Nobilitie and Gentlemen* [1570], p. 39). Like Fraunce, Fenner, and Newton, Sturmius theorizes metaphor as the combination of two signifiers into "one thing," as a rhetorical actualization of the fantasy of a universal fusion. This fantasy is thing-related, ontological. It has to do with the ontological production of the One coeval with the phallus. Like most other Renaissance rhetoricians, Sturmius extols metaphor as a phallic aesthetic category in terms of a superlative. Sturmius installs metaphor as a general equivalent of elocutionary forms, whose yield of "pleas[ure]" exceeds the pleasure afforded by all other such forms. This maximal yield of pleasure allows metaphor to function as a standard of value for those forms.

But the pleasure in terms of which Sturmius theorizes metaphor is not the phallic, visual pleasure in terms of which Fraunce and Hobbes theorize it. The pleasure in terms of which Sturmius theorizes metaphor is the pleasure of the "ear," an aural, orally-generated pleasure, the pleasure harkening to the most primordial satisfactions afforded by the oral incantations of the mother, whose breast, the most primal oral object, is encrypted into all love objects.

The aural pleasure in terms of which Sturmius theorizes metaphor is the non-rational pleasure from which Puttenham seeks to distinguish metaphor. Puttenham does not align metaphor with the "auricular" figures effecting "sweetnesse" of sensation yet "reach[ing]…no higher than th'eare and forc[ing]…the mynde little or nothing" (p. 134). Puttenham associates metaphor with figures "affect[ing] the minde" (p. 148), the seat of rationality and logicality with which the metaphoric copula is ubiquitously aligned. The pleasure of the ear with which Sturmius, unlike most of his peers, aligns metaphor is the pleasure with which, as Stephen Whitworth has argued in "Far from Being," early modern writers of pastoral were most concerned (pp. 160–161).

The concluding lines of the first sonnet in Henry Constable's *Diana* sequence speak of this aural pleasure. These lines affirm: "The voyce is made the eare for to reioyce: / And your eare giueth pleasure to my voyce," (lines 12–14). Constable offers these aural pleasures as a better, more "ioy"–producing substitute for the pleasures of sexually possessing, corporeally ioy-ning a "patient object" (line 6). These pleasures are anticipated yet never obtained by the speaker's "lightening eyes" (line 5), the source of the "ambitious thought" (line 9) of visualized fantasy. Sturmius theorizes metaphor in terms not of a visual possessiveness whose phallic inflection is evident in Constable's choice to poeticize its object as "patient," passively submissive, but of orally-generated aural pleasure. This causes Sturmius's valuation of metaphor as a phallic general equivalent of elocutionary forms to deconstruct to the point of asymptotic approximation to a primal orality beyond the phallus, to the domain of past-oral.

Sturmius and Hoskyns introduce the domain of pastoral into their theorizations of metaphor. This introduction complicates the common association of metaphor with the phallus in early modern rhetoric. It inflects metaphor toward the maternal. Hoskyns's maternalization of metaphor is suggested by his choice to theorize metaphor as Arcadian, past-oral, fl-oral, and aligned with "plent[y]" or copiousness. The category of plenty or copiousness Hoskyns inscribes into metaphor is ubiquitously theorized by early modern rhetoricians in reference to the fertile, gestating female body (Parker, *Literary Fat Ladies*, pp. 15–29). Another resonance of the copiousness Hoskyns associates with metaphor is the mythic concept of the cornucopia (Cave, "*Copia* and Cornucopia"). The concept of the cornucopia reaches back to archaic fertility cults gravitating to the Great Mother (Neumann, *Origins and History of Consciousness*, pp. 49–50).

Metaphor in Hoskyns's theorizations is aligned with the archaic mother as much as with the symbolic Father.

In Hoskyns's *Directions for Speech and Style*, the aesthetic category of metaphor is instituted as a general equivalent of the forms of elocution, rhetoric's isomorph of the economic standard, whose Latin name is *or*, gold. At the same time, metaphor in Hoskyns's theorization deconstructs into the category of or-al, archaic maternality. Renaissance rhetoricians transcode archaic maternality with the infinite, diffuse primal substance of semiosis which must be partitioned into elocutionary forms if signification and the subjectivity predicated upon it are not to be oceanically dissolved, if a symbolic economy of rhetoric is to be at all possible. In Hoskyns's rhetorical theory, metaphoricity deconstructs into the oceanic. The traces of this deconstruction of metaphor into the oceanic appear in Hoskyns's theorization in the form of explicit references to pastoral, the poetic domain whose thematization of polymorphic sexualities is the closest approximation to the psychic state of the oceanic possible from within rhetoric.

The phallic general equivalency of metaphor in early modern rhetoric is neither obvious nor stable. The "rule of metaphor," a phrase coined in the seventeenth-century treatises of Blount and Hoskyns and taken up in the context of contemporary theory as the title of Paul Ricoeur's monumental study of the poetics of this form, is a conflicted, dialectical rule. This "rule" encompasses the status of mastery accorded metaphor in early modern rhetoric and made possible through the masculinizing associations of metaphor with heroic plots, political leadership, active or aggressive male sexuality, and phallocentric unicity. The phrase "the rule of metaphor" indexes the necessity, dictated by rhetoric's logocentric, taxonomic drive to, as Joseph Aickin puts it, "Regulate" what is imagined as the infinite oceanic primal substance of semiosis "with distinguisht Forms" (sig. A2).

In their Aristotelian association with imprinting pattern, the "Forms" into which the primal, amorphic substance of semiosis is partitioned are conceptually paterial (Goux, *Symbolic Economies*, p. 220). The paterial partitioning of the primal substance of semiosis into "distinguisht," discrete forms or categories enables the institution of signification, and of subjectivity as a cut in the signifying chain, as separation. The institution of subjectivity and signification involves the regulation and control of the dissolute. This drive to rule through distinction or separation, to, as Jeremiah Wharton puts it, "distinguish each Part of Speech asunder" (unpaginated), is an abreaction of the anxiety of the fall of signification into oceanic diffusion transcoded with the primal substance of signification.

This drive to rule and master the primal oceanic substance of signification through the erection of metaphor as master trope is belied by the deconstruction of theorizations of metaphor into the poetics of pastoral. These poetics proffer the maximal asymptotic approximation to the imagined primal oceanic substance possible from within the condition of language and subjectivity. The deconstruction of attempts to erect metaphor into the poetics of pastoral is made inevitable by rhetoric's nostalgia for pastoral, a nostalgia always already in dialectical tension with rhetoric's driving anxiety of dissolution.

CHAPTER FIVE

Transferential Approximations: Similes, S(i)miles, Jouissance

Rhetorical treatises of the Renaissance attempt to erect the aesthetic category of metaphor, inscribed with logocentric sameness, One-ness, identity, possessiveness, phallic masculinity, and phallic desire, as their elocutionary and cognitive general equivalent. Yet the attempts at the erection of the metaphorical category of s(e)amless sameness and static identity are simultaneous with their inaugural breakdown. These attempts deconstruct into the category of oceanic anti-identity they seek to foreclose. The attempts to erect metaphor as general equivalent become traces of the irresistible allure of pastoral, of the seductiveness of an archaic femininity.

This seductiveness is manifest in early modern rhetoric in more than the cryptonymic form of the deconstruction of the aesthetic category of metaphor, the would-be phallicized, unitary, s(e)amless and ontological general equivalent of elocution, into the category of the oceanic. This allure of a seductive femininity is inscribed less cryptonymically and anasemically, more directly, in the theorization of the aesthetic category often conceptualized as metaphor's abjected binary, simile. The category of simile is conceptually marked not with the stasis of Being but with the open-endedness of polymorphic desire as becoming.

The attempted, and inevitably self-dissolving, attempt to enthrone metaphor notwithstanding, Renaissance rhetoric and poetics manifest an unprecedented fascination with the aesthetic category of simile. Renaissance rhetoric witnessed the emergence of a new rhetorical subgenre, the collection or compendium of similes. Examples of treatises of this genre include Anthonie Munday's *A Banquet of Daintie Conceits* (1588); Anthonie Fletcher's *Certaine Proper & Most Profitable Similes* (1595); Nicholas

Ling's *Politeuphueia: Wit's Commonwealth, A Treasury of Admonitions, Similies, & Sentences* (1597); Francis Meres's *Witts Academy: A Treasvrie of Goulden Sentences, Similies and Examples* (1595), *Palladis Tamia: Wit's Treasvry* (1598), and *Wits Commonwealth: A Treasurie of Diuine, morall, and Phylosophical similies, and sentences* (1597); John Bodenham's *Belvedere or The Garden of the Muses* (1600); Robert Cawdray's *Treasvrie or Storehovse of Similies* (1600); Conrad Lycosthenis's *Similivm Loci Commvnes* (1602); Thomas Shelton's *A Centvrie of Similies* (1640); Nicholas Breton's *Jesus Christ: Similies Divine and Moral* (1647); John Spenser's *Things Old or New or a Storehouse of Similies* (1658); and the section "A Garden of Tulips, or the Pleasant Prospect" in Edward Phillips's *Mysteries of Love and Eloquence* (1658).

The preoccupation with the similaic is evident even within the most influential articulation of humanist pedagogy in English, Roger Ascham's *Scholemaster* (1570). Ascham makes the principle of *imitatio* the cornerstone of his humanist pedagogy (p. 47). He theorizes *imitatio* in terms of the category of the similaic as *similis materei similis tractatio* (ibid.). Ascham goes on to recommend the notation of similitudes articulated by earlier authors as a means of practicing *imitatio*. The most accomplished humanist, he writes, "Erasmus, the ornament of learning, in our tyme" (ibid.), "prescribed to him selfe" such notation and "left to posteritie" its record or trace, a "notable booke" entitled *Similia* (ibid., p.52). Ersamus's *Similia*, commended by Ascham as an *exemplum* of the humanist practice of *imitatio*, was one of the earliest Renaissance compendia of similes, published in 1528.

The obsession with the similaic is manifest in the literature no less than in the rhetorical theory of the period. The most conventional, and most often analyzed, poetic technique of the Renaissance, the Petrarchan blazon, frequently appears in similaic, rather than metaphorical form. A good example is sonnet #64 of Spenser's *Amoretti*, where the speaker declares of his beloved:

> Her lips did smell *lyke* vnto Gillyflowers,
> Her ruddy cheekes *lyke* vntto Roses red:
> Her snowy browes *lyke* budded Bellamoures,
> Her louely eyes *lyke* Pincks but newly spred.
> Her goodly bosom *lyke* a strawberry bed,
> Her neck *lyke* to a bounch of cullambynes:
> Her breest *lyke* lillyes, ere theyr leaues be shed,
> Her nipples *lyke* yong blossomd Iessemynes. (lines 5–12, emphases mine)

Shakespeare, ever critical of the Petrarchan blazon, is always careful to point out the similaic form of the poetic device for whose psycho-conceptual underpinnings he has much contempt. In the opening line of his parodic sonnet #130, Shakespeare's speaker declares: "My Mistress' eyes are nothing *like* the Sun." In the opening line of sonnet #18, Shakespeare's speaker implies he shall never *"compare"* his beloved "to a Summer's day." Elsewhere, he condemns Petrarchan blazons wholesale as "false *compare*" (sonnet #130, line 14), or "couplements of proud *compare*" (sonnet #21, line 5, emphases mine).

Shakespeare's aesthetics involves an intense psycho-conceptual engagement with simile as the basis of an erotic poetics of anti-identity. This poetics of anti-identity is at the basis of Shakespeare's radical philosophy of *dramatis personae* not as loci of self-same, conceptually metaphoric identity but as malleable, changeable, re-inscribeable "characters."

Shakespeare's radical philosophy of character is manifest in the meta-dramatic frame of the largely forgotten *Taming of a Shrew*, where the drunkard "Slie" receives the new "character" of a lord from a nobleman whose name, "Simon," or in short "Sim," underscores his alliance with the similaic. The remolding of Slie's character is a rhetorical act paradoxically amounting to the evacuation of the specular, narcissistic self-identity suggested by the "characters" i-m-i, I am I, a phonic echo of the Greek *eimi*, to be, from what would otherwise be the word "similie," simile in common Renaissance spelling. In the Folio version, the familiar *Taming of the Shrew*, the conceptual relevance of simile to the play is underscored by explicit mention (Act 5, scene 1, line 57).

Shakespeare conceived of the hollowed-out similaic subjectivity represented by Slie as coeval with desire. This is confirmed by another largely forgotten Shakespearean text, "A Lover's Complaint," where "similes / Hollow'd with sighs" are invoked as signs of seduction (lines 228–229). Crossing the hollowing out of subjectivity as desire with the hollowing out of simile, this poem resoundingly designates the field of the similaic rather than the metaphoric as the field of erotism. Shakespeare's "A Lover's Complaint" anticipates Lacan's theorization of desire as a function which can only ever deploy itself in the "want-to-be," marked by the "void of the verb 'to be'" (*Écrits*, p. 259), the identity-designating copula of metaphor (Sharon-Zisser, "'Similes Hollow'd with Sighs'"). Representing the similaic space of anti-identity as itself "Hollow'd" out, evacuated of the egoic signifier "I," the typographical trace of phallic self-identity (Lacan, *Écrits,* p. 287), the poem gestures toward the doubly erotic space of simile (–I). This space of a simile hollowed of an "I" is a space of rhetorical, affective, and corporeal osculation whose product is a "smile," a mark of an affectively and corporeally experienced *jouissance*.

In *Measure for Measure*, the similaic copula is used to speak of the "desire [of the] like" (Act 4, scene 1, line 52), of incest and homoeroticism wherein "like" quits/coits "like" (Act 5, scene 1, line 409). *As You Like It* is a play whose title links two gender-neutral pronouns by means of two similaic copulas into a potentially infinite libidinal sequence semantically speaking the possibility of all forms of liking and li(n)king, all forms of sexuality and desire.

In all these texts, Shakespeare recovers similaic rhetoric and anagrammatically rewrites it as the erotic. For Shakespeare, the similaic is the site of a poetics wherein, in the words of sonnet #62, the endless generation of identity through narcissistic "self-love" is rejected. What is celebrated or "praise[d]" instead is the "quit"-ing or separation of self and other subtending the similaic as the condition of a paronomastic coit-ing. The simultaneous quit-ing qua coit-ing and cut-ting phonically indexed by the sonnet is what enables a glimpse of "anti-quit-y," of archaic *jouissance* (lines 10–14).

Like sonnet #62, Shakespeare's *As You Like It* treats the connection between the archaic, "antique world" of pastoral (Act 2, scene 3, line 58) and simile. In this play, "the melancholy Jaques" (Act 2, scene 1, line 41) is the character who articulates the pain of consciousness as a cut in infinite continuity. When the melancholy Jaques projects this pain onto an external spectacle of a "sequestered stag" (Act 2, scene 1, line 33), he is said, in the play's only reference to a rhetorical form, to "moralize [the] spectacle...into a thousand *similes*" (Act 2, scene 1, lines 44–45, emphasis mine).

For all of his intense engagement with the similaic, Shakespeare was not the only early modern writer to point to the conceptual relation of this aesthetic category with the dynamics of a non-possessive, non-phallic eroticism. In "Colin Clovts Come Home Again," part of the non-phallic, non-Petrarchan, pastoral portion of his *oeuvre*, Spenser too alludes to the similaic as subtending the amatory structure of the domain of pastoral. The god of pastoral, the god of the shepherds, Spenser writes in this poem, is Eros. Eros is "Borne without Syre or couples" (line 800). He incarnates desire because he is de-syred, marked only by "the absence of the sign of the father" (Whitworth, "Far from Being"). What the god of polymorphic desire beyond the phallus as sign of the father teaches, Spenser adds, is "each one his *like* to love" (line 863, emphasis mine).

In 1587, A few years before Spenser published "Colin Clovt" (1591), Ulpian Fulwell had published a "pleasant Enterlude" entitled *Like Will to*

Like. This title combines "like," a signifier of the similaic copula and of an affective inclination acknowledged in the first lines of the interlude as the obverse of "mis-like," with "will," a signifier designating desire and the incarnation of drive in the male body. The combination of "like" and "will" in Fulwell's title thematizes the principle of non-anaclitic attraction, declared in the first lines of the interlude: "Cicero in his book de amicitia these woords dooth expresse, / Saying nothing is more desirous then like is unto like" (unpaginated).

In these inaugural lines of Fulwell's interlude, the non-anaclitic attraction of like to like is declared through an appeal to an archaic Ciceronian text, *De amicitia*. This text inspired other aesthetic expressions of male homoeroticism in the Renaissance, such as Pontormo's painting of fraternal intimacy, which adopts the title of Cicero's text (Whitworth, *The Name of the Ancients*). Fulwell foregrounds the affective and erotic resonances of the similaic copula as what "adioyne[s] like to like always." He indicates some of the corporeal-sexual resonances of the similaic copula "like." Fulwell's interlude includes a ribald sexual reference to one of the characters as "tom lick hole" (unpaginated).

The preoccupation of early modern writers with the similaic is not limited to the ribald or to the male homoeroticism foregrounded by Fulwell, Pontormo, and Spenser. Most of the lyrics of Aemilia Lanyer, including "The Author's Dreame to the Countess of Pembroke," "To the Lady Arabella," and "To the Queen's Most Excellent Majesty," take the form of an apostrophe of one woman to another and extensively explore the intersubjective dynamics of female homoeroticism. Lanyer invokes the similaic in relation to the sexual, and especially the erotic. Lanyer's "Description of Cooke-ham" is a poem wherein the woman-speaker's affective attachment to Margaret Clifford, Countess of Cumberland, is said to be thematized in "those rich chaines" constituting the poem as aesthetic object (line 211). Those poetic "chaines" transcode with imagined loving caresses between speaker and addressee projected onto the natural scene of Cooke-ham, where "Hills, vales, and woods" are "All interlac'd with brookes and christall springs (lines 68–71), and where "Trees with leaves, with fruits, with flowers clad, /Embrac[e]…each other, seeming to be glad" (lines 23–24). Those externalized fantasies of relational moments of amatory "interlacing" are generally characterized as instances wherein "all things…did hold like *similies*" (line 22, emphasis mine). In this meta-similaic statement, affect, erotics, rhetoric, and sexual fantasy are "interlaced" by means of a similaic copula.

John Donne's "Sapho to Philaenis" is a male's sexual fantasy of female homoeroticism. In this poem, Donne too thematizes female homoeroticism as a similaic liking of the like. When the Lesbian poet who is Donne's dramatized speaker articulates her narcissistic attraction to her companion Philaenis (literally, "female friend"), she does so by means of the similaic copula. Sapho states: "thy right hand, and cheek, and eye, only / Are *like* thy other hand, and cheek, and eye" (lines 22–23). She proceeds to protest: "the *likeness* being such, /Why should they not *alike* in all parts touch?" (lines 46–47, emphases mine). For Donne in "Sapho to Philaenis," the similaic becomes the affective and sexual basis of female homoeroticism and its adequate rhetorical expression. Likeness "begets" the "strange selfe flatterie" (line 51), the narcissistic deployment of the libido involved in female homoeroticism.

In Renaissance rhetoric and poetics, simile is singled out for attention among many dozens of rhetorical forms although it is never accorded the status of general equivalency attributed to metaphor. Renaissance poetics involve repeated instances of insistence on the conceptual connection of the similaic and the erotic, especially in two types of circumstances, which often overlap. (1) Insistence on the connection between the similaic and the erotic appears in Shakespeare's *Measure for Measure* and *As You Like It*, in Spenser's "Colin Clovts Come Home Again," in Fulwell's *Like Will to Like*, in Aemilia Lanyer's "To Cooke-ham," and in Donne's "Sapho to Philaenis," where the erotic is inflected as the homo-erotic, whether male or female. (2) Insistence on the connection between the similaic and the erotic appears in *As You Like It* and "Colin Clovts Come Home Again" when the similaic is deployed in the domain of pastoral as, in Spenser's terms, the domain of Eros. What could explain this marked and conscious preoccupation with the similaic in the rhetoric and poetics of the Renaissance, especially in connection with pastoral and with homoeroticism?

Preoccupation with the similaic is symptomatically indexed in the writing of Abraham Fraunce. Fraunce's career as a man of letters was diachronically and dialectically split between an engagement with the erotic poetics of pastoral and with the ostensibly hyper-rational theory of rhetoric and oratory striving to set up metaphor as a phallic general equivalent "loftie and full of maiestie" (*The Arcadian Rhetorike*, unpaginated). In *The Arcadian Rhetorike*, Fraunce theorizes rhetoric in terms of the similaic, as "both *vnlike* that of Poets, and alwaies *vnlike* itself" (unpaginated, emphases mine). Rhetoric, Fraunce implies, seeks to be "vn-like" the polymorphism of the unconscious thematized in pastoral texts, yet in doing so becomes only "vnlike itself," alienated from its conscious goal. In this statement in *The Arcadian Rhetorike*, Fraunce makes simile, of all rhetorical forms, an index to the inevitable infiltration of the polymorphic erotics of pastoral, erotics constitutively beyond the phallus, into the would-be phallic and hyper-rational theory of rhetoric. What about the aesthetic category of simile as it was theorized by early modern thinkers of language led Fraunce to make it an index to the constitutive failure of Renaissance rhetoric to repress the seductive poetics of pastoral?

The answers to such questions, Renaissance rhetoricians and poets suggest, could never be found by limiting appeals to history. The similaic, they repeatedly suggest, is a category harkening back to the first principles of origin. Renaissance rhetoricians and poets inflect the similaic as beyond the vicissitudes of the linear chronology from which origin constantly recedes, although not beyond the more complex category of psychically-inflected temporality. The logical principle of simile, syncrisis, Elisha Coles declares at the outset of his treatise by this name, published in 1677, "is as Ancient as Nature itself" (unpaginated).

Francis Meres opens his compendium of similitudes, *Wits Commonwealth*, by declaring the principle of "*triasmus omnia*," the pervasiveness of the triangle of desire exceeding the solipsistic illusions of a wholeness born of couples of which Spenser too speaks (sig. A1). Like Spenser, Meres transcodes this principle of non-dyadic desire with the similaic. For Meres, this non-dyadic similaic desire "is as old as father Time" (ibid.). This principle is as old as the most archaic fathers of philosophy, Pythagoras and Thales, whose thinking on *triasmus omnia*, a thinking preceding the ontological tradition fixated on the thinking of Being qua presence by which it was repressed, Meres quotes in his dedication (ibid., sigs. A2–A3).

In calling the philosophy of Thales, Pythagoras, and other pre-Socratics I mention in this book "non-ontological," I do not mean these philosophers were not concerned with the question "what is?" Instead, I indicate the absence of an obsession with definiteness and totality. For instance, I read the Pythagoreans' engagement with the categories of Harmonia and Number, involving the problematic of separates, as bracketing out the issue of Being qua plenitude which became the focus of the metaphysics of Plato and Aristotle and of the much of the ensuing philosophical tradition. In the sense of the absence of an obsession with Being, the philosophy of the Pythagoreans, of Thales, of Heraclitus, of Anaximenes, and of other pre-Socratics I mention in this book is non-ontological.

Shakespeare too invokes pre-ontological, pre-Socratic thinking in conjunction with the similaic. The response of Rosalind, the heroine of his similaically-entitled *As You Like It*, to the song dedicated to her by her lover Orlando, is "I was never so berhymed since Pythagoras's time" (Act 3, scene 1, line 170). Early modern rhetoricians and poets repeatedly refer to the similaic in conjunction with the ancient, the antique, the archaic. They refer to the similaic in conjunction with the category of the archaic as the site of a non-ontological philosophy not fixated on the category of Being. Early modern rhetoricians and poets are concerned with the similaic in conjunction with a supplemental, at least triple desire exceeding the illusion of complementarity.

The connections between the similaic, the archaic, and supplemental eroticism in early modern rhetoric and poetics have an important theoretical consequence. The pervasive preoccupation with the similaic in early modern rhetoric and poetics, while temporally localizeable, is a simultaneously philosophical and psychological rather than historical phenomenon. Because it is a psychological and philosophical phenomenon, the early modern preoccupation with the similaic does not require an analysis alert to any cultural contexts which might "ground" and thus conceptually empty it. The early modern preoccupation with the similaic demands and deserves an analysis alert to its conceptual and psychic resonances. The deployments of the similaic in Renaissance poetics already tell us what those resonances might be: non-ontological, non-phallic, affective, erotic, related to the polymorphic sexuality thematized by pastoral. The philosophical analysis of those resonances cannot stop short at the formal or even the metaphysical. It must extend into the psychic. It must be a philosophically-inflected psychoanalysis.

The poetic deployments of the similaic by Renaissance authors to designate the interlacing of the rhetorical and logical function of likeness, affective lik-ing, and corporeal/linguistic li(n)king indicate where this psychoanalysis must begin: in the theorizations of the signifier "like" or its grammatical equivalent "as." "Like" and "as" formally subtend simile as its copula. They distinguish simile from the aesthetic category to which simile is often related in early modern rhetorical theory, metaphor.

Most rhetorical treatises of the Renaissance and their medieval precursors theorize simile in relation to metaphor. In Jacobus Iznelgrinus's *Rethorica Nova* (ca. 1450) *translationem* and *comparationem* are mentioned in conjunction with one another (p. 13), as they are in Philippus Callimachus's *Rhetorica* (ca. 1470) (unpaginated). In Lorenzo Guglielmo Traversagni's *Margarita Eloquentiae Castigatae* (ca. 1480), *translatio* is described as a form made possible by *similitudo* (p. 197). Alberic of Montecassino describes metaphors as grounded in similitudes (p. 46). In G. Perez De Ledesma's *Censura de la Eloquencia* (1648) similes and metaphors are said to have but a slight difference from one another (p. 123). In the English Renaissance, Richard Sherry cites "similitudes" as the generating principle of metaphors (*Schemes and Tropes*, p. 33), and Hobbes in his *Art of Rhetoric* (1681) describes a similitude as "differ[ing] from a Metaphor only by such Particles of Comparison as...As, Even as, So, Even so, &c" (p. 106). These medieval and Renaissance theorizations of simile in relation to metaphor have their classical antecedents in Aristotle's description of the difference between metaphor and simile as "but slight" (*Rhetoric* 1406b) and Longinus' theorization of comparisons and similes as "[c]losely related to Metaphors" in *On the Sublime* (sec. 32, line 3).

Examples of simile provided by Renaissance rhetoricians foreground its predication on the copula so ubiquitously theorized as the grounds of its difference from metaphor. Hobbes's examples of similes in *The Art of Rhetoric* include "They who choose their Magistrates by Lot, are *like* them that choose for their champions those on whom the Lot shall fall" (p. 93), and "the Baeotians were *like* to so many Okes in a Wood, that did nothing but beat one another" (p. 111). Bernard Lamy cites as an example the beginning of the first Psalm, "He shall be *like* a Tree by th' Waters side" (p. 232). Sherry's examples in *The Treatise of the Figures of Grammer and Rhetorike* include "one flew upon his enemies, *like* a dragon or a lion" (fol. liii). Peacham's examples in *The Garden of Eloquence* include "her bodye is *lyke* the slender yew, her fyngers *lyke* the whyte palm braunches, the bee strypte, her eyes *like* glistening pearles, her lyppes *lyke* the carnation Rose, her cheekes *like* the whyte & lillye, besprynkled with ruddy iuyce, her lookes *like* a golden fleece, her countenance chereful, *like* the smiling Mother upo [sic] her tender babe, her neck & brestes *like* to whyte Alabaster" (unpaginated). John Smith's examples include "[t]his comfort in danger is *like* the honey that Samson found in the Lyons jaws, or *like* lightning in a foggy night" (p. 211). The examples of similes provided by Joshua Poole in his *Practical Rhetorick* include "Fortune is *like* the Country-men in the Fable who...out of the same mouth blew both cold and hot" (p. 108, emphases mine).

In contradistinction to the metaphoric copula to which it is often said to be formally related, the similaic copula "like" does not designate a grammatical tense, certainly not the ontologically-weighted present tense early modern grammarians associate with the signifier "is" structuring the metaphoric copula. This implicit distinction between a metaphoric copula designating a tense and a similaic copula not designating a tense suggests a split between the category of simile and the category of time in early modern aesthetics. The allusions to the connections between simile and a lost timeless archaic in the texts of Shakespeare, Meres, and Coles suggest the same split.

Yet as early modern thinkers of language were aware long before Lacan theorized the unconscious as "a temporal structure" which nevertheless "does not lend itself to ontology" (*Seminar XI*, pp. 29, 32), ontology and presence are not one and the same as temporality. Temporality or "Tyme," Richard Sherry says in *A Treatise of Schemes and Tropes*, "signifieth two thynges." (1) First of these is the "playn," ontologically definitive temporality of the "time present, past, or to come." (2) The second meaning of "Tyme," for Sherry, is the proleptic, non-ontologically definite temporality of an "opportunity to do a thynge." This mode of temporality, Sherry says, can only be a "coniecture." In this mode, Sherry adds, "tyme is taken for an opportunity of tyme" (unpaginated). In Renaissance rhetoric, simile is related to this second, conjectural temporality of "opportunity."

The similaic copula significantly lacks the ontologicality and presence early modern theorists of language inscribe into its metaphoric counterpart. The similaic copula is conceptually linked with a kind of non-present temporality best described, in Lacanian terms, as unconscious. The non-present temporality Sherry and Lacan speak of manifests itself in the want-to-be, in the gap between an alluring "image of the past" and a "future" which is nothing but the past always already on the verge of its second coming (Lacan, *Seminar XI*, pp. 31–32). This non-present temporality is the conjectural temporality of desire.

In William Walker's *Treatise of English Particles* (1655), this erotic temporality is the third meaning adduced to the signifier "like" as a particle. Walker's treatise is devoted to "particles," linguistic components theorized in terms of the "Arteries in the body, running through the whole, add[ing] life and motion...to every part" (unpaginated). Walker theorizes particles in terms of a connecting, animating, and kineticizing copulative function. Kineticism, Bataille was to say, is the hallmark of the erotic ("The Solar Anus," *Visions of Excess*, p. 7). In *Symptoms, Inhibitions, and Anxiety*, Freud speaks of Eros in similar terms. Eros, Freud writes, is a striving toward the love object and the yearning for linking contact with this object (p. 49). The functions in terms of which William Walker theorizes the category of the particle are structurally subtended by a constitutively erotic intentionality to link. The classification of "like" as one of the "particles" already eroticizes it.

In the third theorization of "like" as a constitutively erotic "particle," Walker glosses it as a signifier "import[ing] a likelihood or probability of some event hapned, feared, or desired" (p. 179). Walker's third gloss of "like" situates it in an ambiguous temporality. This temporality is suspended between the certainty of a past "event" and a "feared or desired" event which may never happen.

This temporality, in which the present tense subtending the metaphoric copula is absent, significantly lacks explicit theorization as a tense in most early modern treatises on grammar. Most early modern grammar treatises recognize, besides the present and future (simple) tenses, three preterite (past) tenses: preterimperfect, preterperfect, and preterpluperfect (R[obinson], p. 59; Miege, p. 50; Aickin, p. 13; Busby, p. 13; Wharton, p. 43; Poole, *English Accidence*, p. 10; Jonson, *English Grammar*, p. 10). They do not define what modern linguists would come to call the "conditional" as a tense.

A few early modern grammar treatises do not avoid the theorization of the conditional, and they theorize this category in significant terms. In Guy Miege's *English Grammar* (1688), the future tense is said to be split "into two, first and second, that being Absolute, and this conditional" (p. 50). Cooper too talks of the "conditional," but theorizes it as a mood rather than a tense (pp. 142–143). R[obinson] theorizes the conditional temporality of likelihood as the "promissive," (p. 50), accentuating its conceptual link with what is longed for or desired. In the few cases in which the conditional is theorized in early modern grammar treatises, it is characterized in terms of the less than "absolute" or definite and the alluringly possible. When the conditional temporality is theorized in early modern grammar treatises, it is constitutively eroticized.

The suspended, ambiguous temporality lacking a referent Walker associates with the particle "like" exemplified by Renaissance rhetoricians as a copula of simile is inscribed in most Renaissance treatises on grammar through its absence. The absence of the theorization of non-referential temporality in early modern grammar treatises implicitly theorizes this temporality in terms of a structuring lack. This lack structuring non-referential temporality is what would enable Lacan to designate this temporality as the "field of the unconscious" (*Seminar XI*, p. 36).

William Walker exemplifies the ambiguous, suspended, lacking, and hence erotic temporality by means of the phrases "we are *like* to have war," "I am *like* to lose my credit," "I am *like* to be hanged," and "you are never *like* to see me more" (pp. 179–180, emphases mine). All these examples articulate purely conjectural, non-definite events. The exemplification of the conjectural temporality of likelihood in Walker's treatise seems to be at odds with Walker's first characterization of this temporality as what had definitively "hapned." This exemplification of likelihood seems to be at odds with Walker's choice to characterize likelihood in all three instances by means of the preterite tense.

The preterite tense expresses defineable things (Whitworth, "Passing for Mean," p. 71). Early modern grammarians theorize this tense as definitively, ostensively "denot[ing]" (Aickin, p. 10) or "expressing" (Miege, p. 50) a "time past" (Aickin, p. 10; Miege, p. 50). This time consists of events whose having taken place is an ontologically verifiable certainty.

William Walker's choice to theorize the erotic temporality he associates with the similaic particle "like" as semantically and formally preterite is as anasemically telling as the obsession of most Renaissance grammarians with the three configurations of the preterite and their simultaneous avoidance of the theorization of the temporality of likelihood. The obsession with the grammatical categories of the past is simultaneous with an avoidance of a category of a future less than "absolute," a future eternally in the "promissive." This simultaneity inflects the seemingly polarized obsession and avoidance as having psychically and conceptually much to do with one another. The obsession with the multiple forms of the preterite, with the past, in early modern grammatical theory bespeaks the retheorization of the preterite as the content of the untheorized erotic temporality. The conditional, erotic temporality rarely theorized in early modern grammar theory becomes implicitly theorized as what Stephen Whitworth calls a "memory for the future" ("Passing for Mean," p. 84).

In William Walker's third theorization the particle "like," this particle is associated with "likelihood or probability," with what has not yet occurred. At the same time, this theorization involves a doubly foregrounded appearance of the preterite, of an "event" syntactically and semantically declared to have "happned." Within this theorization, the definite and the non-definite seem to be held in dialectical tension. This dialectical tension inflects Walker's third function of "like" as a particular temporality. This temporality involves the happening of an encounter. The psychological significance of the happening of an encounter, Lacan teaches, is considerable. The happening of an encounter, for Lacan, is a necessary condition of happiness. "Happiness," Lacan comments, "is after all 'happen'; it, too, is an encounter" (*Seminar VII*, p. 13).

Yet the absence of representations of past events among Walker's examples suggests this happy happening took place at a mythic time which never was. This temporal situation of happy happenings in William Walker's text inflects them as what Ned Lukacher calls "primal scenes." A primal scene, Lukacher writes, is an "intertextual event displaced from the ground of ontology" and henceforth "situated in the differential space between historical memory and imaginative reconstruction" (p. 24). Within the dialectical temporality implied by Walker's third theorization of "like," the primal scene of happy happening is completely displaced from the ground of ontology and resituated as an aspiration. This primal scene of happiness is resituated as the impossible, unreachable aim of what Stephen Whitworth calls "desire's eternal futurity" ("Passing for Mean," p. 73). Lacan identifies this impossible aim. He calls it "the oceanic aspiration" (*Seminar XI*, p. 31).

Walker's third theorization of the similaic copula in the form of the eroticized particle "like" as "likelihood or probability" aligns it with the structure of desire as an aspiration to return to an inaccessible oceanic origin which never was. The origin resituated as aim in Walker's third theorization of "like" is the origin other early modern rhetoricians transcode with the primal substance of semiosis. The aspiration to this inaccessible oceanic origin has as its inevitable obverse the "fear" of the loss of individuating boundaries of which Walker too speaks.

Walker's theorization of the similaic "like" in terms of a constitutively erotic "memory for the future" aligns it with the ontologically undecideable temporality of desire. This theorization aligns the similaic "like" with the grammatical mood of desire. This mood is inevitably less than definitive, absolute, and categorical. It is the mood of "likelihood and probability," the mood early modern grammarians implicitly contrast with the "indicative" mood structuring the metaphoric copula and name the "optative" or "potential," and sometimes the "subjunctive."

Busby theorizes the subjunctive as the general class and the potential and optative as its special cases. He describes the optative as signaled by an "Adverb of wishing," a signifier of desire (p. 12). Miege offers the same classification, specifying the optative class of the subjunctive as the mood wherein "we make wishes" (p. 54). In Wharton's *English Grammar*, the only mood designating the non-definite, non-categorical, non-ontological modality of "likelihood or probability" of which Walker speaks in relation to the similaic particle "like" is the potential. Like in Walker's theorization of the particle "like" as an erotic mood, in Wharton's treatise this mood is designated as "signif[ying] a…desire" (p. 43).

R[obinson]'s *English Grammar* and Poole's *English Accidence* offer a slightly different theorization of the non-definite mood. In the treatises of

R[obinson] and Poole, the subjunctive, theorized by other early modern grammarians as the general class of the optative and potential, is taxonomically and conceptually isolated from these moods. R[obinson] and Poole theorize the subjunctive as different from the optative and potential because unlike the optative and potential moods it necessarily "hath some conjunctions...joined with it" (Poole, p. 10). Consequently, the subjunctive "doth not by itself perfect a sentence, unless it be subjected to another speech, or have another speech subjected to it" (R[obinson], p. 58). In the grammatical treatises of R[obinson] and Poole, the subjunctive, not the optative mood is eroticized, in its theorization as a mood which "wisheth" or "desireth" (Poole, p. 10; R[obinson], p. 58).

In Peacham's *Garden of Eloquence* too, "*optatio*" as a rhetorical category is eroticized. Peacham theorizes *optatio* as a figure occurring "when we wishe for that, that we would gladly haue" (unpaginated). The Eros with which Poole, R[obinson], and Peacham associate the optative is by definition a "power binding subjects together" (Lacan, *Seminar I*, p. 112) and hence intersubjective and relational. The erotization of the optative underscores its conceptual link with the subjunctive taxonomically isolated from it by Poole and R[obinson] on the grounds of its necessary formal implication in a relation of subjection. The erotization of the optative associates it with the potential as the grammatical mark of the eternal intention of desire toward the oceanic aim, the eternal intention to "find again" an archaic object who "has never been lost" (Lacan, *Seminar VII*, p. 58).

In early modern grammatical theory, the optative, potential, or subjunctive moods are sometimes wholly or partially collapsed into one another. In other cases, these moods are taxonomically isolated from one another yet implicitly linked through their common conceptual predication on erotic relationality. Yet in all cases, what is theorized in relation to the optative, potential, or subjunctive mood is a less than categorical modality. This non-categorical modality of what Walker calls "likelihood or probability" disables an indicative, ontological ostension toward a referent purportedly given in the definite temporalities of the present or preterite theorized in relation to the metaphoric copula "is" (see Chapter Four above). Instead, the non-categorical modality incessantly gestures toward a necessarily barred referent it may never access.

The optative, potential, and subjunctive moods as theorized by the early modern grammarians bear out Bataille's theorization of poetry at large as "not a knowledge of oneself, and even less the experience of a remote possible (of what, before, was not), but the simple evocation through words of inaccessible possibilities" (*The Impossible*, p. 162). Early modern theorizations of these less than definite moods bear out Agamben's similar eroticized definition of lyric poetry as "always transfixed on the verge of a day that has always already set," as a text "necessarily empty" yet linguistically creating "something like a lived experience" it forever seeks (*The Idea of Prose*, pp. 52–53). The optative, potential, and subjunctive moods in their early modern theorizations are avatars of the constitutively erotic orientation toward an object simultaneously "exposed and sealed off," an orientation functioning, Agamben writes, as "the idea of love" (ibid., p. 61).

In Walker's treatise on particles, the modality established for the particle "like" with which early modern rhetoricians exemplify a similaic copula is constitutively amatory and erotic in its ontological undecideability, its suspension in a future eternally about to happen. R[obinson] suggests this when noting the optative mood "hath sometimes the signification of the future tense" (p. 58).

The constitutively amatory and erotic underpinnings Walker foregrounds in his third theorization of the particle "like" as a temporality and modality have significant consequences for his second theorization of the particle "like" as a verb "denoting to approve, delight in, be pleased with, glad of &c" (p. 179). The connection between the function of the particle "like" as modality and as verb is more than paronomastic and homophonic. "Like" as a verb is theorized by Walker in relation to pleasure, "delight," and joy. Walker exemplifies this verb in the phrases "you will like the doing of it," "if you like it," and "I like it well" (p. 179), bearing out its theorization as pleasure-related. "Like" as modality is theorized by Walker in relation to a constitutively erotic proleptic temporality too. Centuries later, Lacan would diagnose the two psychic functions Walker inscribes into the similaic signifier "like" as conceptually related to one another. Lacan perceives a conceptual link between "archaic...pleasure" and the subject's desire, necessarily orienting itself toward objects standing in for this archaic pleasure (*Seminar VII*, pp. 42, 58). Given this conceptual link, the connection between Walker's second theorization of the particle "like" as pleasure-signifying verb, and his third theorization of this particle in terms of the temporality and modality of "desire" as a memory for the future, and its inevitable corollary, "fear," is, beyond homophony, a profoundly categorial, philosophical connection.

Another categorial connection between the particle "like" and the concept of desire is revealed in early modern theorizations of the optative, potential, or subjunctive moods with which Walker associates this particle.

These intentional, non-definite, and hence erotic moods, early modern grammarians affirm, are formally relational. Given the definition of Eros as the intentionality of subject to love-object, the formal relationality of the non-definite moods increases their eroticism. Unlike the solipsistic, self-contained, and hence phallic indicative mood, the non-definite moods have another part of speech "joined to them" (Aickin, p. 11). The part of speech joined to the non-definite moods is a conjunction, or an adverb (Aickin, p. 11; Busby, p. 12; R[obinson], p. 58).

The first among the parts of speech joined to the non-definite moods, the conjunction, is a "part of speech joining words, and sentences together" (Wharton, p. 57; Busby, p. 26; R[obinson], p. 101). According to Ben Jonson, the function of the conjunction is "knitting diverse speeches together" (*English Grammar*, p. 48). The conjunction is inherently copulaic, or as Wharton (p. 57) and Busby (p. 26) put it, "Copulative." The conjunction is hence constitutively erotic.

The second part of speech theorized by early modern grammarians as related to the non-definite modality associated, in Walker's treatise, with the particle "like," the most common similaic copula, is the adverb. Early modern grammarians theorize the adverb too as copulaic and relational. Wharton speaks of the adverb as "*joined* to a Verbe, or a Noun" (p. 53). Aickin defines the adverb as "*joyned* to Verbs and Adjectives" (p. 15). Busby says the adverb is "*joyned* to a Verb, Noun, or Participle" (p. 25). R[obinson] declares the adverb to be "*joyned* to the Verbe" (p. 97; emphases mine). In all these cases, Renaissance grammarians conceptualize the adverb, designated as a formal part of the modality they theorize as erotic in its proleptic intentionality, as performing the function of linguistic joining.

The function of linguistic joining is the function Sherry theorizes as fundamental to elocution. Elocution consists, Sherry writes, of "wordes…considered by themselues, and…*joyned* together in speache" (*Schemes and Tropes*, unpaginated, emphasis mine). Because linguistic joining, for Sherry, is seminal to elocution, it is seminal to the effect he says elocution generates. In the dedication of his *Treatise of Schemes and Tropes*, Sherry speaks of elocution as generating "corporall…pleasure," the sensuous joy indexing eroticism (unpaginated). Sherry's distinction between "woordes…considered by themselues" and words "joyned together in speache" suggests his implicit recognition, long before the psychoanalysis of Jacques Lacan and Michèle Montrelay, of the constitutively limited, partial, morcel-like nature of the surfaces organized by an assembling pulsion (Montrelay, p. 91). Montrelay speaks of this assembling pulsion as Eros. Sherry speaks of it as generating pleasures with which Eros is associated.

The joy of joining separates can only be experienced within the gap or hollow differentiating signifiers, and signifiers from signifieds, the gap or hollow differentiating subjects as cuts in the signifying chain. This hollow is desire (Lacan, *Écrits*, pp. 299, 311). The erotic joy of the signifier is produced by joining, thereby depending on the cut, bar, or limit invoked by Renaissance grammarians in their theorization of the adverb. This joy is necessarily always partially proleptic, a "fragment of *jouissance*," of the lost archaic "infinite placenta-time" (Montrelay, p.137). The lost archaic joy is projected into the future as the aim of desire, inscribed in early modern theorizations of the optative, potential, or subjunctive moods. Renaissance grammarians recognize the erotic character of the adverb they theorize as a component of those eroticized moods Walker theorizes as subtending the modal inflection of the similaic particle "like." The adverb functioning as the conjunction forming these moods, they write, is an "Adverbe of wishing" whose Latin equivalent is *"utinam"* (would that) (Busby, p. 12; R[obinson], p. 58).

The conceptual connection sketched in early modern theory of grammar between the adverb as a joining signifier and the signifier "like" exemplifying the similaic copula in many Renaissance treatises on rhetoric exceeds the theorization of the adverb as a component of the proleptic, ontologically indefinite moods subtending the modal inflection of "like" as theorized by Walker. The theorization of the category of the adverb in early modern treatises on grammar includes the function of wishing featured in the theorizations of the proleptic, erotic moods of a "likelihood" suspended in the state of being wished-for. The theorization of the category of the adverb in early modern grammar treatises includes the functions of "Likenesse" (Poole, *Accidence*, p. 28; Wharton, p. 56; Busby, p. 25), and "Comparison" (Poole, *Accidence*, p. 28; Wharton, p. 56), or, as Cooper puts it in his *Grammatica Linguae Anglicanae*, *"Comparandi"* (p. 163). In Ben Jonson's *English Grammar*, the function of "likenesse" is theorized as expressed by the adverb alongside the constitutively erotic function of "wishing" (p. 68). The adverbial function of likeness in Jonson's grammatical treatise is articulated as apposite to and synonymous with the name of an elocutionary category: "similitude" (ibid.).

In early modern treatises on the aesthetics of rhetoric, the functions of comparison and likeness theorized by early modern grammarians as components of the adverb are conceptualized as constitutive of the elocutionary category of similitude or one of its corollaries. This is the case in Wilson's *Arte of Rhetorique*, where similitude is defined as "a likeness when two things, or more than two are so *compared* and resembled together that they...in some property seem like" (p. 213). This definition is echoed verbatim in the dedication to Cawdray's *Storehovse or Treasvrie of Similies* (sig. A2). In Sherry's *Treatise of Schemes and Tropes*, similitude is defined as a "*coparation* [sic]" or "*comparyng* of a thyng...for some thyng that is lyke or unlyke" (unpaginated). In Smith's *Mysterie of Rhetorique Unvail'd*, similitude is defined as "a form of speech whereby the Orator or speaker *compares* one thing with the other" (p. 211). In Peacham's *Garden of Eloquence*, similitude is defined as occuring when "the image of a thing or person, is painted out by *coparing* [sic] and resembling forme with forme, quality with quality, and one likenesse with another" (unpaginated), and as a "*comparing* of thinges, persons, deedes, examples, contraries, lyke or unlyke" (unpaginated). In Lamy's *Art of Speaking*, "comparison" is used as a synonymous apposite to "Similitude" (p. 241). In John Hoskyns's *Directions for Speech and Style*, similitude is said to consist of sentences "of several proper terms *compared*" (p. 9). In Joachimus Camerarius's *Elementa Rhetoricae*, similitude is said to be subtended by "*comparationis*" (p. 221). In Charles Butler's *Oratoriae Libri Duo*, the "*comparata*" (compared terms) said to constitute a similitude are described as being "*similia et Dissimilia*" (similar and dissimilar, like and unlike) (sig. C32). In Bartolomeo Cavalcanti's *La Retorica*, "*similitudine*" is said to be a "*comparatione espressante de una cosa d'un altra*" (an expressed comparison of one thing unto another) (p. 253, emphases mine).

In all these cases, the functions of comparison and likeness, theorized by early modern grammarians as components of the category of the adverb subtending the constitutively erotic non-categorical moods conceptually related to the particle "like," are theorized as formative of the rhetorical category of simile. The adverbial component of the non-categorical moods further inflects the connection in early modern language theory between the similaic copula "like" and the modality of "likelihood" pointed out in Walker's *Treatise of English Particles*, as extending from the homophonic and paronomastic into the conceptual.

The modality of a memory toward the future associated by Walker with the particle "like" is constitutively erotic. The category of the adverb is theorized as a component of this non-categorical modality. The category of the adverb is eroticized taxonomically, because it is a component of a non-categorical modality. This category is eroticized structurally and constitutively, because it is a joining or joined part of speech. The erotization of the modality of a memory toward the future is redoubled by the constitutive erotization of one of its components. The conceptual connection of this modality with the similaic copula "like" intensely eroticizes this copula.

The connection between the adverbial and the similaic in Renaissance theory of language is, beyond even the functional-conceptual, etymological. Adverbs of quality (Jonson, *English Grammar*, p. 68; R[obinson], p. 100; Aickin, p. 18; Wharton, p. 56; Miege, p. 78) are theorized as formally distinct from the adverbial functions of likeness and comparison. They are, at the same time, theorized as "end[ing] in ly" (Miege, p. 78), "made of Adjectives by adding ly" (Wharton, p. 56), or "formed from Nounes, for the most part, by adding ly" (Jonson, *English Grammar*, p. 68). The suffix "ly" in relation to which the adverb is theorized in early modern grammar treatises derives from the Old English *"lic."* This Old English signifier is the etymological root of the particle "like" in its signification of likeness, the signification inscribed by Renaissance rhetoricians into the similaic copula.

The similaic copula "like" is related to the category of the adverb as theorized by Renaissance grammarians etymologically and functionally. The adverb is theorized as relational. Because of its relationality, the adverb is dependent on the bars separating the entities put into relation. Categories dependent on such bars, Montrelay says, "put *jouissance* into play so as to limit it" (p. 39). This makes the adverb as theorized by early modern grammarians too a participant in a dialectic of the deployment and limitation of *jouissance*. The adverb is all the more implicated in this dialectic in its overdeterminately eroticized inflection as a signifier of "wishing," a component of the optative, potential, or subjunctive moods formally expressive of desire's eternal futurity. The etymological and functional relation of the similaic copula "like" to a category as intensely eroticized as the adverb, especially in its inflection as a signifier of "wishing," increases the erotization of the similaic copula.

The conceptual consequence of the erotization of the adverb is the eroticization of the similaic copula with which the adverb is etymologically, functionally, and conceptually related. In one anonymous Renaissance treatise on linguistic aesthetics, *Words Made Visible: or Grammar and Rhetorick Accommodated to the Lives and Manners of Men* (1679), this conceptual consequence is expressed by means of a mythologeme. In this treatise, two characters dramatize the category of the adverb. One character is designated by a Greek word, the other by a Latin word. The Latin word is the same "adverb of wishing," *"utinam"* (would that) used by Busby and R[obinson] to theorize the erotic optative mood. The Greek word is

"Ithmy," a signifier derived from *ithuo*, to desire eagerly. The names of the eroticized characters who dramatize the adverb are Greek. These names are mythologically eroticized. The two characters impersonating the adverb in *Words Made Visible* are the Heavenly Twins, Castor and Pollux.

Castor and Pollux are the Dioscuri, mortal and immortal sons of Leda. Like the love between Demeter and Persephone celebrated in the mysteries of Eleusis, the love of Castor and Pollux for one another effects a transference powerful enough to transcend the boundaries between mortality and immortality. According to the archaic myth, as told by Homer, Apollodorus, and Theocritus, the Twins were involved in a battle with Lynceus over plundered cattle driven from the pastoral realm of Arcadia, in the course of which Castor was killed and Pollux fell unconscious. His father Zeus then carried Pollux to heaven. Since "Pollux was unwilling to accept immortality while Castor lay dead, Zeus granted that both of them should live alternate days amongst the gods and among mortals" (Apollodorus, bk. 3, sec. 12, line 2). In Pindar's Ode 10.50, strophe 455, the Heavenly Twins are said to "each fulfill...an equal destiny, since Polydeuces preferred this life to being wholly a god and living in heaven, when Castor was killed in battle."

Ancient sources foreground the eroticism of the myth of the Heavenly Twins. The name of the immortal twin, Pollux, or Polydeuces, resonates with the word *"polu-euktos"* (much prayed for, much desired). A fragment by Ibycus refers to the Twins in the context of a song about "love's...power," a power driving the gods to "give much prosperity to those whom they wish to have it" (*Greek Lyric*, p. 227). Demosthenes speaks of the Twins in his *Erotic Essay* in the context of a discussion of what makes one deemed worthy of the company of gods, describing them as "beloved of the gods" because of their courage (bk. 6, sec. 1, line 30). In Cicero's *De divinitate*, the Dioscuri are said to have been identified by the Spartans with the morning and evening stars (bk. 2, sec. 32, line 68). The morning star is conventionally Venus, goddess of love, who becomes conflated with the immortal twin whose name is the name of desire.

In other ancient texts, what is foregrounded is the incestuous nature of the eroticism associated with the Twins. In Euripides' *Electra*, the heroine declares: "I turn away from Castor, who sought me in marriage before he joined the gods, *for I was his relative*" (line 310, emphasis mine). Euripides' Electra names incest as the cause of desire rather than desire's prohibited aim. Theocritus' hymn to the Dioscuri tells the story of their wedding two sisters, Hilaira and Phoebe, to whom they are cousins (*The Greek*

Bucolic Poets, p. 129).

Above all, the story of the love between the Twins is the story of the multiple attraction to the like. The attraction between them is homoerotic, fraternal, and geminaic. Their story is a story of polymorphic desire such as thematized in the genre of pastoral. The introduction of the mytheme of Castor and Pollux into the dramatized rhetorical treatise *Words Made Visible* foregrounds the psychic and conceptual relationship of Renaissance rhetoric and pastoral, which I have shown to be evident in each one of the rhetorical categories analyzed in this book. In *Words Made Visible*, the relation of rhetoric to pastoral as a poetic adequation of the imaginary state of fusion with the primal, maternal oral object is implicitly recognized in an act of naming. In this dramatized treatise, the oral aspect of rhetoric, pronunciation, is given the prosodic name of the pastoral genre, "Eclogus" (p. 104).

Other than the Heavenly Twins, ec-logic traces of pastoral desire exceeding logicality, the only mythological character featured in the treatise is the god of eloquence Mercury, who is dramatized as "a Messenger of King Syntaxis" (sig. A2). This choice of casting has a crucial conceptual consequence. It inflects the pastoral mythologeme of desire for the like at its extreme as no less fundamental to the category of rhetoric than the mythologeme of Mercury who is identified as the god of this discipline.

The Heavenly Twins are mythic manifestations of the desire of the like at its extreme. Their mythologeme is subtended by the functions of likeness and/as libidinal liking and li(n)king. In *Words Made Visible*, the Heavenly Twins are conflated with the category of the adverb. This category, in particular in its inflection as an adverb of wishing, is, I have shown above, multiply eroticized. The conflation of the adverb with the Heavenly Twins underscores the erotization of the adverb and inflects this erotization as similaic, related to the multiple desire of the like: incestuous, fraternal, geminaic, and homoerotic.

The category of the adverb with which Castor and Pollux are conflated in *Words Made Visible* is multiply implicated with the function of likeness. The adverb is related to the similaic copula "like" in two ways. (1) The adverb is related to the similaic copula "like" etymologically, because of the derivation of its qualitative inflection from the Old English *lic*. (2) The adverb is related to the similaic copula functionally, because it is one of the components of the optative mood of "likelihood." The conflation of adverb and the Heavenly Twins in *Words Made Visible* more than underscores the erotization of the similaic copula. This conflation causes the similaic copula to become inscribed with desire as a general category, and specifically with a desire of the like. *Words Made Visible* is an early modern rhetorical text wherein the similaic copula is implicitly inscribed with the desire of the like related to the aesthetic category of simile in the early modern literary texts of Shakespeare, Lanyer, Donne, Spenser, and Fulwell.

The appearance of Castor and Pollux alongside the god of rhetoric Mercury in *Words Made Visible* foregrounds the co-implication of rhetoric and pastoral eroticism in the early modern thinking of the relations between love and language, thinking unconsciously echoed by contemporary psychoanalysis. This appearance has mythological roots. Mythological sources relate the Heavenly Twins to the god of eloquence, Hermes or Mercury. In Pindar's *Nemean Ode*, Castor and Pollux are mentioned as "guardians of Sparta," who "along with Hermes...administer the flourishing institution of the games" (sec. 10, line 50). Apollodorus recounts a version of the birth of Helen of Troy, according to which she was not conceived by Leda, the mother of the Dioscuri, but emerged from an egg given Leda for safekeeping "by a shepherd" (bk. 3, sec. 10, line 7). According to Etruscan sources, this shepherd, a representative of the domain of pastoral whose thematizations from their beginnings sing of polymorphic eroticism is none other than Castor, and, in other cases, Hermes, with whom Castor thus becomes interchangeable (Caskey-Beazley, vol. 3, p. 72). Castor and Pollux are implicated with the rhetorical no less than the erotic from the most archaic roots of their fictionalization.

The rhetorical inflection of the erotic mythologeme of the Heavenly Twins is even more pronounced in an early modern text, Giordano Bruno's mythological-astrological-philosophical *Expulsion of the Triumphant Beast* (1584). Bruno's text relies on the mythologization of the Heavenly Twins as the Morning and Evening Stars to conflate them with the eroticized constellation of Gemini. The stars of the geminaic constellation are said to "show...the reciprocal love of two effeminates" (p. 112), and to charm Saturn into lusting after them as his "bed warmers" (ibid., p. 229). In Bruno's text, the Heavenly Twins are rhetoricized at the time they are eroticized. Their place in the heavens is pronounced by the goddess of love Venus to be the place of "Intimacy, Kiss, Embracing, Caressing" (ibid., p. 22), of the psychic and phenomenal manifestations of linking generated by Cupid or Eros, who is himself conflated with them as a "twin" (ibid., p. 229). The place of phenomenalized erotic linking occupied by the Twins in Bruno's text is said to be the place of a love specifically designated as rhetorical, "Figurative Love" (ibid., p. 84). This rhetorical love is situated in the non-phallic, omphalic domain of figure, the domain implicitly theorized in early modern rhetorical texts as the domain of polymorphic desire. This is the domain within which the aesthetic category of simile is ubiquitously classified in Renaissance rhetoric. Bruno's association of the Heavenly Twins with the category of figure in an (homo-)eroticized inflection homoeroticizes the ubiquitous classification of simile as a figure. More generally, Bruno's text and its mythological sources (homo-)eroticize and rhetoricize the characters dramatizing the category of the adverb, and more implicitly, the category of simile, in *Words Made Visible*. The fictionalizations of the mythologeme of Castor and Pollux in Bruno's text and its sources anagrammatically foreground the conceptual link between the rhetorical and the erotic.

Words Made Visible is not the only rhetorical text to mention Castor and Pollux. Castor and Pollux are among the few mythological characters other than the god of eloquence Hermes or Mercury featured in classical and early modern rhetorical texts. They are part of a mythologeme not imported into rhetorical theory but constituting an integral part of this theory. This mythologeme reverberates in the rhetorical tradition almost as often as the myth of the invention of rhetoric by the orator-civilizer. This is the myth of the invention of the art of memory, the fourth part of rhetoric according to the ancient five-part division, by the poet Simonides, a contemporary of Pythagoras. For the early modern English rhetoricians, the name of Simonides would have resonated with the name of the aesthetic category of simile.

The most detailed retelling of this myth in early modern rhetoric appears in Wilson's *Arte of Rhetorique*. In Wilson's account, the lyric poet Simonides is said to be the "father" (p. 236) of the art of memory. Pliny talks of memory as the art of sameness and metaphoricity "which allow[s] anything once heard to be repeated in *identical* words" (*Natural History*, bk. 7, sec. 24, line 89, quoted in *Greek Lyric III*, p. 351, emphasis mine). In Pliny's text, memory becomes associated with the static, solipsistic One early modern rhetoricians were to inscribe into the fusional, ontological copula of metaphor.

In early modern rhetorical theory, the art of memory Simonides is said to have invented is conceptually related to the aesthetic category of metaphor. Like metaphor, memory is theorized as unitary, fusional, and phallic. In early modern rhetorical theory, and, as Mary Carruthers has shown, in early modern rhetoric's classical and medieval sources, memory is theorized as a conceptually phallic procedure tellingly imaged as the imprinting of letters or a signet ring upon paper or wax. Cicero refers to mnemonics as the inscription of "letters" onto a "wax writing tablet" in

De oratore (bk. 2, sec. 6, line 355). Quintilian talks of mnemonic "impressions" made "upon the mind" as "analogous to those which a signet-ring makes on wax (*Institutio oratoria*, bk. 11, sec. 2, line 17).

The theorizations of memory in the ancient texts of Cicero and Quintilian reverberate in early modern texts. In *The Art of Memory*, John Willis speaks of memory as involving the "imprint" of "occurrent things" on the mind (p. 29). Shakespeare's sonnet #122 refers to memory as "character'd" "tables" (lines 1–2).

This theorization of memory as imprinting taps into what Goux calls the sexualized "symbolic of the symbolic," the ubiquitous thinking of an amorphic, conceptually mater(nal) matter yearning for the shaping imprint of a conceptually paternal pattern (*Symbolic Economies*, p. 232). The "archontic" impulse of the art of memory, Derrida says, "is paternal and patriarchic" (*Archive Fever*, p. 5). In the mythic account of the origin of memory as reformulated by Wilson, the pa(t)ternality of this art is incarnated in Simonides, who is designated its "father."

Phallic mnemonics, conceptually related to the aesthetic category of metaphor, do not emerge in isolation in early modern rhetoric. These mnemonics emerge at a moment of crisis, of an "originary, structural breakdown" (Derrida, *Archive Fever*, p. 12) of the concept of the archive together with the concept of forgetting they attempt to repress. "Oblivion," states the early modern rhetorician John Willis, author of several treatises on memory, is "such a principle of Memory as Privation is of Generation" (*Mnemonica*, p. 29). According to Cicero, the first rhetorician to recount the myth of the invention of mnemonics, when the science of mnemonics was "being introduced for the first time," an Athenian sage, Themistocles, protested he would prefer a "science of forgetting" from which he could learn "to forget what he wanted" (*De oratore*, bk. 2, sec. 54, lines 299–351). Wilson (*Arte of Rhetorique*, p. 235) repeats this story. John Willis asserts the art of memory may be complemented by "an Art of Oblivion" consisting of "deposition, or discharging things committed to mind" (*Mnemonica*, pp. 30–31).

Forgetting is conceptualized in early modern rhetorical theory and its classical sources as a constitutive moment of "discharge." Psychoanalytic theory inadvertently but significantly echoes Willis's theorization of forgetting in relation to "discharge." In psychoanalytical terms, discharge is "the evacuation into the external world of the energy brought into [the psychical] apparatus by excitations of either internal or external origin" (Laplanche and Pontalis, p. 121). Discharge is involved in the clearing of psychoneuroses "precipitated by frustration leading to the damming-up of the libido" (ibid., p. 11). Discharge opens up a dammed-up libido into a wanting or, in Willis's terms, "privation." Privation, Lacan would later say, is one of the forms of lack, the structure subtending desire as "the interval that demand hollows within itself" (*Écrits*, p. 263). Forgetting as a moment of privation, lack, and desire lets archontic, phallic mnemonics happen. "Oblivion," Wilson writes, is an "infection" that is "cankered" (*Arte of Rhetorique*, p. 233). He invokes archontic mnemonics as a "sovereign preservative" against its powers (ibid.).

The pathologizing of forgetting makes its forgetting imperative for Wilson. The reason for this pathologizing is suggested by Wilson's characterization of forgetting as an effect of "heat and moisture" (ibid.). The two effects said to generate forgetting are psychologically charged. Heat is a well-worn metonymy for lust. Moisture is a phenomenal trace of dissolving fluidity, the defining characteristic of the psychic state of fusion theorized by Freud as the "oceanic" and transcoded by early modern rhetoricians with the primal substance of semiosis. Wilson associates forgetting with sexual attraction and oceanic diffusion.

The combination of attraction and diffusion as the somatic bases of forgetting inscribes this rhetorical-psychological category with the two contrary pulsions underwriting the eternal return of desire. Forgetting is said to "draw things" together yet to be unable to "long hold them" (ibid., p. 234). Forgetting in Wilson's theorization is inscribed with an unpredictable erotic dynamic. This dynamic is not based on desubjectifying phallic possessiveness. The eroticism Wilson inscribes into the category of forgetting is based on a passion resulting in the mutual overreaching of subjects "drawn" together so powerfully they cannot contain it. This structure of desire is non-phallic, non-solipsistic, and intersubjective. Lacan would theorize this structure of desire as transferential (*Seminar I*, pp. 109–112). The retelling of the mythologeme of Simonides in Wilson's treatise involves an implicit theorization of forgetting as a rhetorical-psychological category associated with transferential eroticism.

In Wilson's retelling of the mythologeme of the invention of memory, forgetting qua transferential eroticism is opposed to the category of memory, theorized as a pa(t)ternal and phallic art. The phallic and unitary attributes of the category of memory align it with the aesthetic category of metaphor, theorized in terms of these same attributes (see Chapter Four above). Memory is aligned with metaphor phonically too, in its first syllable.

In Wilson's treatise, Simonides is associated with the pat(t)ernal and phallic art of memory. Because the theorization of memory in Wilson's treatise is bound up with the theorization of forgetting as the inextricable obverse of memory, Simonides is associated with the category of forgetting. Forgetting is conceptually related to memory as memory's abjected Other, isomorphically with the way in which simile is related to metaphor, itself an isomorph of memory, in much early modern rhetorical theory. In Wilson's treatise, isomorphism works to associate Simonides with the similaic as an isomorph of forgetting.

Simonides is related to the similaic by more than isomorphism, and by more than the phonic resonance between the name of simile and his name. I have shown above how the similaic is conceptualized in early modern theory of language as related to the erotic mood of the optative, of likelihood. This mood is theorized as expressing desire as a memory for the future. The optative mood in its early modern theorization is a proleptic anti-memory not fixated on an ontologically definitive, dead past. The optative is not predicated on memory. It is conceptually opposed to the erection of "memorials," poetically described by Simonides as "lifeless in place of living" (*Greek Lyric III*, p. 565). Instead, the optative mood in its early modern theorizations yearns toward what is eternally about to happen. The optative is an anti-memory, conceptually coeval with forgetting as theorized in Wilson's treatise in relation to the mythologeme of Simonides. The alignment of Simonides with the optative conceptually aligns Simonides with the category related to the optative: the similaic.

Part of the mythologeme of Simonides as it appears in Wilson's treatise is conceptually related to the similaic because like the similaic as theorized in early modern grammar treatises, it is connected with the category of an eroticized, proleptic anti-memory. The mythologeme of Simonides is related to the similaic for another reason. Like the category of the similaic, this mythologeme includes the category of the at least double which exceeds the solipsistic One and is thereby able to engage in joy-enabling joining. I have shown above how in early modern theory of language the similaic is conceptually, phonically, and etymologically related to the category of the adverb. Because the adverb is a joined and joining function, it is predicated on scissions and limits, the structures constitutive of all manifestations of the erotic (Montrelay, p. 85).

Putting scissions and limits into play, the category of the adverb activates the erotic so as to generate linguistic fragments of *jouissance*. The association of simile with the adverb in early modern language theory conceptually links simile with the psychic function of generating *jouissance* through separation. This function is predicated on the suspension of the One. In Wilson's rhetorical treatise, the association of the similaic not with the One but with the at least double is explicit. Wilson describes simile as "a likeness when *two things, or more than two*, are…compared and resembled together" (p. 213, emphasis mine).

The mythologeme of Simonides too is predicated upon the function of the at least double. Wilson's account of the mythologeme of Simonides reformulates similar accounts in Cicero (*De oratore*, bk. 2, sec. 86, lines 351–353) and Quintilian (*Institutio oratoria*, bk. 11, sec. 2, lines 11–16), and their source, Callimachus' *Aetia* (quoted in *Greek Lyric III*, pp. 345–346). This mythologeme is itself double and hence conceptually related to the at least double aesthetic category of simile as Wilson theorizes it.

In Wilson's account of the mythologeme of Simonides, structurally related to his theorization of the similaic as the at least double, Simonides features in two different types of roles. The first of these roles is conceptually phallic. Simonides is the author of many elegies commemorating heroes who died in battle, and the inventor of epinician odes, sung in honor of athletic champions (*Lyra Graeca*, pp. 253, 333). Both these genres involve adulation of phallic glory. In Wilson's text, Simonides appears in the capacity of authoring an epinician ode and reciting it at a banquet held in celebration of "a triumphant champion called Scopas" (*Arte of Rhetorique*, p. 236). He is called out from the banquet just before the roof caves in to crush all the remaining attendants. Simonides is the only one to survive among the attendants of Scopas' banquet. He is able to identify the dead according to the visual pattern he has in his memory of the places they had occupied at the table. His identification of the dead according to the pattern he has in his memory makes the work of mourning possible. In his capacity as author of epinician odes and inventor of mnemonics, Simonides is aligned with phallic functions which in early modern rhetorical theory are aligned with the category of metaphor.

Yet in Wilson's text, Simonides is featured in another story. This story is superfluous to the representation of Simonides' role as the founder of the art of memory. This story opens Wilson's account. In this story, Simonides, who is described by a Scholiast as generally "accustomed to use digressions" in his singing of "sweet song [that] breathed delight" (quoted in *Greek Lyric III*, p. 361), "digress[es]" from the epinician ode (*Arte of Rhetorique*, p. 236). He digresses into a song not of triumph but of desire. The song into which Simonides digresses from the phallic epinician ode he composes to adulate the triumph of Scopas is a sensuous paean.

Simonides' digression belongs to the amatory portion of his poetry, in which he celebrates the beauty of "the lovely-haired Apollo of the golden locks" (*Greek Lyric III*, p. 399), or the "inebriate revel-lover, who struck all night long his boy-lover lyre" (ibid., p. 577), or "Maias of the lovely eyes...outstanding in beauty among the...violet-haired daughters who are called the heavenly Peleiads" (ibid., p. 447), or the "unharvested brine...the irresistible rush of the sea" (ibid., p. 415), or a "girl, sending forth words from her crimson lip" (ibid., p. 469).

Simonides' invention of mnemonics is based on the visual. His medium in the story of the invention of memory is cognitive "images" (*Arte of Rhetorique*, p. 237). Such images, Frances Yates and Mary Carruthers have shown, remain the infrastructure of the art of memory in its medieval and early modern theorizations. I have shown in the fourth chapter of this book how early modern rhetoricians associate the visual with the metaphoric and the phallic. In early modern rhetorical theory, mnemonics are conceptually phallic because of their predication on pattern, and because of their predication on the visual.

But in Simonides' digressive song, his medium is not the visual. His medium is the vocable, the sonorous, the oral, a medium "speak[ing] all the time of the blindness that constitutes it" (Derrida, *Memoires of the Blind*, p. 4). Stephen Whitworth has shown how the oral function in a variety of psychic parameters is conceptually central to the genre of pastoral. The oral function of pastoral is foregrounded in one of the earliest instances of pastoral, a hymn by Theocritus. Song, Theocritus writes, is "the fairest" of "God's prerogatives" (*The Greek Bucolic Poets*, p. 275). In Theocritus' hymn, all singers of song are said to be "dear unto the sons of Tyndareus" (ibid.). The sons of Tyndareus are the Heavenly Twins Castor and Pollux, the Dioscuri, to whom Theocritus' hymn is dedicated. In one of the earliest instances of pastoral, Castor and Pollux are related to pastoral, sonorous song. They are fictionalized as the guardians of such song.

Simonides' digression from a phallic epinician ode into past-oral song associates his mythologeme with the mythologeme of Castor and Pollux. In *Words Made Visible*, the mythologeme of Castor and Pollux is conflated with the category of the adverb. In early modern grammar theory, the adverb is conceptually related to the optative mood of likelihood, itself phonically resonating with the similaic copula "like." Simonides' digression from the epinician ode to past-oral song confirms the relation between the digressive portion of the mythologeme of the invention of memory in which he appears and the similaic.

In the early modern cultural context in which Wilson's rhetorical treatise was composed, Castor and Pollux are featured in Giordano Bruno's *Expulsion of the Triumphant Beast*. In this text, Bruno describes their relation as "Perverse Desire" (p. 84), a category which was to become significant in modern psychoanalysis. The category of the "perverse" in its Freudian and Lacanian inflections is distinct from the category of "perversion" in the Lacanian inflection I relied on in Chapter Two above. For Freud in *Three Essays on the Theory of Sexuality*, "perversity" and "perversion" are synonymous, and designate a deviation from heterosexuality. In this text, however, Freud uses the phrase "polymorphous perversity" to refer to the entire range of structures of sexual attraction (p. 57). Lacan was to call the range of structures of sexual attraction the "eternal polymorphism" of the libido, and to conceptually relate this range in its entirety to the domain of pastoral (*Seminar VII*, p. 92). For Lacan, especially in *Seminar IV*, perversion is a structure of desire defined by its seeking the *jouissance* of the other. Perverse desire as theorized in *Seminar I* is distinct from perversion. Perverse desire is a structure of desire sustaining itself only in the absence of its object. Lacan identifies the structure of perverse desire as "mak[ing] up one aspect of the drama of homosexuality" (*Seminar I*, p. 221). Homosexuality is at work in the myth of the Dioscuri. In Bruno's text, where the Twins are described as the "bed warmers" of Saturn, another type of eroticism is at work: servile eroticism. In Lacan's terms, the myth of the Dioscuri involves perversion, and possibly perversity. This is already indicated by Bruno's non-judgmental characterization of their relation as "perverse."

The category of the perverse associated with the Twins in Bruno's *Expulsion of the Triumphant Beast* is at work in Wilson's retelling of the Simonides myth. In Wilson's text, the Twins are formally related to Simonides' digressive, past-oral song by virtue of their fictionalization by Theocritus, in an instance of pastoral song, as the guardians of such sung thematizations of the multiple forms of eroticism Freud was to call polymorphous perversity. In Wilson's text, the Twins are thematically related to Simonides' past-oral song. They are the contents of this song.

The song itself is structurally perverse. It involves a "digression" which disconcerts the phallic figure of the hero whom it addresses to the point he denies Simonides "a piece of his reward" (Wilson, *Arte of Rhetorique*, 236). The digression in Simonides' song is perverse in the Freudian sense of the non-heterosexual in its contents too. The contents of this digressive song intensify the link between the digressive portion of mythologeme of Simonides and the category of the similaic as theorized in Renaissance rhetoric.

In the digressive, structurally perverse song, Simonides tells the homoerotic story of the Heavenly Twins Castor and Pollux. In *Words Made Visible*, Castor and Pollux embody the category of the adverb of wishing Renaissance grammarians theorize as part of the eroticized optative mood transcodable with forgetting as theorized by Wilson and Willis and with the modality of likelihood conceptualized by William Walker as a deployment of the signifier "like," commonly exemplified as a similaic copula. In the mnemonic texts of Wilson and Willis, Castor and Pollux are associated with the psychic-rhetorical category of forgetting. In *Words Made Visible*, Castor and Pollux are associated with the adverb of wishing. In early modern rhetorical theory, forgetting and the adverb of wishing are inscribed with non-phallic eroticism, and they are conceptually linked with the similaic copula. In a number of cases in early modern rhetorical theory, the appearance of Castor and Pollux is symptomatic of a simultaneous preoccupation with the similaic, with non-phallic, transferential eroticism, and with a less than normative sexuality.

The attraction between the Twins is so powerful as to effect a transference crossing the boundary between mortality and immortality. This attraction involves desire for the like at its extreme. The desire between the Twins is homoerotic, the desire for the "sweet love of boys" (*Greek Lyric III*, p. 579) "most handsome to look at" (ibid., p. 549) Simonides sings of. The desire between the Twins is incestuous and geminaic. Like forgetting as Wilson describes it, the attraction between the Twins is a powerful force of "drawing" together (*Arte of Rhetorique*, p. 234) what the mnemonic impulse classifies and separates. This is a libidinal rather than hyper-rationally archontic linking or coupling, which cuts through and "dissipates" boundaries (ibid., p. 236). The geminaic constellation with which Bruno associates the myth of the Heavenly Twins, Bruno points out, diverges from the paternal principle upon which the archontic art of memory rests. The stars of the geminaic constellation "do not form a pattern" (*Expulsion*, p. 111).

The seemingly superfluous "digression" of Simonides' song in *The Arte of Rhetorique* and its classical sources establishes polymorphic desire as a site of a forgetting functioning as the forgotten prelude to the myth of the invention of memory. This prelude haunts the myth. In the myth, Simonides is transposed from his role as a poet who sings the similaic desire indexing forgetting in perverse contravention of the hero's phallic presence, to the role of the passively "placed" guest in the feast erecting this hero's triumphs and underscoring his potency. After his transposition from the phallic role he perversely failed to fulfill, Simonides is entirely lured out of the phallic domain of One, the domain later transmuted into the domain of memory. Simonides is lured out of the mnemonic, archontic, phallic domain of One not by a single suitor with whom he could form a deludingly complemental dyad. He is lured out but by "two young men," defined in some versions of the myth as Castor and Pollux themselves, who "desire" him "most earnestly" (Wilson, *Arte of Rhetorique*, p. 236), or, as Quintilian puts it, "urgently."

The homoerotic desire for the double rather than the phallic One inscribed by Wilson into the category of forgetting returns to trouble the domain which is to become the archontic, "paternal and patriarchic" domain of memory. This return of perverse desire inscribed with forgetting makes the emergence of memory possible. The double, homoerotic desire of the young men is an instance of what Lacan would call perverse desire, a desire involving aphanisis. For Lacan, perverse desire can "only be grasped at the limit," and "loses its object" at "the moment when it catches up with it" (*Seminar I*, p. 222). Wilson's fictionalization of the (missed) encounter between Simonides and the Twins anticipates the Lacanian theorization of perverse desire as aphanisis, as graspable at the limit. The two young men voice their desire for Simonides at the limit, "at the door" (Wilson, *Arte of Rhetorique*, p. 236). Simonides comes to respond to their desire at the limit, "on the threshold" (ibid.). Yet all Simonides encounters at the limit is the disappearance of the doubled object of desire of his desire. He learns the redoubled object of his desire had vanished, suspending itself *as* desire at the limit where it was spoken. This is the only point where desire, as Lacan theorizes it, can be recognized. Desire, Lacan says, "always becomes manifest at the joint of speech, where it makes its sudden emergence, its surge forward" (*Seminar II*, p. 234).

Simonides' moment of recognition of a polymorphic desire with which Wilson inscribes forgetting is simultaneous with the collapse of the phallic space of hero-worship from which Simonides had been allured by this desire. The collapse of the phallic space of hero-worship effects an effacement of the identity of the bodies within it, which Simonides then re-members by means of the visual. For all of Wilson's fears of the "infection of cankered oblivion" (*Arte of Rhetorique*, p. 233), in his text, the emergence of memory as what makes mourning possible is simultaneous with an effacement, a forgetting. This forgetting is at least double. It is a forgetting of corporeal identity and of polymorphic desire which, in this text, is transcoded with the work of forgetting.

In Wilson's text, Castor and Pollux are fictionalized as components of the mythologeme of forgetting, a category whose eroticism Wilson recognized long before De Man (p. 69). In Wilson's text, the eroticism inscribed into the category of forgetting bespeaks a transferential desire of the like. In *Words Made Visible*, Castor and Pollux personify the category of the adverb, a category early modern grammarians functionally and conceptually relate to the eroticized optative mood of likelihood, subtended by the similaic copula "like" and etymologically related to this copula. The myth of Castor and Pollux as it appears in the early modern mnemonic texts of Wilson and Willis and in *Words Made Visible* establishes significant conceptual links. The mythologeme links similaic, polymorphic, transferential, non-phallic eroticism, in particular in its deployments as a desire of the like, and forgetting, an art mythically connected with the lyric poet Simonides. The relation of Simonides to the similaic is foregrounded by the phonic resonance of his name.

The link between Simonides and the similaic is foregrounded by phonic resonance but not limited to the phonic. Simonides is linked with the similaic conceptually too. The phonic resonance between the name of the poet Simonides and the aesthetic category of simile is made possible by the Latin name for the form of figurative comparison. Yet the conceptual relation between Simonides and the similaic precedes the emergence of Latin. The conceptual relation of Simonides and the similaic harkens to one of the founding texts of philosophical ontology, Plato's *Protagoras*.

The *Protagoras* quotes the only surviving record of the epinician ode Simonides is said to have sung to Scopas (339a5) in the myth of the invention of memory and forgetting as it appears in the rhetorical tradition from Cicero to Willis. In the mythologeme reverberating in the rhetorical tradition, Simonides is said to have at some point digressed from this epinician ode into a past-oral celebration of the desire of the like as fictionalized in the myth of the Dioscuri. Significantly, the contents of the epinician ode from which Simonides is said to have perversely digressed digress from the adulation of phallic glory required by the epinician genre invented by Simonides. Instead of celebrating the glory of Scopas as a hero, Simonides' epinician ode to Scopas involves a philosophical meditation of the relationship between the categories of Being (*emmenai*), with which early modern rhetoricians were to transcode the ontological copula of metaphor, and becoming (*genesthai*) (Plato, *Protagoras*, 339b-c).

Protagoras and Socrates, who discuss this Simonidean ode, agree on its philosophic import. Simonides, they say, clearly distinguishes between the categories of Being and becoming (340d). Protagoras and Socrates interpret Simonides as theorizing becoming a good man (*arethos*) as difficult but possible (*dunaton*) and statically, permanently being a good man as impossible (*a-dunatos*). According to Simonides' epinician ode, Socrates and Protagoras believe, statically and permanently being a good man is beyond human power, an attribute of gods alone (344c–e). Simonides' perverse epinician ode in praise of Scopas is interpreted by Socrates and Protagoras as situating human existence in the domain of possibility, of potentiality, of what might be. Renaissance grammarians theorized this domain of possibility as the domain of the erotic mood of the optative, of likelihood, a mood phonically and conceptually related with the similaic "like."

In classical Greek, as in early modern English, the modality of likelihood and the category of similaic likeness are phonically, etymologically, and conceptually related. In classical Greek, the signifier for likelihood is *eiko*; one of the signifiers for simile is *eikon*. In classical Greek language and thinking, as in early modern English theorizations of grammar, the modality of likelihood, of potentiality, is constitutively erotic. The signifier *dunatos* through which Simonides sings the domain of the possible or potential as the domain of human existence is phonically and etymologically related to *dunamos*. The signifier *dunamos* denotes potentiality and kinesis. Long before Bataille's insistence on the correlation of the kinetic and the erotic, ("The Solar Anus," *Visions of Excess*, p. 7), the Pythagoreans thought of kineticism as subtending the "reaching out" toward an object, the "movement of the soul" (Iamblichus, p. 87). Aristotle conceptualizes the relation between the kinetic and the constitutively erotic potential recognized by his Pythagorean predecessors and suggested in Simonides' song. In his *Metaphysics*, Aristotle speaks of "the potential" (*dunatos*) as a function "whose nature is to move [*dunamos*] or be moved" (1048a27).

Many centuries after Simonides, Heidegger was to speak of "[t]he world's darkening" as "never reach[ing] /...the light of Being" and to enjoin us to "head toward a star — this only" (*Poetry, Language, Thought*, p. 4). Many centuries after Simonides, Lacan was to theorize the reaching out toward Being from a condition of lack as desire (*Seminar II*, p. 223). Long before Heidegger and Lacan whose formulations echo the poeticized thinking of Simonides, Simonides' song poeticized human existence as situated in the domain of becoming, of dynamic erotic striving.

For Simonides, human existence is marked by the dynamic erotic striving such as characterizes the relation between Castor and Pollux of which he proceeds to sing. Human existence, for Simonides, is not situated in the domain of what statically and permanently is, the domain of the gods relinquished by Pollux in order to be joined with his mortal twin.

In another fragment of his epinician song cited in the *Protagoras*, Simonides speaks of the inhabitants of the domain of striving and becoming as possible objects of "love" (*phileo*) (345c). He implicitly establishes the domain of striving and becoming as the domain of Eros. This erotic domain of becoming, Socrates says in his commentary on this fragment of Simonides' song, is the domain of the "middle" or "in between" (*mesos*) (346d). In the famous speech on love in the *Symposium*, the middle or mean Simonides transcodes with becoming qua eroticism is the category with which Diotima transcodes Eros (202e).

The title of Plato's famous dialogue on love would have resonated, for early modern men of letters, with the Latinate name of the aesthetic category of the similaic. The Greek word *sumposion* (drinking together) bespeaks an activity of pleasurable joining. The category of the similaic too rests on the function of joining because of its subtension by a less than fusional copula and its conceptual relation with the copulaic category of the adverb. In Greek, the function of joining structuring the activity of banqueting and the elocutionary category of simile is expressed by the prefix *sum* (with). This copulaic prefix structures such signifiers as sym-phony (*sum-phonia*) or sym-metry (*sum-metria*). In inverse anagrammaticality, the copulaic prefix *sum* structures the signifier mus-ic (*mousike*), the art of symmetrical tone combinations productive of the aural pleasures of symphony. This art is related to love in the *Symposium* (187b, 196e, 205c). Its name is derived from the name of the Muses, a name "deriv[ed] from a root that indicates ardor" (Nancy, *The Muses*, p. 1). The Greek prefix *sum* which would have resonated with the similaic for early modern men of letters has everything to do with aural eroticism.

The domain of Eros, as theorized in Diotima's speech in the similaically-resonant *Sym-posium* and in the Simonidean digression in the *Protagoras* is the domain of transferential bonds of philiation. The philiation of which Diotima speaks in the *Symposium* is a function Pythagoras theorizes as an excessive and supplemental copulatory function (Iamblichus, p. 29). For Pythagoras as for Diotima in the *Symposium*, bonds of philiation are created in the interaction between subjects who dynamically strive toward one another as imaginary substitutes for Being within the potentiality proffered them in the domain of becoming.

The song to Scopas which establishes the connection between Simonides and the mythologeme of Castor and Pollux poeticizes a non-ontological, erotic thinking of becoming as *philia*. In the *Protagoras*, this non-ontological eroticism of becoming is implicitly opposed to the category of Being. I have shown in the fourth chapter of this book how in early modern language theory, the category of Being, of the ontological, is inscribed into the copula of metaphor. In the next chapter, I show how in early modern language theory, simile is theorized as metaphor's abjected binary. The category of simile in early modern rhetoric is implicitly inscribed with the binaries of the categories attributed to metaphor.

In Simonides' song to Scopas, mentioned in the myth of the invention of mnemonics in the early modern treatises of Willis and Wilson and cited in the *Protagoras*, the binary of the category of Being ubiquitously attributed to metaphor is erotic becoming. The category of simile in the early modern texts retelling the mythologeme of Simonides is inscribed with non-ontological erotic becoming.

Long before Lacan was to theorize the unconscious, as locus of desire, as non-ontological (*Seminar XI*, pp. 29–32), Simonides, and the early modern rhetoricians who retell his mythologeme or the associated mythologeme of Castor and Pollux, sketched conceptual connections between desire and becoming rather than Being. The early modern rhetoricians implicitly link desire and becoming with a linguistic category Lacan fails to echo. In the texts of Willis and Wilson and in *Words Made Visible*, as in the archaic text of Simonides and the ancient mythologizations of Castor and Pollux, desire and becoming are linked with the similaic.

Plato's text is committed to ontology, to the theorization of Being. It cannot comfortably accommodate Simonides' poetic thinking of becoming as erotic philiation. In Plato's text, Socrates expounds this poeticized thinking from the Simonidean fragments. Shortly afterwards, however, Socrates proceeds to disavow those fragments and what is inscribed within them as "childish trifles" (*leros...paidie*) (347d), not worthy of the attention of philosophers. The justification Socrates provides for his disavowing devaluation of Simonides' poetic thinking of becoming is the non-deonticality of the medium of song in which this thinking of becoming is articulated. The proper linguistic medium of the philosophers, Socrates asserts, is rational conversation, wherein truths can be established with deontic certainty (347e). This deontic modality, Socrates states, is what poetic articulations notoriously lack.

The phrase "*autois hautois...ontas*," with which Socrates asserts the purported superiority of the rational conversation of the philosophers over poetic song overdetermines the ontologicality and the self-sufficiency he ascribes to rational conversation. This phrase conflates the signifier for the ontic (*ontas*) with the signifiers for the self (*autos*) and with the signifier for the absolutely self-reflexive (*hautois*). What Socrates attributes to rational discourse befitting the articulation of deontic, absolute truths is ontologicality and/as autarchy. Ontologicality and self-sufficiency are attributes early modern theorists of language were to inscribe into the copula of metaphor. These attributes associate metaphor with the possessive, de-subjectifying solipsism of phallic desire.

Socrates in the *Protagoras* theorizes poetry as distinctly non-phallic. Socrates describes poetry as deployed in a feminized domain of *"auletridas," "psaltridas,"* and *"orchestridas"* (aulos-playing-girls, harp-playing-girls, dancing-girls) (347d). This domain is aural/oral and choreographic. Because the domain of poetry as conceptualized by Socrates is oral/aural, it is conceptually related to the primal past-oral object Renaissance rhetoricians were to transcode with the primal substance of semiosis. Because this domain is choreographic, it is associated with the veiled phenomenal manifestations of the primal oral object in the choreographic rituals of Eleusis and Dionysus, inscribed, in early modern rhetorical theory, into the elocutionary category of figure. Dionysian rituals are invoked by Socrates in relation to poetry in his dismissive reference to the domain of song as a "drinking party" (*sumposiosis*) (347c). Socrates dismisses song and/as the Dionysian in terms of the copulaic signifier (*sum*) which for early modern men of letters would have resonated with the name of simile.

Socrates aligns the domain of song, of past-orality, with the Eleusinian and Dionysian mysteries and with the non-phallic, conceptually feminine sexualities these mysteries mythologize. In so doing, Socrates aligns song with aesthetic and mythological categories early modern rhetoricians were to inscribe into the elocutionary category of figure. Unlike the elocutionary category of trope, figure is a non-phallic, omphalic category (see Chapter Two above). Figure is the category in terms of which early modern rhetoricians were to classify simile.

In those early modern treatises distinguishing between figures and tropes, simile is almost invariably classified as a figure. This is the case in Thomas Wilson's *Arte of Rhetorique*, where "similitude" (p. 213) is cited as the twenty-fourth among the figures or schemes, whose definition as "Ornaments to Commend and Set Forth the Oration" underscores their association with the feminine-seductive dimension of semiosis. Sherry lists "Parable, which some call similitude," "Icon, called of the Latines [sic] Imago [which is] much lyke to a similitude" among the "figures of a sentence," in a text whose title, *A Treatise of Schemes and Tropes*, declares its commitment to the figure-trope binarism structuring the domain of elocution. Simile is mentioned among the figures in Henry Peacham's *Garden of Eloquence* too (sig. B2). In George Bersmann's *Erotemata Rhetorica*, *imago*, listed as one of the forms of similitude, is designated as a *figura orationis* (p. 484). In Conrad Lycosthenis's *Similivm Loci Commvnes*, simile is defined as an *ornationis verborum* (p. 72), in terms of the category of ornament seminal to the theorization of figure (see Chapter Two above). In Soario Cypriano's *De Arte Rhetorica* (p. 40), Joannnes Alstendius's *Rhetorica* (p. 410), and Vossius's *Rhetorices Contractae* (p. 34), simile is referred-to as a "scheme" (*de schematibus in verbis similis soni*). Simile is classified as a figure in Bernard Lamy's *Art of Speaking* (p. 111) and Dominico Decolonia's *De Arte Rhetorica* (p. 105). In the anonymous *Rhetoricae Synopsis* of 1693, an entire chapter (chapter 35) is devoted to "figures of similitude" (*Figuris Assimilatum*), including *comparatio, imago, exemplum,* and *collatio* (p. 74).

Socrates' dismissal of song as an instance of the Dionysian aligns song with a category early modern thinkers on language would come to associate with the Dionysian: figure or scheme, the taxonomic locus, in early modern rhetoric, of the similaic. For the early moderns, Socrates' dismissal of song as an instance of the Dionysian would amount to a disparaging of the category of the schematic or figural into which they inscribe the Dionysian, and to the potential dismissal of the similaic as a part of the schematic.

Socrates' dismissal of song as failing the categoricity of philosophical discourse aligns song with what early modern logicians such as Fraunce would theorize as the non-axiomatic. In the fourth chapter of this book, I showed the conceptual connections, in early modern language theory, between the axiomatic, the ontological, and the metaphoric. In terms of the categories of early modern rhetoric, Socrates' dismissal of song as non-axiomatic would amount to the implicit theorization of song as non-ontological and non-metaphoric. Socrates' is a disavowing dismissal of a particular song, the song of Simonides. This song thematizes the non-ontologicality it generically performs. Simonides' song aligns the non-ontologicality of which it sings with an erotic becoming manifest in the optative domain of the possible (*dunatos*) or likely (*eiko*). In ancient Greek, as in early modern English, the domain of the likely (*eiko*) is, grammatically and conceptually, the domain of the similaic like (*eikon*). The Socratic disavowal of the past-oral, poeticized thinking of becoming in its relation to the similaic as non-argumentative and hence non-philosophical reverberates in the early modern thinking of language, which nevertheless in many ways undoes this disavowal. This is evident in the theorization of similitude in Smith's *Mysterie of Rhetorique Unvail'd*. Similitudes, Smith writes, "are not argumentative." They do not "prove any doubtful thing" (p. 211). They are, instead, situated in the conjectural, optative temporality of opportunity or likelihood, the temporality of desire.

The particular contents of Simonides' song on becoming conceptually link the eroticized category of song with the structure of erotic becoming as *eiko*, the ancient Greek equivalent of the similaic. In the *Protagoras*, Socrates disavows the contents of Simonides' song, and the aesthetic category of song in its entirety. Like all disavowals, Socrates' disavowals confirm what they deny. These disavowals establish the similaic as the structure subtending the thinking of constitutively erotic becoming. The tradition of philosophical ontology, from the *Protagoras* onwards, has been committed to Being and to the repression of the thinking of erotic becoming. In the Simonidean song Socrates disavows, erotic becoming is aligned with the similaic. From the moment of the articulation of Socrates' disavowal, the similaic became the unconscious of the ontological tradition. The place of the similaic as the unconscious of ontology was determined long ago, but it has hitherto not been recognized, even in Lacan's observation concerning the non-ontologicality of the unconscious, of the unconscious' being the locus of desire as a "want-to-be" (*Seminar IV*, pp. 29–32).

The centrality of the similaic to the categories of desire and the unconscious is implicit already in Simonides' archaic singing of becoming. The centrality of the similaic to the categories of desire and the unconscious is manifest in the preoccupation with and theorization of the similaic in early modern literature and theory of language. This centrality is implicitly and probably unconsciously suggested in Lacan's theorization of Being, the category early modern rhetoricians inscribe into the ontological copula of metaphor. Being, Lacan says, is never given to intersubjectivity. This is because in intersubjectivity "there is no sexual relation" (*Seminar XX*, p. 45). The sexual relation does not give access to completeness and plenitude, does not confirm the possibility of a self-contained dyad wherein two become One. Nor is Being given to language, which is always "beside the referent" (ibid., p. 44), able only to approximate the referent. For Lacan, existence is situated not in the domain of the ontological, of Being (*être*), but of what is *"par-être."* The phrase *"par-être"* denotes "beside Being" and, as Lacan points out, phonically resonates with *"paraître"* (ibid., pp. 44–45), a word denoting appearing or seeming.

Lacan's situation of existence in the *"par-être"* inflects existence as similaic. Appearing and seeming, the functions of *"par-être"* associated by Lacan with what is otherwise than Being, are the manifestations of the non-deontic modality, the non-indicative, optative mood of likelihood associated with the similaic copula "like" in early modern theory of language. In inverse reading, which Lacan does not suggest,"*par-être*" resonates with *être pareille* (being like). Lacan's "*par-être*" resonates with one of the most archaic names of simile, para-bola (see, for instance, Puttenham, p. 205; Sherry, *Schemes and Tropes* [unpaginated]; Peacham, *Garden of Eloquence*, sig. U2). Lacan's insight concerning the place of the subject of desire and the unconscious in the non-ontological domain of para-Being, the domain tending toward Being but only ever approximating Being as its beyond (*Seminar XX*, p. 45) is no postmodern innovation. This insight inadvertently echoes and finds its anticipation and confirmation in the verses of Simonides, at the most archaic beginnings of the thinking of the relations between ontology, subjectivity, and language. This insight inadvertently echoes the extensive, complex links drawn, consciously or unconsciously, in early modern literature and theory of language, between the aesthetic category of simile resonating with Simonides' name, and the uncertain, paradoxical temporality of desire as a memory for the future.

For all of Lacan's insistence on the centrality to psychoanalysis of the category of "the signifier, brought back to life from the ancient art of rhetoric by modern linguistics" (*Écrits*, p. 298), he never mentions simile in his theorizations of the transcodings between linguistic and psychic structures. Early modern authors and theorists of language do mention simile, extensively so. The early modern theorizations of simile harken to an archaic Simonidean pre-text and to even more archaic pre-texts thematizing the multiple desire of the like of the Heavenly Twins sung in the Simonidean pre-text. In early modern theorizations of simile and their archaic pre-texts, the category of simile is implicitly associated with an erotic memory for the future. Early modern theorizations of simile and their archaic pre-texts offer modern psychoanalysis the rhetorical structure of simile as the linguistic substrate of the category of the erotic qua memory for the future.

Simonides' is not the only archaic pre-text for the category of a memory for the future. The poetry of Simonides, as distinct from the mythic retellings of his invention of the visual, archontic art of memory, echoes an archaic thinking of non-ontological mnemonics, related not to a dead past but to an origin projected onto an eternal futurity. Simonides' visual mnemonic methods gave rise to a tradition of archontic mnemonics predominating, as Mary Carruthers and Frances Yates have shown, throughout the Middle

Ages and Renaissance. Simonides' times witnessed the articulation of a non-ontological mnemonics of the type implicit in his poeticization of becoming and reverberating in the early modern theorizations of forgetting alluding to his mythologeme. These are the mnemonics of the Pythagoreans.

Pythagorean mnemonics are posited as a continuation of the mnemonics of Simonides (Curtman, p. 13). They are known to us, as they would have been to early modern poets and thinkers on language, mainly from the fragments of Philolaus and Plato's *Phaedo*. In the *Phaedo*, Socrates' interlocutor in the discussion of Pythagorean anamnesis is a disciple of Philolaus called Simmias. Like the name "Simonides," the name "Simmias" would have resonated, for early modern men of letters, with the Latinate name of the aesthetic category of simile. Like the anti-mnemonics inscribed into the eroticized rather than morbid portion of the mythologeme of Simonides through the mythologeme of Castor and Pollux, Pythagorean mnemonics are emphatically non-visual. Pythagorean mnemonics are cognitive and epistemological. They are based on a "meditation" utilizing particular linguistic structures, including those of "repetition" and "prosopopeia" (Curtman, p. 17).

The cognitive and linguistic structure most central to Pythagorean mnemonics is what underpins Simonidean anti-mnemonics: analogy. In Pythagorean mnemonics, the object of recollection is not, as in archontic, historicist mnemonics, any ontologically definitive event or situation, such as the position of a body in space, the object of recollection in the myth of Simonides' invention of the art of memory. In Pythagorean mnemonics, the object of recollection is the essence of the soul at its origin. This essence does not have any particular content. It is a structure or form, predominantly the structure or form of Number (Iamblichus, pp. 65, 73; Nicomachus, p. 57; Cameron, pp. 20, 86).

The Pythagoreans considered the knowledge of Number to be at the archaic origin of the soul. This knowledge, they believed, is lost to the soul at birth (Cameron, pp. 25, 36). The life of the soul, according to the Pythagorean doctrine of metempsychosis or the transmigration of souls, is eternal. In each of its incarnations, the soul has an opportunity to recollect the truth of Number constituting its origin and essence (ibid., pp. 22, 25, 36, 89, 91). The medium of this recollection of Number is the physical world, the place of incarnation (ibid., pp. 51, 58, 60). The physical world offers "beautiful shapes and forms" to the sight and "beautiful rhythms and melodies" to the ear (Iamblichus, p. 26). In archontic mnemonics, supposed to have been invented by Simonides, the phenomenal manifestations of the physical world serve as means for recollection. But in the non-archontic terms of the Pythagoreans, because the essence of the soul is structural, not ontological, the phenomenal manifestations of the physical world could not ever be the means for recollecting it. Instead, the structural essence of the soul must be captured through the perception of structural "number-ratios" between phenomenal manifestations (ibid., p. 51). The Pythagoreans speak of these structural number ratios through which the essence of the soul is revealed as "analogies" (ibid., pp. 51, 54–55, 58, 60). In Socrates' discussion of the Pythagorean doctrine of recollection with the similaically named disciple of Philolaus in the *Phaedo*, he calls the structural principle of Pythagorean mnemonics the "like" (*homoion*) (74a). In Pythagorean fragments and in the *Phaedo*, Pythagorean mnemonics, whose focus is structure, not content, are conceptualized as subtended by the function of likeness constituting the similaic copula.

Like Simonidean anti-memory, Pythagorean mnemonics do not look to a dead, factual, historical past. They look to an archaic origin projected into an indefinite future. Pythagorean mnemonics are subtended by a constitutively erotic temporality. They too are conceptually related to the similaic. For early modern thinkers, Pythagorean mnemonics are related to the similaic phonically, through the resonances of the name of Simmias, the Philolaic philosopher who represents them in the *Phaedo*. Pythagorean mnemonics are conceptually related to the category of simile more closely than Simonidean anti-memory. The similaic is inscribed in Pythagorean mnemonics through the modality of likelihood, etymologically connected with the signifier for simile in ancient Greek as it was to be in early modern English. The similaic is inscribed in Pythagorean mnemonics in another way: in the invocation of the logical relation of homology or likeness expressed by the similaic copula as the formal principle of these mnemonics.

In Pythagorean philosophy, the concept of Number is the archaic essence of the soul, an essence the soul may recollect through the principle of analogy or similitude. The concept of Number in Pythagorean philosophy is closely related to the concept of Harmonia. The word "Harmonia" derives from *hermosmena*, a signifier meaning to join or bind, a function early modern grammarians were to inscribe into the similaic through the conceptual connection of the similaic with the copulaic category of the adverb. The signifier *hermosmena* from which the Pythagorean category of Harmony derives has another meaning. It means "to betroth," to bind erotically. The function of erotic binding at the linguistic root of the Pythagorean category of Harmony is conceptually central to the category of simile in early modern rhetoric. Early modern grammarians inscribe the relation of erotic binding into the copula "like" in their theorizations of the adverb. The adverb, as theorized in early modern grammar treatises, is structurally and conceptually connected with the constitutively erotic optative mood of likelihood referenced by the signifier "like" and with the function of joining. The adverb is copulaic and erotic. It is inscribed with the same psychic and linguistic functions etymologically informing the Pythagorean concept of Harmony. The resonance of the Pythagorean category of Harmony in early modern theorizations of the adverb inscribes Harmony into the similaic copula structurally and conceptually connected with the adverb.

The connection between Pythagorean Harmonia and erotic binding has a mythological aspect. According to Iamblichus' fourth-century *Pythagorean Life*, Pythagoras believed the principle of "universal harmony" to have been personified by the Dioscuri (p. 69). The mythologeme of the Dioscuri narrates a powerful incestuous, homoerotic desire binding the mortal and the immortal. In *Words Made Visible*, this mythologeme is associated with the category of the adverb. In the rhetorical treatises of Wilson and Willis, this mythologeme is associated with the category of forgetting. The categories of the adverb and of forgetting are conceptually related to the similaic in early modern thinking on language. Within this thinking of language, the similaic becomes implicitly aligned with Pythagorean Harmonia by mythological resonance too.

The fragments of Philolaus of Croton are some of the only remaining primary traces of Pythagorean mnemonics. Number and Harmonia, Philolaus says in those fragments, do not "admit falsehood" (quoted by Cameron, p. 78). For Philolaus, Number and Harmonia become linked with one another as substrates of truth (Cameron, p. 27). Because they are conceptualized as substrates of truth, Number and Harmonia in the thinking of Philolaus are transcoded with another aspect of truth in Pythagorean thinking: the truth of the original structure of the soul.

The concept of Harmonia is closely related to the procedure of analogy through which the Pythagoreans recommend it be found out. In the most extensive of Philolaus' extant fragments, he speaks of Harmonia as a relation of the joining of separates on the basis of correspondence, proportion, and symmetry (Kirk and Raven, p. 327). At a later date, Epicurus speaks of Harmonia in similar terms. Epicurus' Fragment 250 talks of *"summetrikai harmoniai"* (symmetrical harmony). Epicurus' theorization of Harmonia in terms of symmetry harkens back to the

Philolaic theorization of Harmonia. Philolaus and Epicurus who echoes him conceptualize Harmonia in terms of the principle of symmetry. In Philolaus' text, the principle of symmetry is apposite to the principle of analogy. In the thinking of Philolaus, and more implicitly, in the thought of Epicurus, Harmonia is conceptualized in relation to the principle of analogy. This is the principle whose use Philolaus and other Pythagoreans Socrates mentions in the *Phaedo* recommended to recover Harmonia behind the manifestations of the phenomenal world. In the thinking of Philolaus, Harmonia is related to the similaic structurally too. It is conceptualized in terms of the structure of analogy subtending the elocutionary category of simile.

In Plato's *Symposium*, the conceptual connection between Harmonia and the formal relation subtending simile is made even clearer. Eryximachus, one of the speakers in this similaically-entitled dialogue on Eros, theorizes Harmonia in reference to the thinking of yet another representative of the pre-ontological, pre-Socratic tradition to whose repression Platonic philosophy and its derivatives are committed, namely, Heraclitus.

The thinking of Heraclitus was not foreign to early modern rhetoricians. Puttenham mentions Heraclitus in the context of his defense of a way of thinking not committed to the cathexis of the extrinsic and, like contemporary new historicism, caring "for nothing but matters of pollicie, & discourses of estate" (p. 84). Dismissing this limited and limiting cathexis of the definite, Puttenham calls for a hermeneutics recognizing, as does psychoanalysis, that truth lies in the details, or, as Puttenham puts it, in "trifles" (ibid., p. 85). The hermeneutics Puttenham recommends is courageous enough to follow the seductions of anagrams and other forms of the free play of the signifier beyond the phallic and paternal prohibitions of any "Pope or Patriarch or other seuere censor" to the site of "recreations of mans wit" (ibid.), which modern psychoanalysis calls the unconscious. Only such a hermeneutic which suspends the cathexis of the "graue" and definite, Puttenham implies, yields one "pleasure"(pp. 82, 85). This hermeneutic rejoicing in trifles and responding to seductions, Puttenham adds, is no invention of his, but "come[s] from many former siecles" (ibid., p. 85). As proof, Puttenham cites a Heraclitean fragment claiming the "matters of man" to be beyond "reason" (ibid.). In Puttenham's text, the pre-Socratic, non-ontological philosophy of Heraclitus is regarded an archaic source of a way of thinking suspending the rational, the definite, and the ontological, and indulging in the free play of language as a means of accessing the truth of the psyche.

Puttenham would and may have found confirmation for his view of Heraclitean philosophy as committed neither to politics not to ontology but to play and pleasure in Plato's *Symposium*. Interpreting Heraclitus' statement on Harmonia as the unity of disjuncts in this dialogue, Eryximachus states: "harmony is a symphony, and symphony a homology" (*harmonia sumphonia estin, sumphonia de homologia*) (187b). Eryximachus transcodes Harmonia with the name for the similaic relation, the name of homo-logy. Homology is the category Socrates uses in the *Phaedo* to talk about analogy or similarity as the structural basis of Pythagorean anamnesis. Eryximachus transcodes homology with the sym-phonic, a signifier denoting the sounding together in concord. Like "*symposium*," the name of the dialogue within which Eryximachus makes his statement, the symphonic is a category which would have phonically resonated for Renaissance humanists with the name of the aesthetic category of simile.

Symphony is related to simile structurally and conceptually too. The concept of symphony is subtended by the idea of the joining of separates. In the case of symphony, what are joined are separate sounds. The idea of the joining of separates subtending the concept of symphony is inscribed by early modern grammarians into the category of the adverb, conceptualized as a copulaic function. In early modern language theory, the category of the adverb is linked with the similaic "like" etymologically, phonically, and conceptually, through the optative mood of "likelihood" of which the adverb is a part. Through its connections with the copulaic category of the adverb as theorized in early modern language theory, the category of simile is conceptually linked with the category of symphony as articulated in one of the most archaic philosophical fragments, re-articulated by Eryximachus in one of the most influential archaic philosophical texts on desire.

Eryximachus' re-articulation of the Heraclitean fragment on Harmonia increases the similaic import of the category of Harmonia. Harmonia is seminal to the pre-Socratic, Pythagorean theory of recollection. This category is theorized in the pre-Socratic thinking of Heraclitus as not merely similaic but at least doubly similaic. The Pythagoreans recommend the use of analogy, the logical relation subtending simile, as the means of discerning archaic origin. Heraclitus inscribes origin itself as predicated upon the structures of correspondence, proportion, symphony, and symmetry. All of the four structures mentioned by Heraclitus in relation to simile enable the relation of analogy. The last two of these structures, symphony and symmetry, resonate with the Latinate signifier for analogy, similitude.

Early modern theorists of language looked back to the pre-Socratic, Pythagorean, Heraclitean, Simonidean origin of pre-ontological thinking. They looked back to a philosophical tradition preceding the Platonic-Socratic repression of the thinking of becoming. The philosophical prelude echoed by early moden theorists of language is the thinking of memory not as the visualized reconstruction of a static and dead past but as the eternal futurity such as subtends desire. These early modern thinkers on language were well aware of the connections their ancient mentors had sketched between the categories of simile and the categories of symmetry, proportion, symphony, and harmony.

Early modern language theorists are clearer about those connections than are the pre-Socratics. This probably has to do with the Latinate name of simile. The Latinate signifier "simile" phonically resonates with "symphony" and "symmetry," derived from the Greek. These phonic resonances would have further foregrounded for early modern men of letters, if unconsciously so, the conceptual connections forged in ancient Greek between the two categories of symphony and symmetry and the category of homology, the Greek term for the similaic. Richard Sherry recognized the connection between the Greek-based signifier "homology" and the rhetorical category of simile. Sherry, famous in his time for his knowledge of Greek and Latin, foregrounds this connection between homology and simile when glossing the elocutionary category of "homiologia" as *"Sermo ubiuqe sui similis"* (*Schemes and Tropes*, unpaginated).

Sherry recognizes the conceptual connections between the elocutionary category of simile and the Pythagorean-based categories of symmetry and harmony in other ways. In the context of his discussion of "Vertue" as a subdivision of the aesthetic category of "Scheme" in terms of which he classifies similitude, Sherry theorizes the relation of "analogia," another structure subtending similitude. The Latin equivalent Sherry suggests for the relation of analogy is not similarity but "Proportio" (unpaginated). This is the Latinate signifier for the relation the pre-Socratics had named symmetry or harmony. The signifier "Proportio" is phonically, anagrammatically, and conceptually associated with the aural pleasures of symphony and musicality. Not surprisingly, the next "Vertue" of schematic speech Sherry theorizes is the musicality of speech, the "swete and pleasaunt modulacion or tunablenes of wordes" he names "tasis" (unpaginated).

The "Vertue" Sherry theorizes after tasis is similaically inflected too. This virtue of speech is "Sinthesis." The signifier "Sinthesis" means "bringing together." Its Greek prefix, *sun*, is a variant of the prefix *sum* (with) structuring the signifiers sym-metry and sym-phony. Synthesis as an aesthetic principle is related to the categories of symmetry and symphony in Aristotle's *Poetics*. In the *Poetics*, Aristotle mentions "*sunthesin melopoiian*" (the synthesis of song, or melody) (1449b35). He theorizes the synthesis of song as marking the language of "rhythm and melody," and, according to another primary version, of harmony. Such language, Aristotle says, is "sensuously attractive" (*hedusmenon*) (1449b25–30).

The category of synthesis, whose Greek name resonates with simile's Latinate name, is conceptually related to simile as a copulaic aesthetic category. Sherry recognizes the principle of synthesis is conceptually related to the similaic. He theorizes synthesis as "an apte setting together of wordes, whych causeth all the partes of an oracion to bee trymmed al *alyke*" (*Schemes and Tropes*, unpaginated, emphasis mine). Synthesis, for Sherry, is a copulaic relation, a relation of the "setting together" of words. Simile too is implicitly conceptualized in early modern language theory as a copulaic category, because of its etymological and conceptual relation to the adverb. Sherry foregrounds the similaic inflection of the category of synthesis by describing it in terms of the similaic copula, as the cause of likeness. Synthesis, for Sherry, is the reason why the synthesized "partes" end "alyke."

Sherry sequentially links analogy-as-proportion, the musicality of speech, and synthesis-as-likeness. In his *Treatise of Schemes and Tropes*, all three of these aesthetic categories are aspects of the alluring "Vertue" or "grace" of schematic speech. Schematic speech, for Sherry, is transcodable with the mythological Primordial Maiden of Eleusis as the archetypal object-cause of desire (see Chapter Two above). Sherry retraces and intensifies the anagrammatic, phonic, and conceptual connections between the similaic, the copulaic, the symmetrical, the symphonic, and the musical as fundamental components of the sensuality of language. In Sherry's theorization of the "vertues" of speech, which harkens back to pre-Socratic theorizations of Harmonia echoing in the aesthetics of Aristotle, language is a medium of Eros.

Similar conceptual links between harmony, proportion, music, symmetry, and simile are drawn in the metalinguistic text of Sherry's near contemporary, the poet, composer, and theorist of language Thomas Campion, who shared Sherry's love of language and of musicality. In his *Observations in the Art of English Poesy* (1602), Campion relates the "ioyning of words to harmony" with the principles of "Simmetry and proportion" subtending "Musick" (p. 1). The inter-related aesthetic principles of joining, harmony, symmetry, and proportion, Campion says, are to be found in the category of rhyme. Much like Sherry, who had characterized the aesthetic principle of synthesis qua harmonic joining in terms of the similaic copula, Campion proceeds to characterize the category of rhyme in terms of the similaic as *"similter desinentia"* (ibid.).

The connection between analogy as the structural principle subtending simile, and proportion as the structural principle subtending symmetry and harmony is evident in early modern lexicography. In Thomas Blount's *Glossographia* (1656), "analogy" is expounded as "proportion," "correspondence," and "harmony." Blount's glossographical gesture links the structural principle of similitude with the categories of symmetry so crucial to the pre-Socratic thinking of Philolaus. Foregrounding this link, John Florio glosses "Analogia" (p. 26) and "Simmetria" (p. 500) as "proportion," and "Proportione" as "a *resemblance*" (p. 405, emphasis mine), in terms of the signifier he uses to gloss the aesthetic category of "similitude" as "Likenesse [and] resemblance" (p. 500). Florio sketches a semiotic chain wherein the similaic and the symmetrical, conceptually related to one another since the most archaic, pre-Socratic beginnings of the thinking of erotic becoming and phonically resonating with one another in early modern Italian and English semantically dovetail and slide into one another.

Such semantic dovetailing is even more explicit in John Bullokar's *English Expositor* (1616). In Bullokar's text, "symmetrie" (sig. O4) is transcoded with "Analogie" (unpaginated). Like symmetry, analogy is glossed in terms of "proportion." Symmetry in Bullokar's text is specifically transcoded with the "likenesse," cited as an equivalent of the signifier "Similitude" and lexically attributed to analogy (unpaginated). Bullokar suggests this dovetailing of the similaic and the symmetrical has a psycho-structural significance related to "like" as a signifier of the similaic copula. Bullokar's *Expositor* includes a word denoting the incarnation of symmetry, the "Symmetrian" (unpaginated). The next word glossed is "Sympathie" (unpaginated). Like synthesis, the signifier of the sensually attractive other in Aristotle's *Poetics*, sympathy is structured by the relation of being with expressed by the prefix "sym." The signifier "sympathy" semantically expresses the relation of being with too. Bullokar glosses sympathy as "a *likenesse*…or a *like* disposition of affection" (unpaginated, emphases mine). For Bullokar, sympathy is a symmetrical similitude functioning, in terms of William Walker's second theorization of the particle "like," as a reciprocal intersubjective li(n)king.

The categories of the similaic and the symmetrical have conceptual and affective links harkening to the pre-Socratic philosophy of the Pythagoreans. In this pre-Socratic philosophy, the category of Being, which would become the focus of philosophy in Plato and the ensuing tradition of metaphysics, is suspended. In early modern rhetoric and its antecedents, Being is inscribed into metaphor as master trope and general equivalent (see Chapter Four above). In early modern rhetoric and its antecedents, simile is the abjected binary of metaphor. The pre-Socratic philosophy of the Pythagoreans becomes implicitly aligned, by isomorphism, with simile as what the ontologized category of metaphor abjects. Pythagorean philosophy is considerably focussed on the categories of Harmonia and symmetry. The isomorphic positioning of Pythagoreanism in the history of the thinking of Being and of simile in the early modern thinking of elocution enables the alignment of the categories of similitude and symmetry. This alignment by isomorphism confirms a conceptual alignment made in Pythagorean anamnesis theory, where similitude qua analogy and symmetry are principles of uncovering the truth of the structure of the soul. Given the conceptual and affective links between similitude and symmetry, and given the phonic resonances between these two categories enabled by the simultaneous reliance of early modern European languages on Latin and Greek, the category of the similaic appears to have a prominent place in one of the most influential rhetorical treatises of the English Renaissance, Puttenham's *Arte of English Poesie*.

Simile is a significant category in Puttenham's treatise. This is made evident by Puttenham's extensive theorization of "Omiosis or Resemblance" (pp. 201–206). Like the early modern lexicographers and like Sherry, Puttenham transcodes resemblance with "similitude," "likening" and, significantly, "proportion" (pp. 201–206). The place of simile in Puttenham's theory of elocution is much more prominent than even his extensive theorization of resemblance suggests. The third part of Puttenham's tri-partite treatise, in which simile is theorized, is entitled "Of Ornament" (pp. 114–258). Despite its conventional privileging of metaphor as the "most commendable" of aesthetic forms (p. 250), Puttenham's theory of elocution is idiosyncratic among Renaissance treatises on rhetoric. Most other Renaissance rhetoricians postulate the phallic category of "trope" and theorize metaphor as the general equivalent of elocution within this category. Puttenham forgoes the phallic category of trope. He theorizes all elocutionary forms, including metaphor, as "ornaments" or "figures," in terms of a non-phallic taxonomic aesthetic category he and his peers associate with seductive myths of omphalic, feminine desire as perversion (see Chapter Two above).

Given this suspension of the phallic category of trope, we should not be surprised to see how despite Puttenham's token privileging of the conventionally tropological category of metaphor, he foregrounds the figural category of simile, which many of his peers theorize as the abjected binary of metaphor. Puttenham devotes much more space to his theorization of simile than to his theorization of metaphor. Puttenham's foregrounding of the similaic is evident already in the first of the two theoretical sections of his treatise which follow the introductory historical-speculative section on "Poets and Poesie" (pp. 1–51). The first theoretical section in Puttenham's treatise is fully devoted to a single aesthetic category. This category is "Of *Proportion* Poeticall" (pp. 53–113, emphasis mine).

In the third section of his treatise, Puttenham, like Sherry, Florio, Bullokar, and Blount, transcodes the category of poetical proportion with similitude (p. 204). The conceptual contents of Puttenham's section on proportion confirm the implicit foregrounding of the similaic suggested in its title. Proportion in poetry, Puttenham writes in this section, involves the creation of "good symmetrie" (p. 75). In early modern English, symmetry is a formal relation phonically resonating with the similaic. Ancient philosophers such as Heraclitus, Philolaus, and their successor Epicurus transcode symmetry with harmony. Following their lead, Puttenham does the same (pp. 53, 64). Symmetry is a copulaic relation structured by the relation of homology the early moderns came to name similitude. For Puttenham, the implicitly similaic symmetricality-as-harmony he ascribes to poetic proportion, the structural relation lexicographers of his time habitually use to gloss analogy, the basis of the similaic relation, has a sensuous-affective consequence of which Aristotle had already spoken. Puttenham refers to proportionable, and hence symmetrical speech, as "harmonicall" (pp. 54, 61). Proportionable, symmetrical speech, Puttenham writes, echoing the Eryximachian gloss of Heraclitus in the *Symposium* which conflates harmony and homology with symphony, is what "Maketh your meeter symphonicall" (p. 66).

For Puttenham, such symphonical-symmetrical "harmonicall" speech is what "breedeth to th'eare a great compassion" (p. 61). A subject's particular aurally sensuous sym-phonic combination of phonemes with (*sum*) each other gives rise, he suggests, to a passionate, affective combination or com-passion between the subject and her/his interlocutors. Like Bullokar was to do, Puttenham speaks of this compassion in terms of its Greek-based equivalent, "simpathie" (p. 57). The signifier "sympathie" phonically resonates with the categories of symphony and symmetry with which Puttenham transcodes it. This signifier phonically resonates with the similaic, with which Puttenham more implicitly transcodes it through the category of proportion he identifies with simile in the following section of his treatise (p. 204).

The intersubjective relation of sympathy Puttenham implicitly associates with similitude through the categories of symmetry and symphony is conceptually related with the similaic as a non-metaphorical and thus, in terms of the categories inscribed into metaphor in early modern thought on language, non-ontological and non-visual category. This is confirmed in Puttenham's explicit theorization of poetical proportion, with which he proceeds to conflate similitude, as a primarily aural/oral relation. For Puttenham, proportion does not appeal to the phallicized eye/I with which Sidney and Fraunce transcode metaphor (see Chapter Four above). Proportion appeals to the ear (p. 64), one of the orifices receiving the archaic satisfactions proffered by the mother as primordial past-oral object (see Chapter One above).

Puttenham recognizes the thematization of the primordial oral object in the poetry of pastoral. He theorizes pastoral as "the first and most aunciant forme of artificiall Poesie," embodying the most archaic, "first amorous musicks" in collective literary, and, more implicitly, individual history (p. 50). Poetic proportion, Puttenham writes but a few pages later, is "a kind of Musicall vtterance" (p. 53). In so doing, Puttenham conceptually aligns the relation of proportion, with which he later conflates similitude, with the formal relations of symmetry and symphony, and with music as their aural/oral aesthetic medium. Puttenham explicitly relates the medium of music to pastoral poetics as expressing the "auncient" or archaic and the "amorous" or erotic, intensifying the links between the aesthetic categories of simile and pastoral sketched as early as the archaic poetry of Simonides.

Like Sherry, Puttenham retraces archaic links between the similaic, the symmetrical, the symphonic, and the musical. In early modern English, phonic resonance and anagrammaticality, an aesthetic relation that Puttenham himself theorizes as part of similaic proportion (pp. 82–85), reinforce these links. The relevance of phonic resonance and anagrammaticality to Puttenham's aesthetics is confirmed by the explicit emphasis on the phonic and oral/aural in those aesthetics. Puttenham goes further than Sherry's alignment of similaic symmetry with the alluring sensual "grace" of non-tropological, non-phallic, omphalic, schematic language. Sherry theorizes similaic symmetry as what makes schematic language, when articulated by a particular subject, sensually attractive, in

Aristotle's terms, to others. Puttenham theorizes similaic symmetry as what constitutes and enables intersubjective sympathy. Like Sherry, who echoes Aristotle, Puttenham suggests the orally/musically-generated similaic sympathy between subjects has everything to do with Eros in general. Going further than Sherry, Puttenham suggests the orally/musically-generated similaic sympathy between subjects has everything to do with the primordial, past-oral satisfactions of the "first amorous musicks" too. Long before Kristeva would say amorous passions are modeled on the primal rhythmic-sonorous-erotic articulations of mother to child, Puttenham theorized primal love as musical. Long before Lacan would point out the conceptual relation of the archaic, polymorphic libido to pastoral, Puttenham recognized the conceptual and psychological relation of this genre to the "auncient" and archaic. Unlike Kristeva and Lacan, for all the linguistic slant of their psychoanalytic theory, Puttenham recognized the particular rhetorical structure underpinning the musical orality of archaic love. This rhetorical structure, he implies, is symmetrical similitude.

Puttenham's emphasis on the musicality of the relation of proportion he later conflates with similitude has an important consequence for the inter-subjective dynamics he inscribes into the aesthetic category of simile. This consequence exceeds the relation of the dynamics of sym-pathy to the "first amorous musicks," the primal past-oral encounters with the (m)Other for which the polymorphic forms of eroticism the genre of pastoral thematizes are poetic adequations. Music, Puttenham states, echoing the Pythagorean philosophy of Philolaus and his later followers such as Nicomachus, author of the first-century *Manual of Harmonics*, is an aesthetic domain subtended by symmetrical proportion, by the harmony enabled by symmetrical proportion, and "by number" (p. 53).

The category of number in Pythagorean philosophy is characterized as abstract and immutable, a stable structure persisting through phenomenal vicissitudes. Number in Pythagorean philosophy is differential too. Number is the constituent of a system isomorphic with language, with grammar, with rhetoric, and with intersubjectivity. All such symbolic systems are characterized by Pythagoras as "correspond[ing] to" Number (Iamblichus, p. 73). All these systems are predicated upon discontinuities. The differentiality and discontinuity of numbers enables them to be organized into the ratios, the proportions structurally subtending musical chords and making harmony possible (Nicomachus, pp. 73, 85; Iamblichus, p. 53).

According to the Pythagorean aesthetics reverberating in Puttenham's theorization of poetical proportion as the basis of harmony in speech, such harmony depends on differentiality and discontinuity among its constituents, including the tone and the semitone (Iamblichus, p. 53). For Nicomachus, the "satisfying consonance" of harmony is the product of a symbolic system "varied" enough for its constituents to be "intercalated" into a range of tonal proportions (ibid., p. 73). Echoing this Pythagorean principle, Puttenham theorizes harmony in speech as possible only among "things that haue conueniencie by relation" (p. 53), things that can be related to one another as separates. According to Thomas Campion too only "Number[s]" as *"discreta quantitas"* can be joined in "due proportion" to produce "harmony" (*Obseruations in the Art of English Poesy*, p. 1).

The harmonious relation of separate "things," Puttenham goes on to say, the relation enabling the "beautiful," the aesthetic, is "proportion" (p. 53). Later in his text, Puttenham conflates proportion with similitude. Other early modern thinkers on language share Puttenham's recognition of the conceptual links between proportion and similitude. In *The Lawier's Logike*, Fraunce theorizes "Proportion" as another name of "likenesse" such as is expressed in "compared arguments" or "similitudes" (p. 72). In Thomas Blunderville's *Arte of Logike* (1599), "Proportion," conceptualized as a feature of arguments being "compared together" (p. 97), is cited as a subdivision of arguments "From Similitude or Likenesse" (p. 113). Unlike Fraunce and Blunderville, Puttenham adds an aesthetic conclusion to the observation of the conceptual affinity between proportion and similitude. He goes on to explain the technical condition of the fundamental aesthetic relation between proportion and similitude. This condition, Puttenham says, is "measure" (p. 53). For Puttenham, the proportion making harmony possible is conditional upon the relational linking of separate and different "things" we can "measure" with respect to one another on the basis of number.

Looking back to Pythagorean aesthetics, Puttenham inscribes the relational linking of separates on the basis of measure into the category of proportion qua similitude. This relational linking of separates is theorized in early modern treatises on grammar. In early modern grammar treatises, the relational linking of separates is expounded as subtending the relation early modern rhetoricians conceptualize as the structural basis of simile, namely, comparison. In early modern grammatical theory, the relation of comparison which subtends similitude is theorized as a relation of measure or degree. This theorization is made with respect to the category of the adjective. An adjective, Aickin writes, "hath no other variation, than that of Degrees," one of which is the "Comparative" (p. 8). Aickin situates comparison within the conceptual domain of the variant or differential and the gradational or measurable. This is the sphere in which Puttenham had situated the relation of proportion he conflates with the category of simile, a category subtended by the relation of comparison of which Aickin speaks. Wharton too speaks of comparison as an attribute "belong[ing] to Adjectives" and expressible "by degrees" (p. 36). Poole in *The English Accidence* (p. 6), Miege (p. 35), R[obinson] (p. 46), Jonson in *The English Grammar* (p. 58), and Busby (p. 8) too speak of comparison in the context of their theorization of the adjective. They all make measure or "degree" the condition of comparison. In all of those cases, early modern grammarians attribute the relation of comparison, related by rhetoricians of the time to simile, to the syntactic category of the adjective. Early modern grammarians place the similaic relation of comparison within a domain whose constituents are relatable to one another by measure because of their constitutive separation and difference from one another. This is a domain where relation is made possible by differentiation.

Within the domain of comparison and/as degree sketched by the early modern grammarians, the relation enabled by the differentiality of its constituents may "increase, or be diminished" (R[obinson], p. 46; Busby, p. 8). According to Blunderville, in this domain, the relation between different constituents may proceed "from the More to the Lesse, or from the Lesse to the More, or from Like to Like" (p. 94). According to R[obinson], in this domain "excesse" and its absence are possible (R[obinson], p. 46). This domain is shifting, dynamic, plural in its potentialities, and relational. By virtue of all those formal attributes, the domain of comparison is structurally, constitutively erotic.

This eroticism of the domain of comparison is suggested in Ben Jonson's *English Grammar*, where the comparison by degree is described in psychic rather than formal terms as an "affection" of the adjective (p. 58). Puttenham, like Fraunce and Blunderville in their treatises on logic, conflates gradational relationality with proportion as an attribute of similitude. Early modern grammarians theorize the category of gradational relationality. For them, this shifting, dynamic and hence affective/erotic relationality of comparison can exist only within the differential, wherein the fundamental structural condition is separation.

In so theorizing proportion-as-comparison or similitude in terms of the affective/erotic linking of separates, Puttenham, Fraunce, Blunderville, and the early modern grammarians delineate the dynamics of erotic linking of which modern psychoanalysis was to speak. Eros, Lacan was to write, "tends to unite," yet this "tendency to union" can "only ever be apprehended in its relation to the contrary tendency, that leads to division, to rupture, to redispersion" (*Seminar I*, p. 79). This tendency to division, to separation, is simultaneously the condition for erotic union. Separation (se *séparer*), Michèle Montrelay explains, is what takes place so as to allow for a pair-ing that is an adornment of one subject (*se parer*) with the Other at the locus of the unconscious (p. 151). The dynamics of the pairing of separates delineated by early modern thinkers on language in relation to the category of comparison provide this psychoanalytical maxim with a poignant historical resonance and a linguistic grid. The dynamics of comparison in early modern language theory inflect the pair-ing of se-para-tes of which Lacan and Montrelay speak as a com-pair-ing, conceptually aligned with the aesthetic category of simile.

Early modern theorists of language and the Pythagoreans whose thinking they echo did not conceive of the similaic linking of separates as a static procedure. Like contemporary psychoanalysts, early modern language theorists conceived of the linking of separates as a dynamic procedure. In Pythagorean philosophy and early modern language theory, the similaic linking of separates mutually transforms the entities linked and makes their linking into what the ancients called a symphony or symmetry, and the early moderns called a similitude.

The early modern grammarian Elisha Coles, again looking back to archaic Greek thinking, and even beyond it, to a principle said to be "As Ancient as Nature itself," named this mutually transformative, dynamic similaic linking of separates "syncrisis." "Syncrisis" is the title of Coles's treatise. Coles glosses this signifier as a "comparing" (unpaginated). Coles's etymological gloss looks back to the "Ancient." This Greek signifier begins with the prefix *sun* (with), a variant of *sum*, which for early modern thinkers would have resonated with the Latinate term "*simile.*" "Syncrisis" combines the similaically resonant "*sun*" with the term "*krisis*" (to distinguish), etymologically enacting the principle of the linking of separates.

The conceptual overlap between syncrisis and simile persists later in the rhetorical tradition. John Newberry, an eighteenth-century rhetorician, provides a precise etymology of "syncrisis" in his Rhetoric *Made Familiar and Easy* (1748), when theorizing simile as "*syncrisis*, a judging between" (p. 46).

In Aristotle's *Topics* (102b15) and in his *Rhetoric* (1368a21), "*sunkrisis*" appears in the sense of "comparison." Expounding the principles of encomium in the *Rhetoric*, Aristotle instructs the rhetorician what to do if the praised personage fails to provide the rhetorician with sufficient material. In such a case, Aristotle says, the rhetorician must compare (*sunkrinein*) the praised personage with others. Aristotle's use of the term "syncrisis" echoes a yet more ancient, pre-Socratic, pre-ontological source. At the beginning of his major text on ontology, the *Metaphysics*, Aristotle uses the term in his discussion of the thinking of his predecessors, including Thales, Heraclitus, Anaximenes, and Anaxagoras (984a). Aristotle presents his thinking of Being as supplanting Anaxagoras on pre-ontological first principles (*oun archaia*) in Fragment 4 (Kirk and Raven, p. 358). Anaxagoras, he says, claimed "first principles" to have been "generated" (*gignesthai*) and "destroyed" (*apollusthai*) "in this sense only, by combination [*sunkrisei*] and differentiation [*diakrisei*]" (984a15). In the pre-Socratic thought of Anaxagoras, as expounded by Aristotle, the principle of syncrisis-as-combination, which is conflated with comparison in Aristotle's *Topics* and *Rhetoric*, is transcoded with the principle of generation, of dynamic change. Aristotle's term for dynamic change is *"gignesthai,"* a verb derived from the same root (*gignomai*, to become) as *"genesthai,"* the verb featured in the Simonidean song on becoming discussed in the digression in Plato's *Protagoras*.

Aristotle mentions Simonides shortly before his exposition of pre-Socratic philosophy as a thinker who described "perfect knowledge" as "beyond human power," as not "within man's reach"(982b). Simonides, Aristotle implies, is a thinker who, similarly to the pre-Socratics as Aristotle describes them, bracketed off the category of the perfect, of the All, of Being, and who situated human existence within the domain not of the ontological but of "knowledge," of the necessarily imperfect epistemological.

In early modern language theory, the signifier "syncrisis" appears as synonymous with comparison, the structural relation subtending the aesthetic category of simile and associated with it in treatises on rhetoric. In Aristotle's *oeuvre*, "syncrisis" is conceptually aligned with comparison and with the archaic, first principle of linking-as-becoming articulated in the pre-Socratic, pre-ontological thinking of Anaxagoras and of Simonides. The aesthetic category of syncrisis as simile in early modern language theory resonates with the archaic first principle of linking as non-ontological becoming articulated by Simonides. Simile as theorized in early modern rhetoric is aligned with Simonides by more than phonic resonance and more than the mythologeme dramatizing a multiple desire of the like.

The conceptual links made in Coles's treatise on comparison between simile and the archaic principle of syncrisis anticipate yet another formal-conceptual principle Lacanian psychoanalysis would formulate, namely, transference. Transference as Lacan defines it is not the re-projection of submerged feelings during analysis Freud had theorized (Laplanche and Pontalis, p. 455). Instead, transference is an intersubjective procedure. Like syncrisis as Coles theorizes it, looking back to its ancient thinking as a form of linking qua dynamic becoming, transference causes a transformation in the entities it links. In transference, a process "link[ing]...subjects together," "something takes place which changes the nature of the two [subjects linked]," something which "transforms them" (Lacan, *Seminar I*, pp.108–109).

Like the linking of syncrisis as Coles theorizes it, the linking of transference is effected by the medium, the copula, of "speech" or language (ibid.). Since for Lacan, speech is a constitutively erotic medium, the only medium wherein desire becomes manifest (*Seminar II*, pp. 221, 234), the intersubjective linking involved in transference is, like the linking of syncrisis as the pre-Socratics, in Aristotle's account, conceived of it, inherently erotic. For Lacan, transference is the process set into motion by "human subjects communicating" (*Seminar I*, p. 108). Transference subtends and constitutes Eros and love (ibid., pp. 110, 112). What constitutes love is transference, not the sexual relation, not the signs of physical pleasure in the body of the other, which, Lacan repeats, are "not the sign of love" (*Seminar XX*, pp. 4, 146).

For Lacan, the copula of transference is the medium of full speech in its entirety, namely language insofar as it is articulated in "an authentic and full manner" (*Seminar I*, p. 109). Lacan does not designate any linguistic structure as the copula of transference. Yet his theorization of transference suggests this copula is closely related, in conceptual terms, to a linguistic structure described by early modern rhetoricians and pre-Socratic philosophers. This linguistic structure is the copula of syncrisis or simile, a structure which, for all of Lacan's recognition of the significance to psychoanalysis of the "ancient art of rhetoric" (*Écrits*, p. 298) as a resource for the theorization of links between linguistic and psychic structures, Lacan does not mention.

Since for Lacan, Eros as a force of linking depends on disconnection, and is a cut, as much, and at the same time, as it is a copula, the transformative work of transference he transcodes with Eros, like the transformative work of syncrisis as theorized by Coles and the pre-Socratics, presupposes separation. The copula on which Eros is predicated can never signal the ontological stasis of union in Being into which it is swallowed up. Instead, the copula of transference links subjects on the basis of Eros, of libidinal attraction, and at the same time safeguards their distinctness from one another. This distinctness guarantees the post-conjugal separation of subjects from one another as "partial" (Montrelay, p. 90). The copula of transference generates a transferal, or diffusion, of imaginary content across the boundaries of the subjects it links, boundaries by definition incomplete and discontinuous, just like the erogenous zones, their embodied reflection (Lacan, *Écrits*, pp. 299, 314). The copula of transference as theorized by Lacan is what Heidegger describes as the threshold qua pain, pain being what "tears asunder [and] separates" yet functions as the "joining agent." (*Poetry, Language, Thought*, pp. 50–54). The threshold qua pain coeval with the copula of transference is an affective copula effecting an "intimacy," which can only be less than a "fusion." This transferential intimacy is an "intimacy of striving," of subjects' continually "overreaching" themselves in a similaic attempt to approximate, simulate, be with (Greek *sum*) one another (ibid., pp. 202–204). The copula of transference delineates the boundary separating two subjects while it functions as the elocutionary erogenous zone, a mediator of a transferential coupling, an oscular scission in boundaries through which erotic content is diffused. The copula of transference is, in Heidegger's terms, a rift of wrenching, separating pain functioning as a "threshold" (ibid., p. 204) through which the intersubjective amatory exchange or transference between two subjects yearning toward one another takes place.

These attributes of the copula of transference as theorized by Lacan are those of syncrisis, similitude, or comparison as theorized by early modern rhetoricians and grammarians. For early modern thinkers on language, the similaic copula, just as the copula of transference in Lacan's theorization, is the imperfect, the not-All, what is less than the fusion in Being attributed to the copula of metaphor. Like the copula of transference theorized by Lacan, the similaic copula in its early modern theorization effects constitutively erotic li(n)king of separates marked by libidinal *liking*. Like comparison in its early modern theorizations, this transferential, li(n)king liking is dynamic and procedural. It involves a transferal of imaginary content between the subjects it links. This trans-ferral is trans-formative. Its result is the replenishment and rejuvenation of the subjects trans-ferentially li(n)ked together by amatory liking and their psychic changing by what they receive from one another and what constitutes their "pact" (Lacan, *Seminar I*, p. 108).

Early modern thinkers on language too speak of the psychic changing or transformation of exchanged content generated by the amatory li(n)king of separates. Puttenham theorizes the aesthetic category of apostrophe, the result, he writes, of a passionate "fly[ing out]" of one speaking subject toward another, as an "exchaunge" which "breedeth" a "certaine recreation to the hearers minds" (pp. 198–199), strikingly anticipating the Lacanian theorization of transference as a psychically transformative erotic exchange. More implicitly yet more extensively, Puttenham and other early modern thinkers on language theorize mutually transformative amatory exchange in relation to another linguistic category. This linguistic category is conceptually close to apostrophe in Puttenham's theorization and to the apotropaic as theorized by Derrida (*Glas*, p. 46). It is what I call apo(s)trophaic, beyond the phallus in its repressive function and constitutively omphalic, umbilical. This is the category of similitude, comparison, or likening.

In theorizing transference as a constitutively erotic and omphalic transformatory intersubjective exchange of full speech, Lacan was not only recasting a Freudian category, as he claims to be doing. He was also, perhaps unconsciously, tapping into early modern theorizations of linguistic form preceding Freud by more than three centuries. These early modern theorizations of the linguistic categories of apostrophe and similitude must not be considered rudimentary forms of the Lacanian category of transference. More formally specific and detailed than the Lacanian theorization of transference and Montrelay's theorization of the umbilical, the early modern theorizations of simile and apostrophe provide the psychoanalytical categories of transference and of omphalic linking with a precise linguistic grid of the kind Lacan always sought for the psychic structures he described in "the ancient art of rhetoric," though, not being a student of that art, he did not always pinpoint.

In terms of the categories of early modern rhetoric, the omphalic copula of transference may be called inherently similaic. This copula involves a erotic pair-ing of se-par-ates leading to a mutually adorning (*se parer*) com-paring. This is a li(n)king occasioned by libidinal liking and leading to the likening of two subjects who similaically simulate one another. This likening necessarily never reaches the point of fusion, the point of what Derrida calls "consum(mat)ion" in which the copula is "gulped down" (*Glas*, p. 66). The formal attributes of the psychic process of transference whose structural grid is similitude as theorized by early moderns include the likening and mutual simulation of two subjects. This likening/simulation is at the same time the limit of transference.

Likening/simulation marks the necessary gap between transference and the fusion which would annihilate it. Likening/simulation marks the necessary constitution of transference as a dynamic becoming of striving rather than a static fusion in Being.

Transference, and the structure of simile which early modern language theory proposes as its formal grid, is a process constitutively not of consum(mat)ion but of approximation, the structure Levinas theorizes as the fundamental intersubjective relation (*Outside the Subject*, pp. 19, 41). For Levinas, the ethical status of approximation is guaranteed by its non-ontologicality. The relation with the other, Levinas writes, "is not...ontology" (*Basic Philosophical Writings*, p. 7). Where the intersubjective relation is concerned, "to be or not to be is not the question" (*Autrement qu'être*, 4). The ethical relation of approximation is marked by an "inadequation" to Being, by an incapability and unwillingness to "equal its beyond" (*Outside the Subject*, p. 73), in which "I" and "Thou" would become the ontologically "Same" (*Basic Philosophical Writings*, p. 13).

Levinas theorizes ethical intersubjectivity as an approximation which does not yearn for the stasis of the Same but recognizes the subtension of intersubjectivity by the "conjunction...of analogy" (*Autrement qu'être*, p. 4). Long before Levinas, early modern thinkers on language theorized the relation of analogy structuring the linguistic categories of comparison and similitude as a relation which does not deploy itself within the domain of the "Aequall" (Fraunce, *Lawier's Logike*, p. 75), of the axiomatic, of the seamless Same. The relation of analogy, early modern thinkers on language recognized, deploys itself within the shifting domain of Number wherein the governing principle is "degree" or "measure."

The functions of "degree" and "measure" are conceptualized in early modern theory in relation to linguistic categories aligned with similitude. The category of "degree" is often mentioned as constitutive of comparison (Fraunce, *Lawier's Logike*, p. 72; Blunderville, p. 96; Poole, *English Accidence*, p. 6; Jonson, *English Grammar*, p. 58; Aickin, p. 8; Wharton, p. 36; Busby, p. 8). "Measure" is the relation Puttenham theorizes as constitutive of the category of "proportion" (p. 70), and later transcodes with "similitude" (p. 204). The domain of similitude as theorized by the early moderns is the domain of what Campion calls *"discreta quantitas"* (unpaginated). In this domain, the entities linked may be made alternately closer or more distant. They may be brought "from the More to the Lesse, or from the Lesse to the More" (Blunderville, p. 94). The entities linked within the domain of similitude, early modern language theorists imply, may be made more or less proximate. The different degrees or measures of their approximation to one another yield a variety of pleasant symmetries, harmonies, and symphonies. Yet, early modern language theorists imply, the entities linked within the domain of similitude may never be fused, equated, consum(mat)ed, made seamlessly Same.

The domain of the early modern similaic, the generic subtitle of Fulwell's similaically/erotically entitled *Like Will to Like* implies, is the domain of the "pleasant Enterlude." This is the domain of playfulness (or fore-playfulness). It is the domain of rhetorical qua erotic pleasure. This pleasure remains in the inter-rim, in the gap or even the unbridgeable abyss between the subjects it keeps distant and distinct while it links and transforms them.

The aesthetic category of simile as theorized in early modern language theory is emphatically predicated, conceptually and phonically, on the Greek prefix "*sum*" (with). The prefix "*sum*" is not etymologically linked with simile, yet it does etymologically subtend the categories of proportionate symmetry and symphony with which Puttenham links simile. This prefix is constitutively erotic. It is erotic because, like the category of syncrisis predicated on its variant, *sun*, it links yet separates. The prefix *sum* is erotic because it is a copula only insofar as it is a cut. The conceptual, phonic, and etymological association of simile and related categories with the prefix *sum* increases the erotization of simile.

The phonic, etymological, and conceptual association of the category of simile in early modern rhetoric with the Greek *sum* has a significant philosophical consequence. This association inflects the aesthetic category of simile as involving a revocation or suspension of the ontological, of the category of Being. In the history of ancient philosophy, the thinking of Being supplanted the thinking of syncrisis as becoming. Isomorphically, in the history of language, the Greek prefix *sum* was overlain by the Latin *sum*. The Latin *sum* conflates the first-person pronoun and ontological copula. It bespeaks solipsistic self-identity and Being, categories that early modern rhetoricians transcode with simile's phallic binary, metaphor. Simile is aligned by isomorphism with the pre-Socratic thinking of syncrisis as becoming, as otherwise than Being.

The acoustic-conceptual harkening back of the early modern theorizations of simile beyond the Latin *sum* (I am) to the more archaic Greek *sum* (with) is philosophically and psychologically significant. This is a harkening back beyond the ontological, solipsistic, possessive, desubjectifying structure of phallic desire early modern thinkers on language transcode with the aesthetic category of metaphor, to the pre-ontological Lacan would come to conflate with the unconscious (*Seminar XI*, p. 29).

This is a harkening back to the pre-ontological thinking of syncrisis as an archaic first principle of the transferential and transformative omphalic linking of separates.

Like the other language theorists of his time, Shakespeare too wrote of the similaic as a transferential and transformative linking of separates. In his famous soliloquy, Shakespeare's Hamlet conflates "the consummation / devoutly to be wish'd" with the fallacious question of Being stated at the beginning of the soliloquy (Act 3, scene 1, lines 56, 63–64). Shortly after the appropriately monological articulation of this devout wish for ontological consummation, Hamlet speaks to an other, to Ophelia. What he voices to Ophelia is the literally lethal "I loved you not" (Act 3, scene 1, lines 118–119), a disavowal of his desire for her. The structure of Shakespeare's text, where the monological insistence on Being is followed by a devastating disavowal of desire, inflects the disavowal as a consequence of the obsession with Being.

Unlike Hamlet, early modern theorizations of simile do not bespeak an obsession with Being, with ontological "consummation." Early modern theorizations of simile associate this aesthetic category with a never fully consum(mat)ed omphalic linking. Such linking is not predicated on the Latin *sum*. It does not reduce the entities it links to seamless Sameness such as Levinas would associate with the ontological (*Basic Philosophical Writings*, p. 12). In the dynamics of omphalic linking adumbrated in early modern theorizations of simile the entities linked remain in a state of eternal erotic tension towards one another. This erotic tension is what guarantees the possibility of their transferential being with one another in the sense articulated by the Greek prefix *sum*.

In the state of syncritical, transferential, erotic tension inscribed into the aesthetic category of simile in its early modern theorizations, the entities linked can never form a uniform "I am," a *sum* in the Latin sense. Nor can they form a sum, a perfect whole resulting from the addition of two complements, the "sum of good" Shakespeare speaks of in sonnet #109 (line 12) and transcodes with the "all" (line 14).

The transferential linking of separates inscribed into the aesthetic category of simile in its early modern theorizations does not form a sum, an all, a whole made up of two complements. The idea of a whole of two complements is featured in totalizing, nostalgic imaginary captations of love such as Aristophanes' famous account of lovers as two halves of one whole in Plato's *Symposium* (189c–193d). In early modern language theory, the form of linking inscribed into the aesthetic category of simile is not the fusion of two "into a single piece" of which Aristophanes speaks

(192e). It is not an a-twain-ment which becomes an at-one-ment such as Shakespeare sings of in "The Phoenix and Turtle." The "love in twain" of Shakespeare's Phoenix and Turtle "Had the essence but in one" (lines 25–26). Their is an a-twainment qua at-one-ment offering redemption from the pain of difference and separation. Their a-twainement qua at-one-ment proffers what Alexandre Leupin calls the delusory "double fantasy of continuity and totality" ("The Impossible Copula").

Whereas Shakespeare's "Phoenix and Turtle" suggests a fantasy of continuity and totality wherein "Number...in love was slain" to produce a s(e)am-less Sameness in which there is "division none" (lines 26–27), early modern theorizations of simile reject this fantasy by positioning the similaic within the domain of "degree" and "measure," within the domain of "number" (Puttenham, p. 53). In this similaic domain of number, which is necessarily a domain of separation and difference, any "two" entities linked, as Shakespeare puts it in sonnet #36, "must be twain," despite, because of the erotic, transferential copula of "undivided love" binding them (lines 1–2). In this domain of number postulated by early modern theorizations of simile, erotic linking can never be a complemental a-twainment qua at-one-ment, a consum(mat)ion in which number and separation are "slain," as they are in the delusory fantasy of fusion that informs early modern theorizations of metaphor in terms of the totalizing, possessive, de-subjectifying structure of phallic desire. Similaic linking is necessarily not complemental, combining two halves into a perfect, continuous whole. Similaic linking is supplemental, always exceeded by a remainder constitutively extrinsic to it. This excess or remainder is the differences between the subjects/signifiers linked. Those differences are registered in the omphalic copula of simile which is never "gulped down" like the metaphoric copula as theorized by Derrida and by early modern language theorists, but remains a supplemental excess.

The supplemental, separating structure of the linking inscribed into the aesthetic category of simile in its early modern theorizations guarantees the possibility of the harmonic symmetry and symphony Puttenham links with the similaic acoustically and conceptually. The supplemental, separating structure of similaic linking guarantees the flourishing and thriving of this symmetrical, symphonic harmony not despite but because of the absence of totalizing consum(mat)ion. The approximatory, transferential nature of the similaic copula as conceptualized in early modern language theory makes such totalizing consum(mat)tion impossible.

Similaic linking as theorized in early modern thought on language guarantees more than a supplemental symmetry born of the open-ended, potentially infinite harmonizing of separates where totalizing, complemental, ontological, metaphorical consum(mat)ion is impossible. Similaic linking guarantees what, as Alexandre Leupin points out in "The Impossible Copula," has been fallaciously associated with consummation in nostalgic imaginary captations of complemental union from Aristophanes' account of love as the fulfilling fusion of halves in Plato's *Symposium* to Freud's account of the rejuvenating coalescence of organisms in *Beyond the Pleasure* Principle (p. 60). Similaic linking guarantees *jouissance*.

Aristophanes imagines *jouissance* as the product of the fusion of the two into the sum of One, as the product of a total consum(mat)ion which consumes separateness. Before Aristophanes, Eryximachus speaks of a symmetrical, symphonic, harmonic erotic being with (Greek *sum*), which Aristophanes' fantasy of total fusion would make impossible (187d). Early modern thinking of simile is aligned with the erotics of Eryximachus, not Aristophanes. In it, the condition for *jouissance* is the revocation of the fantasy of total consum(mat)ion, of the production of the perfect sum of One, of the Latin *sum* (I am) bespeaking ontology and the solipsistic narcissism marking the phallic desire early modern thinkers on language inscribe into the aesthetic category of metaphor.

The approximatory, omphalic, and transferential erotics associated with simile in early modern language theory are the stated concern of Shakespeare's "A Lover's Complaint." This poem ends with a woman's rhetorically/erotically performed climactic *jouissance*. The combination of the orgasmic pleasure of a woman with an approximatory, non-consummational similaic erotics well accounts for the critical foreclosure of this dazzling poem, despite its attribution to Shakespeare. The poem inflects the climactic *jouissance* with which it ends as what can only ever be produced within the field of the similaic rather than the metaphoric. In reversal of Hamlet's declaration of his addiction to Being, Shakespeare's "A Lover's Complaint" situates *jouissance* in the domain of what "seems," another term phonically and conceptually resonating with the similaic, rather than what "is" (*Hamlet*, Act 1, scene 2, lines 73–76). "A Lover's Complaint" situates *jouissance* in the domain of the not-All rather than the All, of the some rather than the sum, of the "a-twain[ment]" (line 6) which never becomes an at-one-ment.

Shakespeare's "A Lover's Complaint" makes non-consum(mat)tional *jouissance* conditional upon the further hollowing out of the already hollow, differential, approximatory structure of simile as theorized by rhetoricians of the period. In order for *jouissance* to be possible, the poem suggests, "similes" must be "Hollow'd with sighs" (lines 227–228). Sighs are a corporeal-affective expression of what Heidegger would philosophize as "the dif-ference" between subjects, which "tears asunder" yet "joins together what is held apart in separation" (*Poetry, Language, Thought*, p. 204). They are a corporeal-affective expression of the recognition of the possibility of the totalizing, (con)summational sum resulting in a solipsistic *sum* (I am). The signifier "sigh" whose hollowing out from simile is the psychic-linguistic task the youth in the poem sets his object and the poem sets its readers, phonically resonates with the totalizing, egoic signifier "I." This signifier bespeaks the ontologicality articulated by the Latin *sum*, and is the typographical trace of the phallus (Lacan, *Écrits*, p. 83).

The non-metaphorical rhetorical-erotic field of the similaic is conceptualized in early modern language theory as the field of a non-egoic, transferential and omphalic rather than phallic desire. The poem requests this rhetorical-erotic field be recursively "Hollow'd" out with "sighs" bespeaking the recognition and embracing of separation, the revocation of the complemental sum, and phonically resonating with the phallic "I." When this rhetorical-erotic hollowing out takes place, the field of the similaic becomes the field of simile (–I). The result is a "s(i)mile," a mark of an affectively and corporeally experienced *jouissance*.

Granting poetic resonance to early modern theorizations of similaic linking, Shakespeare's "A Lover's Complaint" inflects the climactic, orgasmic s(i)miles of *jouissance* as the result not of a totalizing con(sum)ation but of the embracing of the "sighs" marking the "Hollow" separating any two subjects, the hollow which is desire itself and which is the condition of a being with in the more archaic sense of *sum*: of supplemental, open-ended, intersubjective and thus ethical and erotic rather than ontological harmony and symmetry.

Chapter Six

*Simile and Maternality:
From the Abject to the Orgasmic*

In early modern poetics and language theory, simile is inscribed with an approximatory rather than consummatory structure of desire. In this structure of desire, the entities involved remain twain and linked by what Derrida calls the "third term," the copula. Unlike in the structure of "communion" (or fusion) Derrida describes, in the structure of approximatory desire inscribed into simile in early modern language theory, the copula does not "disappear" (*Glas*, p. 66). The structure of approximatory, similaic desire inscribed in early modern poetics and language theory is, as suggested by Wilson's theorization of simile as involving "two things, or more than two" (*Arte of Rhetorique*, p. 213), more than double. Desire of this structure is at least triple, marked by the necessary presence of the separating yet connecting third term. This structure of desire is isomorphic with the principle of syncrisis in its archaic, pre-Socratic theorization reverberating in Coles's early modern treatise on simile whose title is the name of this principle.

Given this inscription of the the pre-Socratic principle of the at least double into early modern conceptualizations of the aesthetic category of simile, we should not be surprised to find a celebration of the principle of *triasmus omnia*, the omnipresence of the numeral three, in the most philosophical of the many compendia of similes published in sixteenth-century Europe, Francis Meres's *Wits Commonwealth* (sig. A4). In the introduction to this compendium, Meres celebrates the principle of *triasmus omnia*. In doing so, Meres celebrates the arithmetical substrate of one of the most pervasive of psychic structures, the shifting triangle of desire, characterized by an open-ended supplementarity exceeding the illusory unity of the dyad as sum.

Meres celebrates the principle of three, of the triangle, while alluding to the pre-Socratic philosophy of Thales and of Pythagoras (sig. A4), who is known to have been influenced by Thales (Iamblichus, p. 5). This reference is not incidental to the principle of three. Pythagoras' theory of harmonics uses the signifier "harmony" as a name for the number three. This theory proposes another at least triple structural category. Pythagorean harmony theory speaks of the category of the *mese* or "middle note" as what guarantees "consonance" or harmony and a "varied scheme" of sound (Nicomachus, p. 73). This Pythagorean acoustic is dynamic, expressive of infinite possibilities, and pleasurable. It shares the attributes of eroticism.

Meres recognizes the erotic subtext of his celebration of the "old," archaic, pre-Socratic principle of *triasmus omnia*, the principle he transcodes with similitude (sig. A4). Attaining one's "wished desire," he writes, involves one's being able to "reioyce for three things" (sig. A4), for an excessive, joy-giving joining exceeding the sum of two.

In another treatise, *Gods Arithmeticke*, Meres celebrates a form of joining quite at odds with the celebration of the triangle of "wished desire" in *Wits Commonwealth*. In the moralistic *Gods Arithmeticke*, Meres commends the principle of heterosexual joining generated "When God had married Adam and Eua together [and] said to them both, increase, multiplie, and replenish the earth" (sig. A2).

Meres's writing is split between the celebration of the excessive triangle of desire and the moralistic commendation of matrimonial heterosexuality. The excessive triangle of desire is adumbrated in Meres's compendium of similes. The triangle of desire is associated with similaic aesthetics. The matrimonial heterosexuality Meres commends in *Gods Arithmeticke* is not associated, in this treatise, with any particular rhetorical form.

The implicit association of the similaic copula with an excessive and open-ended eroticism in Meres's *Wits Commonwealth*, and the split in Meres's thinking between an excessive and open-ended eroticism associated with the similaic copula and dyadic, reproduction-oriented heterosexuality raise important questions concerning the relation between rhetorical and sexual forms. These questions are made all the more pertinent in view of the frequent early modern thematizations of simile in relation to male and female homosexuality. The similaic copula as theorized by Meres, Puttenham, Shakespeare, Fulwell, Fraunce, Blunderville, and the early modern grammarians is an excessive supplement, an apex of an erotic triangle, a middling mean allowing for infinite varieties of non-consummational erotic symmetry. What are the consequences of this theorization for the relationship between simile and particular forms of sexuality, such as heterosexuality, homosexuality, and incest?

Early modern writers such as Shakespeare, Fulwell, Donne, Lanyer, and Spenser use the common semanteme of the similaic copula, "like," to thematize forms of sexuality based on the attraction to the like. These forms of sexuality are constitutively excessive of the non-erotic, reproductive function of matrimonial heterosexuality Meres terms "Gods Arithmeticke." Does the inscription, in early modern thinking on language, of the similaic copula with a structure of desire exceeding the illusory complementarity of the pair inflect the common semanteme of the similaic copula, "like," only toward forms of sexuality based on the attraction to the like? A careful examination of the theorization of simile in early modern treatises on rhetoric and their ancient sources will lead us to a complex answer to the last of these questions.

Early modern literary texts include many affirmations of homosexuality articulated by means of the signifier "like." Examples include Fulwell's "nothing is more desirous than like unto the like" (unpaginated), and the declaration "Like doth quit like" at the end of Shakespeare's *Measure for Measure* (Act 5, scene 1, line 409). This declaration echoes Isabella's articulation of her Lesbian attraction to Marianna, the woman to whom she is introduced as one who "comes to do [her] good": "I do desire the like" (Act 4, scene 1, lines 51–53). Yet the answer to the question of whether the category of simile in early modern language theory is inflected only or even predominantly toward sexualities of the like is not the affirmative suggested by these articulations of homosexuality by means of the similaic copula "like."

Despite these literary connections between the similaic copula "like" and homosexuality, simile is theorized in early modern treatises on rhetoric in reference to an object excessive of the reproduction-oriented "loue between man & wife" Meres celebrates in *Gods Arithmeticke* (p. 6). The constitutively excessive object allied with the form of simile is not necessarily either homosexual or heterosexual. The excessive object allied with simile in early modern language theory is the primal (incestuous) maternal object, the source of desire and anxiety. This is the same (a)object early modern thinkers on language transcode with the primal substance of semiosis (see Chapter One above).

The maternalization of simile in Renaissance rhetoric is in part a function of the theorization of simile as the abjected binary of metaphor, the aesthetic category elevated to the rank of general equivalency (see Chapter Four above). Because metaphor is the general equivalent of elocution, it functions as a homologue of the phallus. Since in symbolic economies "the phallic referent is positively charged in contrast to the part object or the negative charge of the female organ" (Goux, *Symbolic Economies*, p. 90), simile becomes contrasted with metaphor as an encryption of the female genitals, of the sex of the mother.

The maternalization of simile in Renaissance rhetoric is more than structural, and it has an ancient history whose roots extend to Aristotle's formative theorization of this aesthetic category in the third book of his *Rhetoric*. Aristotle's association of simile with the genitals of the mother is in part a function of the elevation of the aesthetic category of metaphor with which simile is related to the rank of general equivalency. One of the means of the elevation of metaphor to general equivalency in Aristotle's text is Aristotle's tendency to mention simile only "within a larger context of metaphor" (McCall, p. 51). This tendency amounts to the implicit theorization of simile as secondary, dependent, conceptually feminine. Most predominantly, the maternalization of simile in Aristotle's text is function of an isomorphism between Aristotle's economy of elocution and his articulation of sexual difference.

According to Aristotle, simile differs from metaphor "only in that particular that has been stated," a particular he later judges to be "less attractive" (*Rhetoric*, 1410a). Critics such as Marsh McCall (p. 41) and theorists such as Paul Ricoeur (p. 26) have ventured exegeses of this theorization justifying or explicating its obvious devaluation of simile in ostensibly neutral and descriptive terms of cognitive effect. These exegeses overlook the vocabulary Aristotle uses to theorize the difference between simile and metaphor. This vocabulary is primarily libidinal, not epistemological.

The primary fault Aristotle finds in the "particular" distinguishing simile from metaphor is its making simile "less attractive" in relation to the logocentric pleasures of the "mind" metaphor has to offer (*Rhetoric*, 1410a). Simile's difference from metaphor is theorized as a difference from *logos*. "The dominion gained by the category of mind over the category of matter," Goux says, is isomorphic with the subordination of the female sex to the male sex (*Symbolic Economies*, p. 90). Simile's difference from metaphor is contextualized as a sexual difference. This is a difference from *logos* transcoding with a difference from maleness and paternity. This difference is the difference of maternity. For Aristotle, the consequence of the sexual difference of simile from metaphor is simile's diminished sex-appeal, its being "less attractive."

Aristotle's devaluation of simile with respect to metaphor works by means of categories of desire and sexual difference. These categories are expounded in greater detail elsewhere in Aristotle's *oeuvre,* notably in the *Metaphysics* and *The Generation of Animals. The Generation of Animals* describes male and female as "the same in species" (731a). In terms of Aristotle's definition of species in the *Metaphysics* (1058b), this sameness in species makes male and female equivalent in terms of their defining formal attributes. They are "versions of each other" (Lacquer, p. 29). Within the context of affiliation with the same species, male and female are anatomically distinct from one another. A human being, Aristotle states in *The Generation of Animals*, is made male or female "only in virtue of a certain...part." This part is "in the female the so-called uterus, in the male the testes and the penis" (716b). The difference between the sexes is genital, hinging on the designation of the womb, the maternal organ, as the part "most peculiar to the female" and of the penis as the organ "distinctive of the male" (Lacquer, p. 31).

This anatomical difference between male and female is far from neutral (Lacquer, pp. 8–11). It is embroiled with the identification of the male with rationality and of the female with irrationality in the *Politics* (1259b–1260a). In Aristotle's one-sex model, men and women are arrayed "along an axis whole *telos* [is] male" (Lacquer, pp. 5–6). In this model, the formal, anatomical attribute of the female's organ of reproduction being putatively "always internal," rather than "external" like the male's, makes the female not merely the "contrary" of the male but the male's incapacitated "privation" (*Metaphysics*, 1055b). In Aristotle's account, the interiority of the female's organs of reproduction makes for a lack of heat rendering them incapable of contributing "seed" to the process of conception (*Generation of Animals*, 729a). This interiority of the female genitals as conceived by Aristotle limits their role in generation to the supply of matter "from which is made the resulting product" (ibid., 730b).

The male, for Aristotle, is the efficient and active cause, imprinting the inert matter of the genetrix with phallic form. In Aristotle's account of generation, Goux observes, "the mother-matter inclines toward change, for it desires what is missing, what it lacks: it desires [the] form" supplied by the phallic imprint of the male (*Symbolic Economies*, pp. 118–119). In Aristotle's account of sexual difference, the female body in its maternal inflection is theorized as a site of lack and privation. The female body is a "deviation" from the more perfect body of the male (*Generation of Animals*, 767b). For Aristotle, a woman, in particular in her biological role as mother, is a deficient male, defined by what she lacks.

Aristotle's sexual economy, in which the anatomical difference between the male and the female genitalia is a hinge for the devaluation of the maternalized female body and the diminishing of its potential to become an object of male desire, is transcodable with Aristotle's economy of metaphor and simile. Just as a woman in Aristotle's anatomy is rendered deficient and devalued "only in virtue of a certain part," her genitals (*Generation of Animals*, 716b), simile in Aristotle's *Rhetoric* is devalued because of "that particular." The similaic copula becomes transcodable with the female genitals in their maternal function. Just as Aristotle theorizes the female organ of generation as deficient and lacking with respect to the organ of the male, Aristotle theorizes the similaic copula as a lack, a failure to "assert that 'this is that'" (*Rhetoric*, 1410a).

Crossing rhetorical, logical, grammatical, anatomical, biological, ontological, and gendered vocabularies, Aristotle theorizes the similaic copula as a quintessential lack whose corporeal site is the female organ of sexual copulation. Even more significantly, the corporeal site of the similaic copula as Aristotle theorizes it is the site of maternity, the function early modern rhetoricians would transcode with the primal substance of semiosis. The isomorphism between Aristotle's accounts of sexual difference and of the difference between metaphor and simile renders the similaic copula transcodable with the female organs of copulation and procreation, with the springs of maternality in the female body.

In its formative Aristotelian theorization, simile is conceptualized biologically and sexually more than erotically. In Aristotle's *Rhetoric*, simile is not transcoded with a structure of desire, such as the transferential desire undergirding many of early modern theorizations of simile. Instead, simile in Aristotle's *Rhetoric* is transcoded with a particular sexual object, the maternal object. The mother inscribed into Aristotle's theorization of simile is not the symbolic mother, the primal, prototypical object of desire (Evans, pp. 118–119) informing early modern theorizations of figure, the elocutionary category in terms of which simile is commonly classified. The mother inscribed into Aristotle's theorization of simile is the imaginary mother, imagined as horrifying and abject because of the threat she poses to individuation (ibid.). The inflection of maternality inscribed into Aristotle's theorization of simile is, in his terms, the "less," even least attractive for the subject.

Aristotle's sexual-erotic economy is not far from Lacan's. Echoing Aristotle, Lacan says: "the female sex is characterized by an absence, a void, a hole, which means that it happens to be less desirable than is the male sex for what he has that is provocative" (*Seminar III*, p. 176). Lacan often relies on Aristotelian philosophy. The fifth chapter of *Seminar XX*, for instance, is entitled "Aristotle and Freud: the Other Satisfaction," and includes an extensive discussion of Aristotle's *Nicomachean Ethics* (pp. 51–63). Lacan insists on the linguistic structure of psychic and sexual functions. Yet he does not offer a rhetorical grid for his Aristotelian sexual-erotic economy in which the female is genitally lacking and hence less desirable. Many centuries before Lacan, Aristotle and the early modern rhetoricians who echoed him had provided such a grid, namely, the category of simile inscribed with maternal genitality.

The rhetorical trace of the deficient attractiveness of the similaic copula is its relative length. Aristotle pronounces the similaic copula he transcodes with the female genitals "less attractive" than the metaphoric copula "just because it is longer" (*Rhetoric*, 1410b). Early modern rhetoricians echo the Aristotelian characterization of the similaic copula as longer. The assertion "A Similitude is a Metaphor dilated" appears in John Smith's *Mysterie of Rhetorique Unvail'd* (p. 211) and Hobbes's *Art of Rhetoric* (p. 110). The early modern treatises echoing Aristotle's association of length in discourse with the similaic copula and the maternal genitals become inscribed with the Aristotelian conceptual complex involving simile, maternality, the various forms of expansion of the female flesh, and the protraction of discourse. In early modern rhetoric, such protraction of discourse is theorized predominantly in relation to the categories of *copia*, dilation, and amplification.

Not one of these three categories is gender-neutral. All three involve etymological, semantic, and conceptual links with the gynecological and maternal, the functions Aristotle inscribes into the similaic copula. *Copia* is associated with simile in the early modern rhetorics of Hoskyns and Blount, in Soario Cypriano's *Arte Rhetorica* (1682), and in the anonymous *Rhetoricae Synopsis* (1693). *Copia* is a rhetorical-aesthetic category resonating with an "imagery of abundance" (Cave, "Copia and Cornucopia," p. 56). Richard Rainolde, for instance, transcodes *copia* with "aboundaunce and plentuousneses" in the *Foundacion of Rhetorike* (fol. ij). The term "*copia*" touches upon natural plenty, personified in the goddess Ops, and abundance (Cave, *The Cornucopian Text*, p. 3). All of these associations tap into the feminine archetypes of matter/*mater*, nature, and fertility.

Copia is problematically maternalized. It involves an "underlying notion" of "abundance, fertility, and fruitfulness" (Cave, "Copia and Cornucopia," p. 59) crystallized in the image of the cornucopia. At the same time, *copia* is associated with "military strength (pl. *copiae*, 'forces')" and, more generally, with "mastery, whether social or linguistic" (Cave, *The Cornucopian Text*, p. 3).

This pairing of maternality-as-fecundity and mastery stresses the explosivity of the notion of *copia* for the early modern rhetorical imaginary. In the early modern rhetorical imaginary, *copia* comes to stand for a maternal body and for an empowered maternal body, such as the body of the imaginary, devouring mother early modern rhetoricians transcode with the primal substance of semiosis. *Copia* is theorized in terms of images of plenty. These images inflect *copia* as a maternalized category exceeding the mechanisms seeking to contain it. *Copia* is always already the "prolixity *(loquacitas)*" and "over-elaboration" Terence Cave cites as its "inversions" (*The Cornucopian Text*, p. 5). *Copia* in its early modern theorizations is a form of signification "above all unstructured" (Jardine, p.131). Like the category of the devouring mother Renaissance rhetoricians associate with the primal substance of semiosis, the aesthetic category of *copia* dissolves boundaries. *Copia* ultimately involves not a celebration of eloquence but its crisis.

The crisis of signification of which theorizations of *copia* are symptoms is a crisis of the phallic masculinity invested in the would-be logocentric theory of early modern rhetoric. This crisis occasions the deployment of second-order attempts, such as the notion of *brevitas*, to contain *copia* and bring it within the horizon of an ending. *Brevitas* may be generated as a "rival attraction" to *copia* (Cave, *The Cornucopian Text*, p. 16). But the attraction *brevitas* offers is of another order. What brevity offers is the attraction of phallic mastery, not of an unpredictable excess constitutively evading such mastery. In Alberic de Montecassino's *Flores Rhetorici* (ca. 1080) *brevitas* is opposed to a maternal *"facundia"* (fecundity) (p. 37). Similarly, in Angel Day's early modern *English Secretoire* "breuity" is opposed to the maternal "ryfe and plentifull coinceite of inuention" (pp. 7–10). In early modern rhetorical theory, *copia*, a category technically referencing the length in discourse Aristotle inscribes into the similaic copula, is "figured as female" (Parker, *Literary Fat Ladies*, p. 31). *Copia* in early modern rhetorical theory is maternal, as suggested by Cave's study and argued by Patricia Parker (*Literary Fat Ladies*, p. 31). Given the association of *copia* with the maternal, the theorization of simile's distinction from metaphor as a distinction of length in treatises such as those of Smith and Hobbes overdetermines simile's gynecologization.

In early modern rhetorical theory, simile is theorized in terms of another category referencing length in discourse, *dilatio*. Thomas Wilson, for example, talks of similitude as a means to "dilate our cause" (*Arte of Rhetorique*, p. 214), and Richard Sherry describes "parable and comparacion" (both transcoded with simile [see Chapter Five above]) as strategies wherein arguments may "be dilated" (*Schemes and Tropes*, unpaginated). John Smith and Thomas Hobbes use the category of dilation to theorize simile's distinction from metaphor (see above).

The aesthetic category of dilation associated with simile in early modern rhetoric is even more inflected toward gynecologization than the parallel category of *copia*. Patricia Parker has shown in a number of studies ("Dilation and Delay," "Deferral, Dilation, *Différance*," and *Literary Fat Ladies*, pp. 8–35), how in the rhetorical tradition of the Middle Ages and the Renaissance, the term *dilatio* meant more than protracted discourse. Rhetorical dilation has a number of conceptual contexts. These include "deferral in time and expansion in space," the "deferral of coitus or consummation" ("Deferral, Dilation, *Différance*," pp. 85–86), the "mediate or earthly," and the interpretation of a "closed and hermetic scriptural text," often imaged as an act causing the text to "increase and multiply" its meanings (*Literary Fat Ladies*, pp. 14–15). Almost all of these contexts involve the enlargement or extension of a measurable or material entity: time, earth, country, maternalized female body, or text. This set of conceptual associations makes rhetorical dilation, technically involving the length in discourse Aristotle disparagingly associates with the similaic copula, into a mark of an expanding materiality. In the early modern rhetorical imaginary, such expanding materiality is inscribed into the primal substance of semiosis qua archaic mother. Dilation becomes conceptually associated with the primal substance of semiosis, and conceptually maternalized. The signification of dilation as the growing breadth of the vagina during childbirth gives the maternalized rhetorical category of dilation a specifically obstetrical inflection.

This obstetrical inflection is at work in the third term for rhetorical protraction. Amplification, as Thomas Wilson, for one, theorizes it, consists "in augmenting and diminishing of any matter" (*Arte of Rhetorique*, p. 152). The verb to "augment" signifies an economic operation of hoarding. It is also used in early modern gynecological discourse to signify the "increase of the uterus" (Smellie, p. 117). An economic vocabulary referencing the fluctuations (augmenting and diminishing) of wealth in an early capitalist economy mingles with a gynecological vocabulary referencing the expansion and contraction of the "matter" of female flesh in pregnancy and childbirth. Gynecological vocabulary is the more foregrounded. Wilson goes on to describe amplification by means of an obstetrical scenario as an operation involving the "tak[ing]" of words "[o]ut of the…matter" (p. 152). Similarly, Richard Rainolde describes the state of a discourse being "ample and large" in terms of the obstetrical scenario of the "sett[ing] out" of "small thynges or woordes" by an entity represented in terms of conceptually maternal "aboundaunce and plentuousnes," and specified as obstetrically "dilat[ing]" (fol. ij).

The rhetorical category of amplification in early modern rhetoric is distinctly gynecologized. This category is often associated with simile. Early modern texts wherein amplification is theorized as a characteristic of simile include Joachimus Camerarius's *Elementa Rhetoricae* (p. 219), Richard Sherry's *Treatise of Schemes and Tropes* (unpaginated), Soario Cypriano's *De Arte Rhetorica* (p. 58), John Hoskyns's *Directions for Speech and Style* (p. 18), Thomas Blount's *Academie of Eloquence* (p. 71), and Dominico Decolonia's *De Arte Rhetorica* (p. 57). In these texts, the category of amplification said to be characteristic of simile is inscribed with an obstetrical scenario. This scenario overdetermines the gynecologization of simile.

The gynecologization of simile becomes most manifest in Robert Cawdray's *Treasvrie or Storehovse of Similies*. In this treatise, one of the signifiers coupled in simile is imaged as "drawn" from "the secrets and bowels of nature" (sig. A2). Cawdray imagines the source of one of the components of simile as a predominantly feminized, uterine realm of itemized material phenomena, including, significantly, "bloud, milke...and women in trauaile, in childbirth" (ibid.).

In early modern rhetoric, the formative Aristotelian theorization of the "longer" similaic copula in terms of the female genitals in their maternal inflection receives extensive conceptual resonance. This conceptual resonance is the effect of the transcoding of the aesthetic categories for length in discourse — *copia*, dilation, and amplification — all of which are associated with aesthetic category of simile, with the biological, gynecological, and obstetrical aspects of maternality. These are the same abject aspects of maternality informing early modern theorizations of the primal substance of semiosis in terms of the imago of the imaginary, devouring mother who resists individuation and separation (see Chapter One above).

The transcoding, in early modern rhetoric, of the aesthetic category of simile with the abject and threatening aspects of female sexuality in its maternal inflection gives rise to an anxiety of inundation and loss of control similar to the anxiety manifest with respect to the primal substance of semiosis. Just as in the case of the primal substance of semiosis, this anxiety generates mechanisms of defense whose function is to allay it. Those mechanisms usually take one of two forms. (1) One defense mechanism involves the partitioning of the aesthetic category of simile associated with the sex of the mother into a hierarchical binarism consisting of a devalued ("far-fetched" or catachretic) configuration and privileged (illustrative) configuration. (2) The second defense mechanism is the invention of a new rhetorical sub-genre, the compendium of similes, where illustrative similes are restricted and restrained.

The first mechanism attempts to circumvent the anxiety induced by the inscription of maternal femininity into the aesthetic category of simile by splitting this femininity into two polarized configurations. (1) The denounced, catachretic configuration is associated with a non-regulated and independent female sexuality. (2) The sanctioned, illustrative configuration is associated with a female sexuality committed to subservience within the regulatory framework of a reproduction-oriented heterosexual marriage such as Meres celebrates in *Gods Arithmeticke*.

The second mechanism, the compendium of similes, reveals the limitations of the first. Early modern compendia of similes include only illustrative and hierarchical similes. Those illustrative similes are linguistic forms of a hierarchical structure. This hierarchical structure is designed to fulfill a psychic function: allaying the anxieties concerning the sex of the mother with which simile is associated in the Aristotelian tradition. The necessity to further confine illustrative similes supposed to allay the anxiety of the sex of the mother within the space of the compendium is telling. The postulation of the compendium of illustrative similes shows the insufficiency of the sanctioning of simile's hierarchical configuration, and of the reproduction-oriented matrimonial heterosexuality with which the hierarchical configuration is transcoded, to counter anxiety. Compendia of similes reveal the insufficiency of the hierarchical configuration of simile to allay the anxiety of the abject and devouring aspects of maternality transcoded with the primal substance of semiosis and resurfacing in gynecologically-inflected theorizations of simile.

The limitations of the compendia of similes as a mechanism whose role is to allay the anxiety surging from the psychic confrontation with the sex of the mother inscribed into the similaic copula are revealed also in what these compendia exclude, namely, catachretic similes. This exclusion reinforces the devaluation of catachretic similes and of the non-regulated female sexuality transcoded with catachretic similes. At the same time, this exclusion leaves female sexuality outside mechanisms of defense and control. The female sexuality inscribed into catachretic similes excluded from Renaissance compendia is a perilous excess, ever intensifying the anxiety of psychic confrontation with the sex of the mother these compendia are driven to allay.

Both mechanisms deployed in early modern rhetoric to circumvent the anxiety of female sexuality in its maternal inflection inscribed into the aesthetic category of simile necessarily and constitutively fail this end. Ultimately, what these mechanisms index are the psychic risks inherent in the inscription of maternality into aesthetic form. In early modern rhetorical theory, these risks are primarily the risks of simile. The risks of simile are consequent upon the symbolic and the imaginary functions of the maternal. The psychic deployments of the maternal are split between a menacing and devouring image and the structural substrate of all objects of desire. Given those two deployments of maternality, the inscription of maternality into an aesthetic category associates this category with the abject aspect of the m(O)ther, such as is inscribed into the primal substance of semiosis, and with the m(O)ther's seductive aspect, such as is inscribed into the aesthetic category of figure in terms of which simile in early modern rhetoric is ubiquitously classified.

The structural deployment of maternality as the psychic substrate for all objects of desire has a correlate in the field of sexuality, and a correlate in the field of eroticism. The seductive aspect of the m(O)ther structurally subtends any small other, any object, incestuous, homoerotic, heteroerotic, or autoerotic, to which the subject orients her or his desire. Given the subtension of all forms of object-choice by the m(O)ther, the inscription of maternality into aesthetic form opens the way to the theorization of this form in terms of the polymorphic libido beyond the phallus in its repressive function.

Because the psychic category of the archaic mother is constitutively in excess of the phallus and beyond it, the inscription of maternality into an aesthetic form has an additional, erotic consequence. This inscription opens the way to the theorization of the aesthetic form associated with maternality in terms not of a particular sexuality but of a particular structure of non-phallic desire. This non-phallic desire is not possessive, and not fixated on consum(mat)ion and the delusory fantasy of the sum of two. This, as I have shown in the fifth chapter of this book, is the structure of desire early modern grammarians, logicians, rhetoricians, and writers inscribe into the aesthetic category of simile.

In this chapter, I follow the attempts made in early modern rhetoric to allay the anxiety of the psychic confrontation with the sex of the mother consequent upon the transcoding of the similaic copula with the female genitals. These attempts are registered in the splitting of simile into a sanctioned illustrative configuration and a prohibited catachretic or "far-fetched" configuration, and in the invention of the compendium of illustrative similes. I trace the necessary failure of these attempts, and explore the psychic and conceptual consequences of this constitutive failure to allay the anxiety of the maternal accruing to simile in the fields of sexuality, desire, and, inseparably, language.

The attempt to allay the anxiety of the sex of the mother accruing to simile by means of the prohibition of its "far-fetched" configuration is ancient. An injunction against the use of "far-fetched" similes appears as early as the *Rhetorica ad Herenium*, estimated to have been written around 86–82 BC (McCall, p. 58), where a simile is said to be "defective" (*vitiosum*) when it "lacks" (*nec habet*) a "proper ground for the comparison" (bk. 2., sec. 9, line 46). Referring to similes as "defective" because of what they "lack," the *ad Herenium* reaffirms the available Aristotelian association of the similaic copula with the "deficient" female genitals. The *ad Herenium* displaces this association, making it a staple not of similes in general but of a particular type of similes: those yoking together two semantically distant (*dissimile*) signifiers. Here the dis-simile, the form of figurative comparison failing to obey the rules of decorum and tangling customary contiguities, is, in Aristotelian fashion, associated with female sexuality as a "lack" of the penis and the phallus, with maternity as real privation and symbolic castration.

Associated with the lack of the general equivalent of the phallus, the simile coupling two semantically distant signifiers as theorized in the *Rhetorica ad Herenium* comes to embody the threat of the collapse of the symbolic order gravitating to the phallus in its repressive function. This threat is articulated in Cicero's theorization of the *simile dissimile* in *De finibus* (bk. 4, sec. 27, line 76). Cicero's theorization is accompanied by an example whose content involves the image, designated as "transgressive" (*peccat*), of a child beating its parent. This image signals the dissolution of paternal authority, the enabling condition of a symbolic economy Deleuze would term "masochistic." Masochism is a symbolic economy from which the father is abolished and which is presided over by the mother who receives "the possession and privileges of the phallus" (Deleuze, *Coldness and Cruelty*, p. 127). Cicero's image of the *simile dissimile* is echoed in Shakespeare's *Measure for Measure*, a play concerned with the consequences of the absence of paternal authority. In *Measure for Measure*, a similar image of "the baby beat[ing] the nurse" is evoked as characterization of a situation wherein the monarch removes himself from a social context in which, consequently, "quite athwart goes all decorum" (Act 1, scene 3, lines 30–31).

The association of the "defective" *simile dissimile* with a transgression of linguistic decorum and with the abolition of paternal authority and the institution of a symbolic economy gravitating to an empowered or phallic woman is underscored in Quintilian's *Institutio oratoria*. There, the example provided for similes whose use requires policing by paternal "judgment" involves just such a woman "who is liberal of her money to many [*pecuniam suam pluribus largitur*]" and "liberal of her beauty [*forma*]" (bk. 5, sec. 11, lines 26–27). The woman in this example is libidinal. Her sexuality is foregrounded though the reference to her beauty as material form and through her association with largesse and multiplicity. The first of these categories evokes generosity, and the largeness or dilation of female flesh in pregnancy and childbirth. The second is conceptually bound up with the notion of plurality Luce Irigaray diagnoses as a staple of a female economy of desire and polarizes to phallic unicity (*This Sex*, pp. 1–26).

Within the bounds of Quintilian's example, this sexualized female is allowed sovereignty over her sexuality (*pudicitiae*). In contravention of patriarchal strictures, the female in Quintilian's example of the faulty simile is made sovereign over money. The transcodability of money with female sexuality apparently worries Quintilian, who proceeds to defensively disavow it. The "force" of "liberality" (*largitur*) in "money and chastity" (*pecuniae et pudicitiae*) is, Quintilian protests, "quite different" (*diversa*). Diversity, identified by Luce Irigaray as s staple of female libidinality, is made the formal standard for the condemnation of a simile whose contents give woman control over pleasure and money, and require her to be "commended" (*laudanda*). Quintilian condemns these troublingly masochistic contents and the form in which they are inscribed. A woman who scrambles the property relations of the symbolic order by possessing money and being sexually liberal, he implies, is not to be "commended" but to be subjected to "judgment" and policing. Quintilian conflates rhetorical concerns about the indecorous comparison of dissimilars with phallocentric worries about the possibility of female sexual and economic autonomy whose consequence might be the undermining of the patriarchal traffic in women. In so doing, Quintilian strikes a note echoed in early modern rhetoric, whose condemnations of the "far-fetched" simile are informed by the fear of a transgressive woman, possessed of sexual or economic autonomy, whose exercising could dissolve the elementary structures of kinship.

At stake in the injunctions voiced against "far-fetched" similes in classical rhetoric is a fear of the semiotic, economic, and material scrambling of the symbolic order in its regulatory, repressive function. The coupling of dissimilars sets in motion a questioning of the chain of semantic differences making articulation in the framework of the symbolic possible. In the *Rhetorica ad Herenium* and the *Institutio oratoria*, "far-fetched" similes are troubling in another way. They are associated with female licentiousness whose ultimate consequence is imagined to have dire consequences. Homosexual female licentiousness elicits anxieties of the end of generation. Heterosexual female licentiousness is bound up with an anxiety of the absolute indeterminability of biological paternity and hence the production of a social situation "in which everyone would be everyone else's...sibling" (Shell, *The End of Kinship*, p. 42). In such a social situation, the differences of kinship making the observation of the incest taboo possible would be erased. The rhetorical corollary of such dissolution of the structures of kinship would be the collapsing of the semiotic code based on the difference among signifiers into a chain of endless repetition, a figure which early modern rhetoricians unequivocally condemn. Repetition, Obadiah Walker writes, is to be "avoided" (p. 33).

Condemnations of repetition in early modern rhetorical treatises and their antecedents often manifest fears of foreclosure of the divine command to "increase and multiply" underlying the fantasy of heterosexual complementarity Meres celebrates in *Gods Arithmeticke*. The fears surfacing in theorizations of repetition relate to the end of generation in the linguistic and the biological senses. In Julian of Toledo's *De Vitiis et Figuris*, dated to *ca.* 680 AD, repetition is labeled "faulty" (*vitiosa*), and described as an offence against the "plenitude" (*plenam*) of signification. Repetition, Julian writes, renders signification "vacuous" (*vacui*) (pp. 13–14). Polarizing repetition to the "plenitude" of speech, Julian makes repetition the logical opposite and conceptual rival of the tradition of *copia*, the "rhetorical counterpart" of the biblical command to "increase and multiply" so as to ensure the plenitude of the earth (Parker, *Literary Fat Ladies*, p. 15). Repetition in this theorization is what undermines plenitude. It is an agent of vacuity emptying the womb and ultimately the earth. The association of repetition with extinction is echoed in George Gascoigne's *Instructions Concerning the Making of Verse* (1575). Repetition, Gascoigne warns, "hunte[s] the letter to death" (p. 36).

The reason for the canceling out of generation associated with the form of repetition is suggested in Richard Sherry's *Treatise of Schemes and Tropes* (1550). In Sherry's treatise, homiologia, one of the forms of repetition, is theorized as a "great...faulte" because it makes "the matter all alyke, and hath no varietie" (unpaginated). This theorization suggests a semiotic state of absolute identity in the "matter" of language whose social counterpart would be the absence of the kinship structure making it possible to distinguish between permissible and forbidden partners for sexual intercourse. In such a social situation, all potential "mat(t)ers" would be equally available, to females and males, and every act of sexual intercourse would be potentially incestuous. Sherry's reference to repetition as a linguistic form in which all is "alyke," via the similaic copula associated with the female genitals, highlights two conceptual relations. (1) Sherry's theorization makes repetition a figure of incest and female homoeroticism. (2) Sherry's theorization aligns the "far-fetched" simile with the image of a promiscuous woman whose sexual libertinism could bring about a situation of libidinal polymorphism involving these forms of sexuality.

The insinuation of Lesbianism in connection with simile has as a possible *locus classicus* in Demetrius' theorization of comparison in *On Style*, written in the first century AD, where one of the examples for similes conveying "charm" is Sappho's reference to "the man that stands out among his fellows" as "Pre-eminent, as mid alien men is Lesbos' bard" (frag. 92, quoted in *On Style*, bk. 3, line 146). This Sapphic poetic fragment steals manhood. It uses the similaic copula subtending analogy to claim a conceptually phallic pre-eminence for the poet of female homoeroticism. This copula becomes a rhetorical site of female empowerment and Lesbian desire.

The conceptual connection forged in early modern rhetorical texts and their earlier intertexts between the similaic copula transcoded with the female genitals and the prospects of incest and female homoeroticism is echoed in Shakespeare's *Measure for Measure*. This play is preoccupied throughout with sexual transgressions, including "a kind of incest" (Act 3, scene 1, line 138) and female homoeroticism. Both transgressions involve the character of Isabella and both exploit the sexual inscriptions into the similaic copula "like." Incest and Lesbianism involve the sexual intercourse of persons who are "like" in belonging to the same social group. To the extent those forms of sexuality involve women, they are predicated on the "like" in the genital sense forged by Aristotle.

Isabella's involvement in the dynamics of incest in this play has been analyzed exhaustively in Marc Shell's *The End of Kinship*. But the play also suggests Isabella's association with female homosexuality, for example in her encounter with Mariana, who is greeted by Isabella's "I do desire the like" (Act 4, scene 1, line 53), a line expressing same-sex desire by means of the sexually-charged similaic copula. Associated with Lesbianism and incest, including by means of the similaic copula, Isabella in *Measure for Measure* indexes a phallic phobia. This phallic phobia is fixated on the horror of the removal of the phallus in its repressive function, removal of the kind involved in the abdication of the Duke at the beginning of the play. Such removal is feared to open the way to the proliferation of polymorphic sexualities. In the polymorphic sexual economy the play explores, "likes" would be permitted to coit, and the differential taxonomies of phallocentric elocution would dissolve into repetition.

This rhetorical possibility and its sexual corollary is suggested in the line repeated in the play's title: "Like doth quit like, and Measure still for Measure" (Act 5, scene 1, line 149). This line links repetition, likeness, and the female genitality inscribed in the similaic copula. It encapsulates the linguistic and sexual potential of "far-fetched" or transgressive female conduct which renounces patriarchal strictures in favor of a form of pleasure in which "like" could "quit" — a term paronomastically evoking the "coit" of sexual intercourse and the "cut" enabling any intercourse — "like."

The collapse of signification is at issue in another early modern intertext linking simile and repetition through the theorization of Lesbianism and Sapphic poetry, Donne's "Sapho to Philaenis." Barbara Correll has analyzed "Sapho to Philaenis" as a "crisis poem," in which "Donne projects a zero-sum signifying economy of lesbian erotics" ("Symbolic Economies and Zero-Sum Erotics," p. 493). In this poem, the elocutionary form used to represent Lesbian desire is not the "far-fetched," usually metaphoric, figuration of Donne's heteroerotic poems, but simile. Donne's Lesbian speaker says to her beloved: "when gods to thee I do *compare*, / Are graced thereby; and to make blind men see, / What things gods are, I say they are *like* to thee" (lines 16–18, emphasis mine). "Likeness" as a signifier of and for Lesbian erotics is represented in the poem as able to "beget" only "strange self-flattery" (line 51), a repetition whose sexual sub-text is a female homoeroticism ultimately indistinguishable from the "masturbatory consolation" (Correll, p. 499) of autoeroticism. In Donne's poem, repetition born of sexual and rhetorical similitude is a rhetorical fault leading to an "indecipherable and illegible insignificance" (ibid.). As Correll points out, the "eroticized simile" in which Sapho compares her woman beloved to gods "breaks down to narcissistic tautology" (ibid., p. 498), wherein Sapho says to Philaenis: "thy right hand, and cheek and eye only / Are like thy other hand, and cheek, and eye" (line 16–24). In "Sapho to Philaenis" as in *Measure for Measure*, the similaic "like" is the signifier of female homoeroticism, and its rhetorical consequence is repetition, a form drawing signification "toward...paralysis" (Correll, p.

499). Repetition in "Sapho to Philaenis" and in *Measure for Measure* is the rhetorical trace of a sexual economy from which the male power to "beget" is absent and which is feared to lead to biological extinction.

Anxious to disallow such a sexual economy, early modern rhetorics seek to strictly police the far-fetched simile associated with it. The comparative coupling of dissimilars, Joachimus Camerarius writes in his *Elementa Rhetoricae* of 1540, is "ridiculous" (p. 221). This term implies a fear of the object of ridicule so profound it necessitates the disavowing deployment of laughter and derision. The coupling of dissimilars, Camerarius instructs, is to be "abhorred" (p. 221) just as much as the sexual licentiousness of the whore paronomastically resonating in this moralistic judgment.

A similar association of the "far-fetched" simile and unregulated female sexuality appears in John Hoskyns's *Directions for Speech and Style* of 1641. Writing at a time when the rhetorical coupling of dissimlars was a fashionable literary technique, perfected in the poetry of John Donne, Hoskyns, at one point in his theorization of similes, appears to commend it. He does so in an economic vocabulary. This economic commendation echoes the Quintilianian example of the *dissimile simile* as a phallic woman controlling her sexuality and her capital. A rhetorician would "most profit," Hoskyns writes, "by inventing matter of agreement in things most unlike, as London and a tennis court" (p. 18). Hoskyns inflects the stylistic act of comparing dissimilars as possibly leading to the accumulation of capital.

This stylistic act is feminized by two factors. The coupling of dissimilars as theorized by Hoskyns is feminized by the tradition associating the "far-fetched" simile with a sexually aggressive female. The coupling of dissimilars as theorized by Hoskyns is feminized because of its association with the rhetorical category of "invention." Invention, the first part of rhetoric in the classical five-part division, is conceptually linked with the fertility of the female body (Parker, *Literary Fat Ladies*, pp. 114–115), not least in its theorization as the "matter" of speech reiterated by Hoskyns. For Hoskyns, the comparison of "things most unlike" (p. 18) is not a rhetorical fault associated with moral vice but a means for economic profit in a milieu of exchange.

Yet the theorization of the rhetorical strategy of the coupling of dissimilars in terms of the feminized notions of "matter" and "invention" inscribes this strategy with the danger of an uncontrollable physicality associated with the maternalized female body transcoded, in early modern rhetoric, with the similaically-inflected aesthetic categories of *copia*, dilation, and amplification. In early capitalist economy, uncontrollability, risk, and "hazard," another term Hoskyns uses to theorize the comparison of "things most unlike" (p. 18) are the foregrounded characteristics of the money form (Agnew, p. 4). Combining the vocabularies of gynophobia and capitalism, of the volatility of the maternalized female body and of the money form, Hoskyns's theorization of "far-fetched" similes slips from an advertisement of profit to an anticipation of loss.

This anticipation of loss underlies Hoskyns's flanking of his endorsing theorization of comparison by two statements disavowing the profitability of comparison. The "comparison of things different," Hoskyns writes later in his treatise, "is most commendable when there seems to be much affinity in the matter compared" (p. 20). This theorization of simile still links it with the "matter" of the maternal body, tapping into the tradition of configuring simile in gynecological terms, a tradition at least as ancient as Aristotle's *Rhetoric*. This theorization of simile forgoes the economic terminology and the semantic distance between the compared terms involved in the preceding theorization. Hoskyns's second theorization of simile substitutes the moral terminology of "commendab[ility]" for the terminology of capital. In this theorization, Hoskyns substitutes "much affinity" between the compared signifiers for their being "most unlike." In the context of the anxiety of castration embodied by a volatile female body as uncontrollable as the money form, these substitutions are measures of restraint employed to circumvent this threat or "hazard" of castration whose specter is raised by the Hoskyns's first theorization of "things most unlike."

The clearest disavowal of Hoskyns's acclaiming of the comparison of "things most unlike" as a source of profit appears in the statement immediately preceding this acclaim, where the comparison of "things seeming unequal" is denounced as "not so favorable" (p. 18). This denunciation is informed by an anxiety of a phallic and libidinalized femininity qua perilously circulating money form, inherited from Quintilian's association of the *dissimile simile* with an unthrifty and sexually licentious woman. The anxiety of monetary loss articulated by Hoskyns indexes a deeper castration anxiety whose focus is an imaginary captation of an empowered woman. This anxiety is later intensified by Hoskyns's theorization of the "far-fetched" simile in terms of the economic category of "profit" and, simultaneously, the psychically inflected category of "matter," a trace of maternality (ibid.).

Castration anxiety is most evident in the example Hoskyns provides for the "far-fetched" simile, a "widow compared to a ship" (ibid.). The first signifier in this example is an image of a means of transportation, trade, and escape from oceanic dissolution, an image of psychic control and economic empowerment. The second signifier refers to a woman not legally bound to a husband. Bringing together independent femininity, psychic control, and economic empowerment, Hoskyns's example for a "far-fetched" simile epitomizes the fear of economic uncontrollability masking a deeper castration anxiety with which this rhetorical category is inscribed, in Hoskyns's text, and in its classical source, Quintilian's *Institutio oratoria*.

Associated with a phallic femininity embodying the threat of castration, the "far-fetched" simile as theorized in early modern rhetoric and its classical antecedents becomes the epitome of linguistic transgressions indexing psychic and sexual transgressions usually discussed under the separate rubric of "catachresis" or "abuse." Technically, catachresis denotes the coupling, by identification or comparison, of semantically distant signifiers. Technically, catachresis includes "far-fetched" metaphors and "far-fetched" similes. Psycho-conceptually, the connection between catachresis and simile is stronger than the connection between catachresis and metaphor.

The conceptual connection between catachresis and the "far-fetched" simile is occasionally made manifest in the theorizations of catachresis by means of reference to the similaic copula. In *The Garden of Eloquence*, Peacham theorizes catachresis as an "abuse of *like* words" (unpaginated, emphasis mine). In *A Treatise of Schemes and Tropes*, Richard Sherry theorizes "abusio" as the case when "for a certayne and proper worde, we abuse the *lyke* or [what is] nie unto it" (unpaginated, emphasis mine). In both these cases, catachresis is theorized in terms of a common signifier for the similaic copula, a copula transcoded with the maternal genitals in Aristotle's formative theorization which resonates in early modern rhetorical theory.

Peacham and Sherry theorize catachresis as an "abuse" of the "like" qua the sex of the mother. "Abuse" in Renaissance English signified "vice" and "corruption" (Stubbes, title page). This signifier had a distinctly sexual inflection. One of its components, "use," was synonymous with sexual intercourse (see, for example, Stubbes, p. 100). The theorization of catachresis as an "abuse" of the "like" amounts to an imaginary captation of this category in terms of non-sanctioned "use," of participation in illicit sexual intercourse such as adultery or incest, listed as "abuses" in Phillip Stubbes's *Anatomie of Abuses* (1584) (p. 99).

The anxiety of adultery and what Stubbes considers the related "abuse" of incest is manifest in Sherry's theorization of catachresis. This theorization turns on an opposition sexual as much as it is linguistic. On the devalued, abjected side of this opposition, Sherry lists the "abuse" of a "lyke": the "use" of the female genitals which is "abusive" or transgressive either because it is adulterous or because it involves the sexual equivalent of the semantic proximity indicated by the term "nie," incest. The privileged side of the opposition involves "certeyne and proper" signification, the equivalent, in terms of sexual vocabulary, of the socially sanctioned marital fidelity of a presumably not consanguinous husband and wife, the relationship of man and woman as a presumably perfect sum Meres calls "Gods Arithmeticke."

For Sherry, rhetorical "abuse" is inseparable from the sexual "abuses" or excesses of incest and adultery, the same forms of sexuality inscribed in other texts into the form of the "far-fetched" simile. Rhetorical abuse is the linguistic isomorph of the "proper" (married) woman in the narrative embedded in Stubbes's injunction against adultery, who has sexual intercourse with a man, who, similarly ignoring the strictures of matrimonial propriety and property relations, "put[s] away his owne wife...vsing her at his pleasure" (p. 100). In a promiscuous society such as the allegorical ailing and alienized "Countrey of Ailgna" in Stubbes's *Anatomie of Abuses*, the object of the adulterer's "pleasure" may well be his biological kin.

The connection enabled by the term "abuse" between linguistic excesses and sexual excesses such as incest is articulated in Thomas Blount's *Academie of Eloquence*. In this treatise, the theorization of catachresis is prefaced by a statement describing it as "now grown in fashion, as most abuses are" (p. 5). This statement echoes in a metalinguistic context complaints made in moralistic contexts such as Stubbes's *Anatomie*, of "Abuses," including adultery and incest, having "crept into euery one of...seuerall exercyses" (p. x). Blount proceeds to relate the verbal "abuse" of catachresis to the sexual "abuse" of incest when theorizing catachresis as "the expressing of one matter by the use of another" (p. 5). This is a substitutional narrative of "use" in the sexual and in the linguistic sense. In this narrative, intercourse with "another" is an "expressing" or substitution for incestuous intercourse with the "matter" of the maternal body.

The biological consequence of the "abuse" of incest Sherry and Blount associate with catachresis is breeding within one's kin, a generational repetition whose linguistic counterpart is the "vice" of repetition wherein signification is foreclosed through the erasure of semantic differences. In early modern English rhetoric, this conceptual link between the ostensibly unrelated forms of catachresis and repetition is articulated in Thomas Wilson's theorization of "abusion" in *The Arte of Rhetorique*. Catachersis is not theorized here, as it usually is, as the coupling of two disparate signifiers, but as what initially seems the contrary of such coupling: the case "when for a certain proper word we use what is most nigh to it, as in calling some water a fishpond" (p. 200). Catachresis here is not the "far-fetched" coupling of dissimilars but the association of a given signifier with one "most nigh" or immediately contiguous to it. This coupling of contiguous signifiers approximates what rhetoricians before and after Wilson theorize as the feared consequence of such coupling: the association of a given signifier with itself, namely, repetition.

Wilson's theorization of catachresis, the form habitually associated with adultery in early modern rhetoric, highlights the dissolution of the structures of kinship anxiously imagined as the possible consequence of adultery. The feared consequence of adultery is copulation and potential reproduction within the same or incest. The linguistic counterpart of incest is repetition, a rhetorical category threatening to dissolve the differentiation between signifiers which makes communication possible, whose economic counterpart in early modern England is usury, the breeding of money out of money.

In his *Discourse on Usury* (1572), Wilson virulently condemns usury by association with incest. Usury, Wilson writes, is a transaction in which "moneye bringeth forth moneye" (p. 275). It is breeding within the same. Elsewhere in his treatise, Wilson condemns usury by means of an analogy with the other sexual category inscribed into catachresis in early modern language theory, namely, adultery. The usurer and the adulterer, Wilson says, "do more abound than eyther theefes or murtherers" (p. 223).

In Wilson's economic treatise as in his language theory, adultery and incest are conceptually connected. Adultery is imagined to erase boundaries between households and thereby move toward a situation in which any sexual encounter might be incestuous. Wilson denounces adultery as creating the potential for incest and the covetousness necessitating usury in the grim warning of a Preacher: "Wo be unto you that ioine house to house, and land to land, even unto the bounds of the place. Do you think to live alone upon the earthe?" (p. 221). Usury for Wilson is a crux of economic and sexual excesses or abuses whose end is imagined to be genocidal. In Wilson's economic treatise, the feared consequence of usury is the end of generation. In his *Arte of Rhetorique*, this consequence is not associated, as it usually is, with repetition. In Wilson's *Arte of Rhetorique*, the end of generation is associated with catachresis. In Wilson's linguistic theory, catachresis occupies the structural and imaginary place occupied by repetition in other early modern linguistic theories. This is the place of "abuse," whose imagined corollary is the end of generation feared to be the consequence of adultery and incest. The exchangeability of the rhetorical categories of catachresis and repetition in Wilson's rhetorical theory underscores the link forged between these two categories in the early modern rhetorical imaginary through the category of the sexually transgressive woman.

For Wilson, catachresis is a form of what Marc Shell calls "verbal usury" (*Money, Language, and Thought*, p. 49), a form whose principle of joining words in transgression or excess of normative significations is feared to lead to semiotic genocide. The sexual analogue of this form is imagined to be what Deleuze calls a "masochistic" symbolic economy from which the phallus is abolished. The abolition of the phallus from a symbolic economy "masochistic" in Deleuze's sense opens the way to polymorphic sexualities exceeding the phallic norm of possessive, reproduction-oriented matrimonial heterosexuality. A polymorphic sexual economy opened up by the abolition of the phallus would include the same sexualities whose feared consequence, as conceptualized in early modern moralistic tracts, is biological annihilation.

The conceptual link between catachresis and the abolition of the phallus feared to destroy the structures of kinship upholding the symbolic in its regulatory, repressive deployment is underscored in Renaissance treatises published in England yet written in Latin rather than the vernacular, namely Mark Beumley's *Rhetoricae* (1598) and Johanne de Kerhuel's *Idea Eloquentiae Rhetoricae* (1673). In these treatises, catachresis is theorized in terms of the category of parricide (Beumley, p. 7; de Kerhuel, p. 22). In de Kerhuel's treatise, the introduction of the category of parricide is psychologically justified by the theorization of catachresis as *"ex natura"* (p. 22), unnatural. De Kerhuel theorizes catachresis as an aesthetic form exceeding the natural qua normative. Catachresis in his theorization is structurally parallel to the economic excess of usury and the sexual excesses of homosexuality and incest, situated in the beyond of the phallic norm.

De Kerhuel seems most concerned with a particular sexual excess he associates with catachresis: *"sororis intersector"* (p. 22). Technically, de Kerhuel is referring to a conjunction of semantically proximate signifiers, underscoring the slippage of catachresis to repetition. Psycho-conceptually, he is referring to the intersection of, or physical encounter between, sisters. He is referring to a simultaneously Lesbian and incestuous sexuality, such as the sexuality indicated between the cousins Rosalind and Celia in Shakespeare's similaically-entitled *As You Like It*. This Lesbian and incestuous sexuality involves a double transgression of the phallic norm of reproduction-oriented heterosexual copulation within the marital framework Meres celebrates in *Gods Arithmeticke*. The form of sexuality evoked in de Keruhel's theorization of catachresis exceeds the incest taboo mediated by the symbolic Father and exceeds the heterosexual matrimonial norm requiring the presence of a male qua agent of the Name of the Father in the act of copulation. This double transgression of the phallic norm amounts to symbolic parricide.

For de Kerhuel, catachresis embodies the nightmare of polymorphism in signification and in sexuality possibly unleashed with the "licentiousness" — a term used to theorize catachresis in the anonymous *Rhetoricae Synopsis* of 1693 (p. 23) — consequent upon symbolic parricide. For de Krehuel as for the Port Royal rhetoricians, catachresis is the most licentious, "the freest Trope of them all," the trope whose use involves the "liberty to borrow the Name of a thing, though quite contrary to what we would signifie" (p. 80). In the Port Royal *Rhetoric*, catachresis is made into the form of verbal usury and sexual license or liberty. This last term, in its conflation of moral libertinism (from the Latin *liberi* [free]) with *liberi* (sons and daughters in relation to their parents) underscores the anxiety of incest generated by a vision of radical promiscuity in which "the *pater* (father) [would be dissolved] in the *liber* (son)" (Shell, *The End of Kinship*, p. 40).

The abolition of paternal authority associated with the rhetorical form of catachresis opens the way to a sexual excess less radical but more immediately threatening to the regulation of property than incest in its Lesbian configuration suggested in de Kerhuel's *Idea Eloquentiae Rhetoricae*. This is the sexual excess of adultery. The Port Royal *Rhetoric* reveals a concern with adultery. In this treatise, the aesthetic category of catachresis is associated with "liberty" and with a narrative of "borrow[ing]" a name (p. 80). The notion of "borrowing" as the temporary transfer of property from one person to another in expectation of reciprocity and taliation appears elsewhere in early modern rhetorical theory, for example in theorizations of metaphor as "a friendly and neighbourly borrowing of a word" (see Chapter Four above). The borrowing such theorizations associate with the aesthetic category of metaphor is described as non-transgressive of the norms undergirding relations of friendship and as affirming relations of neighborhood by respecting the physical boundaries dividing the domestic space of one "neighbour" from the domestic space of another.

Set against the background of these inscriptions of economic borrowing into early modern rhetorical theory, the Port Royal *Rhetoric*'s theorization of catachresis appears to involve "borrowing" of an entirely different order. This borrowing is not based on reciprocity and mutual agreement to the exchange by borrower and lender. This borrowing is unilateral, predicated upon the borrower's assumption of the liberty to appropriate a commodity located in another person's domain. This "borrowing" does not respect and reaffirm the boundaries between the property of one "neighbour" and the property of another, but breaks down this boundary.

In Barnabe Rich's *Ladies Looking Glasse* (1616), such unilateral breaking down of boundaries between one neighbor's property and another's is described as involved in an act of neighborhood adultery. Rich fictionalizes adultery as a sin "heinous in respect of our Neighbour, hose hedge we break down...whilst we do purloyn and defile and dishonour what is his most proper possession...[and] invade and incroach upon his Inheritance also by making our Bastard his Heir" (pp. 43–44).

The liberal borrowing described in the theorization of catachresis in the Port Royal *Rhetoric* is informed by the notion of an act of sexual libertinism and economic transgression which may have dire consequences for the inheritance of the man whose wife is "borrowed." This act involves the defiling of the wife's "honour." Even more significantly for the concerns of a patriarchal economy, adultery, the borrowing of another's wife, involves the borrower's usurpation of the place of the lawful husband. This sexual usurpation, Barnabe Rich implies, amounts to the adulterer's illicit assumption of the husband's "name." The feared consequence of such assumption is the transferral of the name, and the attendant inheritance, of the betrayed husband to a bastard.

Similar concerns with the economic consequences of adultery inform another seventeenth-century theorization of catachresis. In John Newton's *Introduction to the Art of Rhetoric* (1671), catachresis is theorized as a "change of a word, as when a word or name is put for another, not by any proper relations, but by a kind of force" (unpaginated). In this narrative of "change" or substitution, one word/actant usurps the place of "another" with whom he does not have "any proper relations," such as the sanctioned relations obtaining between a husband and wife and ensuring the transferral of proper(ty) from one man to another through the mediation of a woman. Newton's narrative of catachresis is transcodable with a narrative of adultery in which one man usurps another's position as husband. In Newton's theorization of catachresis, the equivalent of the female body lacks agency and is absent from the surface structure of the narrative, except in the insinuation of its being an unwilling participant in the narrative of adultery as power struggle between two men. In this theorization of catachresis, the rhetorical equivalent of the female body is "put" or inserted into a narrative of exchange by a "force." This insinuation of the exertion of force on a passive female body gives the adultery inscribed into the category of catachresis a sinister inflection. It renders Newton's theorization of catachresis a narrative of adultery and/as rape. Yet Newton's theorization of catachresis seems to be concerned not with any violence done to the female body in the context of the act of adultery. Instead, Newton is interested in the consequences catachresis qua adultery might have for that owner's "name," which might pass on to an illegitimate son.

In the context of the sub-text of adultery inscribed into the early modern theorizations of catachresis, this category becomes, as George Bersmann's *Erotemata Rhetorica* (1601) puts it, *"vitiosum,"* a vice of style (p. 173), a *"transgressio,"* and a *"perversione"* (p. 297). Catachresis is theorized as a perilous deviation from the order of decorum in speech and sexuality. Within a phallocentric libidinal economy hinging on the fantasy of heterosexual complementarity and on a possessive, phallic desire supposed to ensure such complementarity, catachresis is what, in the words of a later rhetorician, one should "never venture upon" (John Lawson, *Lectures Concerning Oratory* [1758], p. 260).

"Far-fetched" figuration is conceptualized in early modern rhetorical theory as a coupling of semantically disparate signifiers. In early modern rhetorical theory, this coupling is theorized as possibly destabilizing the code of semantic contiguities enabling signification. The imagined correlate of this semantic destabilization is unregulated, excessive sexuality, especially female sexuality. The combined sense of linguistic and sexual excess inscribed into the notion of "far-fetched" or catachretic speech is made explicit in Puttenham's theorization of the "fareffet" in *The Arte of English Poesie*:

> as when we had rather fetch a word a great way off then to use one nerer hand to expresse the matter as wel and plainer. And it seemeth the deviser of this figure, had a desire to please women rather than men, for we use to say by manner of Proverbe: things farrefet and deare bought are good for Ladies: so in this manner of speech we use it, leaping over the heads of a great many words, we take one that is furdest off, to utter our matter by. (p. 193)

Puttenham's image of "farrefet" or catachretic speech as involving the speaker's "leaping over the heads of many words" to reach the one "furdest off" implies an idea of language as a chain of contiguous signifiers, akin to Umberto Eco's notion of the "semiotic code" of semantic contiguities (p. 261). In Puttenham's text, the signifiers constituting the semiotic code are feminized. Far-fetched signification is theorized by Puttenham as a libidinal quest of the male author and the predominantly male implied audience implicit in the pronoun "we." In this libidinal quest, a body "nerer hand" or readily available as an object of desire is discarded in favor of the pursuit of a body a "great way off," whose inaccessibility, in the familiar Petrarchan erotic dynamic, only increases its desirability.

The Petrarchan erotic dynamic informing Puttenham's theorization of the "farrefet" is, in Lacanian terms, perverse. Perversity, for Lacan, is a style of desire characterized by "an inexhaustible captation of the desire of the other" (*Seminar I*, p. 221). This style of desire is conditional upon "the disappearence of the object" (ibid., p. 222), upon this object's remaining, in Puttenham's terms, "furdest off," eternally perpetuating an erotic striving.

Puttenham's theorization of the "farrefet" anticipates the Lacanian theorization of perverse desire, and offers the linguistic grid for this structure of desire. Yet Puttenham's gendering of this structure of desire is different from Lacan's. Lacan theorizes perverse desire as making up "one aspect of the drama of homosexuality" (ibid., p. 221). Puttenham's theorization of the farrefet is distinctly heterosexual. In this theorization, the speaker and his implied audience are male. The object of eternal, perverse, erotic pursuit is a female. This is suggested by Puttenham's reference to the "deviser of this figure," in a revealing slippage from rhetorical surface-structure to psycho-sexual sub-text, as one who has "a desire to please women rather than men" (p. 193).

The perverse heterosexual desire for a woman inscribed by Puttenham into the category of the "farrefet" is economically perilous. The object of this desire, Puttenham implies, is "deare bought." The libidinal striving this object generates propels the subject to excessive expenditure. In *The Worth of a Penny*, Peacham cautions against excessive expenditures involved in erotic pursuits outside the limits of marriage. Perverse extra-marital pursuits of inaccessible objects, Peacham cautions, might deplete the economic resources of the household, which the adulterer might "give or sell" in order to be able to provide them (p. 4). Puttenham's theorization of the "farrefet" crosses rhetorical, amatory, and economic vocabularies. The precipitate of this crossing is a linguistic structure indexing a psychically and economically perilous style of extra-marital heterosexual desire sustainable only in the eternal inaccessibility of its object.

In early modern rhetoric, far-fetched figuration in general and catachretic figuration in particular are theorized in terms of sexual transgressions exceeding the matrimonial norm. These transgressions include homoerotic and heteroerotic adulterous liaisons outside the marital framework and incestuous liaisons within this framework. The insistent effort made in rhetorical treatises of the Renaissance to prohibit "far-fetched" figuration and "far-fetched" similizing in particular is conceptually inseparable from the effort made within the symbolic in its repressive deployment to regulate sexuality through reproduction-oriented marriage resting on the phallic fantasy of complementarity, of the "two," as Meres puts it in *Gods Arithmeticke*, "turn[ing] into one" and enjoying "vnitie...for euer" (p. 19).

The conceptual gesture most commonly deployed in early modern rhetorical treatises to mark out "far-fetched" figuration as prohibited is isomorphic with the patriarchal splitting of the image of woman into the polarized extremes of chaste virgin and whore. In early modern rhetorical theory, far-fetched or catachretic figuration is made the binary opposite of a different type of similizing. In this second type of similizing, the anxieties evoked by simile's association with female sexuality in its maternal inflection are militated against by simile's association with a particular structure of heterosexual relations. This is the structure of the reproduction-oriented marriage resting on the phallic fantasy of complementarity. In some cases in early modern rhetorical theory, the anxieties of non-regulated female sexuality associated with simile are militated against by the limitation of simile to a particular generic space.

Simile, whose occasional theorization as a phallicized maternal body makes it a source of anxiety, is binarized into a catachretic configuration and an illustrative configuration. The catachretic configuration of simile confirms the psycho-sexual risks inscribed into simile qua the sex of the mother and even intensifies those risks by associating simile with the sexual excesses of homoeroticism, incest, and adultery. The illustrative configuration is isomorphic with a patriarchal dyad. This binarism is articulated in Dudley Fenner's *Artes of Logike and Rhetorike* (1588) and echoed verbatim in Hobbes's *Art of Rhetoric* (1681):

> [The] change of signification must bee shamefest and as it were maydenly, that it may seem...to be led by the hand to another signification...Yet sometimes this manner of speech swerveth from this perfection, and then it is the abuse of fine speech, called Katachresis...when the change of speech is hard, strange and unwonted. (Fenner, sig. C3; Hobbes, p. 138)

Ostensibly distinguishing between two types of figuration, one sanctioned, the other "unwonted," this passage rests on an opposition between two polarized images of "maydenly" or female conduct. In one image, the "mayden" is "shamefest" and "led by the hand." In the other image, the "mayden" is abusively excessive, "swerv[ing]" from the norms of decorum. The excessive female conduct inscribed here into the form of "Katachresis," is, "like Shakespeare's, another unruly and undomesticated 'Kate'" (Parker, *Literary Fat Ladies*, p. 108).

The full title of Fenner's treatise is *The Artes of Logike and Rhetorike...Together with example for the use of the same for methode in the gournement of the famelie, prescribed in the woorde of God*. This title links the prescriptions of rhetoric to those of the patriarchal and theological Name of the Father. Fenner's title links the transgressions of rhetorical prescriptions to transgressions in the spheres of gender and sexuality. In Fenner's treatise, catachresis is theorized as "abuse." "Abuse," for Fenner, is a rhetorical term and a gendered term. It appears in relation to "Katachresis" in the rhetorical section of the treatise and in relation to female transgression in the treatise's description of the "Order of the Householde" (unpaginated). For Fenner, "abuse" is an "excess" of rhetorical decorum and of the conceptually equivalent limits, internal and external, of the "Householde" or "Oiconomia" (unpaginated).

Fenner's "Katachresis" qua abuse becomes the rhetorical equivalent of the unruly female who seeks to "vsurpe" the husband's "authoritie and chiefdome in all matters" (unpaginated). Such a woman is described in Fenner's treatise as renouncing her subordinate position within the household and the stricture requiring her to "tarry...at home" (unpaginated). For Fenner, catachresis is the rhetorical equivalent of a woman who ventures far beyond the physically and sexually restricted latitude of the patriarchal household to the public domain (Parker, *Literary Fat Ladies*, p. 105). The catachretic woman as theorized by Fenner is a potential or actual adulteress who exceeds the norms of sexuality enforced to ensure patriliny and informed by a phallic fantasy of complementarity.

Fenner's catachretic woman is the polar opposite of the "shamefest" maiden. In Fenner's treatise, the "shamefest" woman is depleted of subjectivity or agency. She is described as passively "led" by the phallic metonymy of the "hand" of a male endowed with agency and authority. In the familial section of Fenner's treatise, this figure of "authoritie" is the male "Chief" or "gouernor of the famelie" (unpaginated), the family's general equivalent, the Father. The female conduct Fenner inscribes into the binary of catachresis qua female sexual excess is the conduct of a woman who, as he puts it in the familial section of his treatise, observes her duty to be "subiecte to her husbande" and "to yield helpe" to him (unpaginated). This subjection is primarily sexual. The "help" of a wife to her husband, Meres writes, echoing Thomas Aquinas's *Summa Theologiae*, is help in the work of procreation (*Gods Arithmeticke* [p. 14]).

Fenner and Hobbes identify the "far-fetched" catachresis as the rhetorical equivalent of the unruly woman. They do not identify the antitype of the sexually excessive woman, the rhetorical equivalent of the submissive and shamefast woman. Other early modern rhetorical treatises theorize this antitype of catachresis as a type of simile whose use is sanctioned. This configuration of simile, the isomorph of a woman who is "led by the hand" or subordinated to her husband, is what Renaissance rhetoricians usually call "illustration," "illumination," "explanation," or "elucidation." All these terms adumbrate a hierarchical semiotic structure, in which one signifier is placed in the subservient function of complementing the meaning of another.

Aristotle's *Rhetoric*, the *locus classicus* for the influential association of the similaic copula with the maternal genitals, nevertheless mentions one configuration of simile, the "illustrative parallel" (1393b4–8). Aristotle does not denigrate this configuration as he does the category of simile in general in his biologized discussion of the difference between simile and metaphor, wherein simile is made into "a subordinate and less desirable form of metaphor" (McCall, p. 30). Aristotle's silence on the value of the illustrative comparison, when set against his explicit denigration of simile as "less attractive" with respect to metaphor, amounts to a sanctioning. This sanctioning is a likely return to Plato's philosophy, which despite its known animosity to rhetoric as a material obstruction or distortion of Truth, includes a number of references to "illustrative comparison" as a permissible strategy of argumentation (McCall, p. 23).

Quintilian's *Institutio Oratoria*, another *locus classicus* for early modern rhetorical theory, cites "illustration" (*inlustrandae*) as one of the functions of similitude, cautioning "anything that is selected for the purpose of illustrating something else must itself be clearer than what it is designed to illustrate [*inluminat*]" (bk. 8, sec. 3, lines 73–74). The illustrative simile is theorized here as a comparative coupling of an illustrating signifier and an illustrated signifier. Elsewhere in the *Institutio Oratoria*, Quintilian advises rhetoricians to draw the illustrating signifier from the realm of "animals" or "inanimate objects" (bk. 5, sec. 13, lines 23–24), the realm of matter conceptually associated with the maternal body. The relation of the maternalized illustrating signifier to the illustrated signifier is a relation of conceptual and structural subordination. The order in which the signifiers appear in the surface structure of the similitude, Quintilian argues, is irrelevant to this structural subordination; the illustrating signifier may either precede (*praecedit*) or follow (*sequitur*) the "*res*" it illustrates (bk. 5, sec. 2, line 77).

This seminal theorization of the illustrating similitude as a hierarchical structure in which a maternalized component is semantically subservient to a dominant "*res*" involves a "strange loop," a short-circuiting of its own logic. Like the strange loop involved in the collapsing of metaphor and trope (see Chapter Four above), this loop functions as a symptom. The strange loop involving the maternalized form of simile and its maternalized component is an anasemic breaking point in the text. In this anasemic breaking point, what is articulated in the surface of the text's envelope comes close to the contents of the unconscious kernel driving the text.

Elsewhere in his text, Quintilian uses the term "*similitudo*" to refer to the category of simile in general. This category formally consists of two signifiers joined by the similaic copula. In this passage, Quintilian uses the term "*similitudo*" to refer to only one of simile's two signifiers, the signifier illustrating the "*res*." This tangling of the levels of signification, in which the same term is used to denote a rhetorical category and one of its components is conceptually necessary to Quintilian's theorization of simile as it is to the many later rhetoricians who echoed Quintilian's theorization. This tangling shows how the effort to create a legitimate place for simile within the space of rhetoric despite the troubling association of simile with the maternal body and female sexuality in general leads to the displacement of this association to one of the components of an illustrative simile. The hierarchical structure of the illustrative simile makes possible the attempted control of this troubling maternalized component by the ostensibly superior "*res*" qua general equivalent or "*rex.*"

This displacement of the maternity associated with the figure of simile in general to one of the components of simile and the theorization of this component as requiring the discipline provided by the other component is similar to another ubiquitous psycho-conceptual manoeuvre of Renaissance rhetoric. This is the displacement of the idea of the feminizing materiality of signification in general onto the theorization of the category of figure, and the concomitant disavowal of femininity in the theorization of the category of trope (see Introduction, and Chapters One and Two above). In the two cases, the displacement of troubling femininity inevitably produces conceptual contradictions in the aesthetic theory within which it is made. In Quintilian's rhetorical theory, such a conceptual contradiction is revealed in the strange loop involving *similitudo* as simile in general and the illustrating signifier of an illustrative simile in particular.

The conceptual contradictions effected by displacement and symptomatically indexing it are manifest in Quintilian's rhetorical theory in an other way: the inclusion of the ostensibly well-policed form of the illustrative simile among the strategies of legal persuasion (bk. 3, sec. 9, line 4). This inclusion has the unsettling effect of ushering a form associated with the female body into the constitutively logocentric, phallocentric domain of the Law. This inclusion activates the phallocentric nightmare, already fictionalized in Quintilian's time in the *Liber lamentationum matheoluli*'s story of Carfania, a "Roman matron who demonstrated her control of oratory by arguing cases in court (Parker, *Literary Fat Ladies*, pp. 106–107). This story conflates a woman litigating a legal *causa*, the term that Quintilian uses in the above passage for legal deliberations, with a woman's revealing her *"casus"* or private parts in court (ibid.). In Quintilian's text, the illustrative simile necessarily malfunctions as a linguistic structure wherein the sex of the mother associated with simile is kept in check. The illustrating signifier to which maternal sexuality is displaced defies phallocentric control. This signifier functions as perilous excess, generating symptoms of illogicality and impropriety within the rhetorical text.

In the English Renaissance, the gynophobic displacement of the sex of the mother associated with simile in its Aristotelian theorization to the subordinate signifier of an illustrative simile generates similar symptoms. Echoing Quintilian's theorization of the illustrative simile's drawing from the semantic repertoire of inanimate creatures, Richard Sherry theorizes similitude as an aesthetic category involving a "comparing of a thing that has no life or body to our cause and purpose" (*Schemes and Tropes*, unpaginated). Sherry's text too seeks to contain the maternal sexuality inscribed into the category of simile in its entirety by a double manoeuvre of displacement and containment. In Sherry's theorization of the illustrative simile, as in Quintilian's, maternal sexuality is displaced to a signifier drawn from the maternalized material domain.

In Sherry's text too, this maternalized signifier is supposed to illustrate and hence semantically subserve another signifier. In Sherry's theorization of the illustrative simile, the sex of the mother defies control. Maternal sexuality irrupts into the ostensibly controlling signifier. This signifier is designated as a "cause," a term whose early modern resonances include the "case" of the female genitals (Parker, *Literary Fat Ladies*, p. 106), already associated with the similaic copula through the influential Aristotelian inscription.

In Sherry's theorization of the illustrative simile, the illustrating signifier is not contained and controlled by the signifier it illustrates. Instead, the illustrating signifier contaminates the illustrated signifier with the naming of the sex of the mother. This contamination symptomatically indexes the necessary failure of the phobic attempt to bring the sex of the mother under the control of the phallus deployed as bar. This failure is necessary constitutively, since maternal sexuality is by definition in excess of the phallus in its repressive function. This failure is necessary structurally, since the copula by means of which the maternalized illustrating signifier is linked with the illustrated signifier it is supposed to semantically subserve is itself already excessive, inscribed with the sex of the mother.

The maternal sexuality inscribed into the similaic copula and into the illustrating signifier in "illustrative" similes makes all such similes into instances of what the *Similium loci communes* (1602) calls a *"causa similitudinem"* (p. 88). The phrase *"causa similitudinem"* seeks to co-opt similes into the linear logic of cause and effect. But what the phrase effects is only the symptomatic confirmation of the conceptual connection of the category of simile, via the similaic copula, with the female genitals, for which *causa* was a "familiar code term" (Parker, *Literary Fat Ladies*, p. 28).

A French text of the same period, Pierre de Courcelles's *La Rhétorique* (1557), is more frankly explicit about the psychic and sexual stakes involved in the notion of rhetorical "illustration" to which other rhetoricians of his time insist to confine similes. The function of similitudes, Conrad Lycosthenis writes in his *Similium Loci Communes* (1602), is to provide "explication" (*explicatum*) (p. 27), and in particular "illustration," a term he insistently repeats in relation to similes (for example, pp. 26, 78, 88, 89). In de Courcelles's text, "illustration" is made the function of similes and of the art of rhetoric at large. The purpose of this art, de Courcelles writes, is *"illustrer & rendre nostre* [sic] *langue maternelle plus coppieuse & riche"* (to illustrate and render our maternal language more copious and rich) (unpaginated). This formulation is striking because of its explicit identification of the conceptual link between rhetoric and the maternal body, the conceptual link early modern rhetorical theory in general seeks to elide. This formulation is initially perplexing too. It does not cite "illustration" as a means of arresting the *copia* or proliferation of language, a rhetorical category "figured as female" (Parker, *Literary Fat Ladies*, p.

31) and hence closely allied with the maternalized form of simile. De Courcelles's formulation cites "illustration" as a means of perpetuating and even augmenting maternal language, making it yet more fertile and more "rich."

De Courcelles's use of the economic term "rich" is symptomatic. Making illustration an instrument of *copia*, this term suggests, is tongue-in-cheek, just like de Courcelles's reference to rhetoric as *"ce petit art"* (this small art) in the same paragraph. Like Puttenham's *Arte of English Poesie* and Girolamo Mascher's *Fiore della retorica*, de Courcelles's *La rhétorique* is informed by Petrarchan poetics. De Courcelles's text reproduces the familiar Petrarchan situation of a male speaker addressing a female object of desire who is rendered all the more desirable by her coldness and cruelty, which make her, in Deleuze's terms, phallic (*Coldness and Cruelty*, p. 69). In de Courcelles's text, the Petrarchan dyad of a phallic woman and an ardent but frustrated suitor is fictionalized through a hierarchical opposition. On one side of this opposition is the *"petit art de rhétorique,"* a gift of love embodying the speaker's masochistic desire and bespeaking his symbolic castration with respect to his superior and inaccessible love object. On the other side of this opposition is the desired woman, the *"Tres-illustré* [most illustrious] *Princesse Madame Charlotte de Bourbon"* ("Dedication"). The condition of the woman's being "illustrious" — superior to the speaker economically and socially, but above all psychically, in her being phallic — is posited in De Courcelles's text as the motivation for the speaker's presenting her with the art of rhetoric.

The presentation of the rhetorical text to the princess is an act of gift. This act does not demand reciprocation. It "remains foreign to the circle of the debt" (Derrida, *Given Time*, p. 69). Nevertheless, the acceptance of this love-gift by the desired "Princesse" and even the thought of this acceptance are fantasized to effect a change in her and consequently also in the subject who desires her. Such acceptance would amount to an erotic transubstantiation, a displaced intercourse wherein the princess would revoke the symbolic phallus of her inaccessibility and magically undo the speaker's symbolic castration.

Because de Courcelles's rhetorical text is a gift, it is an "erotic form" (Hyde, p. 73) "bespeak[ing] relationship" (ibid., p. 69). The rhetorical text is endowed with a fantasized power to dissolve the hierarchical dyad involving an "illustrious," phallic princess and a masochistically desiring rhetorician. The rhetorical text is fantasized as transforming gift.

De Courcelles emphasizes the magical transformative qualities fantasized for his art of rhetoric. This art, he says, is a *"liqueur"*

("Dedication"). It is a liquid substance taken into the body. This conflation of rhetorical text and liquor is symptomatic of the fantasy of insemination informing its presentation to the princess.

This act of presentation qua insemination structures the dedication to de Courcelles's text. Since a dedication, as Derrida puts it, is a *"dative or donor* movement that displaces the text" (*Given Time*, p. 87), the act of presentation qua insemination makes everything within the dedication into a gift. The conflation of rhetoric and liquor marks the dedication by what Derrida calls "the economic motif of drunkenness and the superfluous," wherein speech is "superabundant, excessive, generous,...luxurious" (*Given Time*, p. 104). In de Courcelles's time, rhetoricians called such speech "copious."

De Courcelles's conflation of rhetorical text and liquor may seem to undermine the claims of the rhetorical text to systematicity and the preservation of a phallocentric economy. This conflation aligns the rhetorical text with the potentially unlimited libidinality involved in "the enjoyment and expenditure" of a substance whose only use appears to be sensory stimulation (Derrida, *Given Time*, p. 109). Yet where the consumption of substances like liquor or tobacco is concerned, Derrida says, "there is no gratuitous expenditure, no superabundance, no overflowing of pure luxury" (ibid., p. 109). This is so because the consumption of such substances "can correspond to an aim, can belong to an end-oriented system" and accomplish "symbolic functions" (ibid.).

In de Courcelles's dedication, the function of the fantasized conflation of rhetorical text and liquor is not the undoing of the text's commitment to a phallic Law through a renunciation of restrictions on sensual enjoyment. The function of this conflation is to reaffirm this commitment, to reforge the alliance between the princess and the *"langue maternelle,"* the potentially anarchic excess which had been distorted by the princess's phallic status and ultimately to control this excess. The conflation of rhetorical text and liquor realigns the princess, via the symbolism of drunkenness, with an excessive and undisciplined body. Fictionalizations of this excessive body in the early modern "literature of excess" emphasize its possible undoing of male superiority (Roper, p. 153).

The excessive fantasized body of the princess appears to necessitate discipline. This discipline is inscribed in de Courcelles's text. This text speaks of the princess's *"parfait cognnoyassance* [sic] *De verite"* (perfect recognition of truth") ("Dedication"). The princess recognizes, de Courcelles suggests here, the "truth" implicit in the rhetorical text with which the speaker identifies himself.

Rhetoric, de Courcelles initially says, is a "small" art. Yet through inebriate fantasy, rhetoric in de Courcelles's text becomes a means of disciplinary reinversion. In this fantasy, the body of an initially inaccessible phallic woman is finally fantasized as excessive and unruly, demanding control and recognizing the "truth" of the authority of the initially castrated suitor. Rhetoric is fantasized as the means of wrenching a female body from the condition of being *"tres illustré"* in which it exerts phallic power over a desiring male, to a configuration of "illustration," denominated the major objective of rhetoric. In the illustrative configuration, the no longer phallicized woman is subjected to the control of phallocentric "truth."

De Courcelles's inebriate fantasy of the conversion of an "illustrious" phallic woman to a controlled woman inscribed into the rhetorical category of "illustration" through rhetorical insemination is telling. What is at stake in the rhetorical notion of "illustration" incorporated into the theorization of the sanctioned configuration of simile in early modern rhetoric, this fantasy suggests, is the control of the feminized, maternalized copiousness of language. De Courcelles's text makes the category of illustration the rhetorical substrate of phallic control. Illustration becomes the rhetorical antidote to maternalized *copia*.

The category of illustration frequently appears in early modern rhetorical theory in conjunction with another common category for *copia*: amplification. To "Amplifye and Illustrate," John Hoskyns writes in *Directions of Speech and Style* (1641), are "two of the principal Ornaments of Eloquence" (p. 17). This formulation is echoed verbatim in Thomas Blount's *Academie of Eloquence* (1659) (p. 11). Hoskyns and Blount manifest a common paradoxical gesture in Renaissance rhetorical theory. This theory teaches to "expand a discourse" and demands the control of expansion to keep *copia* "from getting out of bounds" (Parker, *Literary Fat Ladies*, p. 13). This paradoxical gesture symptomatically indexes the dialectical relation of attraction and repulsion, desire and anxiety, of Renaissance rhetoricians to the maternalized substance of semiosis and its inscriptions in aesthetic categories.

The textual site of this manifestation of attraction and repulsion in relation to the maternal is symptomatic. Hoskyns and Blount articulate the dialectical gesture of requiring *copia* and demanding its circumscription in their theorization of "similitudes." Because of the link articulated in Aristotle's *Rhetoric* between similes and the maternal body, similes are a conceptual embodiment of the maternalized category of *copia*. Hoskyns and Blount single out the technically illustrative similes in which there is "much affinity between the things compared" as "most commendable" (Hoskyns, p. 20; Blount, p. 12). This commendation of simile in the treatises of Hoskyns and Blount indexes a fascination with the maternality inscribed into the category of simile ever since Aristotle. The commendation of the illustrative configuration of simile indexes the simultaneous anxiety of the maternal. Like the category of *copia* with which simile is psycho-conceptually aligned, the category of simile in the rhetorical theory of Hoskyns and Blount can only be commended when it is simultaneously subjected to phallic control.

The psycho-conceptual alignment of simile and *copia* or amplification is manifest in other early modern rhetorical treatises. Specifically stating the link between simile and *copia*, Soario Cypriano prefaces his discussion of simile in *De Arte Rhetorica* (1612) by the title "*De Amplificatione & Similitudine.*" The intensity of the anxiety occasioned by the conjunction of two rhetorical categories highly charged with the sex of the mother is suggested by Cypriano's immediately proceeding to commend only a particular configuration of simile, the hierarchical illustrative example (*illustre exemplum*) (p. 58). More explicit about the idea of the abject and excessive informing the rhetorical notion of amplification or *copia*, the anonymous *Rhetoricae Synopsis* (1693) pits the illustrative (*illustrandum*) similitude against a condemned figural magnification (*magnum*). Magnifying similes, the author of this treatise writes, are "sordid" (*sordidis*) and "vulgar" (*vulgaris*) (p. 75), terms bespeaking the abject and indexing an anxiety of the maternal informing the category of the abject.

In the seventeenth-century treatises cited above, the "illustrative" simile is commended as a rhetorical antidote to the perils of abjection inscribed into the figure qua its association with the maternal genitals. In the illustrative simile as theorized in those treatises, the signifier performing the complementary semiotic function of enhancing the signification of the other, of "illustrat[ing] a doctrine" (John Spenser, *A Storehouse of Similies* [1658], p. 4) is made into the rhetorical equivalent of the excessive female body under matrimonial control.

The category of the illustrative simile as theorized in early modern rhetoric ultimately fails to perform the psycho-conceptual task of serving as an antidote to the perils of abjection associated with simile. The category of the illustrative simile fails to allay the anxieties of inundation and loss of individuating boundaries induced by the transcoding of the similaic copula with the female genitals in their maternal inflection. The category of illustrative simile does affirm a form of sexuality reassuring to an imaginary predicated on de-subjectifying phallic desire, namely, reproduction-oriented matrimonial heterosexuality. This form of sexuality is reassuring for an imaginary solipsistically fixated on phallic mastery. This form of sexuality is reassuring because in it the female body is made subservient to the body of the male for which it is to supply male offspring who would ensure patriliny.

Reproduction-oriented matrimonial heterosexuality is reassuring to an imaginary predicated on phallic desire for another, psychic reason. This form of sexuality is reassuring because it is informed by a fantasy of complementarity wherein male and female subjectivities form, in terms of what Meres calls "Gods Arithmeticke," a perfect consum(mat)ion, a perfect sum. Yet the illustrative simile can be reassuring to an imaginary predicated on phallic desire only at the price of the postulation of its abjected binary, its mirror image. This mirror image is the catachretic simile.

In early modern rhetoric and its classical antecedents the catachretic simile is inscribed with a non-regulated female sexuality exceeding phallic strictures. The female sexuality inscribed into the category of catachresis exceeds the phallic fantasy of possessing and controlling the female body as an instrument of reproduction. The female sexuality inscribed into the category of catachresis is polymorphic, diversely deployed as empowered, incestuous, adulterous, and homoerotic. The affirmation of the phallic fantasy of complemental heterosexual consum(mat)ion in which female sexuality is regulated by the phallus in terms of the aesthetic category of the illustrative simile depends on the risky postulation of an aesthetic category inscribed with polymorphic female sexualities beyond phallic regulation. The catachretic simile threatens to shatter the fantasy of heterosexual complementrarity informing the illustrative simile with alternative forms of being with.

The category of the illustrative simile postulated by early modern rhetoricians as an antidote to the anxieties of the abject, devouring maternality inscribed into simile is psychically precarious. Given this precariousness, we should not be surprised to find in early modern rhetorical theory another mechanism attempting to circumscribe the abject, devouring maternality inscribed into the form of simile in Aristotle's formative theorization and its early modern echoes. Early modern Europe was the site of the emergence of a rhetorical sub-genre seemingly devoted to the regulation of similes. This is the compendium of similes. Early modern compendia of similes valorize the regulated, illustrative configuration of this category. This rhetorical valorization indexes the valorization of the regulated female sexuality with which illustrative simile is inscribed in early modern rhetorical theory.

One of the earliest English texts of this genre is Anthonie Fletcher's *Certaine Very Proper and Most Profitable Similies* (1595). This title bespeaks a drive to regulate the maternal sexuality with which simile is transcoded by bringing this sexuality under morally and behaviorally "Proper" regulation. The intensifiers "Very" and "Most" index the obsessiveness of this drive. Under the strictures of "Proper" conduct, the female body with which simile is transcoded would be subject to homosocial exchange. This body would be a proper(ty) whose transacting is the source of psychological "Profit" for two men and economic "Profit" for the man who receives it (Irigaray, *This Sex*, p. 172; Rubin, p. 192).

Fletcher's title tells us more about the psychological "Profit" inherent in the relegation of similes to the textual space of the compendium. This relegation, Fletcher's title suggests, would provide for the conversion of the existence of similes as "Certaine" or sundry semiotic entities, to a mode of existence in which they would be subject to "Certaine," definitive and authoritative rule. Psycho-conceptually speaking, this rule is the rule of the phallus.

The same motivation of bringing a potentially unwieldy rhetorical form, made into a site of gynophobia through its association with female genitality and maternity, underlies Conrad Lycosthenis's *Similivm Loci Commvnes*, published in Geneva in 1602. The title of this treatise combines two psychologically loaded rhetorical categories. First of these is the category of simile, inscribed with the female genitals. The second rhetorical category in Lycosthenis's title, the *"Loci Commvnes"* or "common places" carries similar psycho-sexual resonances. The rhetorical category of the "common place" is associated with the "private place" of the female body adultery might make "common" (Parker, *Literary Fat Ladies*, p. 105). The title of Lycosthenis's compendium of similes is doubly inscribed with female genitality.

The inscription of the category of the female into Lycosthenis's compendium is intensified by the inscription of the feminine in a short comment, printed in small type on the margins of this voluminous text. In this comment, Lycosthenis reiterates simile's affiliation with the maternalized amplification or dilation of speech. He calls simile *"multiplicatione"* (p. 801). The category of the multiple is feminized (Irigaray, *This Sex*, p. 26). This feminization of the multiple is archaic. It is articulated in the table of opposites attributed to the Pythagoreans in Aristotle's *Metaphysics* (986a22–25).

Lycosthenis proceeds to call simile *prolixa* (p. 801). He names simile by means of the same term collapsing length and feminizing liquidity Hobbes uses to theorize simile as inferior and feminized in relation to metaphor. "What a Metaphor does, a Similitude does the same," Hobbes writes, "but with lesse grace, because with more prolixity" (p. 115). The feminization of simile in the margins of Lycosthenis's text is a maternalizing feminization. This is overdetermined by Lycosthenis's theorization of simile as fecund (*foecundus*) (p. 801).

The maternalizing theorizations of simile on the margins of Lycosthenis's text mount what Derrida calls a "limitrophic violence" on this text (*Margins of Philosophy*, pp. xxiv–xxv). The objective of Lycosthenis's text is to subject similes to a process of regulation. In the context of this process, only those similes conforming to the hierarchical mold of an illustration (*illustrationem*) of divine doctrine (*divina doctrina*) are allowed entry into the textual space of the compendium (Lycosthenis, p. 801).

The associations of simile with proliferation and flux on the margins of Lycosthenis's text are symptomatic. The text's regulatory project, these associations suggest, has not been and cannot be carried out successfully. The maternalized female sexuality inscribed into the form of simile breaks through the envelopment the text attempts to construct for it. The sex of the mother inscribed into the category of simile remains an uncalculated excess the compendium's phallic economy cannot contain.

In Anthonie Fletcher's earlier English compendium, simile is required to undergo a similar transformation from unregulated excessiveness to a subjection to phallic control. In Fletcher's treatise, unlike in Lycosthenis's, this transformation is not vaguely attributed to the machinations of a "divine doctrine." This transformation is designated as the conceptual work or "labor" (sig. A2) of the rhetorician as an emissary of the Law of the Father. Fletcher represents himself as a "minister of the word of God," who "collect[s]" similes (sigs. A1–A2). The "gather[ing] together" or rounding up of categories inscribed with female genitality into a "little booke of similes" by a self-proclaimed agent of the Name of the Father makes his book the textual equivalent of private property qua the restricting space of the Father (Irigaray, *This Sex*, p. 185).

The inscription of the "collect[or]" of similes as phallic disciplinarian of the female body is evident in his theorization of his rhetorical project by means of the image of "the finger of God" (sig. A1), an image conflating phallic ostension, the common graphic trace of the discourse of the early modern (school) master (see Chapter Four above), with the name of the theological Father. This image makes the rhetorician's fingers and the pen held in them phallic extensions of the Christian Father.

Yet the theological Father is inscribed in Fletcher's treatise as more than a phallicized general equivalent, more than a symbolic Father function. The theological Father is inscribed in Fletcher's treatise as homosexual object. In Fletcher's treatise, the collector's erotic energies are not primarily directed at the maternalized similes he seeks to collect and control. These erotic energies are primarily directed to a homoerotically inflected "love in Christ Iesu" (sig. A2). Shakespeare sings of devotional love of this sort, calling it "dear religious love" (sonnet #31, line 6). Lacan would theorize love of this devotional structure as constitutively homosexual (*Seminar III*, pp. 29–31).

In Fletcher's treatise, the homosexual inflection of the collector's devotional love is registered is his articulated need to "testifie it" (sig. A2). Semantically, the reference to testimony speaks a commitment to religion and to the Law, wherein testimony is a fundamental procedure. Etymologically and phonically, this reference is sexualized. Testimony "comes from the Latin *testis* or witness, which relates to testes, testicles" (Willbern, p. xvii). The religious love of Fletcher's collector of similes, like the "religious love" of the speaker in Shakespeare sonnet #31, originates not in the site of Law but in the site of male sex.

In the self-characterization of Fletcher's collector of similes, homosexual desire predominates. The intensity of the collector's homosexual passion for Christ makes the female genitality inscribed into the similes he collects much less than alluring. Contact with similes, Fletcher's speaker says, involves "paine" (sig. A2). The intensity of the collector's homosexual passion suggests this willingness to engage in the pain or unpleasureable contact with female genitality inscribed into the category of simile does not derive from heterosexual masochism, wherein female sexuality is alluring only insofar as it inflicts physical and psychic pain. Instead, this willingness derives from homosexual masochism, from the desire to serve as devoted "minister" (sig. A2) to a sublime homosexual object even and especially when this service involves pain. In this case, the pain comes from unpleasurable contact with simile qua maternal sexuality.

The imaginary captation of the compendium as the "finger of God" inflects its articulator as engaged in displaced intercourse with similes qua maternal bodies. But this intercourse is not pleasurable. The testical drive propelling this displaced intercourse is not occasioned by female bodies but by a sublime male object. The speaker imagines himself as a phallic extension of this sublime male object, and engages in imaginary displaced intercourse with similes qua maternal bodies in the interests of "ministering" and mediating the sublime object's wish to control them.

The collector of similes "lai[s] open and displaie[s]," these similes, with some revulsion (sig. A1). The common rhetorical motif of the phallic opening up of the feminized body of a text by a male exegete is here mobilized to a religious discourse whose virulent misogyny toward earthly women soon reveals a homosexual desire for the body of Christ. The imaginary captation of simile qua maternal body as "displaied" makes its disciplinary penetration an act of public rape. In this act, simile is "displaied," exhibited; and simile is "dis-plaied," made part of a sexual interaction in which play, and foreplay, has no part. In Fletcher's compendium, the regulation of similes is not carried out within a heterosexual dyad. The regulation of similes is carried out within an erotic triangle in which the driving passion is homosexual. This regulation is not motivated by a quest for phallic control on the part of the collector of similes. The regulation of simile in Fletcher's compendium is a masochistic enterprise, grudgingly carried out by the collector of similes so as to satisfy his sublime homosexual object.

The psycho-sexual dynamics of Fletcher's compendium involve a fourth term, namely, the implied "Christian Reader" (sig. A1). The similes are collected and laid open in order to make this reader "fearful...of...forbidden things" (sig. A1). The goal of the ritualistic spectacle of the disciplinary rape of simile qua maternal body adumbrated in Fletcher's compendium is to mark as forbidden any unregulated — adulterous, prostitutional, fornicatory — heterosexual intercourse driven by sexual attraction rather than by the duty to procreate. Heterosexual intercourse in excess of what Meres calls "Gods Arithmeticke" is marked in Fletcher's compendium as morally "forbidden," repulsive, and "lothsome" (sig. E). Erotically oriented rather than reproductively oriented heterosexual intercourse in excess of the phallic fantasy of complementarity inscribed into the categories of metaphor and of illustrative simile is brought into Fletcher's text as a spectacle. This spectacle yields control over the raped and displayed female body associated with simile. The purpose of the spectacle of the rape of simile, however, is not to play into sadistic fantasies but to elicit the implied reader's revulsion.

What Fletcher offers as an alternative for male libidinality to the "forbidden" acts of fornication and adultery is its channeling toward God. The second stated objective of his compendium is the theorization of "notable vertues" not as didactic prescriptions but as expressions "lively" and seductive enough to make the "Godly reader," provided he be "of Christian inclination," "mightily inflamed with a love unto them" (sig.

A2). The feminized body of the non-regulated, "far-fetched" simile becomes not even the passive conduit for the affirmation of homosocial ties. It is a body to be violated by males in ritualistic rape. The purpose of this rape is not the provision of pleasure or even control. The purpose of this rape is the exhaustion of heterosexual drives and the re-channeling of libidinal energies to a "might[y] inflam[mation]," a homosexual passion, for God the Father.

In Fletcher's dedication, the "Christian inclination" of the implied readers becomes transcodable with these readers' being, like the collector of similes, "very desirous" (sig. A2) of a sublime homosexual object. The cultivation of such homosexual passion requires the constant staving off of female seduction by insistence on regulation of women's sexual activity in the hierarchical institution of the patriarchal marriage, of which the illustrative similes "collected" and restrained in Fletcher's treatise are the rhetorical-aesthetic analogues.

Robert Cawdray's voluminous *Treasvrie or Storehovse of Similies*, published half a decade after Fletcher's compendium, shares its psycho-conceptual concerns, as is most apparent in its undisguised plagiarism of parts of Fletcher's text. Cawdray appropriates Fletcher's image of the rhetorician's pen as a phallic extension of the "finger of God" which concedes to carry out the unpleasurable and even "pain[ful]" task (sig. A3) of laying "open" the feminized body of simile in an act of ritualistic rape designed to divert the desire of the "Reader...of a Christian inclination" (sig. A3), from "forbidden things" (sig. A2) such as seductive female bodies to a libidinal condition where the reader is "inflamed with...a loue" for a sublime homosexual object (sig. A2).

Like Fletcher, Cawdray adumbrates the relinquishing of male heterosexual desire. Like Fletcher, Cawdray suggests two alternatives to male heterosexual desire. The first and most significant alternative to male heterosexual desire in Cawdray's compendium, as in Fletcher's, is an intense ("inflamed") homosexual desire for the *logos* or "word of God" (sig. A2). The second alternative to heteroerotic passion in Cawdray's compendium, as in Fletcher's, is a de-eroticized control over a female body in a power dyad isomorphic with the illustrative similes he confines in his book.

Cawdray is more explicit and outspoken than his source and predecessor regarding the psycho-conceptual motivations of the genre of his text. The title page of Cawdray's compendium identifies the illustrative similes "collected" in the compendium as including "common places." The "common place" is the early modern name of a rhetorical category and of the private parts of the female body.

The sexual resonance of the rhetorical category of "common places" is underscored in another Elizabethan treatise on rhetoric, John Sturmius's *Ritch Storehouse or Treasvrie for Nobilitye and Gentlemen* (1570). This treatise describes "common places" as "things" a man "owne[s]" (p. 23). It suggests a man "should gather and dispose" these "things" (p. 23). The injunction to "gather" indexes the act of collecting and circumscribing structuring the compendium genre. This act, I suggested above, is motivated by the transcoding of similes with the sex of the mother. The injunction to "dispose" invokes the rhetorical category of "disposition." This is the category of rhetorical ordering imbricated with the "reigning gynecological conception of the male as 'disposing' the female in generation" (Parker, *Literary Fat Ladies*, p. 116). Sturmius's injunction to subject rhetorical "common places" to two procedures loaded with connotations of controlling female genitality underscores the genital inflection of these "common places."

In Sturmius's treatise, the anxiety-generated drive to restrict and control the female genitality inscribed into the rhetorical category of the "common place" is indexed by the reference to the treatise as a confining "Storehouse." This term appears in the title of Cawdray's compendium of similes/commonplaces too. In Cawdray's and Sturmius's titles, "Storehovse" is apposite with the name of another "place," namely a "Treasvrie."

The terms "Treasvrie" and "Storehovse" abound in conceptual associations. They denote spaces where commodities or goods are placed in order to prevent their uncontrolled and unregulated circulation. In this respect, "Treasvrie" and "Storehovse" are structurally analogous to the household as the physical space of the patriarchal marriage bond, one of whose functions is to provide a material guarantee for the wife's fidelity by her enclosure (Irigaray, *This Sex*, p. 187; Parker, *Literary Fat Ladies*, p. 105).

"Treasvrie" and "Storehovse" have semantic links with the ideology of the household. "Storehouse," a term featured yet again in the title of a later compendium of similes, John Spenser's *Things Old and New or: a Storehouse of Similies* (1658), is the rhetorical signifier for the discursive space of the "common places" of language, upon their conceptual association with the private "places" of the female body adultery, fornication, or incest might make "common" to several lovers. "Storehovse" is the rhetorical equivalent of the space of the household whose material and institutional boundaries were expected to block the slippage of women from private to "common" property.

The implicit analogy between the collection of illustrative similes in a discursive "Storehovse" and the patriarchal effort to contain women's sexual activity by insisting on their shamefastness and subordination to their husbands and on their confinement to the household is made explicit in Thomas Fuller's address "To the Reader" in John Spenser's *Things Old and New or: a Storehouse of Similies* (1658). This treatise ends with Fuller's mock-protest, "the reader will catch cold by keeping him too long in the porch of this preface, who now (the door being opened) may enter into the *house* itself" (unpaginated). This mock-protest interpellates the implied male reader as a phallic force penetrating a domestic space. This space conflates the category of a house, the woman of the household, and the illustrative simile whose semiotic structure replicates the power hierarchy structuring the patriarchal household.

The analogy between storehouse and household is underscored in Ralph Lever's *The Arte of Reason, Rightly Termed Witcraft* (1573), a treatise of logic and rhetoric. Lever explains:

> There are…generall wordes whiche maye well be called storehouses, not solely for the doze of wordes which they conteyne…and for the good order they keep in placing of wordes in their particular roumes, with breefe rules (as notes setle on packets) declaring theyr nature and properties. (pp. 38–39)

In this text, the rhetorical "storehouse," like the patriarchal household, is a space whose partitioning into distinct "roumes" is a disciplinary apparatus for the physical and restrictive "conteyn[ment]" of its occupants "in good order." Lever's text recognizes the precariousness of logocentric control proferred by the rhetorical "storehouse." Far from being a stably self-contained unit in which the contained bodies are subjected to the "good order" of "reason," the rhetorical "storehouse" is a repository for such bodies as commodities or "properties" offered for sale.

The rhetorical "storehouse" is isomorphic with early modern accounts of the household not as a hermetically sealed or "impermeable" hierarchy of husband and wife (Roper, p. 154) but "as a skin so thin that it can hardly hold its…denizens together: the master patriarch, most likely to fall prey to any kind of vice, the mistress, only too ready to surrender herself to concupiscence" (ibid., p. 24). In such accounts, husband and wife mark(et) themselves as bodies available for libidinal circulation which circumvents the normative paradigm of the regulated exchange of women between men and can give rise to complications regarding the division of property.

The rhetorical term "storehouse" combines "house" as "basic unit of social organization" (ibid.), lauded as a disciplinary apparatus with a "role of policing morals" (ibid., p. 154), and "store" as a reservoir of commodities and the site of their exchange. This combination suggests the social and economic need, within a phallocentric economy, to police domesticity and prevent the slippage of "house" to "store." At the same time, the combination indexes the inevitability of this slippage within the coordinates of capitalism.

The category of the rhetorical "storehouse" bespeaks a wish to control sexual and monetary excess while betraying an anxiety such control may be impossible. This category indexes the desire and the anxiety implicit in the denomination of the treatise's project of conveying the "Arte of Reason" as "Witcraft." The signifier "Witcraft" paronomastically invokes the disciplinary fantasy of monetary and sexual control through "wit" qua logocentricity. At the same time, the signifier "Witcraft" paronomastically evokes the category of "wit(ch)craft." Witchcraft is imagined in Renaissance texts as involving sexual excess. This excess trasgresses the "heterosexual norm" into forms of "non-reproductive intercourse" including the most extreme form of "sex with the mother herself" (Roper, p. 25).

A later text devoted to the regulation of the female body through the dissolution of its empowerment as object of desire, Edward Philips's *Mysteries of Love and Eloquence* (1658), more openly admits the shortcomings this project. Phillips denominates the strategies of persuasive wooing he recommends to courtiers "the *witchcraft* of their persuasive Language" (title page, emphasis mine). This reference to witchcraft acknowledges the relevance of the body of the witch, imagined in the Renaissance as a woman "governed by uncontrollable lust" (Brauner, p. 40), to a textual apparatus whose ultimate objective is the establishment of a marriage in which all traces of such excessive female libidinality would be effaced.

The category of the rhetorical "storehouse" is imbricated in a psychic dynamic combining the revulsion from sexual and economic excess and the fantasy of its control. In this context, labeling a text a "Storehovse of Similies" involves an articulation of a drive to control the excesses of female sexuality long associated with simile and an admission of the impossibility of fulfilling this drive. In Lever's text, this admission is implicit in the reference to similitude as a form which "properlye [has] no place" since it is a destabilizing form by means of which "you maye as soone prove a wrong matter as a right" (p. 195). Simile has no "place" in Lever's treatise on logic because simile is in excess of the text's function as a regulating apparatus of logic.

The relation of simile to Lever's logocentric text is analogous to the relation of the witch in the early modern imagination to the phallocentric institution of the patriarchal household. The witch was imagined to threaten the household by "seduc[ing] men with her wanton sexuality, bewitching them and rendering them impotent" (Brauner, p. 40), by sucking out their "seminal fluid" for which she allegedly had an "insatiable hunger" (Roper, p. 208), and by depleting the post-partum maternal body of the fluids necessary for the nourishment of the household's offspring (ibid., p. 207).

In the context of early modern imaginary captations of witchcraft, and of the isomorphism suggested by Lever's text between the category of the witch and the category of simile, the inclusion of the form of simile within a treatise on logic would be an act of considerable risk. This inclusion could disrupt the logocentricity of the treatise on logic and cause the treatise to slip from a paterialized text on "The art of Witcraft," to a text contaminated by what was imagined as a form of excessive female libidinality: the art of wit(ch)craft.

"Treasvrie," the second term used to name Cawdray's project of "collecting" and controlling the "aboundant increase" (sig. A2) or *copia* accruing to simile in its technical definition as a mode of dilation or "amplification" and in its conceptual associations with the female genitals and the maternal body involves similar conceptual entanglements. Like the term "Storehovse" with which "Treasvrie" is coupled by both Cawdray and Sturmius, "treasury" denotes "treasure-chest, hoard, or store" (Cave, *The Cornucopian Text*, p. 6), the place where a commodity is kept. In this case, the commodity is designated as precious or valued, a "treasure." Yet in the English Renaissance, the differences between the commodities imagined as stored in a "storehouse" and those imagined as stored in "treasury" were not so polarized after all. "Treasure" was a term commonly used to refer to a woman's private parts which must be kept locked up and chaste.

This sense of "treasure" as regulated female genitality is bitterly evoked by Katherina in Shakespeare's *Taming of the Shrew*. Speaking to her father, Katherina refers to her sister Bianca as "your treasure" (Act 2, scene 1, line 32). Bianca is the epitome of the early modern idea of a submissive or "shamefast" woman. Bianca's initial characterization hinges upon her acquiescence to the patriarch's repeated injunctions to stay within the material limitations of his household. "Get you in," Baptista, stemming the possible development of an erotic dynamic between Bianca and one of the suitors who fetishize her as a Petrarchan object of desire, commands her (Act 1, scene 1, line 75). He is answered by her servile affirmation of paternal authority: "Sir, to your pleasure humbly I subscribe" (Act 1, scene 1, line 81). "Go in, Bianca," he demands again in Act 1, scene 1, line 90. This time, Baptista is answered not by words but by the dramatic gesture of "Exit Bianca," in which Bianca even more obsequiously renounces the female right to speak even her submission. The father's next "Bianca, get thee in" (Act 2, scene 1, line 30), immediately before Katherina's reference to Bianca as her father's "treasure" (Act 2, scene 1, line 32) is again met by silent submissiveness.

In the context of Shakespeare's play, the reference to female chastity and obedience to paternal authority whose manifestation in staying "in" the bounds of the patriarchal household as a "treasure" underwrites the conceptual link between the term "treasure" and the female genitals as a commodity which requires restriction because of its value to the patriarchal symbolic economy.

"Treasure" is woman's sexuality as commodity in a homosocial exchange. The space containing the "treasure" qua female sexuality, the "Treasvrie," is the space circumscribing this sexuality. The term "Treasvrie" is invoked to name texts containing illustrative similes. The semiotic structure of these similes is hierarchical. It is isomorphic with the structure of the patriarchal household. The "Treasvrie of Similies" is structurally coterminous with the space of the patriarchal household as treasury in the sense of a "repository or reserve of wealth...from which money comes and to which it returns" (Goux, *The Coiners of Language*, p. 23).

A treasury differs from all other repositories of wealth in terms of its contents. What a treasury contains is not circulating currency but a "treasure" removed from circulation and hoarded for special needs (ibid., p. 26) such as transactions "for which conventional tokens are no longer acceptable" and which require the payment to be made by means of the treasure (ibid., p. 35). The homosocial traffic in women is just such a transaction. In the structure of homosocial exchange, a woman's exchange-value depends on her prior hoarding as undefiled "treasure" in the paternal household as treasury.

Cawdray represents the confinement of the illustrative simile as a female body treasured for homosocial exchange as "profitable," "pleasaunt," and "delightful" (title page). This confinement is more than economic. It is an operation of a libidinal economy, whose yield is pleasure. The recipient of this pleasure is male. This is made clear in the dedication to the treatise, addressed to two men: Sir John Harington and James

Harington, his brother (sig. A2). The dedication advertises the text following it as a "worke" deserving "to be aduisedly read, attentiuely considered," and "effectually ruminated" because there is no "estate of *men* for whom [it] is not necessarie" (sig. A2, emphasis mine). Cawdray goes on to commend his book to an entire catalogue of males. For Princes, he writes, "it is prettie,"

> for Preachers profitable, for sage Counsellors it is singular, meete for Magistrates, lawdable for Lawyers, a Iewell for gentlemen, a staffe to leane on for students, good to further godlinesse, and therefore apt and profitable for all *men*. (sig. A2, emphasis mine)

This catalogue overdetermines the gender identity of the compendium's implied readers. It lists practitioners of institutional offices: preachers, counsellors, magistrates, and lawyers. In the English Renaissance, these were offices from which women were in principle systematically excluded. The catalogue of implied readers includes "gentlemen," for whom the similes "collected" within the compendium would provide a "Iewel": a treasured commodity conceptually equivalent to the guarded chastity of a virgin and the guarded fidelity of a wife. Finally, Cawdray's list of implied readers mentions students, another an all-male social group of his time, for whom the contents of the text are promised to provide a "staffe to lean on," a temporary, prosthetic phallus.

The compendium attempts to produce the pleasure of phallic control over the sex of the mother. The sex of the mother is inscribed into two rhetorical categories Cawdray mentions early on in his text. The sex of the mother is inscribed into the rhetorical category of the "common place" mentioned in the frontispiece to the treatise. It is inscribed into the "aboundant increase" or *copia* of language Cawdray invokes in his dedication (sig. A2). Rhetorical "common places" and rhetorical *copia* are conceptually transcoded with the aesthetic category of simile allied, like them, with female sexuality through centuries of the rhetorical tradition. In the frontispiece, the "common places" aligned with the sex of the mother are distinguished from and subordinated to "Heads," in a semiotic gesture isomorphic with the subjection of a woman's genitals to the control of her husband as her "head" in marriage. The copious matter of language concretized in Cawdray's voluminous compendium is subjected to the regulating operation of "collecting" and confining, declared in the frontispiece of this treatise.

Within the treatise, the aesthetic category of simile is subjected to phallic control. Cawdray recognizes the conceptual maternity of the category of simile. He refers to the similaic contents of his compendium as "matter," a signifier resonating with the Latin *mater* (sig. A2). He speaks of simile's tendency to "breede and increase in all degrees" (ibid.), in terms of the biological functions of maternity. In Cawdray's compendium, simile qua maternalized body is subjected to increasingly violent procedures. In the dedication to the compendium, Cawdray speaks of simile as a category of which the reader should make "vse," a term whose early modern resonances are economic, practical, and sexual.

In Cawdray's compendium, simile undergoes a process of commodification. The "matter" of this feminized aesthetic category is "laye[d]...euen before the eyes" of the implied male consumers (sig. A5). Subjected to the "eyes," simile becomes, in Lacan's terms, the gaze as object, given only in its perpetual slipping away (*Seminar XI*, p. 73). Yet in Cawdray's treatise, the ocular encounter between eye and gaze is not erotic. It does not involve the recognition and embracing of the object's slipping away, of the constitutively irreducible gap between subject and object. This gap is the only space of desire, of erotic play. In Cawdray's compendium, there is no erotic play where simile is concerned. Cawdray puts simile on "display" (sig. A2). He makes simile qua maternal body the subject of a controlling, possessive look unable to recognize the other as a subject placed at an irreducible distance wherein intersubjective play becomes possible. Such a reductive and possessive look generates only visual, constitutively phallic, *dis*-play.

In Cawdray's compendium, simile is not a gaze as object but a de-subjectified commodity subjected to phallic look of the implied male reader. In Shakespeare's *Rape of Lucrece*, rhetorical display of the visual beauty of a woman leads to rape (Vickers; Sharon-Zisser, "Re-(de)-erecting Collatine"). In Cawdray's compendium too, the display of simile qua female body leads to a violation of its confines, its rape-like "plaine opening" (sig. A3).

This "opening" is imagined as violent. This is suggested by Cawdray's reference to the display of simile as the simile's being "ripped vp," dismembered (sig. A2). Cawdray later provides a detailed example of the dismemberment of the maternalized body of nature involved in the rhetorical qua sexual but not erotic "vse" of similes (sig. A4). The "comparisons" or illustrating signifiers in similes, Cawdray writes, should be

> fetched-off, and from the secrets and bowels of nature: as namely, from wilde and tame beastes, foules, wormes, creeping and swimming creatures, Hearbs, Trees, the Elements, fire, water, earth, ayre, riuers, brokkes, welles, Cesternes, Seas, stars, pearls, stones, lightning, thunder,

raine, deaw, heate, droeth, cold, winds, blasts, haile, snow, frost, yce, Corne, seede, salt, leuen, nets, snares, and likewise from the humours in a mans body, as bloud, milke, women in trauaile, in child birth, drosse, Iron, Gold, Siluer, and innumerable other things. (sig. A4)

This inventory of possible illustrating signifiers is a formal manifestation of the rhetorical technique of itemizing the parts of the feminized "matter" of language as a "way of taking possession [of that feminized "matter"] by the act of naming or accounting" (Parker, *Literary Fat Ladies*, p. 131).

The "matter" of language from which illustrating signifiers are violently abducted, "fetched-off," as distinct from "fetched-far," is imagined as a sexualized space, the mysterious place of the corporeally interior "secrets" of sexuality. This sexuality is possibly anal, located about the "bowels." This sexuality is at the same time distinctly maternal, connected with the gynecological images of "blood, milke, [and] women in trauaile, in childbirth."

Cawdray's list of possible semantic domains of illustrating signifiers is the rhetorical result of a brutal breaking into and ripping up of maternalized "bowels." This rhetorical-sexual violation provides the simultaneous pleasures of a sadistic and scopophilic prising of the maternal body. It also provides for the control of the maternal body through partition, and for the indefinite perpetuation of this partitioning. Cawdray concludes the violation of the similaic "bowels" by describing this violation as a "familiar" project, and assuring it could proffer "innumerable other things" (sig. A2). He locates the promise of infinite dismemberment of the abject insides of the maternal body at the site of the familiar/familial, at the site of domesticity.

The sadistic dismemberment of the female body involves but one of the two signifiers coupled in the illustrative simile as a controlled, domesticated, and thus sanctioned version of a linguistic form otherwise theorized as dangerously transgressive and destructive in its possible subversive effects. In Cawdray's compendium of similes, the illustrating signifier, transcoded with the sex of the mother, is curbed to a signifier conceptually associated with a disciplining *logos*. In Cawdray's compendium as in Fletcher's, this signifier is identified as the "principles of Christian Religion" and more specifically, as "the word of God," the ultimate Father (sig. A3).

In Cawdray's *Treasvrie or Storehovse of Similies*, like in Fletcher's compendium, the affirmation of the rhetorical equivalent of the subordination of female to male and excessive matter to *logos* does not exhaust the text's psychological trajectory. For Cawdray, too, the sadistic gestures of dismembering the excessive and ultimately maternal body and its restraining by the semiotic emissaries of the Law of the Father are preludes for greater and more liberating pleasures. These are archaic, archetypal pleasures, pleasures Cawdray associates with a "stir[ring]" in "mens drowsie minds" (sig. A2), with the male oneiric.

In Cawdray's compendium, just as in Fletcher's, the male oneiric of implied author and implied reader is a site of devotional, masochistic homoeroticism, of "paines" (sig. A3) incurred in the context of a "mightily inflamed…loue" of Christ (sig. A1). In Cawdray's compendium, similitudes are said to offer a sublime pleasure "surpassing knowledge" (sig. A5). Similitudes lead to the pleasure of an encounter with a sublime other "in whome…all the treasures of wisdom and knowledge" are "hidden" (sig. A3). In its parallelism with the image of "naturall things" (sig. A3) hidden "in the secrets and bowels of nature" (sig. A4), this image feminizes and eroticizes the body of Christ. In Cawdray's compendium, illustrative similes are an instrument for regulating the sex of the mother, inscribed in the similaic copula "like," for controlling male desire for the sex of the mother. The heterosexual desire of the maternal "like" is transmuted in Cawdray's compendium into "an earnest liking" (sig. A3), a similaic homoerotic desire for a feminized Christ, whose conceptual connection with the prototypical feminine object of desire is accentuated by his fictionalization as a container of "mysteries" (sig. A4).

Christ is not the only homoerotic object in Cawdray's compendium. While professing to redirect the reader's heterosexual desire and transmute it toward an "earnest liking" of a sublime male object, Cawdray inscribes his own desire as directed not toward a sublime object but toward the two addressees of his dedication, the brothers John and James Harrington, to whom he owes gratitude for "great kindnesse and fauourable good will (during [his] long trouble, and since)" (sig. A5). The text of the compendium, Cawdray adds, is the "best present" he could give to the Harrington brothers.

Cawdray's compendium is a gift. It is eroticized by its being what Lewis Hyde calls an "emanation of eros" in which libido is given away though once consumed by the recipient is somehow replenished (p. 22). Cawdray underscores this erotization of his compendium as gift. He speaks of himself as "desiring" his addresses to "accept" his "present" (sig. A5).

Cawdray's offering of his compendium as gift inscribes the compendium with his homoerotic desire, his desire as a lover of men. Another early modern compendium of similes, John Spenser's *Things Old and New or a Storehouse of Similies* (1658) includes a similar inscription.

The similes in this treatise are all illustrative, hierarchical. They replicate the structure of the patriarchal dyad. But this replication does not exhaust the psychic function of Spenser's similes. On the title page of the treatise, John Spenser asserts he has "collected" such illustrative similes mirroring the structure of the patriarchal dyad from "the writings and sayings of the learned men of all ages." He has done so, Spenser adds, as a "Lover of Learning and Learned Men" (title page). The collection of illustrative similes and their confinement to the space of the compendium is more than a means of regulating female sexuality and restraining extra-marital male heterosexual desire. In addition, the collection of illustrative similes in Spenser's compendium is offered as an inscription, a textual trace, of male homoerotic desire of a self-professed "Lover...of Learned Men" who has created a textual object of desire by collecting instances of their similaic and hence erotic speech.

In Cawdray's compendium, the homoerotization of the textual object is intensified in the reference to it as a "handful of Flowers, as it were a Nosegay" he has "gleaned" from his "Garden" (sig. A5). The image of the forms of elocution as flowers was standard in the Renaissance. The image of flowers carries a powerful erotic charge (Bataille, "The Language of Flowers," *Visions of Excess*, p. 11). Transcoding this image with the similes collected in his compendium, Cawdray eroticizes the female sexuality he inscribes into the category of simile. What Cawdray offers to the Harrington brothers to whom he dedicates his treatise is rhetorical equivalents of eroticized female bodies. The space of these flowers is eroticized too: it is the Edenic and pastoral space of the garden.

Yet this gift offering of similes qua flowers does not constitute an invitation of the recipients to succumb to the temptations of female sexuality. Instead, Cawdray's gift offering involves an attempt to enclose similes/flowers qua eroticized female bodies. Cawdray's floral similes are enclosed within a "nosegay" uprooting them from the garden as pastoral space of desire. This uprooting from the space of pastoral voids Cawdray's similes of sex-appeal. The erotic function of similes in the dynamic of desire structuring Cawdray's treatise is not to elicit heterosexual attraction. The erotic function of similes is to serve as a copula in an interaction of gift offering between men. The offering of the compendium as gift becomes an invitation to discard heterosexuality for homosexuality, a homosexual seduction to which the female sexuality inscribed into the rhetorical category of simile is irrelevant.

In all of the above cases, the phallic policing of simile by means of the compendium has at best a partial success, acquired at the price of affirming not the rule of the phallus but a general economy predicated on the absence of the phallus, involving the less than normative forms of male homosexual and female *jouissance*.

By "general economy" I am referring to Bataille's notion of a non-restrictive organization of signifiers marked by expenditure rather than production (*The Accursed Share*, vol. I, p. 9). A general economy "can never be reduced to being governed by any given name, concept, or theoretical...configuration" (Plotnitsky, p. 14). I also have in mind Goux's utopian gesture toward "decapitat[ing] the "very thought of a general equivalent" so as to "pave the way for a polymorphic, acephalous...organization that would challenge the monopolies on representation" (*Symbolic Economies*, pp. 46–47). In the context of the concerns of gender marking early modern theorizations of rhetoric, I consider Luce Irigaray's reference to an "economy of abundance," of exchanges "without identifiable terms, without accounts, without end" (*This Sex*, p. 197), another articulation of the category of general economy. The inevitable deconstruction of the two strategies deployed in Renaissance rhetoric to bring the sex of the mother inscribed into the category of simile under phallic control and the consequent affirmation of forms of *jouissance* beyond the phallus in its repressive deployment gestures toward a general libidinal economy.

Neither strategy deployed in Renaissance rhetoric to contain the risks of confrontation with the abject that are the corollary of the formative Aristotelian transcoding of the similaic copula with the maternal genitals succeeds at its allotted restrictive, repressive task. One strategy is the partitioning of the aesthetic category of simile into a sanctioned illustrative configuration transcoded with the hierarchical structure of the patriarchal dyad and a denounced catachretic configuration inscribed with various forms of female sexual excess: phallic femininity, Lesbianism, incest, and adultery. These excessive forms of female sexuality inevitably remain inscribed in the aesthetic category of simile. They function as a horizon of sexual possibility beyond the restrictive hierarchical heterosexual dyad inscribed into the aesthetic category of the illustrative simile.

The second strategy for contending with the risks of simile in Renaissance rhetoric involves the compendia of similes invented and frequently published in the Renaissance. The similes collected in such compendia are exclusively of the hierarchical illustrative configuration. In illustrative similes, the abject maternality inscribed into the aesthetic category of simile in its formative Aristotelian theorization is relegated to the semiotically subservient illustrating signifier. Compendia of similes

Simile and Maternality: From the Abject to the Orgasmic 331

attempt a further restraining of the sex of the mother inscribed into the illustrating signifier of hierarchical similes. They restrict illustrative similes to a textual "storehouse," an isomorph of the patriarchal dyad resting on a fantasy of complementarity. Untrue to this fantasy and symptomatic of the intensification of libidinal drives insistence on this fantasy leads to, compendia of similes frequently involve a redirection of the normative matrimonial heterosexuality toward homosexuality.

The rhetorical gestures of partitioning of similes into a catachretic and an illustrative configuration and of constructing compendia of similes are driven by an anxiety of the abject maternality inscribed into the aesthetic category of simile in a tradition extending back to Aristotle. The postulation of the two configurations of simile, excessive-catachretic and sanctioned-illustrative and the invention of the compendia of illustrative similes are characteristic operations of the symbolic in its repressive inflection. They are rhetorical equivalents of the prohibitions on forms of sexuality in excess of the norm of matrimonial, reproduction-oriented copulation, forms of sexuality beyond the phallus as repressive bar rather than nurturing omphalos or umbilicus. These repressive operations of the symbolic within the theorization of simile in Renaissance rhetoric constitutively fail. They ultimately affirm the excessive forms of sexuality they set out to censor.

The inevitable failure of the repressive phallic operations deployed in Renaissance rhetoric to dispel the anxiety induced by the abject maternality inscribed into the aesthetic category of simile is an index of the constitutive excessiveness of the category of the maternal. This excessiveness puts the maternal beyond repressive phallic regulation. The inevitable failure of the repressive phallic mechanisms set in motion to control the maternal sexuality inscribed into simile is also an index of the constitutive complexity of the category of the maternal, manifest in early modern theorizations of the primal substance of semiosis as archaic maternality (see Chapter One above). This complexity makes the symbolic mother, the structural substrate of any object of desire, including objects the repressive, phallic Law of the Father seeks to bar, into the inseparable corollary of the abject and devouring imaginary mother the subject necessarily seeks to flee. This complexity of the maternal makes desire, always ultimately the impossible desire for the complete satisfactions offered by archaic maternality as aim, the inevitable underside of anxiety.

The aesthetic category of simile has been aligned with the maternal since antiquity. In early modern rhetorical theory, simile is inscribed with excessive forms of male and female sexuality. These forms of sexuality are beyond the phallus in its repressive deployment, beyond the phallic norm of matrimonial, reproduction-oriented heterosexuality informed by the fallacious fantasy of the dyad as a complemental sum. The association of simile in early modern rhetoric with the maternal and with excessive forms of sexuality is significantly symptomatic. This double association indexes the extent to which the yearning for the lost satisfactions afforded by the primal maternal object underlies the orientation of the subject toward any object, be it sanctioned by the phallic norm or in excess of it. This double association indexes the extent to which all forms of sexuality, whether conforming to the phallic norm or in excess of it, are veils for the primal maternal object with which simile has been transcoded since antiquity.

In early modern rhetoric, theorizations of simile riskingly pervert the phallic norm. This perversion is manifest in another way. The perversion of the phallic in its repressive deployment is evident in theorizations of simile in relation to metaphor, echoes of Aristotle's formative *père*-version of simile as the sex of the mother. Within the discourse on trope, the category in terms of which metaphor is most commonly classified and valorized, simile is sometimes theorized as the product or effect of metaphor. Thomas Hobbes, for example, theorizes simile as "a metaphor dilated" (*The Art of Rhetoric*, p. 106), as does John Smith in *The Mysterie of Rhetorique Unvail'd* (p. 211). Metaphor is the phallicized and paternalized general equivalent of elocution (see Chapter Four above). In the treatises of Hobbes and Smith, metaphor is cast in the role of a first principle, of an origin, too. Metaphor is made into paternal origin: a concept transcoded with "father," "master," and "lord" (Derrida, *Dissemination*, pp. 81–84).

This casting of metaphor as paternal origin is problematic. Structurally, Hobbes's positioning of metaphor as the paternal origin of simile reinforces his theorization of metaphor as a pulsion of male potency "beget[ting]...by the Genus" (p. 113). Semantically, Hobbes's theorization of simile as a "metaphor dilated" links metaphor not with a male impregnation of a female body but with the biological consequence of impregnation, namely, the obstetrical "dilation" of the female genitals in the act of childbirth. Gynecologizing metaphor as a dilating substance, Hobbes emasculates the elocutionary category early modern accounts of elocution, including his own, strive to associate with male prowess and phallic desire. Gynecological discourse erupts into and contaminates the discourse on metaphor, the would-be phallicized general equivalent of elocution, demonstrating the necessary failure of Renaissance rhetoric to regulate a substance of semiosis imagined in reference to archaic maternality.

In the early modern rhetorical treatises of Hobbes and Smith, metaphor is theorized as a laboring womb and as its issue. Metaphor, Hobbes and Smith write immediately following their theorization of "similitude" as a "metaphor dilated," is a "similitude contracted into one word" (Hobbes, p. 106; Smith, p. 211). "Contraction" is a concept used to describe the motions of the laboring womb since Hippocrates (Dean-Jones, p. 212). In the theorizations of metaphor in the early modern treatises of Smith and Hobbes, similitude functions as a contracting womb. Metaphor functions as the product or offspring of simile as womb. The masculinity of this issue is suggested by its denomination as "one," the signifier "of form, of the individual, of the (male) sexual organ" (Irigaray, *This Sex*, p. 26).

This theorization of metaphor as the male issue of simile as contracting womb appears to counterbalance what precedes it. In this theorization, metaphor and simile are neatly re-placed in the gender slots of male and female they may be expected to occupy within early modern rhetorical theory in light of their respective classifications as trope and figure. This re-placement too disintegrates and deconstructs. The theorization of metaphor as simile's male issue discards the aligning of metaphor with paternal origin. In Hobbes's earlier theorization of simile as the dilatory product of metaphor, the imaginary captation of metaphor as paternal origin bolsters the attempt to erect metaphor as rhetoric's phallic general equivalent. This attempt to erect metaphor as a phallic general equivalent deconstructs because it is simultaneous with the alignment of metaphor with dilation, and hence with the maternal. In Hobbes's theorization of metaphor as the male issue of simile not even this doomed attempt at erection is tried out.

Other early modern rhetorical treatises divorce metaphor from its phallocentric role as paternal origin by narrativizing it as simile's offspring. Hobbes's contemporary John Hoskyns, author of *Directions for Speech and Style* (1641), similarly disrupts the neat fit between the oppositions of cause/effect and high/low early modern theorizations of metaphor as the origin of simile offer yet subvert. In his text, "similitude" is theorized as the "ground of all emblems, allegories, fables, and fictions" (p. 11). Simile is thereby positioned as the logical precedent and the stable foundation of forms of language discussed under the heading of "metaphor." This genealogical narrative is common in early modern rhetorical theory. It is featured almost verbatim in Thomas Blount's *Academie of Eloquence* (1659), where "similitude" is quoted as the source of "An Emblem, an Allegory, [and] a Fable" (p. 3).

Richard Sherry's theorization of metaphor as "a word translated from the thynge that it properlye signifieth, unto another whych may agree with it by a similitude," in his 1550 *Treatise of Schemes and Tropes* (unpaginated), indicates a similar relationship between simile and metaphor. In Sherry's theorization, "similitude" is the semantic basis for the implementation of the displacement narrative structuring metaphor. Sherry's treatise attempts to masculinize metaphor in two ways. Sherry associates metaphor with colonial conquest undergirded by the structure of phallic desire. Sherry masculinizes metaphor by dubbing it the "cheyfe" virtue of speech (see Chapter Three above), by means of a noun used to refer to a male leader and glossed by Derrida as transcodable with paternity and property (*Dissemination*, p. 81). Like Hoskyns and Blount, Sherry theorizes similitude as the material basis making the emergence of metaphor qua masculine power possible.

In Abraham Fraunce's *Arcadian Rhetorike* too, metaphor is theorized as the product of a similitude's "contract[ing]" (sig. B1). Fraunce raises metaphor to general equivalency by praising it as the "most excellent" of tropes (ibid.). In Fraunce's theorization, metaphor is the product of obstetrical contractions occurring in the imaginary body of a form of elocution feminized by its classification as a "figure" rather than a "trope." This obstetrical scenario echoes Cicero's *De Oratore*, where metaphor is similarly theorized as "a short form of *similitudo*, contracted into one word" (*similitudinis est ad verbum unum contracta brevitas*) (bk. 3, sec. 38, line 157). The notion of the production of metaphor as a consequence of the reduction of the bodily size of a simile, which in Cicero's treatise is expressed by means of the obstetrical term "contraction," also informs Demetrius' notion of metaphor as a more "concise" simile in *On Style* (pp. 89–90) and Quintilian's assertion "[o]n the whole metaphor is a shorter form of simile" (*in totum autem metaphora brevior est similitudo eoque distat*) in the *Institutio oratoria* (bk. 8, sec. 6, lines 8–9).

The theorization of the aesthetic category of simile as a maternal body producing the general equivalent of metaphor as its issue featured in early modern rhetoric and its classical antecedents continues beyond the Renaissance. The theorization of simile as mother of metaphor is powerfully manifest, for example, in John Milner's *Rhetoric* (1736) where metaphor is theorized as a "latent simile" (p. 15). The aesthetic category of simile is theorized here in the image of a pregnant female body, in which a preferably male biological issue is latent, promised yet postponed. This theorization paronomastically and, in psychoanalytical terms, parapractically, evokes the image of the female body in its post-partum, la(c)tating configuration. The theorization of metaphor as a "latent" simile in Milner's eighteenth-century treatise on rhetoric continues the gynecologization characterizing simile's early modern theorizations by imagining simile in terms of the corporeal habitat of a privileged body during the period of gestation and with the nutrition of this privileged body during the postpartum period of la(c)tation.

Etymologically, "latency" and "lactation" are not related. "Latency" derives from the Latin *latere* (to be hidden). "Lactation" derives from the Latin *lactare* (to suckle). The dropping of the "c" from the Latin *lactare* in Romance languages (for instance, French *"lait"* and Italian *"latte"* for "milk") enables a paronomastic link resonating in early modern theorizations of metaphor as a "latent" simile. The paronomasia of latency and lactation inflects those theorizations as scenarios of generation, wherein the maternalized body of simile is first the substance in which an infant is "latent" and, post-partum, lactates to continue the infant's nourishment.

Within early modern tropology just as within its antecedents and precedents, simile is allowed into the masculinized and prioritized tropological environment of metaphor only to be displayed as its source. Other than as an analogue of a transacted female body, simile is not featured in early modern tropologies. Other than as an analogue of the transacted female body, simile is, in most cases, mentioned only in the domain of figure, feminized through its association with the seductive body of a temptress (see Chapter Two above).

Two types of exceptions to this phenomenon confirm the feminization of simile. (1) Some early modern rhetoricians prefer not to employ the distinction between trope and figure available to them in the field of memory constructed by their predecessors and practiced by their peers. Such deviations from the trope/figure taxonomy are rare in rhetorical treatises of the Renaissance, although they appear in undeniably canonical treatises such as Puttenham's *Arte of English Poesie*. In the majority of cases, those rhetoricians who discard the trope/figure binarism as a means for organizing their theories of elocution, opt for the term "figure." In this, they follow John of Salisbury's twelfth-century *Metalogicon*, where metaphors and similes are labeled *"schemata"* (p. 53) or "figure[s]" (p. 54). Another treatise which does not adopt the trope/figure distinction is Judah Messer Leon's fifteenth-century ספר נפת צופים (*The Book of the Honeycomb's Flow*), the earliest among the few Hebrew adaptations of classical rhetoric. The fourth book of this treatise is devoted to a listing of "יפויים" or "beautifications," a term habitually associated with figures. Messer Leon's "beautifications" include forms conventionally classified as "tropes" such as metaphor, metonymy, and irony, and forms habitually classified as figures such as asyndeton, apostrophe, and climax. Two

Renaissance treatises which do not resort to the trope/figure binarism are Puttenham's *Arte of English Poesie* and chapters 2 and 3 (*De Stylo*) in Charles Butler's 1633 *Oratoriae Libri Duo*.

(2) There is a second exception in early modern rhetoric to the prevalent gesture of classifying simile as a figure yet allowing it to be featured in the privileged domain of tropes as the material source of the celebrated and would-be masculinized form of metaphor. This exception occurs in treatises retaining the trope/figure binarism and the attendant classification of metaphor as a master-trope, yet resorting to one of the following gestures:

(a) The first gesture is not classifying simile as a figure or a trope, and allowing it to be mentioned in relation to metaphor but not to be classified in its own right. This gesture has an antecedent in Hermann the German's eleventh-century translation of Averroes' *Middle Commentary* on Aristotle's *Poetics*, where comparison is mentioned only as a means for expressing a trope (p. 289). In Abraham Fraunce's *Arcadian Rhetorike*, simile is mentioned only as the ground of metaphor, theorized as "a similitude contracted into one word" (sig. B1). Simile is not mentioned again by Fraunce, either among the master tropes or in the long list of figures. In Mark Beumly's 1598 *Rhetoricae*, similitude is mentioned as the material source of metaphor, theorized as *"similitudo...ad verbum unum contracta brevitas"* (a similitude contracted into one word) (p. 66), yet is absent from the list of tropes and the longer list of figures. This list includes epizeuxis, anadiplosis, climax, polysyndeton, epistrophe, anaphora, epanados, paronomasia, polyptoton, apostrophe, and prosopopeia, but not simile (p. 113). In Otho Cassman's 1600 *Rhetoricae Tropologiae*, simile is mentioned only as the "voice" making the articulation of metaphor possible (p. 125). In Charles Butler's 1629 *Rhetoricae Libri Duo*, simile is mentioned twice in relation to metaphor, in its definition as *"tropus a simili ad simile"* (a trope based on similitude) (p. 3), and as a *"brevis & occulta similitudo"* (brief and occult similitude) (sig. D), but not among the figures. In Thomas Blount's 1664 *Academie of Eloquence*, simile is mentioned only as the ground of the metaphoric forms of allegory and fable (p. 3). In Joannes de Kerhuel's 1673 *Idea Eloquentiae Rhetoricae*, similitude is again cited as the source of metaphor, theorized as a *similitudo ad unum contracta verbum* (a similitude contracted into one word) (p. 17), yet is absent from the list of tropes (metaphor, metalepsis, allegory, periphrasis, hyperbaton, and hyperbole) and from the list of figures (repetition, conversion, conduplication, traduction, synonym, and gradation [p. 23]). In the extensive taxonomy of John Prideaux's encyclopedic *Hypomenmata Logica, Rhetorica, Metaphysica, Pneumatica,*

Ethica, Politica, Oeconomia, "comparison" is cited as the enabling condition of the trope of metaphor (p. 106), yet has no place among either the "figures" (epizeuxis, anaphora, epistrophe, epanalepsis, paronomasia, and polyptoton [p. 107]), or the "schemes" (apostrophe, prosopopeia, and aporia [p. 109]).

(b) The second (rare but nonetheless telling) gesture occurs in early modern rhetorical treatises wherein the trope-figure binarism is retained, yet simile is altogether ignored. For instance, in Dudley Fenner's 1588 *Artes of Logike and Rhetorike*, simile is not mentioned at all. This second gesture may be explained away as part of a "systematization" or "simplification" of rhetoric to a few basic forms subtending all others, advocated and practiced most insistently by Ramist rhetoricians of the Renaissance (Ong, *Ramus and the Decay of Dialogue*; Joseph, pp. 35–36). What such functionalist explanations cannot account for is why, even granted the logical affiliation of simile and metaphor, it is always simile and never metaphor which gets discarded or subordinated in the interest of greater systematicity.

The two exceptions confirm simile's feminization. The first discards the trope/figure distinction in a gesture suggesting an admission of the feminization of figurative language at large and an abandonment of early modern rhetoric's attempt to repress if not foreclose the archaic maternality inscribed into the category of the primal substance of semiosis. The second manifests a desire to deny simile a room of its own. This desire to foreclose simile indexes an anxiety of the abject maternality inscribed into simile in the Aristotelian tradition.

In the two exceptions to the traditional classification of simile as a figure within an elocutionary binarism including figures and tropes, the taxonomic positioning of simile cannot be understood without reference to the maternalization of simile, read as a symptomatic intensification of the maternalization of the primal substance of semiosis. This semiotic structure, wherein simile is restricted, within a masculinized space, to an originary and procreative role but is otherwise absent or banished, reinforces the maternalization of simile.

Early modern tropology seeks to put the aesthetic category of simile in a place isomorphic with the place of the mother in symbolic economies gravitating to the Father function. This is the place of a woman removed from exchange and entrapped in the "private property" of the household where her role "remains on the side of (re)productive nature" (Irigaray, *This Sex*, pp. 185–186). Simile's function as the material/maternal source of the privileged category of metaphor within the masculinized domain of tropes makes it the rhetorical equivalent of a female body exchanged between men *en route* to its becoming a maternal vehicle of reproduction.

The aesthetic category of simile is theorized within early modern rhetoric as a maternalized female body in order to serve as an abjected Other for rhetoric's general equivalent. Yet it does not stably remain in the position of a low-Other in the would-be abjected zone of figures, to which the early modern theory of language attempts to relegate the femininity it attaches to the primal substance of semiosis. Brought into proximity with metaphor in the context of the conceptual operation deployed to enthrone metaphor as the general equivalent of elocution, simile contaminates and destabilizes this general equivalent. In a strain of early modern theorizations of the relationship of simile to metaphor, metaphor appears not as a masculinized "master trope" but as a female body "dilating" to produce simile as its abjected Other.

The aesthetic category of simile troubles and subverts the logocentric drive of early modern rhetoric on a larger scale. Simile shuttles between the classes of "trope" and "figure" early modern rhetoric seeks to polarize and to insulate from one another so as to provide itself with a stabilizing grid on the volatile substance of semiosis imagined in reference to potentially engulfing archaic maternality. Simile is the only aesthetic form to straddle the categories of trope and figure. Simile as theorized in Renaissance rhetoric is a liminal form. It offers itself as a breach in which the aesthetic categories of trope and figure can leak into one another, collapsing the hierarchical binarism they are supposed to form. This liminality of simile associates it with interstitial spaces, the spaces of subversion (Turner, p. 281) and of creative questioning (Jabès, *Unsuspected Subversion*, p. 37).

The theorization of simile in Renaissance rhetoric is a record of the failure to efface traces of the feminine within language. This failure remains, despite unstinting efforts to reverse it. The failure to foreclose the feminine persists despite the attempts of early modern rhetoricians to make good on the loss of the fantasy of an exhaustive partitioning assuring mastery over semiosis qua archaic maternality. The failure to efface the femininity of semiosis is best evident in the two obstetrical scenarios generated in theorizations of simile in Renaissance rhetoric. Simile is sometimes imagined as maternal origin. Simile is imagined as "contracting" to produce the phallicized form of metaphor. It is imagined as an origin in which metaphor is "latent," a term suggesting gestation and paronomastically connoting the post-partum la(c)tation of the maternal body. At other times, simile is imagined as the effect of a metaphor's "dilating."

Theorizations of simile in Renaissance rhetoric set in motion two obstetrical scenarios. Combined, these two obstetrical scenarios form an unsettling, apotropaic narrative in which the categories of origin and product, mother and son, inseminating and distending male organ and dilating womb ceaselessly collapse into one another. These narratives confirm Derrida's theorization of the apotropaic, wherein "phallus is reversed into...vagina" (Derrida, *Glas*, p. 47), distension becomes dilation. The dissolving of distention into dilation adumbrated by early modern theorizations of simile anticipates Montrelay's theorization of the semiotics of the sexual act. *Jouissance*, Monterlay says, is not assignable to any gender or to any partner. In the sexual act, the partners become a substance approximating primal, incestuous *jouissance* (pp. 151–152). The apotropaic narratives generated by early modern theorizations of simile index the coming into being of *jouissance*. They gesture toward a process of transference mediated by the similaic copula which does not castrate nor deplete but replenishes with an archaic femininity, with a fundamentally feminine *jouissance* which does not properly belong to any sex or gender, "of which the owner is unknown" (Montrelay, p. 152).

All attempts made within early modern rhetoric to regulate the maternality inscribed into the aesthetic category of simile by its subordination to a phallic norm inevitably deconstruct. The valorization of the illustrative simile whose structure replicates the structure of the would-be complemental heterosexual matrimonial dyad necessitates the postulation of an abjected binary or excess. This excess is similaic catachresis, a category inscribed with forms of female sexuality in excess of the phallic norm of submissive procreation. The postulation of similaic catachresis results in the inscription of these excessive forms of sexuality into the category of simile. Early modern compendia of similes attempt to further restrain illustrative similes, in which the maternalized signifier is semiotically and conceptually subordinated to a phallic signifier. Compendia of similes seek to restrict similes to a textual space of a "storehouse or treasury" isomorphic with the early modern idea of the patriarchal household as an enclosure where the "treasure" of female sexuality is guarded from the excessive temptations of the outside. Yet the most powerful libidinal trajectory driving compendia of similes is neither phallic nor heterosexual. It is devotional or masochistic and homosexual. Early modern rhetoricians attempt to theorize simile as a feminized figure nevertheless allowed into the masculinized domain of tropes so as to perform the conceptually maternal function of producing the phallicized general equivalent of metaphor. Yet this attempt generates apotropaic narratives gesturing toward a conceptually feminine *jouissance* beyond the phallus and beyond social distinctions.

The inevitable deconstructions of the partitioning of simile, of the compendia of similes, and of the theorizations of simile in relation to metaphor make it possible to suggest an answer as to why early modern theorizations of simile are only seemingly split between an eroticized theorization and a sexualized theorization. The eroticized theorization of simile is traceable to pre-Socratic concepts of symmetry and harmony. This theorization links simile with a non-phallic and transferential structure of desire often inflected as homoerotic. The sexualized theorization of simile harkens back to a post-Socratic, Aristotelian concept of female biological inferiority. This theorization links simile with female sexuality in its maternal inflection. Early modern rhetoricians attempt to bring simile as a maternalized aesthetic category generating an anxiety of the abject under phallic regulation. The deconstructions of these attempts underscore the extent to which, the disavowing theorizations of Aristotle and his early modern followers notwithstanding, the maternality associated with simile is a primarily psycho-erotic rather than biological, corporeal, and sexual category.

The maternal is the substrate of all objects of desire, those sanctioned by the phallic norm and those exceeding this norm. Because of this psycho-erotic significance of the maternal, the association of a given aesthetic category with the maternal inevitably results in the association of this category with multiple objects of desire. Any maternalized aesthetic category becomes necessarily connected with the multifarious forms of the fundamentally polymorphic libido, all of which, as contemporary psychoanalysis has argued, are veils of the primal maternal object.

Long before Freud and Lacan formulated their insight about the maternal as the psychic substrate of all future objects, this insight had been obliquely formulated in Francis Meres's treatise on similitudes, the form early modern rhetoricians ubiquitously transcode with the maternal. His compendium, Meres states in his dedication, proffers "the naked Truth arrayed in Sentences fitting the tast [sic] of Phylosophers; inuested in Similitudes loved of Oratours" (sig. A3). Similitudes as Meres theorizes them are in-vestments, garments. Similitudes are sartorial objects, substitutes for the lost placenta, transcoded by early modern rhetoricians with the category of figure in terms of which similitude is commonly classified in Renaissance rhetoric. These sartorial objects, Meres implies, veil a philosophical "Truth." The designation of this "Truth" as "naked" symptomatically betrays its connection with the primal incestuous object, the mother, who must remain veiled because direct confrontation with it might shatter the boundaries of subjectivity (see Chapter Two above).

The particle "like," a common signifier of the similaic copula, William Walker writes in the *Treatise of English Particles*, is "sometimes...put to signifie after the guise, garbe...etc." (p. 180). In Walker's treatise too, the similaic has to do with the sartorial. Walker transcodes the similaic copula with sartorial veils generated as substitutes for the primal envelope of the maternal body. The psychic function of such veils is conceptually isomorphic with the function of objects of desire qua substitutes for the maternal as the fundamental symbolic substrate of desire. This substrate of desire constitutively remains in excess of phallic efforts to regulate and circumscribe it.

In early modern poetics, in the texts of Shakespeare, Spenser, Fulwell, Lanyer, and Donne, simile is often transcoded with the desire of the like, and primarily with the desire of the like in the form of homoeroticism. These are forms of desire in excess of the phallic norm of reproduction-oriented matrimonial heterosexuality resting on the fantasy of "Gods Arithmeticke," of the sexual relation of male and female as a consum(mat)ion and a perfect sum. The forms of desire aligned with simile in early modern literary texts are oriented primarily toward pleasure rather than duty to the Law of the Father. This transcoding of simile with excessive, pleasure-oriented forms of the desire of the like is not at all conceptually at odds with the ubiquitous transcoding of simile with the maternal in the early modern echoes of Aristotle's formative distinction between metaphor and simile. Instead, the transcoding, in early modern poetics, of the similaic with male and female homoeroticism is a record of the constitutive excessiveness of the category of the maternal with which simile is so commonly transcoded.

This constitutive excessiveness of the maternal, and thus of the aesthetic category of simile with which the maternal is associated, in part accounts for the duplicitous inscription of simile in early modern language theory as the substrate of excessive forms of sexuality and of a transferential structure of desire. In early modern language theory, as manifest in treatises on grammar, logic, and rhetoric, simile is associated with particular homoerotic objects of desire and with a particular transferential and approximatory rather than solipsistic and possessive structure of desire to which the object's gender is irrelevant. In early modern language theory, simile is imbricated with the category of the symmetrical, with an approximatory being-with constitutively erotic because it makes the issue of consummation as an expression of the delusion of intersubjective Oneness irrelevant. The approximatory being-with associated with simile in early modern language theory exceeds the solipsistic, de-subjectifying structure of phallic desire. Similaic desire is in excess of the phallus in its deployment as repressive bar rather than nurturing omphalos. So are the homoerotic objects of desire associated with simile in early modern poetics, in early modern rhetorical theorizations of similaic catachresis, and in early modern compendia of similes. Similaic desire respects the subjectivity and separateness of the other. It forgoes possessiveness, the psychic structure inscribed in early modern language theory into the aesthetic category of metaphor, rhetoric's phallic general equivalent. Similaic desire involves a foregoing of the phallic and ontological category of the general equivalent. It is predicated on the revocation of phallic desire qua denial of the other.

Early modern theorizations of the aesthetic category of simile are only seemingly split among their inscriptions as maternal, as homoerotic, and to a lesser degree, as incestuous and adulterous, and as a structure of non-possessive, approximatory, and transferential desire. All of these categories of sexuality and eroticism are conceptually linked by their excessiveness of the phallus in its repressive deployment as a despotic, prohibitive signifier seeking to enforce a norm of reproduction-oriented heterosexuality based on an illusion of consum(mat)ional complementarity between man and woman.

Early modern rhetoricians attempt to allay the anxiety of loss of boundaries induced by their association of the primal substance of semiosis with the oceanic archaic mother by partitioning this substance into tropes and figures. They attempt to further allay the anxiety of the oceanic by enthroning metaphor as a master trope, a phallic general equivalent subtended by the category of Being, and the structure of solipsistic, desubjectifying phallic desire abusively indifferent to the constitutive separateness of the other. They postulate a debased binary of the phallic general equivalent. This is the category of simile, a category associated with the maternal, with polymorphic forms of sexuality including those barred by the phallus, and with a non-phallic, transferential, and approximatory structure of desire. These attempts to allay the anxiety of archaic maternality rest on the cathexis of the definite and ontological. Like all psycho-conceptual enterprises resting on the verb "to be," the early modern rhetoricians' attempt to allay anxiety through a hyper-cathexis of the definite is, in Lacan's terms, "highly risky" (*Seminar XX*, p. 31).

In the case of early modern aesthetics of language, the corollary of the risk of the cathexis of the definite and ontological is the inevitable postulation of an aesthetics of simile. This is a non-phallic, omphalic aesthetics. Similaic aesthetics is inscribed with eroticism of a particular structure. This eroticism forgoes ontology, forgoes the fantasy of possessive consummation and affirms a transferential and approximatory form of being with. This form of being with, what I call similaic desire, is symmetrical and harmonious because it safeguards separateness at the same time it reaches out to the other.

Early modern theorists of language seek to postulate a phallic symbolic economy of elocution from which the oceanic, inundating nature ascribed to the primal substance of semiosis would be barred. Yet the postulation of a symbolic economy of rhetoric is simultaneously the record of a yearning toward the oceanic. This yearning is evident in the failure of the attempts to erect a symbolic economy of elocution and in the corollary emergence of an aesthetics of simile.

Within the aesthetics of simile, the units of signification into which the primal substance of semiosis is partitioned function as what Montrelay calls fragments of primal *jouissance* put into play within language, within the symbolic (p. 39). These are fragments of archaic *jouissance* whose se-paration is the condition of their re-paration, re-pairing and, as this study has shown, com-pairing by means of the non-fusional copula/cut of simile. These com-pared fragments proffer a pleasurable approximation within language and the symbolic to the archaic *jouissance* identified with the m(O)ther as primal object. Simile, as conceptualized in early modern language theory and poetics, is the aesthetic form wherein the reparational re-pairing of fragments of *jouissance* is most intense. Within the omphalic aesthetics of simile, linguistic fragments of *jouissance* are compared and com-paired by means of a copula bespeaking not the phallic desire inscribed into the copula of metaphor but a non-phallic, omphalic, conceptually feminine eroticism defying and exceeding constraints. The risky aesthetics of Renaissance rhetoric offers simile as a form capable of what Montrelay would suggest is the task of all signification. This task is the engendering of pleasure, bringing language to its point of "maximum incandescence" (p. 80) where it approximates a constitutively feminine orgasmic pleasure not properly assignable to any gender or sexual orientation (ibid., p. 81).

The erotic and omphalic aesthetics of simile postulated in early modern rhetoric saturates early modern poetics, which now require to be read in its light. This aesthetics has significant consequences for psychoanalytical theory too. The erotic aesthetics of simile is declared in the title of Shakespeare's *As You Like It*. This title is a potentially endless chain of objects whose genders and orientations are indefinite ("you," "it") and similaic copulas ("as," "like"). This title simultaneously references a non-regulated pleasure beyond distinctions of gender and sexual orientation, a pleasure consequent upon multiple forms of li(n)king and libidinal liking. Desire, Shakespeare teaches us, as do early modern rhetoricians such as Richard Sherry, Thomas Wilson, George Puttenham, Francis Meres, and Henry Peacham, does not, as Lacan, writing in ignorance of the early modern theorizations of language and desire would have it, manifest a metonymic structure. Desire, early modern rhetoricians and authors teach us, deploys itself in the domain of the open-ended, of approximation, of yearning. Desire deploys itself in the domain of the veil, not of what is hidden behind it. Desire deploys itself as what might come to be. With(in) the similaic.

WORKS CITED

Primary Texts

A

Aickin, Joseph. *The English Grammar: Or, The English Tongue Reduced to Grammatical Rules*. 1693. Menston: Scolar Press, 1967.

Alain de Lille. *De planctu naturae*. In J. P. Migne, ed. *Patrologia Latina*. Vol. 210.

Alberic of Montecassino. *Flores Rhetorici*. Montecassino: Miscellanea Cassinese, 1938.

Alcuin. *The Rhetoric of Alcuin and Charlemagne*. Trans. Wilbur Samuel Howell. Princeton: Princeton University Press, 1941.

Alsted, Joannes. *Rhetorica*. Köln, 1616.

Anon. *La Rhétorique des putains*. Rome, 1794.

Anon. *Rhetoricae Synopsis*. Genève: Samuel de Tournes, 1693.

Anon. *The English Guide to the Latin Tongue*. London: R. Royston, 1675.

Anon. *The Whore's Rhetorick*. 1683. London: Holland Press, 1960.

Anon. *Words Made Visible: or Grammar and Rhetorick Accommodated to the Lives and Manners of Men*. London, 1679.

Apollodorus. *The Library of Greek Mythology*. Trans. Robin Hard. Oxford: Oxford University Press, 1997.

Aquinas, Thomas. *Summa Theologiae*. Trans. Fathers of the English Dominican Province. New York: Benzinger, 1947.

Aristotle. *The Basic Works of Aristotle*. Ed. Richard McKeon. New York: Random House, 1941.

——. *Treatise on Rhetoric*. Trans. Theodore Buckley. New York: Prometheus Books, 1995.

Ascham, Roger. *The Scholemaster*. 1570. Menston: Scolar Press, 1967.

Aristophanes. *Clouds, Wasps, Peace*. Ed. Jeffery Henderson. Cambridge Mass.: Harvard University Press, 1998.

B

Bacon, Francis. *An Essay on Gardens*. Birmingham: School of Printing, 1930.

Barnfield, Richard. *The affectionate shepheard. Containing the complaint of Daphnis for the loue of Ganymede*. London: Iohn Danter for T. G. [Thomas Gubbin], 1594.

Bersmann, George. *Erotemata rhetorica*. Leipzig, 1601.

Beumley, Mark. *Rhetoricae*. London: Johan Wolf, 1598.

Blount, Thomas. *Glossographia: or a dictionary, interpreting all such hard words, whether Hebrew, Greek, Latin...as are now used in our refined English tongue*. London: Tho. Newcomb, 1656.

———. *The Academie of Eloquence, Containing a Compleat English Rhetorique, Exemplified with Common-Places and Formes*. 1654. Gainseville, FL: Scholars' Facsimiles and Reprints, 1971.

Blunderville, Thomas. *The Art of Logike*. 1599. New York: De Capo Press, 1969.

Bodenham, John. *Belvedere or The Garden of the Muses*. 1600. London: Spenser Society, 1875.

Breton, Nicholas. *Similies divine and morall*. London, 1647.

———. *The Wil of Wit, Wits Will, or Wils Wit, chuse you whether*. London: Thomas Creede, 1599.

Bruno, Giordano. *The Expulsion of the Triumphant Beast*. 1584. Trans. Arthur D. Imerti. Lincoln: University of Nebraska Press, 1992.

Bullokar, John. *An English Expositor: Teaching the Interpretation of the Hardest Words Vsed in Our Language*. 1661. Menston: Scolar Press, 1967.

Busby, Richard. *A Short Institution of Grammar*. 1647. Menston: Scolar Press, 1972.

Butler, Charles. *Rhetoricae Libri Duo*. London: John Haviland, 1629.

C

Callimachus, Phillip. *Rhetorica*. ca. 1470. Warsaw, 1950.

Campbell, David A., ed. *Greek Lyric III: Stesichorus, Ibycus, Simonides, and Others*. Cambridge, Mass.: Harvard University Press, 1991.

Camerarius, Joachimus. *Elementa rhetoricae*. Basel, 1540.

Campion, Thomas. *The Complete Works*. London: Dutton, 1924.

Carbo, Ludovico. *De caussis eloquentiae*. Venice, 1593.

Cassman, Otho. *Rhetoricae tropologiae*. Frankfurt, 1600.

Caussin, Nicolas. *De Eloquentia Sacra et Humana*. Paris, 1630.

Cavalcanti, Bartolomeo. *La Rhetorica*. Ferrara: Gabriel Giolito, 1559.
Cawdray, Robert. *A Treasvrie or Storehovse of Similies*. 1600. Menston: Scolar Press, 1969.
Chapman, George. *Selected Poems*. Ed. Eirian Wain. Manchester: Fyfield Press, 1978.
Cicero, Marcus Tullius. *De Divinitate*. Ed. Remo Giomini. Leipzig: Teubner Verlagsgesellschaft, 1975.
———. *De finibus bonhorum et malorum*. Trans. H. Rackham. Cambridge, Mass.: Harvard University Press, 1914.
———. *De inventione*. Trans. H. M. Hubel. Cambridge, Mass.: Harvard University Press, 1949.
———. *De oratore*. Trans. H. Caplan. Cambridge, Mass.: Harvard University Press, 1942.
[Cicero] *Rhetorica ad Herenium*. Trans. Harry Caplan. Cambridge, Mass.: Harvard University Press, 1989.
Coles, Elisha. *Syncrisis*. 1677. Menston: Scolar Press, 1971.
Constable, Henry. *Diana*. 1594. Menston: Scolar Press, 1973.
Cooper, Christopher. *Grammatica Linguae Anglicanae*. 1685. Menston: Scolar Press, 1968.

D

Daniel, Samuel. *Poems and a Defense of Rhyme*. 1599. Chicago and London: University of Chicago Press, 1965.
Day, Angel. *The English Secretoire*. 1586. Menston: Scolar Press, 1967.
———. *Daphnis and Chloe [a translation by A. Day from the French version of Jacques Amyot of the Greek of Longus]. Excellently describing the weight of affection, the simplicitie of loue, the purport of honest meaning, the resolution of men, and the disposition of Fate, finished in a Pastorall, and interlaced with the praises of a most peerlesse Princesse...and therefore termed by the name of the Shepheards Holidaie*. London: Robert Waldegrave, 1587.
De Colonia, Dominico. *De arte rhetorica*. Posnan, 1705.
De Courcelles, Pierre. *La rhétorique*. Paris: Guillaume le Noir, 1557.
De Kerhuel, Joanne. *Idea eloquentiae rhetoricae*. London: S. L. Lownden, 1673.
De Ledesma, Gonzalo. *Censura de la Elocuencia*. 1648. Madrid: El Crotalon, 1985.
Demetrius. *On Style*. Trans. W. Rhys Roberts. London: Dent, 1929.
Demosthenes. *Funeral Speech, Erotic Essay, Exordia, and Letters*. Trans.

Norman W. De Witt and Norman J. De Witt. Cambridge, Mass.: Harvard University Press, 1949.

Dickenson, John. *Prose and Verse by John Dickenson. I. The Shepheardes complaint. II. Arisbas, Euphues amidst his slumbers: or Cupid's Iourney to Hell, etc. 1594. III. Greene in conceipt. New raised from his graue to write the tragique history of Valeria of London, 1598.* Ed. Rev. Alexander B. Grosart. Manchester: Charles E. Simms, 1870.

Dionysius of Halicarnassus. *The Critical Essays.* Trans. R. Usher. Cambridge, Mass.: Harvard University Press, 1974.

Donne, John. *Complete English Poems.* Ed. C. A. Patrides. London: Dent, 1994.

Drayton, Michael. *Idea. The Shepheards Garland, fashioned in nine eglogs.* London: T. Woodcocke, 1593.

———. *Ideas Mirrovr: Amovrs in Quatorzains.* London: T. Woodcoke, 1594.

Du Vair, Guillaume. *Traitté de l'Eloquence Françoise. Oeuvres.* 1641. Geneve: Slatkine Reprints, 1970.

E

Edmonds, John Maxwell, ed. *Lyra Graeca: Being the Remains of all the Greek Lyric Poets from Eumelus to Timotheus Excepting Pindar.* 3 Vols. London: Loeb Classical Library, 1922–1927.

———. *The Greek Bucolic Poets.* London: William Heinemann, 1919.

Epicurus. *The Essential Epicurus. Letters, Principal Doctrines, Vatican Sayings, and Fragments.* Ed. Eugene Michael O'Connor. New York: Prometheas Books, 1993.

Erasmus, Desiderius. *The Collected Works of Erasmus.* Ed. Craig R. Thompson. London and Toronto: University of Toronto Press, 1978.

———. *Parabolae siue similia.* London: Sebastianus Gryphius, 1528.

Erondelle, Pierre. *The French Garden.* 1533. Menston: Scolar Press, 1969.

Euripides. *Electra.* Tras. D. W. Lucas. London: Cohen & West, 1951.

———. *The Bacchae and other Plays.* Trans. Phillip Vellacott. Harmondsworth: Penguin, 1974.

F

Farnaby, Thomas. *Index Rhetoricus.* 1625. Menston: Scolar Press, 1970.

Fenelon, Francis. *Dialogues on Eloquence.* 1679. Trans. Wilbur Samuel Howell. Princeton: Princeton University Press, 1951.

Fenner, Dudley. *The Artes of Logike and Rhetorike.* Middleburgh: Richard Schilders, 1588.

Fletcher, Anthonie. *Certaine Very Proper and Most Profitable Similies*. London: John Jackson, 1595.

Florio, John. *Qveen Anna's New World of Words*. 1621. Menston: Scolar Press, 1968.

Fortunaziano, Consulto. *Ars rhetorica*. ca. 1480. Ed. Lucia Calboli Montefusco. Bologna: Patron Editore, 1979.

Fraunce, Abraham. *The Arcadian Rhetorike*. 1588. Menston: Scolar Press, 1969.

———. *The Lawiers Logike*. 1588. Menston: Scolar Press, 1969.

———. *The Sheapheardes Logike*. 1585. Menston: Scolar Press, 1969.

Fulwell, Ulpian. *A pleasant Enterlude, intituled, Like will to Like*. London: E. Allde, 1587.

G

Gascoigne, George. *Certayne Notes & Instructions Concerning the Making of Verse or Ryme in English*. 1575. London: Alex, Murray, and Son, 1868.

Geoffrey of Vinsauf. *The New Poetics*. *Three Medieval Rhetorical Arts*. Ed. James J. Murphy. Berkeley: University of California Press, 1971.

Greene, Robert. *Ciceronis Amor. Tullies Love. Wherein is discoursed the prime of Ciceroes youth, setting out in lively portratures how young Gentlemen that aime at honour should levell the end of their affections, etc.* London: R. Robinson, for J. Busbie, 1597.

———.*Menaphon: Camillaes alarum to slumbring Eupheus* [sic] *in his melancholy cell at Silexedra*. London: Valentine Simmes for Nicholas Ling, 1589.

———. *Orpharion. Wherein is discovered a musical concorde of pleasant histories...With divers Tragicall and Comicall Histories presented by Orpheus and Arion*. London: E. White, 1599.

Guntherus, Peter. *De arte rhetorica libri duo*. Metz: Samuel Emmeliz, 1568.

H

Hawes, Stephen. *The History of Grand Amoure and La Belle Ducell, Called the Pastime of Pleasure*. London, 1555.

Hermann the German. "Translation of Averroes' 'Middle Commentary' on Aristotle's *Poetics*." In *Medieval Literary Theory and Criticism, ca. 1100 – ca. 1375*. Eds. A.J. Minnis and A.B. Scott. Cambridge: Wolfeboro, 1987, pp. 289–307.

Hobbes, Thomas. *The Art of Rhetoric, With a Discourse on the Laws of England*.

London: William Crooke, 1681.

Hoskyns, John. *Directions for Speech and Style.* 1641. Princeton: Princeton University Press, 1937.

I

Iamblichus. *On the Pythagorean Life.* Trans. Gillian Clark. Liverpool: Liverpool University Press, 1989.

Izelgrinus, Jacobus. *Rethorica Nova. ca.* 1452. Trans. Mary Frances Laughlin. Washington: The Catholic University of America Press, 1947.

J

James I. *Basilicon Doron.* Ed. James Craigie. Edinburgh and London: William Blackwood, 1944.

John of Salisbury. *Metalogicon.* Trans. Daniel D. McGarry. Berkeley: University of California Press, 1955.

Jonson, Ben. *The English Grammar.* 1640. Menston: Scolar Press, 1972.

Jorden, Edward. *A briefe discourse of a disease called the Suffocation of the Mother.* 1603. In Michael MacDonald, ed. *Witchcraft and Hysteria in Elizabethan London.* London: Routledge, 1991.

Julian of Toledo. *De vitiis et figuris.* Ed. W.M. Lindsay. Oxford: Oxford University Press, 1922.

L

Lamy, Bernard. *The Art of Speaking, Written in French by Messieurs du Port Royal and Rendered into English.* London: W. Godbid, 1676.

Lanyer, Aemilia. *The Poems of Aemilia Lanyer.* Ed. Susanne Woods. Oxford: Oxford University Press, 1993.

Lever, Ralph. *The Arte of Reason, Rightly Termed Witcraft.* 1573. Menston: Scolar Press, 1972.

Ling, Nicholas. *Politeuphuia. Wits Commonwealth, A Treasury of Admonitions, Similies, & Sentences.* London: James Roberts for N. Ling, 1597.

Lodge, Thomas. *An Alarvm Against Vsurers.* London, 1584.

———. *Rosalynd: Euphues Golden Legacie. Found after his death in his Cell at Silexedra.* London: Ieffes for T. G. and Iohn Busbie, 1592.

Longinus. *On the Sublime.* Trans. W. Hamilton Fyfe. London, Dent, 1929.

Luther. "Sermon on Trade and Usury." 1524. Trans. Charles M. Jacobs. *Luther's Work.* Ed. Walther I. Brandt. Philadelphia: Muhlenberg Press, 1962, pp. 245–310.

Lycosthenis, Conrad. *Similivm Loci Commvnes*. Genève 1602.
Lyly, John. *Euphues: The Anatomy of Wit*. London: Thomas East for Gabriel Cawood, 1587.

M

Mascher, Girolamo. *Il fiore della retorica*. Venice, 1560.
Matthew of Vendôme. *Ars versificatoria*. Trans. Roger P. Parr. Milwaukee: Marquette University Press, 1981.
Messer Leon, Judah. *The Book of the Honeycomb's Flow [Sepher Nopheth Suphim]*. 1475. Trans. Isaac Rabinovitz. Ithaca, NY: Cornell University Press, 1983.
Meres, Francis. *Gods Arithmeticke*. London: R. Johnes, 1597.
———. *Palladis Tamia. Wits Treasury, being the second part of Wits Commonwealth*. London: Cuthbert Burbie, 1598.
———. *Witts Academy; a Treasurie of Goulden Sentences, Similies, and Examples*. 1595. London: R. Royston, 1636.
———. *Wits Commonwealth: A Treasurie of Diuine, morall, and Phylosophical similies*. 1597. London: W. Stansby, 1634.
Miege, Guy. *The English Grammar; Or, The Grounds and Genius of the English Tongue*. 1688. Menston: Scolar Press, 1969.
Migne, Jacques Paul. *Patrologia Latina*. 218 Vols. Vol. 210. Paris: 1857–1912.
Milner, John. *Rhetoric*. London: J. Gray, 1736.
Milton, John. *The Complete English Poems of John Milton*. New York: New York University Press, 1963.
Montaigne, Michel de. *The Essays of Montaigne; John Florio's Translation*. New York: Modern Library, 1933.
Mulcaster, Richard. *The First Part of the Elementarie VVhich Entreateth Chefelie of the Right Writing of Our English Tung*. 1582. Menston: Scolar Press, 1970.
Munday, Anthony. *A Banquet of Daintie Conceits. Furnished with verie delicate and choyse Inuentions*. London: J. C. for Edwarde White, 1588.

N

Newberry, John. *Rhetoric Made Familiar and Easy to Young Gentlemen and Ladies*. London, 1748.
Newton, John. *An Introduction to the Art of Rhetoric*. London, 1671.
Nicomachus. *The Manual of Harmonics of Nicomachus the Pythagorean*. Trans. Flora R. Levin. Grand Rapids, Mich.: Phanes Press, 1991.

O

Ovid. *The Metamorphoses*. Trans. Horace Gregory. New York: New American Library, 1958.

P

Palavicino, Ferrante. *La Retorica delle puttane*. Rome, 1642.

Patrizi, Franceso. *Della retorica dieci dialogi*. Venice: Francesio Senese, 1562.

Peacham, Henry. *The Garden of Eloquence*. London: H. Iackson, 1577.

———. *The Worth of a Penny; or a Caution to Keep Money*. London: Skeble, 1687.

Phillips, Edward. *The Mysteries of Love and Eloquence*. 1658. Menston: Scolar Press, 1972.

Pindar. *The Odes of Pindar*. Trans. C. M. Bowra. Harmondsworth: Penguin, 1969.

Plato. *The Dialogues of Plato*. Trans. R.E. Allen. New Haven, CT: Yale University Press, 1996.

Poole, Joshua. *Practical Rhetorick*. 1663. Menston: Scolar Press, 1972.

———. *The English Accidence*. 1646. Menston: Scolar Press, 1967.

———. *The English Parnassus*. 1657. Menston: Scolar Press, 1972.

Price, Owen. *The Vocal Organ, or a new art of teaching the English Orthographie, by observing the instruments of pronunciation*. Oxford: W. Hall for A. Curteyne, 1665.

Prideaux, John. *Erotemata logica, rhetorica, metaphysica, pneumatica, ethica, politica, oeconomiae*. London: Lichfield, 1682.

Puttenham, George. *The Arte of English Poesie*. 1589. Menston: Scolar Press, 1968.

Q

Quintilian. *Institutio oratoria*. 4 Vols. Trans. Butler. London: William Heinemann, 1963.

R

Rainolde, Richard. *The foundacion of rhetorike*. 1563. Menston: Scolar Press, 1972.

Raymond, William. *Orator's Manual*. London, 1879.

Rich, Barnaby. *My Ladies Looking Glasse. Wherein may be discerned a wise man from a foole, a good woman from a bad, etc.* London: T. Adams, 1616.

R[obinson], R[ichard]. *An English Grammar: Or, A Plain Exposition of Lillies Grammar in English*.1641. Menston: Scolar Press, 1972.

S

Shakespeare, William. *A Pleasant Conceited Historie, Called the Taming of a Shrew*. Lanham, MD: Barnes and Noble, 1992.

———. *The Riverside Shakespeare*. Boston: Houghton Mifflin, 1974.

Shelton, Thomas. *A Centurie of Similies*. London: J. Dawson, 1640.

Sherry, Richard. *A Treatise of Schemes and Tropes*. 1550. London: Iohn Day, 1550.

———. *A Treatise of the Figures of Grammer and Rhetorike*. London: R. Tottil, 1555.

Sidney, Sir Phillip. *A Critical Edition of the Major Works*. Ed. Katherine Duncan-Jones. Oxford: Oxford University Press, 1981.

Smellie. W. *A Treatise on the Theory and Practice of Midwifery*. London: W. Wilson, 1752.

Soario, Cypriano. *De arte rhetorica*. Paris: Nicolas du Forze, 1612.

Smith, John. *The Mysterie of Rhetorique Unvail'd*. London, 1657.

Smith, William. *Chloris, or the Complaint of the passionate despised Shepheard*. London: Edm. Bollifant, 1596.

Sophocles. *The Theban Plays* [*King Oedipus, Oedipus at Colonus, Antigone*]. Trans. E. F. Watling. Harmondsworth: Penguin, 1947.

Spenser, Edmund. *The Poetical Works of Edmund Spenser*. Oxford: Oxford University Press, 1947.

Spenser, John. *Things Old and New: A Storehovse of Similies*. London: W. Wilson, 1658.

Stirling, John. *A System of Rhetoric*. 1733. Menston: Scolar Press, 1968.

Stubbes, Phillip. *The Anatomie of Abuses*. London: Richard Iones, 1584.

Sturmius, John. *A Ritch Storehouse or Treasurie for Nobilitye and Gentlemen*. London: Henrie Denham, 1570.

T

Tacitus. *Dialogue on Orators*. *Classical Literary Criticism*. Ed. D. A. Russell and M. Winterbottom. Oxford: Oxford University Press, 1972, pp. 111–143.

Traversagni, Lorenzo Guglielmo. *Margarita Eloquentiae Castigatae*. ca. 1440. Savona: Sabatelli, 1978.

Turner, Daniel. *Abstract of English Grammar and Rhetoric*. Dublin: S. Powell, 1741.

V

Vaughan, William. *The Golden Grove*. London: Simon Stafford, 1600.
Vérard, Antoin. *Le Jardin de plaisance et fleur de Rhétorique*. Paris, 1503.
Vida, Marco Girolamo. *De arte poetica*. ca. 1517. Trans. Ralph G. Williams. New York: Columbia University Press, 1976.
Vossius, Gerard. *Rhetorices contractae*. London: John Mairee, 1640.

W

Walker, Obadiah. *Some Instructions Concerning the Art of Oratory*. 1659. Oxford: L. Lichfield, 1892.
Walker, William. *A Treatise of English Particles*. 1655. Menston: Scolar Press, 1970.
Ward, John. *A System of Oratory*. London: Conhill, 1758.
Webbe, William. *A discourse of English poetrie. Together, with the authors iudgment, touching the reformation of our English verse*. London: Iohn Charlewood for Robert Walley, 1586.
Wharton, Jeremiah. *The English Grammar: Or, The Institution of Letters, Syllables, and Words in the English Tongue*. 1654. Menston: Scolar Press, 1970.
Williams, Roger. *A Key into the Language of America: Or, an Help to the Language of the Natives in the Part of America, Called New England*. 1643. Menston: Scolar Press, 1971.
Willis, John. *Mnemonica; or, the art of memory, drained out of the pure fountains of art and nature*. London: Leonard Sowersby, 1661.
———. *The Art of Memory, so far forth as it dependeth vpon Places and Ideas, written first in Latine...and now published in English*. London: W. Iones, 1621.
Willis, Thomas. *Proteus Vinctus*. 1655. Menston: Scolar Press, 1972.
Wilson, Thomas. *A Discourse upon Usury*. 1572. New York: Harcourt, Brace, 1925.
———. *The Arte of Rhetorique*. 1560. University Park, PA: Pennsylvania State University Press, 1993.

Secondary Texts

A

Abraham, Nicolas, and Maria Torok. *The Shell and the Kernel: Renewals of Psychoanalysis*. Trans. Nicholas Rand. Chicago: University of Chicago Press, 1994.

———. *The Wolf-Man's Magic Word: A Cryptonymy*. Trans. Nicholas Rand. Minneapolis: University of Minnesota Press, 1986.

Adorno, Theodor. *Notes to Literature*. 2 Vols. Vol. 1. Trans. Shierry Wever Nicholsen. New York: Columbia University Press, 1991.

Agamben, Giorgio. *Language and Death: The Place of Negativity*. Trans. Karen E. Pinkus and Michael Hardt. Minneapolis: University of Minnesota Press, 1991.

———. *Stanzas: Word and Phantasm in Western Culture*. Trans. Ronald L. Martinez. Minneapolis: University of Minnesota Press, 1993.

———. *The Idea of Prose*. Trans. Michael Sullivan and Sam Whitsitt. Albany, NY: SUNY Press, 1995.

Agnew, Jean-Christophe. *Worlds Apart: The Market and the Theatre in Anglo-American Thought, 1550–1750*. Cambridge: Cambridge University Press, 1986.

Appadurai, Arjun. *The Social Life of Things: Commodities in Cultural Perspective*. Cambridge: Cambridge University Press, 1986.

Apter, Emily. *Feminizing the Fetish: Psychoanalysis and Narrative Obsession in Turn-of-the-Century France*. Ithaca, NY: Cornell University Press, 1991.

Attridge, Derek. *Peculiar Language: Literature as Difference from the Renaissance to James Joyce*. London: Methuen, 1988.

B

Babcock, Barbara, ed. *The Reversible World: Symbolic Inversion in Art and Society*. Ithaca, NY: Cornell University Press, 1978.

Bachelard, Gaston. *L'eau et les rêves: Essai sur l'imagination de la matière*. Paris: José Corti, 1985.

Bakhtin, Mikhail. *Rabelais and his World*. Trans. Hélène Iswolski. Bloomington: Indiana University Press, 1984.

Barthes, Roland. *A Lover's Discourse: Fragments*. Trans. Richard Howard. New York: Hill and Wang, 1978.

———. *The Fashion System*. Trans. Mattew Ward and Richard Howard. Berkeley: University of California Press, 1983.

———. *Mythologies*. Trans. Annette Lavers. New York: Hill and Wang, 1972.

———. "The Old Rhetoric: An *aide–mémoire*." *The Semiotic Challenge*. Trans. Richard Howard. New York: Hill and Wang, 1988, pp. 5–85.

———. *The Pleasure of the Text*. Trans. Richard Miller. New York: Hill and Wang, 1975.

Bataille, Georges. *Erotism: Death and Sensuality*. Trans. Mary Dalwood. San Francisco: City Lights Books, 1986.

———. *The Accursed Share*. 3 Vols. Trans. Robert Hurley. New York: Zone Books, 1991.

———. *The Impossible*. Trans. Robert Hurley. San Francisco: City Lights Books, 1991.

———. *Visions of Excess: Selected Writings 1927–1939*. Trans. Allan Stoekl et al. Minneapolis: University of Minnesota Press, 1993, pp. 10–15.

Baudrillard, Jean. *For a Critique of the Political Economy of the Sign*. Trans. Charles Levin. St. Louis: Telos Press, 1981.

———. *Seduction*. Trans. Brian Singer. New York: St. Martin's Press, 1990.

Benjamin, Walter."The Task of the Translator." *Illuminations*. New York: Shocken, 1969, pp. 69–82.

Brauner, Sigrid. *Fearless Wives and Frightened Shrews: The Construction of the Witch in Early Modern Germany*. Amherst, Mass.: University of Massachusetts Press, 1995.

Brody, Miriam. *Manly Writing: Gender, Rhetoric, and the Rise of Composition*. Carbondale, IL: Southern Illinois University Press, 1993.

Bronfen, Elizabeth. *Over Her Dead Body: Death, Femininity, and the Aesthetic*. Manchester: Manchester University Press, 1992.

Brooks, Peter. *Body Work: Objects of Desire in Modern Narrative*. Cambridge, Mass.: Harvard University Press, 1993.

C

Cameron, Alister. *The Pythagorean Background of the Theory of Recollection*. Menasha, Win.: George Banta Publishing Co., 1938.

Campbell, Mary. *The Witness and the Other World: Exotic European Travel Writing 400–1600*. Ithaca, NY: Cornell University Press, 1988.

Carruthers, Mary. *The Book of Memory: A Study of Memory in Medieval Culture*. Cambridge: Cambridge University Press, 1990.

Caskey, L. D. and J. D. Beazley. *Caskey-Beazley Catalog of Attic Vase Paintings in the Museum of Fine Arts*. Boston: Museum of Fine Arts, 1991.

Cave, Terence. "Copia and Cornucopia." *French Renaissance Studies 1540–1570: Humanism and the Encyclopedia*. Ed. Peter Sharratt. Edinburgh: Edinburgh University Press, 1976, pp. 52–69.

———. *The Cornucopian Text: Problems of Writing in the French Renaissance*. Oxford: Clarendon Press, 1979.

Chabani Maganyi, N. "Making Strange: Race, Science, and Ethnographic Discourse." *Europe and its Others*. Ed. Francis Barker. Colchester: University of Essex Press, 1985, pp. 152–169.

Cheyfitz, Eric. *The Poetics of Imperialism: Translation and Colonization from The Tempest to Tarzan*. Oxford: Oxford University Press, 1990.

Child-Griffin, Clarence. *John Lyly and Euphuism*. Erlangen & Leipzig: Deichertsche Verlagsbuchh. Nachf. (Georg Bohme), 1894.

Cixous, Hélène. "Castration or Decapitation?" *Signs* 7:1 (1981), pp. 41–55.

———. and Catherine Clément. *The Newly Born Woman*. Trans. Betsy Wing. Minneapolis: University of Minnesota Press, 1986.

Conté, Claude. *Le réel et le sexuel: De Freud à Lacan*. Paris: Point Hors Ligne, 1992.

Copjec, Joan. *Read My Desire: Lacan Against the Historicists*. Cambridge, Mass.: MIT Press, 1994.

Correll, Barbara. "Symbolic Economies and Zero-Sum Erotics: Donne's 'Sapho to Philaenis.'" *English Literary History*, 62 (1995), pp. 487–507.

Cowell, Andrew. "The Dye of Desire: The Colors of Rhetoric in the Middle Ages." *Exemplaria*,11:1 (1999), pp. 115–140.

Curtman, Wilhelm Jacob Georg. *Simonides et Pythagoras, artis mnemonicae inventores*. Gissen, 1827.

D

Dean-Jones, Lesley. *Women's Bodies in Classical Greek Science*. Oxford: Clarendon, 1994.

De Beauvoir Simon. *The Second Sex*. Trans. H. M. Parshley. New York: Knopf, 1952.

Deleuze, Gilles. *Coldness and Cruelty*. Trans. Jean McNeil. New York: Zone Books, 1991.

———. *The Fold: Leibniz and the Baroque*. Trans. Tom Conley. Minneapolis: University of Minnesota Press, 1993.

Delrieu, Alain. *Lévi–Strauss lecteur de Freud*. Paris: Point Hors Ligne, 1993.

De Man, Paul. *Aesthetic Ideology*. Minneapolis: University of Minnesota Press, 1996.

Derrida, Jacques. *Aporias*. Trans. Thomas Dutoit. Stanford: Stanford University Press, 1993.

———. *Archive Fever: A Freudian Impression*. Trans. Eric Prenowitz. Chicago: University of Chicago Press, 1996.

———. *Dissemination*. Trans. Barbara Johnson. Chicago: University of Chicago Press, 1981.

———. *Given Time I: Counterfeit Money*. Trans. Peggy Kamuf. Chicago: University of Chicago Press, 1992.

———. *Glas*. Trans. John P. Leavey and Richard Rand. Lincoln: University of Nebraska Press, 1990.

———. *Margins of Philosophy*. Trans. Alan Bass. Chicago: University of Chicago Press, 1982.

———. *Memoires of the Blind: The Self–Portrait and Other Ruins*. Trans. Pascale-Anne Brault and Michael Naas. Chicago: University of Chicago Press, 1993.

———. *Of Grammatology*. Trans. Gayatri Chakravorty Spivak. Baltimore: Johns Hopkins University Press, 1974.

———. *On the Name*. Trans. David Wood et al. Stanford: Stanford University Press, 1993.

———. "Politics of Friendship." *American Imago* 50:3 (1993), pp. 360–376.

———. *Spectres of Marx: The State of the Debt, the Work of Mourning, and the New International*. Trans. Peggy Kamuf. London: Routledge, 1994.

———. *Speech and Phenomena and Other Essays on Husserl's Theory of Signs*. Trans. David B. Allison. Chicago: Northwestern University Press, 1973.

———. *Spurs: Nietzsche's Styles*. Trans. Barbara Harlow. Chicago: University of Chicago Press, 1979.

———. *The Archaeology of the Frivolous: Reading Condillac*. Pittsburgh: Duquesne University Press, 1980.

———. *The Truth in Painting*. Trans. Geoff Bennington and Ian McLeod. Chicago: University of Chicago Press, 1987.

———. *Writing and Difference*. Trans. Alan Bass. Chicago: University of Chicago Press, 1978.

Detienne, Marcel. *The Masters of Truth in Archaic Greece*. San Francisco: Zone Books, 1996.

Dolan, Frances E. "Taking the Pencil Out of God's Hand: Art, Nature, and the Face-Painting Debate in Early Modern England." *PMLA* 108:2 (1993), pp. 224–239.

E

Eco, Umberto. "The Semantics of Metaphor." *Semiotics: An Introductory Reader*. Ed. Robert E. Innis. London: Hutchinson, 1985, pp. 247–271.

Evans, Dylan. *An Introductory Dictionary of Lacanian Psychoanalysis*. London: Routledge, 1996.

F

Fanon, Franz. *Black Skin, White Masks*. Trans. Charles Lam Markmann. New York: Grove Press, 1967.

———. *The Wretched of the Earth*. Trans. Constance Farrington. New York: Grove Press, 1963.

Fineman, Joel. *Shakespeare's Perjur'd Eye: The Invention of Poetic Subjectivity in the Sonnets*.

———. "The Sound of 'O' in *Othello*: The Real of the Tragedy of Desire." *Psychoanalysis and....* Eds. Richard Feldstein and Henry Sussman. London: Routledge, 1990, pp. 33–48.

Folena, Lucia. "Figures of Violence: Philologists, Witches, and Stalinistas." *The Violence of Representation: Literature and the History of Violence*. Ed. Nancy Armstrong and Leonard Tennenhouse. London: Routledge, 1989, pp. 219–238.

Forrester, John. *The Seductions of Psychoanalysis: Essays on Freud, Lacan, and Derrida*. Cambridge, England: Cambridge University Press, 1989.

Foucault, Michel. *Discipline and Punish: The Birth of the Prison*. Trans. Alan Sheridan. New York: Pantheon Books, 1979.

———. "The Discourse on Language." *The Archaeology of Knowledge and the Discourse on Language*. Trans. Alan Sheridan-Smith. New York: Pantheon Books, 1972, pp. 215–237.

———. *The History of Sexuality: An Introduction*. Trans. Robert Hurley. New York: Pantheon Books, 1978.

Freud, Sigmund. *Beyond the Pleasure Principle*. Trans. James Strachey. New York: Norton, 1961.

———. *Civilization and Its Discontents*. Trans. Joan Riviere. New York: Dover Publications, 1994.

———. *Inhibitions, Symptoms, and Anxiety*. Trans. Alix Strachey. New York: Norton, 1989.

———. *Jokes and Their Relation to the Unconscious*. Trans. James Strachey. Harmondsworth: Penguin, 1991.

———. *Three Essays on the Theory of Sexuality*. Trans. James Strachey. New York: Basic Books, 1962.

———. *The Psychopathology of Everyday Life*. Trans. James Starchey. New York: Norton, 1965.

Fumerton, Patricia. *Cultural Aesthetics: Renaissance Literature and the Practice of Social Ornament*. Chicago: University of Chicago Press, 1991.

G

Goldberg, Jonathan. *Sodometries: Renaissance Texts, Modern Sexualities*. Stanford: Stanford University Press, 1992.

Gombrich, Ernst. *The Sense of Order: A Study in the Psychology of Decorative Art*. Ithaca, NY: Cornell University Press, 1989.

Goux, Jean-Joseph. *Symbolic Economies: After Marx and Freud*. Trans. Jennifer Curtis Gage. Ithaca, NY: Cornell Univerity Press, 1990.

———. *The Coiners of Language*. Trans. Jennifer Curtiss Gage. Norman and London: University of Oklahoma Press, 1994.

———. "The Phallus: Masculine Identity and the Exchange of Women." Trans. Maria Amucastegui *et al. Differences* 4:1 (1994), pp. 40–75.

Green, André. *The Tragic Effect: The Oedipus Complex in Tragedy*. Trans. Alan Sheridan. Cambridge, England: Cambridge University Press, 1979.

Greenblatt, Stephen. *Learning to Curse: Essays in Early Modern Culture*. London: Routledge, 1990.

———. *Marvelous Possessions: The Wonder of the New World*. Chicago: University of Chicago Press, 1991.

———. Ed. *New World Encounters*. Berkeley: University of California Press, 1993.

———. *Renaissance Self-Fashioning: From More to Shakespeare*. Chicago: University of Chicago Press, 1980.

H

Halpern, Richard. *The Poetics of Primitive Accumulation: English Renaissance Culture and the Genealogy of Capital*. Ithaca, NY: Cornell University Press, 1991.

Hegel, Georg Wilhelm Friedrich. *The Logic of Hegel*. Trans. W. Wallace. Oxford, 1874.

Heidegger, Martin. *Being and Time*. Trans. John Macquarrie & Edward Robinson. Oxford: Blackwell, 1967.

———. *On the Way to Language*. Trans. Peter D. Hertz. San Fracisco: Harper and Row, 1971.
———. *Poetry, Language, Thought*. Trans. Albert Hofstadter. New York: Harper and Row, 1971.
———. *The Concept of Time*. Trans. William McNeill. Oxford: Blackwell, 1992.
———. *The Question of Being*. Trans. William Kluback and Jean T. Wilde. New Haven, CT: College and University Press, 1958.
Henrion, Jean-Louis. *La cause du désir: L'agalma de Platon à Lacan*. Paris: Point Hors Ligne, 1993.
Hocquenghem, Guy. *Homosexual Desire*. Trans. Daniella Dangoor. Durham, NC: Duke University Press, 1990.
Hofstadter, Douglass R. *Gödel, Escher, Bach: An Eternal Golden Braid*. Harmodsworth: Penguin, 1979.
Hollander, Anne. *Seeing Through Clothes*. New York: Viking, 1978.
Huizinga, Johan. *Homo Ludens: A Study of the Play–Element in Culture*. London: Routledge and Kegan Paul, 1980.
Hyde, Lewis. *The Gift: Imagination and the Erotic Life of Things*. New York: Vintage, 1983.

I

Irigaray, Luce. *Marine Lover of Friedrich Nietzsche*. Trans. Gillian C. Gill. New York: Columbia University Press, 1991.
———. *Speculum of the Other Woman*. Trans. Catherine Porter. Ithaca, NY: Cornell University Press, 1985.
———. *This Sex Which Is Not One*. Trans. Catherine Porter. Ithaca, NY: Cornell University Press, 1985.

J

Jabès, Edmond. *From the Book to the Book: An Edmond Jabès Reader*. Trans. Rosemarie Waldrop. Hanover: Wesleyan University Press, 1991.
———. *The Little Book of Unsuspected Subversion*. Trans. Rosemarie Waldrop. Stanford: Stanford University Press, 1996.
Jacobus, Mary. *First Things: The Maternal Imaginary in Literature, Art, and Psychoanalysis*. London: Routledge, 1995.
Jafari, Jafar and Richard M. Gardner. "Tourism and Fiction: Travel as Fiction, Fiction as a Journey." Aix-en-Provence: Centre des Hautes Études Touristiques, 1991.

Jameson, Frederic. *The Political Unconscious: Narrative as a Socially Symbolic Act*. Ithaca, NY: Cornell University Press, 1981.
Jardine, Lisa. *Erasmus, Man of Letters: The Construction of Charisma in Print*. Princeton: Princeton University Press, 1993.
Joseph, Sister Miriam. *Rhetoric in Shakespeare's Time*. New York: Harvester, 1947.
Jung, Carl Gustav. *Aspects of the Masculine*. Trans. R. F. C.Hull. Princeton: Bollingen, 1989.
———. and Karl Kerényi. *Introduction to a Science of Mythology: The Myth of the Divine Child and the Mysteries of Eleusis*. Trans. R. F. C. Hull. London: Routledge and Kegan Paul, 1951.

K

Kerényi, Karl. *Eleusis: Archetypal Image of Mother and Daughter*. Trans. Ralph Manheim. Princeton: Princeton University Press, 1967.
———. *The Gods of the Greeks*. Trans. John N. Cameron. New York: Thames & Hudson, 1951.
Kirk, G. S. and J. E. Raven. *The Presocratic Philosophers*. Cambridge: Harvard University Press, 1957.
Kofman, Sarah. *Don Juan, ou, Le refus de la dette*. Paris: Galilée, 1991.
———. *Séductions: de Sartre à Héraclite*. Paris: Galilée, 1990.
———. *The Enigma of Woman: Woman in Freud's Writings*. Trans. Catherine Porter. Ithaca, NY: Cornell University Press, 1985.
Kolodny, Annette. *The Lay of the Land: Metaphor as Experience and History in American Life and Letters*. Chapel Hill, NC: University of North Carolina Press, 1975.
Kristeva, Julia. *Desire in Language*. New York: Columbia University Press, 1980.
———. *Powers of Horror: An Essay on Abjection*. Trans. Leon S. Roudiez. New York: Columbia University Press, 1982.
———. *Revolution in Poetic Language*. 1974. Trans. Leon S. Roudiez. New York: Columbia University Press, 1980.
———. *Strangers to Ourselves*. Trans. Leon S. Roudiez. New York: Columbia University Press, 1991.
———. *The Kristeva Reader*. Ed. Toril Moi. Oxford: Basil Blackwell, 1986.

L

Lacan, Jacques. *Écrits*. Paris: Seuil, 1966.
———. *Écrits: A Selection*. Trans. Alan Sheridan. New York: Norton, 1977.

———. *Écrits*. Paris: Seuil, 1966.
———. *Feminine Sexuality: Jacques Lacan and the École Freudienne*. Ed. Juliet Mitchell and Jacqueline Rose. New York: Norton, 1982.
———. *Seminar I: Freud's Papers on Technique*. Trans. John Forrester. New York: Norton, 1988.
———. *Seminar II: The Ego in Freud's Theory and in the Technique of Psychoanalysis*. Trans. Sylvana Tomaselli. New York: Norton, 1991.
———. *Seminar III: The Psychoses*. Trans. Russell Grigg. London: Routledge, 1993.
———. *Le Séminaire IV: La relation d'objet*. Paris: Seuil, 1994.
———. *Seminar VII: The Ethics of Psychoanalysis*. Trans. Dennis Porter. New York: Norton, 1992.
———. *Le Séminaire VIII: Le Transfert*. Paris: Seuil, 1991.
———. *Seminar XI: The Four Fundamental Concepts of Psychoanalysis*. Trans. Alan Sheridan. New York, Norton, 1978.
———. *Le Séminaire XVII: L'envers de la psychanalyse*. Paris: Seuil, 1991.
———. *Seminar XX: Encore*. Trans. Bruce Fink. New York: Norton, 1998.
Lacoue-Labarthe, Philippe. *Typography: Mimesis, Philosophy, Politics*. Ed. Christopher Fynsk. Cambridge, Mass.: Harvard University Press 1989.
Lacquer, Thomas. *Making Sex: Body and Gender from the Greeks to Freud*. Cambridge, Mass.: Harvard University Press, 1990.
Laplanche, Jean and J. B. Pontalis. *The Language of Psychoanalysis*. Trans. Donald Nicholson-Smith. New York: Norton, 1988.
Lefort, Rosine. *Birth of the Other*. Trans. Marc du Ry *et al.* Urbana and Chicago: University of Illinois Press, 1994.
Lemoine-Luccioni, Eugenie. *La robe: Essai psychanalytique sur le vêtement*. Paris: Flammarion, 1968.
Leupin, Alexandre. *Barbarolexis: Medieval Writing and Sexuality*. Cambridge: Harvard University Press, 1990.
———. "The Impossible Copula: Humanities and Judaeo-Christianity." *Rhetoric Society Quartrely* 29:3 (1999), pp. 11–20.
Levinas, Emmanuel. *Autrement q'être ou au–delà de l'essence*. The Hague: Nijhoff, 1974.
———.*Basic Philosophical Writings*. Ed. Adrian T. Peperzak *et al.* Bloomington: Indiana University Press, 1996.
———. *Outside the Subject*. Trans. Michael B. Smith. Stanford: Stanford University Press, 1993.
———. *Totalité et infini: Essai sur l'extériorité*. 1961. The Hague: Nijhoff, 1971.

Lichtenstein, Jacqueline. *The Eloquence of Color: Rhetoric and Painting in the Classical Age*. Trans. Emily McVarish. Berkeley: California University Press, 1993.
Louis-Combet, Claude. *Le don de langue*. Paris: Lettres Vives, 1992.
———. *Le péché d'écriture*. Paris: José Corti, 1990.
Lukacher, Ned. *Primal Scenes: Literature, Philosophy, Psychoanalysis*. Ithaca, NY: Cornell University Press, 1986.
Lyotard, Jean-Francois. *Libidinal Economy*. Trans. Iain Hamilton Grant. Bloomington: Indiana University Press, 1993.

M

Marin, Louis. *To Destroy Painting*. Trans. Mette Hjort. Chicago: University of Chicago Press, 1995.
Marx, Karl. *Capital Vol. 1: A Critical Analysis of Capitalist Production*. Ed. Frederick Engels. 1867. Trans. Samuel Moore and Edward Aveling. New York: International Publishers, 1967.
———. *The Grundrisse*. Ed. David Mclellan. New York: Harper and Row, 1971.
McCall, Marsh. *Ancient Rhetorical Theories of Simile and Comparison*. Cambridge, Mass.: Harvard University Press, 1969.
Mellor, Roy. *Nation, State, and Territory: A Political Geography*. London: Routledge, 1989.
Montrelay, Michèle. *L'ombre et le nom: Sur la féminité*. Paris: Minuit, 1977.
Mulvey, Laura. "Visual Pleasure and Narrative Cinema." *Visual and Other Pleasures*. Bloomington: Indiana University Press, 1989.

N

Nancy, Jean-Luc. *The Muses*. Trans. Peggy Kamuf. Stanford: Stanford University Press, 1996.
———. *The Birth to Presence*. Trans. Brian Holmes *et al*. Stanford: Stanford University Press, 1993.
Neumann, Erich. *Fear of the Feminine and Other Essays on Feminine Psychology*. Trans. Boris Matthews. Princeton: Princeton University Press, 1994.
———. *The Great Mother: Analysis of an Archetype*. Trans. Ralph Mannheim. Princeton: Princeton University Press, 1963.
———. *The Origins and History of Consciousness*. 1954. Trans. R. F. C. Hull. London: Mansfield 1989.
Niranjana, Tejaswini. *Siting Translation: History, Poststructuralism, and the Colonial Context*. Berkeley: University of California Press, 1992.

Nye, Andrea. *Words of Power: A Feminist Reading in the History of Logic*. London: Routledge, 1990.

O

Ong, Walter J. *Ramus, Method, and the Decay of Dialogue*. Cambridge, Mass.: Harvard University Press, 1958.

Otto, Walter Friedrich. *Dionysus: Myth and Cult*. Trans. Robert B. Palmer. Bloomington: Indiana University Press, 1965.

P

Parker, Patricia. "Deferral, Dilation, *Différance*: Shakespeare, Cervantes, Johnson." In Patricia Parker and David Quint, eds. *Literary Theory/Renaissance Texts*. Baltimore, MD: The Johns Hopkins University Press, 1986, pp. 182–207.

———. "Dilation and Delay: Renaissance Matrices." *Poetics Today* 5:3 (1984), pp. 19–35.

———. *Literary Fat Ladies: Rhetoric, Gender, Property*. London: Methuen, 1987.

———. *Shakespeare from the Margins: Language, Culture, Context*. Chicago: University of Chicago Press, 1996.

———. and David Quint, eds. *Literary Theory/Renaissance Texts*. Baltimore: Johns Hopkins University Press, 1986.

———. and Geoffrey Hartman, eds. *Shakespeare and the Question of Theory*. London: Methuen, 1985.

Plotnitsky, Arkady. *Reconfigurations: Critical Theory and General Economy*. Gainesville: University of Florida Press, 1993.

Pocock, Douglass C. *Humanistic Geography and Language: Essays on the Experience of Place*. London: Croom Helm, 1981.

Pratt, Mary Louise. *Imperial Eyes: Travel Writing and Transculturation*. London: Routledge, 1992.

R

Rebhorn, Wayne E. *The Emperor of Man's Minds: Literature and the Renaissance Discourse on Rhetoric*. Ithaca, NY: Cornell University Press, 1995.

Ricoeur, Paul. *The Rule of Metaphor: Multi-Disciplinary Studies of the Creation of Meaning in Language*. 1978. Trans. Robert Czerny *et al*. London: Routledge, 1986.

Robertson, George, et al., eds. *Travelers' Tales: Narratives of Home and Displacement*. London: Routledge, 1994.

Roper, Lyndal. *Oedipus and the Devil: Witchcraft, Sexuality, and Religion in Early Modern Europe*. London: Routledge, 1994.

Rubin, Gayle. "The Traffic in Women: Notes Toward a Political Economy of Sex." In Rayna R. Reiter, ed. *Toward an Anthropology of Women*. New York: Monthly Review Press, 1975, pp. 157–210.

S

Said, Edward W. *Culture and Imperialism*. London: Vintage, 1994.

Schor, Naomi. *Reading in Detail: Aesthetics and the Feminine*. London: Methuen, 1987.

Serres, Michel. *Hermes: Literature, Science, Philosophy*. Ed. Josue Harari and David F. Bell. Baltimore: Johns Hopkins University Press, 1982.

Sharon-Zisser, Shirley. "A Distinction No Longer 'of Use': Evolutionary Discourse and the Disappearance of the Trope/Figure Binarism." *Rhetorica* 11:3 (1993), pp. 321–342.

———. "From 'Guest' to Occupier? Unstable Hospitality and the Ahistoricity of Tropology in the Discourse of Rhetoric." *Philosophy and Rhetoric* 32:4 (1999) (forthcoming).

———. "'*Illustrer nôtre langue maternelle*': Illustrative Similes and Failed Phallic Economy n Early Modern Rhetoric." *Exemplaria* 9:2 (1997), pp. 393–420.

———. "Re(de)-Erecting Collatine: Castrative *collatio* in *The Rape of Lucrece*." *Rhetoric Society Quarterly* 29.3 (1999), pp. 55–70.

———."Richard Sherry." *Dictionary of Literary Biography: Renaissance Rhetoricians*. Ed. Edward Malone. New York: Gale Research (forthcoming).

———."'Similes Hollow'd With Sighs: The Transferential Erotics of the Similaic Copula in Shakespeare's 'A Lover's Complaint.'" *Exemplaria* 11:1 (1999), pp. 195–220. .

———. "Tropes and Topazes: The Colonialist Tropology of the Tropics in John Holmes's *Art of Rhetoric* and *Grammarian's Astronomy*." *Textual Practice* 11:2. (1997), pp. 285–304.

———. "Undoing the 'Tyrranous Advantage': Renaissance Rhetoric and the Subduing of Female Power." *Women's Studies* 24 (1995), pp. 247–271.

———. "Wanting Word of Woman, Subversive Speech of Simile: *Écriture féminine* and the Erotics of Rhetoric." *Intertexts* 3:2 (1999), pp. 33–58.

Shell, Marc. *The Economy of Literature*. Baltimore, MD: The Johns Hopkins University Press, 1978.

———. *The End of Kinship: 'Measure for Measure,' Incest, and the Ideal of Universal Siblinghood*. Baltimore, MD: Johns Hopkins University Press, 1988.

———. *Money, Language, and Thought: Literary and Philosophical Economies from the Medieval to the Modern Era*. Berkeley: University of California Press, 1982.

Shields, Rob. *Places on the Margin: Alternative Geographies of Modernity*. London: Routledge, 1991.

Sibony, Daniel. *Le féminin et la séduction*. Paris: Grasset, 1986.

———. *Le corps et sa danse*. Paris: Grasset, 1995.

Starobinsky, Jean. *Words Upon Words*. New Haven: Yale University Press, 1979.

Stratton, Jon. *Writing Sites: A Genealogy of the Postmodern World*. Ann Arbor, Mich.: University of Michigan Press, 1990.

Sutton, Jane. "The Taming of the *Polos/Polis*: Rhetoric as an Achievement Without Women." *The Southern Communication Journal* 57:2 (1992), pp. 97–119.

T

Taylor, Mark. *Disfiguring: Art, Architecture, Religion*. Chicago: University of Chicago Press, 1992.

Thompson, Roger. *Unfit for Modest Ears: A Study of Pornographic, Obscene, and Bawdy Works Written or Published in England in the Second Half of the Seventeenth Century*. Totowa, New Jersey: Rowman and Littelfield, 1979.

Turner, James. *One Flesh: Paradisal Marriage and Sexual Relations in the Age of Milton*. Oxford: Clarendon Press, 1987.

Turner, Victor. "Comments and Conclusions" In Babcock, Barbara, ed. *The Reversible World: Symbolic Inversion in Art and Society*. Ithaca, NY: Cornell University Press, 1978, pp. 276–296.

V

Van den Abeele, George. *Travel as Metaphor: From Montaigne to Rousseau*. Minneapolis: University of Minnesota Press, 1992.

Vickers, Nancy. "'The blazon of sweet beauty's best': Shakespeare's *Lucrece*." In Parker, Patricia, and Geoffrey Hartman, eds. *Shakespeare and the Question of Theory*. London: Methuen, 1985, pp. 95–115.

W

Whigham, Frank. *Ambition and Privilege: The Social Tropes of Elizabethan Courtesy Theory.* Berkeley: University of California Press, 1984.

Whitworth, Stephen. *The Name of the Ancients: Humanist Homoerotics and the Signs of Pastoral.* Phd Dissertation, University of Michigan, 1997.

———. "Far from Being: Rhetoric and Dream-Work in John Dickenson's *Arisbas.*" *Exemplaria* 11.1 (1999), pp. 167–194.

———. "Passing for Mean: Barnfield and the Aristotelian Poetics of Copulation." *Rhetoric Society Quarterly* 29:3 (1999), pp. 71–86.

Willbern, David. *Poetic Will: Shakespeare and the Play of Language.* Philadelphia: University of Pennsylvania Press, 1997.

Wills, David. *Prosthesis.* Stanford: Stanford University Press, 1995.

Wittig, Monique. *The Straight Mind and other Essays.* Trans. Louise Turcotte. London: Harvester Wheatsheaf, 1992.

Y

Yates, Frances A. *The Art of Memory.* London: Ark Paperbacks, 1966.

Index

A

abject, 28–29, 39–43, 45–46, 58–61, 66, 73, 82, 84, 130, 159, 282, 286–288, 313–314, 327, 330–331, 337, 340

Abraham, Nicolas, 4, 6, 9, 30, 33, 37, 43–45, 121, 142, 152, 157, 173, 181, 186, 188, 218, 334, 336

abuse, 99, 116, 296–299, 304–305

adjective, 264–265

Adorno, Theodor, 183–184

adverb, 225, 228–233, 235, 238, 240, 242, 244, 246, 253–254, 256, 258

agalma, 123–128

Agamben, Giorgio 9, 88, 162, 227

aim, 2, 25, 31, 37, 41, 65, 103, 123, 131–132, 135, 140, 146, 148–149, 152, 155, 159, 225–226, 229, 232, 255, 267, 270, 292, 295, 311, 316, 331

amplification, 283, 285–286, 294, 312–313, 315, 323

anagram, 11, 45, 66–67, 92, 95, 216, 235, 246, 255, 257–258, 262

anapodoton, 6, 57, 61, 64, 66–67, 69

anasemic, 200, 207, 307

anxiety, 14, 25–30, 37, 40–44, 46, 48–50, 58, 69, 73, 107–109, 110, 127, 129–130, 136–137, 139–140, 144, 150, 152, 154–155, 159–161, 163, 191, 194–195, 200, 203, 205–207, 210–211, 222, 279, 286–289, 291, 295–296, 300, 304, 312–313, 322, 331, 337, 340, 342

apocope, 57–58, 61, 66–67, 69

aposiopesis, 54, 57–58, 61, 66–67, 69

apostrophaic copula, 64–66

apostrophe, 5–6, 54, 64–66, 68–69, 154, 217, 270, 335–337

apotropaic, 270, 339–340

approximatory desire, 277

archaic, 3, 7, 12, 14–15, 19–21, 23–25, 27–30, 32–34, 36–46, 48–54, 56, 58, 61–63, 66, 68–71, 73, 76–78, 80–84, 86, 88, 90–91, 93–98, 101, 104, 108, 114, 117–118, 120, 123–124, 127–128, 130–131, 133, 148, 154–163, 167–168, 175, 186, 197, 199–201, 203, 205–206, 208–210, 213, 216–217, 219–220, 222, 226–227, 229, 232, 234, 247, 250–253, 255–256, 259, 262–263, 266–268, 272–273, 276–278, 285, 288, 315, 328, 331–332, 337–339, 342–343

Aristotle, 22, 51, 90, 134, 145, 161, 168, 203–204, 219, 221, 245, 258–259, 261, 263, 266–268,

280–285, 292, 295–296, 306, 312–315, 331–332, 336, 340–341
Ascham, Roger, 171, 190, 214
asyndeton, 54, 67–69, 154, 335
aural, 10–11, 29, 31–32, 35–36, 62, 97, 183, 186, 208–209, 246, 248, 257, 261–262
axiom, 173, 175–180, 182–184, 249, 271
axiomatic copula, 176–177, 179–180, 206

B

Bacon, Francis 35–36
Barnfield, Richard, 31
Bataille, Georges, 1, 5, 9, 34, 42–43, 75–76, 86, 101–102, 109, 114, 155, 181, 222, 226, 245, 329–330
Baudrillard, Jean, 112–114, 117–120
becoming, 110, 133, 181, 213, 244–247, 249–250, 252, 257, 259, 267–268, 271–272, 338
Being, 3, 5, 8, 10, 12, 14, 23, 25–26, 29, 37, 41–42, 44, 49, 55, 57, 60, 63 64, 67–68, 70, 83, 91, 98, 100, 102, 116, 118, 121, 123, 124–126, 130–131, 133, 140, 147, 152, 161, 168–175, 178, 180, 184, 186–187, 189–191, 197, 201–202, 205, 209, 213, 216, 218–220, 223, 229–230, 232, 236, 244–247, 250–251, 259–260, 264, 267, 269–270, 271–273, 275–276, 278, 280–281, 285, 290, 295, 302, 310, 312, 314, 319, 321, 326, 328, 330, 339, 342, 343
Benjamin, Walter, 194
Bersmann, George, 249, 302
Beumley, Mark, 97, 103, 299
Blount, Thomas, 4, 32–33, 169, 183, 186, 189, 191, 193, 201, 205–207, 210, 259, 261, 283, 286, 297, 312–313, 333–334, 336

Bodenham, John, 33–34, 36–37, 40, 214
Breton, Nicholas, 214
Bruno, Giordano, 234–235, 241–242
Bullokar, John, 168, 259, 261
Busby, Richard, 169–171, 182, 223, 225, 228–229, 231, 265, 271
Butler, Charles, 122–125, 191–192, 230, 336

C

Callimachus, 220, 239
Camerarius, Joachimus, 98–99, 101, 114, 194, 230, 286, 294
Campion, Thomas, 11, 258–259, 264, 271
Cassman, Otho, 336
Castor, 232–235, 240–247, 252
castration, 55–58, 61, 66–67, 70, 92, 115, 139, 202, 295–296
catachresis, 192, 296–302, 305–306, 314, 339, 342
Caussin, Nicholas, 194
Cavalcanti, Bartolomeo, 98–99, 101, 103, 114, 193, 230
Cave, Terence, 23, 95, 113–114, 198, 209, 239, 283–284, 323
Cawdray, Robert, 58–59, 194, 214, 230, 286, 319–320, 323–329
Chapman, George, 10, 36
chora, 30, 82, 105
choreographic, 77, 79–89, 91–92, 95, 105–108, 248
choric, 80–82, 105–106
Cicero, 4, 46–47, 52, 80, 90, 106, 108, 113, 155, 195, 203–205, 217, 232, 235–236, 239, 244, 289, 334
Cixous, Hélène, 6, 23–24, 29, 38, 49, 52–53
climax, 68–69, 154, 335–336
clothes, 75, 97–102, 114, 117–118, 120, 127

Coles, Elisha, 21, 25, 30, 219, 222, 266, 268, 277
colonization, 14, 55, 73, 135, 138, 140–141, 144, 148, 151–154, 157–161, 193, 196, 200–201
color, 114–117, 127
Constable, Henry, 4–5, 31, 209
Cooper, Christopher 143, 170, 223, 229
copia, 20–21, 23, 26, 97, 193, 198, 201, 203, 209, 283–286, 291, 294, 309–310, 312–313, 323, 325
copula, 5, 62–69, 71, 109, 168–172, 175–176, 178–184, 199, 201–202, 205–206, 215, 220–223, 228, 231, 235, 244, 246–248, 250, 253–254, 256, 258, 261, 268–270, 272, 274–275, 277, 282, 292, 296, 298, 300, 309, 329, 331, 343
Correggio, 1–4
Correll, Barbara, 8, 45, 62, 75, 112, 117, 137, 145, 169, 245, 288, 293, 302
cryptonym, 213
cut, 54, 57–58, 64–66, 69, 79–80, 95, 136, 141, 148, 178, 188, 204, 210, 216, 229, 242, 252, 261, 268, 272, 293, 343

D

Daniel, Samuel, 11, 100, 105, 155, 177
Day, Angel , 31, 48, 169, 284
de Courcelles, Pierre, 21, 25, 309–312
de Kerhuel, Johanne, 191–192, 194, 299–300, 336
definite, 12–13, 100, 167–168, 171–172, 174–175, 180, 185, 187, 193, 204–207, 219, 222–229, 253, 255, 327, 342–344
Deleuze, Gilles, 9, 95, 114, 289, 299, 310

delivery, 40, 42–43, 45–47, 60–61
demand, 5–6, 11, 24, 37, 44–45, 66–67, 69, 112, 118, 125, 128, 142, 173, 185, 205, 208, 220, 237, 310, 312, 324
Demetrius, 292, 334
Demosthenes, 70, 90, 232
denial, 25, 160, 165, 173, 176, 178, 342
Derrida, Jacques, 5–6, 9, 31, 65, 78–79, 84, 88, 104, 118, 122–123, 126–127, 144, 151–153, 157, 167, 171–173, 178, 188, 201, 236, 240, 270, 274, 277, 310–311, 316, 332, 334, 339
desire, 2–8, 12–15, 23–24, 27, 31–32, 34, 44–46, 62, 64–67, 69–71, 73, 75–76, 78–79, 81–82, 86–90, 92, 95–96, 101–102, 108, 111–112, 115–121, 123–130, 154, 156, 159–163, 167–168, 172–173, 176–179, 185, 191–192, 195, 197, 200–204, 208, 213, 215–217, 219–220, 222–223, 225–227, 229, 231–235, 237–239, 241–245, 247, 250–251, 254, 256–258, 260, 267–268, 273, 276–279, 281–282, 288–290, 292–293, 302–303, 310, 312, 317–319, 322, 324, 326, 328–329, 331, 337, 340–342, 344
Dickenson, John, 4, 10, 21–23, 25–28, 31, 38
dilation, 58, 60–61, 283, 285–286, 290, 294, 315, 323, 332–333, 339
Dionysian, 78–84, 88, 95–96, 101, 105, 107–109, 113, 115, 118, 248–249
Dionysius of Halicarnassus, 106
Dioscuri, 232, 234, 240–241, 244, 254
disavowal, 25, 42, 73, 95, 121, 172, 249–250, 273, 295, 307
discourse of the master, 132, 157,

177, 180, 183, 190–192, 204
Donne, John, 112, 120–121, 124, 218, 234, 279, 293–294, 341
Drayton, Michael, 4, 31
du Vair, Guillaume, 93

E
ecphonesis, 183–185
Eleusinian, 84–85, 87, 95–96, 101, 105, 127, 248
Eleusinian mysteries, 83, 85–87, 90–91, 93–94, 96, 127, 130
elocution, 34, 36, 46–47, 54–55, 62–64, 68–69, 73, 85, 89, 91, 94–96, 103, 106, 108, 130–131, 133, 146, 150, 153–157, 159, 163–164, 167–168, 177, 180, 188–189, 191–192, 197–201, 204, 206, 208–210, 213, 228–229, 246, 248–249, 255, 257, 260, 269, 280, 282, 293, 329, 332, 334–335, 337–338, 343
Erasmus, Desideriks, 20–21, 23, 25–28, 30, 38, 97, 99, 114, 190, 193, 198, 201, 203–204, 214
erotema, 67, 69, 125, 128, 173, 185, 207–208, 249, 302
erotesis, 173, 185
erotics, 217, 219, 275, 293
Euphues, 31
excess, 1, 5, 13, 34, 42–43, 56, 66, 79, 119–111, 116, 181, 222, 245, 246, 265, 274, 278–279, 284, 287–288, 297–300, 302–306, 308–309, 311–313, 316, 318, 322–323, 327–329, 330–332, 339, 341–342

F
Farnaby, Thomas, 51, 57, 66, 97, 114, 135, 156
female sexuality, 14, 50, 286–290, 294, 302, 304, 307, 314, 316–317, 322, 324–325, 329–331, 339–340
Fenelon, Francis, 118
Fenner, Dudley 51, 113–114, 120–122, 126–127, 141–142, 145–146, 155–156, 177, 190, 208, 304–306, 337
fetish, 73, 75–76, 97, 100–103, 114, 118–120, 127, 129, 131, 324
figure, 1–2, 7, 13–14, 19, 21, 26, 32–33, 47–48, 51, 55–58, 60, 62, 66–68, 69, 73, 75–86, 89–106, 108, 110–133, 146–147, 156, 159–160, 163–164, 167, 169, 178, 188, 190–192, 199–201, 202–203, 209, 221, 226, 234–235, 241, 248–249, 260, 282, 284, 288, 291–292, 302–303, 305, 307, 309, 313, 333–340, 342
figure-trope, 248
Fineman, Joel, 64, 70
Fletcher, Antonie, 213, 315–319, 327–328
Florio, John, 57, 63, 117, 169–171, 194, 259, 261
forgetting, 70–71, 94,179, 236–238, 242–244, 252, 254
fragment, 38, 63, 69, 71, 124, 178, 185, 229, 232, 238, 246–247, 252–256, 267, 292, 343
fragmentary, 15
Fraunce, Abraham, 4, 33, 37–39, 47, 51, 62–64, 68, 100, 113–114, 120–122, 124–127, 142–143, 148, 152, 157, 173–181, 183–184, 186–191, 207–208, 218–219, 249, 262, 264–265, 271, 278, 334, 336
Freud, Sigmund, 10–12, 20, 22, 26–28, 36, 53, 55–59, 67–68, 77, 109, 115, 129, 132, 139, 222, 237, 241, 268, 270, 275, 283, 340
Fulwell, Ulpian, 216–218, 234, 272, 278–279, 341
fusion, 27–29, 37, 44, 49, 62, 65, 73,

75, 112, 154, 158, 177–179, 183–184, 208, 211, 233, 235, 237, 246, 269–271, 273–275, 277, 343

G
Gascoigne, George, 291
gaze, 97, 110–111, 326
general equivalent, 53–56, 69, 115, 131, 139–140, 164, 180, 188–191, 197–202, 206, 208–210, 213, 218, 260, 279, 289, 305, 307, 317, 330, 332–334, 338–339, 342
Goux, Jean-Joseph, 9, 22–23, 49, 53–54, 78, 134, 139–140, 179–181, 186–190, 197–198, 200, 210, 236, 280–281, 324, 330
Green, André, 7–9, 52, 65, 99, 138, 141–142, 145, 195–196
Greene, Robert, 4, 31
Guntherus, Peter, 193
gynecological, 53, 58, 112, 179, 283, 285–287, 295, 320, 327, 332

H
Hamlet, 125, 273, 275
harmonia, 219, 253–256, 258, 260
Heidegger, Martin, 65, 161, 169–173, 245, 269, 276
Heraclitus, 219, 255–256, 261, 267
Hobbes, Thomas, 51, 58, 120, 141–142, 145–146, 155–157, 181–182, 184, 196, 208, 221, 283–285, 304, 306, 316, 332–333
homoeroticism, 216–218, 292–293, 304, 328, 341
homosexuality, 2–3, 15, 79, 241, 278–279, 291–292, 299, 303, 317–319, 329–331, 339
Hoskyns, John, 186, 189, 191, 198, 205–210, 230, 283, 286, 294–296, 312–313, 333–334
hysterologia, 59–61

I
Iamblichus, 245–246, 252, 254, 263–264, 278
identity, 28, 60, 73, 100, 106, 108, 136, 144–146, 151–153, 179, 187, 204, 213, 215–216, 243, 272, 291, 325
illustrative simile, 306–309, 313–314, 318, 321, 324, 327, 330, 339
imaginary, 7, 10, 28, 40–41, 43–44, 53–58, 60–61, 63, 66, 88, 102, 117, 127, 130–135, 137–138, 142–144, 148, 150, 152, 156–158, 160, 162–163, 174, 178, 180, 182, 184–185, 195–196, 200, 202, 204–205, 233, 246, 269, 273, 275, 282, 284–286, 288, 295–296, 299, 313–314, 317–318, 323, 333–334
imaginary mother, 331
incest, 2–3, 15, 70–71, 76, 83–84, 86–89, 91, 93–96, 98–99, 101, 107, 114, 125, 127, 216, 232–233, 242, 254, 279, 288, 291–292, 296–300, 304, 314, 320, 330, 339–340, 342
incorporation, 43–46
indicative, 58, 80, 127, 152, 163, 169, 171–173, 184, 225–226, 228, 251
introjection, 30, 42, 44–46, 48–51, 53, 64
Irigaray, Luce, 6, 9, 19, 23, 80, 91, 105, 177, 290, 315–316, 320, 330, 333, 337

J
Jonson, Ben, 182, 185, 194, 203, 223, 228–229, 231, 265, 271
jouissance, 2, 15, 24, 27, 34–39, 45, 50–51, 63, 67, 69, 75, 86–87, 98, 102–104, 117, 120–121, 123–125, 127–130, 133, 152, 154, 157–160,

167, 178–179, 185, 213, 216, 229, 231, 238–239, 241, 275–276, 330, 339–340, 343

K

Kofman, Sarah, 9, 76, 86–87, 89, 100, 102, 112
Kristeva, Julia, 9, 23–24, 27–30, 37–41, 46, 48–49, 52, 59–60, 121, 129, 134, 140, 204–205, 263

L

Lacan, Jacques, 2–3, 5–6, 8–12, 26–27, 29–30, 32, 37, 49–53, 55–57, 61–69, 71, 76, 81, 88, 97, 102, 111–112, 117–118, 120–121, 123–125, 128–130, 132–134, 156, 160, 163, 169–173, 176–178, 180, 182–183, 185, 189–191, 199, 201–204, 215, 222–229, 237, 241, 243, 245, 247, 250–251, 263, 265–266, 268–270, 272, 276, 282–283, 303, 317, 326, 340, 342, 344
lack, 21–22, 26–27, 37, 52, 56–58, 65–69, 71, 97, 103, 122, 124–126, 128–130, 149, 160, 172–173, 176, 187, 201–202, 205, 222–223, 237, 245, 247, 281–283, 289, 301
Lamy, Bernard, 23, 51, 57–58, 60, 66, 145, 152, 199, 221, 230, 249
Lanyer, Aemilia, 14, 217–218, 234, 279, 341
Lesbianism, 218, 279, 292–293, 299–300, 330
letolic, 70–71, 89, 94
Leupin, Alexandre, 274–275
Lever, Ralph, 46, 321–323
Levinas, Emmanuel, 9, 178–179, 186, 204, 271, 273
Lichtenstein, Jacqueline, 55, 104, 106, 115–116
Ling, Nicholas, 214

Lodge, Tomas, 31, 136–137
Longinus, 189, 221
Lycosthenis, Conard, 214, 249, 309, 315–316
Lyly, John, 31
Lyotard, Jean-Francois, 132–133, 138, 150, 152, 157, 168, 192, 197

M

Mascher, Girolamo, 34, 194, 201, 310
master, 2, 53–56, 79, 92–93, 104, 121, 131–132, 135, 137, 142, 153–154, 156–158, 167, 180, 182–184, 186–192, 195, 197, 203–204, 210–211, 214, 283–284, 314, 316, 321, 332, 338
master-trope, 55, 167, 190–192, 198, 211, 260, 336, 338, 342
maternal, 2, 7, 14, 20–25, 27–32, 35, 37, 39–43, 45–46, 48–56, 58–61, 68–71, 73, 75–78, 80–82, 84–89, 91, 93–99, 101, 103–104, 113, 121, 125, 127, 129–130, 132, 134, 154–155, 159–160, 180, 184, 186, 200, 205, 208–210, 233, 277, 279–289, 294–297, 304, 306–310, 312–318, 323, 325–328, 330–335, 337–342
measure, 31, 53, 188, 198, 216, 218, 264–265, 271, 274, 279, 289, 292–294, 295
memory, 46–47, 65, 169, 180, 224–225, 227, 230, 235–240, 242–244, 251–253, 257, 335
Meres, Francis, 214, 219, 222, 277–279, 287, 291, 297, 300, 304, 306, 314, 318, 340, 344
metaphor, 51, 54–56, 58, 61, 69, 93, 154, 164–165, 167–169, 172, 175–195, 197–211, 213–215, 218, 220–222, 235–240, 244, 247–250, 260–262, 269, 272, 274–276,

279–280, 282, 284–285, 293, 296, 300, 306–307, 316, 318, 332–343
metaphoric copula, 168–173, 175–177, 179, 182–185, 191, 193, 199, 201–202, 204, 206–207, 209, 221–223, 225–226, 274, 283
Miege, Guy, 172, 184, 223–225, 231, 265
Montaigne, Michel de, 194
Montrelay, Michèle, 5, 9, 35–36, 39, 64–65, 68–69, 97, 133, 155, 157–158, 178, 228–229, 231, 238, 266, 269–270, 339, 343

N

Name of the Father, 52, 54, 80, 83, 106–108, 112–113, 118, 183, 190, 208, 300, 305, 316
Nancy, Jean-Luc, 9, 78, 80, 171, 177, 187, 246, 285, 290
Newton, John, 177, 208, 301–302
Nicomachus, 252, 263–264, 278

O

oceanic, 20–22, 25–28, 38, 40–42, 48–49, 67–68, 73, 75, 151, 153–154, 158–159, 161, 200–201, 205–206, 210–211, 213, 225–226, 237, 296, 342–343
omphalic, 14–15, 85–88, 90–93, 95–96, 98, 100–101, 114, 127, 234, 248, 260, 262, 270, 273–276, 343
omphalic aesthetics of simile, 14, 343
ontology, 167, 170, 172, 199, 222, 225, 244, 247, 250–251, 256, 267, 271, 275, 343
optative, 172–173, 225–227, 229, 231, 233, 238, 240, 242, 244–245, 249–251, 254, 256
oral, 10, 23, 27, 29–37, 39–45, 62, 69–70, 76–77, 94, 97, 121–122, 186–187, 197, 208–209, 233, 240–241, 244, 248–249, 262–263
orgasmic, 68–69, 117, 154, 275–277, 343
ornament, 103–106, 108–110, 112, 114–115, 118–119, 127
Ovid, 1, 10, 36, 124

P

parergon, 122–123, 126–128
Parker, Patricia, 7–8, 23, 48, 50, 59, 110, 133–134, 147–148, 180, 189, 196, 209, 284–285, 291, 294, 305, 308–309, 312, 315, 320, 327
pastoral, 4, 10, 22, 30–39, 62, 109, 173–176, 186, 203, 206–211, 213, 216, 218–220, 232–234, 240–241, 262–263, 329
Peacham, Henry, 19, 23, 25–26, 30, 32–33, 38, 47, 52, 56–58, 62–69, 90–91, 100, 103, 113–114, 120, 140–141, 148, 157, 169, 180–181, 183, 189, 192–193, 221, 226, 230, 249, 251, 296, 303, 344
perverse desire, 241, 243, 303
perversion, 14, 75–76, 102, 120–121, 125, 127–132, 159–160, 163, 167, 178, 192, 203, 241, 260, 302, 332
perversity, 241, 303
phallic desire, 14, 121, 130–131, 159, 162, 168, 177, 179, 184–185, 191–192, 195, 197, 200, 203, 213, 248, 272, 274–276, 288, 302, 313–314, 332, 334, 342–343
phallus, 3, 14, 54–57, 78–79, 81, 87, 92, 95, 115, 131, 139, 177, 179–191, 197–199, 207–209, 216, 219, 270, 276, 280, 288–289, 293, 299, 309–310, 314–315, 325, 330–331, 339–340, 342
Phillips, Edward, 4, 91–94, 96, 127, 214, 322

Philolaus of Croton, 254
placental, 28, 98, 129
Plato, 20, 30, 54–55, 75, 78, 89, 103–104, 123–124, 128, 161, 173, 176, 199, 219, 244, 246–247, 252, 255–257, 260, 267, 273, 275, 306
pleasure, 7, 11–12, 31–33, 35–39, 41, 53, 62, 68–69, 71, 76–77, 80, 90, 97, 102, 110, 115, 117, 121, 125, 178, 181–182, 186,196, 198, 208–209, 227–229, 246, 255–257, 268, 272, 275, 280, 290, 293, 297, 317, 319, 324–325, 327–328, 341, 343–344
Pollux, 232–235, 240–247, 252
Poole, Joshua, 30, 48, 57, 169–170, 172, 221, 223, 225–226, 229, 265, 271
present, 2, 9, 58, 66, 144, 148, 169–171, 221–223, 226, 328
preterite, 223–224, 226
Price, Owen, 20, 25, 43
Prideaux, Jean, 122–125, 191–192, 336
primal substance of semiosis, 14, 19, 22, 25–29, 38, 40–46, 48–54, 56, 58, 61, 73, 82, 84, 103, 127, 130–131, 133, 151, 153–154, 159–160, 162–163, 167, 184, 199–200, 210, 225, 237, 248, 279, 282, 284–288, 331, 337–338, 342–343
Primordial Maiden, 85–86, 89, 104, 119, 125, 127–128, 130–132, 258
primordial object, 125
proportion, 254, 256–265, 271
Puttenham, George 10–13, 32, 47, 51, 56, 58, 62–64, 66–68, 90–91, 95–96, 98–103, 114–117, 127, 155, 169, 177, 183, 188–189, 195–196, 209, 251, 255–256, 260–265, 270–272, 274, 278, 302–303, 310, 335–336, 344

Pythagoras, 219–220, 235, 246, 254, 263, 278

Q
Quintilian, 77, 97–101, 114, 236, 239, 243, 290, 306–308

R
Rainolde, Richard, 19, 21–23, 25, 90, 103, 283, 285
real, 27, 37, 56, 61, 64, 76, 89, 156–157, 178, 182, 202
real privation, 56–57, 66, 202, 289
Rebhorn, Wayne, 3, 7, 52, 155, 194, 196
repetition, 252, 291–294, 297–299, 336
rhetoric, 19, 24–25, 27, 30, 32–43, 45–58, 60–64, 66–71, 73, 76, 80–81, 89–91, 94–96,98, 100–101, 103, 106, 108, 112–118, 120–123, 125–130, 133–135, 138–141, 143–146, 149–153, 155, 157–161, 164, 167–168, 173–175, 177, 181, 186–192, 195–201, 203, 205–206, 209–210, 213, 216–222, 229, 233–236, 241, 247, 249, 251, 254, 260, 263, 266–268, 270, 272, 279–280, 282–286, 288, 290, 294–298, 300–301, 304–307, 309–314, 320–321, 330–332, 334–341, 343
R[obinson], R[alph], 169, 171, 223, 225–229, 231, 265

S
sartorial, 71, 76, 88–89, 93–94, 96–102, 340–341
scheme, 75–77, 79, 81–82, 85, 89–94, 96–97, 118, 120, 249, 257, 278
seduction, 86, 89–90, 99–102, 104–106, 112–120, 130, 156–159,

161–162, 200, 215, 319, 329
semiosis, 19–26, 36, 39, 43, 46,
    49–50, 68, 73, 75, 110, 131, 153,
    163, 204–205, 210, 248, 312, 332,
    338
Shakespeare, William, 4–5, 8, 14,
    30–31, 59, 65, 70, 125, 186, 207,
    214–216, 218, 220, 222, 234, 236,
    273–276, 278–279, 289, 292, 300,
    305, 317, 323–324, 326, 341,
    343–344
Shell, Marc, 6, 30, 43–45, 139,
    291–292, 299–300
Sherry, Richard, 8, 19–23, 25–28,
    30, 32–35, 38, 47, 51, 56–57,
    59–60, 62–64, 67–68, 76–86,
    89–96, 98, 100, 104, 112–114,
    118, 120, 122, 127, 136–138, 145,
    155, 157, 186, 188–191, 193, 201,
    221–222, 228–230, 248, 251,
    257–263, 284, 286, 291–292,
    296–297, 308–309, 333–334, 344
Sibony, Daniel, 82, 86, 89, 100–101,
    104–105
Sidney, Sir Philip, 4, 30, 33, 37,
    108, 186–187, 262
similaic, 71, 117, 174, 214–220,
    224–225, 227, 229, 231, 233,
    238–242, 244–247, 249–250,
    253–263, 265–266, 269–270,
    272–276, 278, 293, 325, 327–329,
    339, 341–343, 344
similaic copula, 116, 216–218,
    221–222, 225, 227–231, 233–234,
    240, 242, 244, 251, 253–254,
    258–259, 269, 274, 278–279,
    282–289, 292–293, 296, 306–307,
    309, 313, 328, 330, 339, 341, 344
similaic desire, 165, 219, 242, 277,
    342–343
simile, 45, 54–55, 58–59, 61, 66, 69,
    71, 116, 154, 164, 213, 215–216,
    218–223, 230, 234–235, 238–239,
    244–249, 251–268, 270–280,
    282–290, 292–297, 304, 306–310,
    312–319, 322–323, 325–326,
    329–343
Simonides, 235–247, 249–252, 262,
    267
Smith, John, 19, 21–23, 25–26,
    30–31, 33–34, 47–48, 51, 57–58,
    60, 63–64, 66–67, 91–92, 95–97,
    103, 113–114, 120, 127, 136, 141,
    155, 169, 188–190, 198,201, 221,
    230, 250, 283–285, 332–333
Soario, Cypriano, 191, 193, 249,
    283, 286, 313
Spenser, John, 188, 313, 329
Spenser, Sir Edward, 3–4, 14, 30,
    33, 38, 174, 207, 214, 216–219,
    234, 279, 320–321, 328–329, 341
symbolic, 10, 14–15, 22–24, 27,
    29–30, 37–39, 49–54, 56–57,
    60–61, 63, 66, 77–78, 87–88, 94,
    96, 99–101, 104, 109, 112, 114,
    127, 132, 134–140, 144, 154,
    156–157, 179–183, 186–190,
    195–198, 200, 202, 204, 210, 236,
    263–264, 280–282, 288–291, 293,
    299–300, 304, 310–311, 317,
    330–331, 337, 341, 343
symbolic castration, 56–58, 66, 69,
    103, 115, 137, 140, 289, 310
symbolic economy, 53–56, 58, 61,
    69, 71, 73, 131, 138, 153–154,
    161, 289–290, 299, 324, 343
symbolic economy of rhetoric, 54,
    163, 210, 343
symmetry, 31, 254–263, 266, 272,
    274–276, 278, 340
syncope, 60–61, 66, 69, 154

T
Tacitus, 105–106, 108, 114–115
tapinosis, 56, 61
tasis, 32, 257

Torok, Maria, 6, 9, 30, 43–45
transference, 5, 15, 65–66, 130, 178, 232, 242, 268–271, 339
transferential desire, 244, 282, 342
translation, 37–38, 136, 190, 193–195, 197, 336
triangle of desire, 219, 277–278
trope, 14–15, 47, 51, 55–56, 61, 69, 73, 91, 130–145, 148–164, 167–168, 186, 188, 191–194, 197, 199–201, 203, 207, 248, 260–261, 300, 307, 332–338
trope-figure, 337
tropology, 129, 132–133, 135, 138–140, 142, 144, 149–152, 197, 335, 337

U
umbilical, 84–85, 270

V
Vaughan, William, 33, 122–125
veil, 73, 75–76, 87–90, 92–103, 114, 117–130, 160, 248, 332, 340–341, 344
Vida, Marco Girolamo, 20, 32–37, 39–40, 80–81, 95
visual, 92–93, 112, 115, 123, 128, 186, 207–209, 239–240, 243, 251–252, 262, 326
Vossius, Gerard, 191–193, 249

W
Walker, Obadiah, 103, 110, 291
Walker, William, 188, 204, 222–225, 242, 341
Webbe, William, 108–110, 112, 114
Wharton, Jeremiah, 169–171, 183–185, 210, 223, 225, 228–229, 231, 265, 271
Whitworth, Stephen, 3, 10, 30, 57, 64, 173–175, 186, 206, 209, 216–217, 224–225, 240

Willbern, David, 317
Willis, John, 236
Willis, Thomas, 49
Wilson, Thomas, 8, 22–23, 25–28, 30, 40–48, 52, 70–71, 89–91, 94, 140–141, 145, 161, 167, 189, 191–192, 194, 197–198, 201, 230, 235–244, 247–248, 254, 277, 284–285, 298–299, 344